LEFTY FRIZZELL

LEFTY FRIZZELL

The Honky-tonk Life
of Country Music's
Greatest Singer

Daniel Cooper

LITTLE, BROWN AND COMPANY

BOSTON   NEW YORK   TORONTO   LONDON

First Edition

Library of Congress Cataloging-in-Publication Data

Cooper, Daniel (Daniel C.)
    Lefty Frizzell : the honky-tonk life of country music's greatest
singer / Daniel Cooper. — 1st ed.
            p.   cm.
    Includes bibliographical references (p.   ) and index.
    ISBN 0-316-15620-5
    1. Frizzell, Lefty, 1928–1975.   2. Country musicians — United
States — Biography.   I. Title.
ML420.F86C67   1995
782.42'1642'092 — dc20
[B]   95-6326

10   9   8   7   6   5   4   3   2   1

MV NY

*Published simultaneously in Canada
by Little, Brown & Company (Canada) Limited*

Printed in the United States of America

For Joan H. and John C. Cooper,
"I owe them my all"

Contents

Acknowledgments

THIS BOOK would not have been written without the impetus, support, and full cooperation of Lois Frizzell and Marlon Frizzell. Not only did they approach me with the idea, but they provided me with total, unmediated access to the private papers of their father, Lefty, as well as to several hours' worth of taped interviews conducted with their late mother, Alice Frizzell. Moreover, through three years of formal interviews and informal conversation about Lefty, Lois and Marlon always spoke with admirable candor, at times laughing about incidents a less understanding soul might have relayed through bitter tears. In this, they were, in the very best sense, their father's children. Their only request was that I emphasize—through the good stories and the bad, the funny and the not-so-funny—how completely they loved their father and grieve for him to this day. I say so now, unequivocally, lest there be any moments in the book when my own failings as a writer should lead the reader to doubt their love.

Naamon Frizzell, Lefty's father, passed away while this book was being written. The portrait of Naamon that appears in these pages is not entirely favorable, but I believe it is fair and accurate, so far as it goes. Naamon was a good, hardworking provider under difficult circumstances, but he was also a violent patriarch, as he, himself, was the first to admit. Late in life he turned to religion and lived out his final years in the quiet of Honey Grove, Texas, his personality considerably mellowed. Through the course of several interviews for this book, Naamon was always helpful and never less than utterly gracious. He will be missed.

I would like to thank my editor, Michael Pietsch, and my agent, Carol Mann, for their work and invaluable support in making this book happen. Ben Ratliff also took an early interest in the project, for which I am grateful.

Like so many writers and music fans worldwide, I am indebted to the terrific staff at the Country Music Foundation's media library and resource center in Nashville, Tennessee. I owe particular thanks to CMF staff members Paul Kingsbury and Bob Pinson; as well as Ronnie Pugh, Alan Stoker, and Kyle Young. Also in Nashville, Gary Walker and the crew at The Great Escape generously provided me with access to company resources during the critical early stages of this project.

Life's Like Poetry, Bear Family Records' astoundingly lavish twelve-disc boxed-set compilation of Lefty Frizzell's music, was literally at my side throughout the writing of this book. I am exceedingly grateful to producer Richard Weize for putting together such a state-of-the-art reissue of Lefty's work and for allowing me to reprint the discography. Charles Wolfe's comprehensive and pioneering biographical notes, included in the Bear Family set, were also a great resource.

The following people helped me in ways both great and small: Clay Allen, Hoss Allen, Judy Baker, Rocky Baker, Jon Beck, Eddie Bishop, John Bridges, Gloria Byrne (Saginaw Public Library), Bill Chambers, Hugh Cherry, Jeanne Clements (Arkansas Oil and Brine Museum), David Coen, Jane Cooper, Albie Del Favero, Donna DeLong (Loco Hills Post Office), Dr. Joe Dickerson, Bruce Dobie, Nancy Dunn (Historical Museum and Art Center, Artesia, New Mexico), Steve Eng, Colin Escott, Jeremy Fields, Jimmy Fields, Bobby Fluker, Peter Guralnick, Joan Hershberger, Roberta Hollis, Grady Kilgore, Otto Kitsinger, Don Lambert (Arkansas Oil and Brine Museum), Brian Mansfield, Abe Manuel, Jonathan Marx, Corky Mayberry, Anna Mayday (Saginaw Public Library), George McCoy, Don McLeese, Bill Mercer, J. D. Miller, Scott Moore, Dan Murphy (KELD), Ben Nix, Jolly Joe Nixon, Betty Orbeck (Petroleum Museum, Midland, Texas), David Orr (Chaves County Historical Society), Doodle Owens, Bob Parks (KELD), Gerald Prescott (California State University, Northridge), Wyvonne Putman (Navarro County Historical Society), Ken Ritter, John Stainze, Anne Stebbins, Don Steely, Gaylon Thornton, Joe Tonahill, John G. Tucker, Charlotte and Howard Vandevender (Van Howard), Billy Walker, Blanche Whaley, Jonny Whiteside. Thanks also to the staffs at the municipal libraries, county courthouses, and/or historical societies in the following cities: El Dorado and Little Rock, Arkansas; Meridian, Mississippi; Roswell, New Mexico; Gallatin and Nashville, Tennessee; Beaumont, Big Spring, Corsicana, Dallas, Greenville, Jasper, Longview, Mt. Pleasant, Orange, Paris, Port Arthur, and Sulphur Springs, Texas.

To all who consented to be interviewed for this book, thanks for sharing your memories.

To all the singers, pickers, songwriters, producers, deejays, booking agents, promoters, and industry entrepreneurs who created the musical era in which Lefty Frizzell thrived: thanks for living the life. You are all my heroes.

Finally, and most importantly, I thank my beloved wife, Kathryn Schoepflin Cooper, who put up with more neuroses than I care to catalog, and whose art remains my chief source of inspiration.

DISCOVERY

September 26, 1947. In the Jailhouse. Friday Before Supper.

THE OLD CHAVES COUNTY JAIL stands hard by the county courthouse in Roswell, New Mexico, seven scorching miles west of the Pecos River. The Pecos trickles out of the Sangre de Cristo Mountains near Santa Fe and widens south toward Carlsbad, crossing cotton farms, oil fields, and ancient Apache hunting grounds ruined by the white man's cattle. Folks used to say the west side of the Pecos was the lawless side—the wind-scarred banks where the frontier might not begin but frontier justice certainly did. Moving west across Chaves County, the arid land rises to the rich grasslands of Lincoln County, where in the 1870s a pair of British Isles immigrants waged a bloody range war with the homicidal aid of one William Bonney, aka Billy the Kid. Billy Bonney shot up towns and rustled herds all over the Pecos Valley. In 1881, they buried him beneath the same territorial dust that, many years later, blew past Lefty Frizzell's cell in the Chaves County Jail, on the west side of the Pecos River.

A western movie fan, Lefty might have thought about the Kid a time or two. Just nineteen himself, and locked away from his wife and baby, he might have found comfort in thinking that evil was not bred in the bones of a man but grew from the shifting sands west of the Pecos. His wife, Alice, said it herself: "Seem like in western towns, I don't know, there's wild bunches."

Lefty ran with the wild bunches when he sang at the Cactus Garden outside Roswell. He always packed the house at the Cactus Garden. Roughnecks, soldiers, and cotton pickers dragged their sore, cramped muscles to the dancehall on Saturday nights to hear the kid who sang like Ernest Tubb on a daily program on KGFL. High school girls— white and Hispanic—sashayed to the stage, their cotton dresses twisting around their knees as Lefty leaned over and charmed them with his favorite song: "Be Mine Blue Eyes."

Those girls would be all over Lefty after the shows, or when he hung in the parking lot outside the dancehall to hear barnstorming honky-tonk heros like Ted Daffan or T. Texas Tyler. The Cactus Garden management would throw their doors wide open as the barnlike building turned into a steampit of two-stepping cowboys and roustabouts. Lefty and his running buddies would be out in the field, cutting up on the hood of someone's car, Lefty making dangerous time with the young girls while Alice stayed home with their baby. The Texas fiddles and steel guitar would float across the field, circling the words of Ted Daffan's despondent signature tune, "Born to Lose."

And now Lefty was losing Alice. The wild bunches had been too wild and one of the young girls had been too young. Lefty was jailed for statutory rape. He looked over his song—the one he'd just written on a sheet of Chaves County Courthouse stationery. "A True Song To My Darling—Alice. By Sonny Frizzell" (Sonny was the name his family knew him by). "Wrote In The Eveing [sic]—In The Jailhouse. Friday Before Supper."

Lefty read it and strummed the simple chords behind his inner ear. He knew just how he would sing it if he ever got back to the Cactus Garden, or back on the air at KGFL. He'd move in on the microphone and pitch the song straight to Alice's forgiving heart, as if they were the only two lovers left in an unforgiving world. That's how he'd want "I Love You, I'll Prove It a Thousand Ways" to sound if Alice ever heard it on the radio, which didn't seem too likely as Lefty sat behind the stark gray walls of the Chaves County Jail.

As it turned out, three years later, Alice could hear her husband's jailhouse plea on every country radio show and roughneck jukebox all across America. Released in 1950 as "I Love You a Thousand Ways," it was one half of the double-sided smash hit record—the other half being "If You've Got the Money, I've Got the Time"—that launched the career of Lefty Frizzell, the singer Merle Haggard has called "the most unique thing that ever happened to country music." A superstar in his day, possibly the top country star in America for a time, Lefty inspired not only Haggard but scores of other singers and songwriters who would one day establish their own profound musical legacies. Young George Jones would be chastised by his record producer for imitating Lefty Frizzell. Teenage Roy Orbison would sign a friend's high school yearbook as "Roy (Lefty Frizzell) Orbison." Keith Whitley, echoing Lefty many years later, would stay away from mirrors as fate turned his own focus inward.

As great as some of his followers would become, it was Lefty, a honky-tonk legend to rival his friend Hank Williams, who truly revolutionized country singing with his roughhouse, soulful vocal style—equal parts dancehall ardor and dim-lit romance, sentimental hopefulness and tender regret. His gliding, broken vowel phrasing is now so pervasive in country music that young singers take it for granted as if it evolved from the hillbilly ether—as if no one man had given them that sound by singing to save his honky-tonk life.

Had Lefty died the way poor Hank died—young and wasted—he'd probably be remembered the same today. But as it was, Lefty fought through a twenty-five-year career to keep his life together and his soul intact. He fended off all manner of music industry corruption but could not overcome his own worst habits. His troubles were titanic, but his life, ultimately, a compelling triumph as he survived to offer such timeless classics as "The Long Black Veil," "Saginaw, Michigan," and, two years before he died, the original version of "That's the Way Love Goes."

Perhaps the latter song, better than any, revealed the man Lefty Frizzell really was. For even in the Chaves County Jail at the age of nineteen, in trouble with the law and his wife for what would not be the last time, Lefty's heart was open to the thousand ways that love might go, and to the music made not by himself but God.

WILDCATTING

Chapter 1

Lawyer: "Where were you born and reared?"
Lefty: "Corsicana, Texas, in an oil field behind an oil well."

On May 5, 1923, roughnecks drilling the J. K. Hughes Development Company's No. 1 McKie oil well hit paydirt in the Powell Field nine miles southeast of Corsicana. Dark crude mushroomed over the hundred-foot Powell Field derrick and misted for miles, ruining a dry load of wash on the line behind a nearby farmhouse. The No. 1 well spewed unchecked for four days at a rate of eight thousand barrels per day. On the fifth day, the well blew. Thirteen roughnecks and roustabouts had just begun their morning tour on the derrick floor when the explosion burned all thirteen men alive. Acrid flames lashed at the empty Powell Field skies for eleven days straight. No one could shut down the murderous fire.

Among the oil field men who labored in the ash and heat was probably one William Frizzell, who had brought his family to Corsicana in the middle of the Mexia Fault Zone oil boom. The rush started on August 21, 1921, when two monster gushers—one producing a thousand barrels per *hour*—hit in Mexia, twenty-nine miles south of Corsicana. Within days, 30,000 black-gold diggers had flooded Mexia, a quiet blackland farming community of scarcely two thousand residents. The roustabouts and prospectors slept in cars, hotel lobbies, and on newspapers in the street. Crapshooters, strippers, and whiskey-swilling card sharps followed in their wake. The "undesirables" turned the industrious Cotton Belt Railroad community into a Southern Baptist's vision of whoremongering Bedlam. Saloons and cathouses rose as fast as the derricks. The Winter Garden was thrown together in Mexia, the

Chicken Farm in nearby Wortham. In Luling, on the southern tip of the fault, action got so hot at the Gander Slue that the Texas Rangers rode in on the joint. They dragged the "entertainers" out into the street and chained them to trees like dogs.

The oil-crazed hordes shrugged their shoulders and headed north. The boom spread along a half-mile-wide gauntlet of derricks toward Corsicana in Navarro County. By early 1923, Corsicana had been overrun by workers and speculators from as far away as New York and Chicago. The Frizzells, who had come to Texas from Smackover, Arkansas, were just so many faces in the jostling crowd.

William Frizzell's ancestors had crossed the Atlantic from Scotland in the early nineteenth century and landed in Michigan. From the Great Lakes region, they followed the Acadian path south through the Mississippi Valley, spreading out and settling on farms in Tennessee, Arkansas, Louisiana, and East Texas. A hardy people, Frizzells routinely lived to celebrate their ninetieth birthday. Most had a wide-bridged nose and beefy cheeks: "If you ever seen one Frizzell, you seen 'em all," William's son Naamon Frizzell would say.

William's father, Plez (short for "Pleasant") Frizzell, grew up a farmer in Ouachita County, Arkansas. Plez was the son of John Wiley Frizzell and Anna Rogers, who was rumored to be three quarters Cherokee. In 1877, Plez married Sarah Elizabeth Adams, a Ouachita County woman of equal parts Dutch and Irish descent. Plez and Elizabeth raised five boys and three girls with names straight out of the storybook frontier: Mollie Mary, Etta Allie, Clabe, Pearl, Flem, Fleet, Troy. The fourth child, christened in a moment of nomenclatural calm, was William Monroe Frizzell, born on September 5, 1885. He, too, was brought up a rugged farmer on the Old Frizzell Place, learning like his daddy to cultivate cotton, corn, potatoes, and timber.

Timber dominated the Arkansas economy at the turn of the century. Sawmills rose out of dark forest thickets along the Louisiana border and drew railroad tracks to otherwise isolated pockets of backwater commerce. Cotton survived, but as deposed King. The lumber camps paid a dollar a day to a rough, unsentimental breed of men—some white, some black, and some an uneasy mixture of both. They worked grueling, dangerous shifts in the forest mills, with few prospects beyond the next day's logs and the steady fear of rampaging saws. William Monroe stayed a farmer and married a local girl, Velma Leola Wheelington. Her father sold William eighty acres of sandy land near the Ouachita River, about three miles from the Old Frizzell Place. The couple had six children—three sons followed by three daughters. Naamon Orville was the second son, born November 11, 1908. The family made do raising beans, corn, ten acres of timber, and a bale or two of cotton.

Like everyone in Ouachita County, the Frizzells had heard people talk about oil. Wildcatting entrepreneurs and sober-looking geologists had poked around southern Arkansas for years, drilling gassers and dry dusters all over the lower counties. The region's production was so paltry that in 1919, a Tulsa developer needed just $250 to lease 12,522 acres around El Dorado, in nearby Union County. The first six months, his total payback was a single well that produced 40 million cubic feet of gas and a humiliating eight barrels of oil. The El Dorado townspeople—the ones who had collectively suckered him out of his $250—patted their billfolds and smiled.

The Busey No. 1 discovery well blew the smiles clean off their faces. A gargantuan gusher, the Busey No. 1 came in January 10, 1921. The well spewed thousands of barrels of high-grade petroleum over a forest clearing and down on top of a pathetic cotton patch. A new industrial era had begun in Union County. The same men who had cut logs for six bits a day now drove sixteen-head mule or oxen trains through the forest quagmire and cleared land for drilling. All through the forest, derricks were hammered together only to be blown apart by wild wells.

Five thousand out-of-towners clogged the streets of El Dorado by February and turned the downtown Garrett Hotel into the unofficial land lease exchange. By September, the land offered two years before at $250 per 12,000 acres was renting for $2,000 per single acre. Tents, shanties, luncheon counters, and dry goods storefronts were thrown together a few feet from the thickening mud of Washington Street. The beleagured town fathers worked frantically to contain the populace and hold the line against the influx of parasitic boomtown outlaws. The Washington shanty zone, called "Hamburger Row," was shut down for sanitation problems six months into the boom. At one point, hooded vigilantes calling themselves "The Saints" marched through town to quell a rash of local murders. In Ouachita City, the Ku Klux Klan demolished all the whiskey joints with sledgehammers and axes, then burned the town to the ground.

But Union County went truly berserk when the Smackover Field was discovered a few miles northwest of El Dorado. Twenty-five thousand petty entrepreneurs and callused proletarians swarmed the 139 shocked residents of Smackover, a forest flag stop on the Missouri-Pacific railroad line. The hapless town sunk into a demonic pit of grayish muck and moral sleaze. Spindly derricks rose above the storefronts while Model Ts spun their wheels in the impassable streets, flinging mud to the boardwalks down Smackover's rickety esplanade. The vehicle owners paid larcenous towing fees, while others walked across the railroad tracks to the cathouse district—affectionately known as "Death Valley." There, as one old-timer recalled, "It wasn't nothing to have four or five people killed every night."

What better place to raise a family? In 1921, William Frizzell sold his eighty-acre spread and moved his people to Smackover, where he enlisted in the blue-collar army driving the oxen teams. For a time he ran a blacksmith shop; then he went to work on the rigs. His son Naamon joined him in the oil field, driving a four-horse team pulling a "Fresno" earth scraper. At five six and 150 pounds, thirteen-year-old Naamon was already the thick-chested fireplug he would be for life. He had also embarked on the career that would drive him in and out of Southwest oil patches for the next thirty years.

The Frizzells stayed less than two years in Smackover before moving on to Corsicana to find work in the Powell Field boom. William and family moved into a farmhouse outside Tuckertown, the bawdy company village raised to accommodate the Powell Field workers. Quick riches combined with the deadly work on the rigs to pulverize moral distinctions in the high-pressure industrial universe of Tuckertown. Family shotgun houses stood board to board with brothels and gin mills. Wells exploded, survivors drank, young wives were widowed. Tuckertown once burned completely to the ground. Naamon, still a teenager at the time, ran a dry goods store for a Syrian man who paid for his high school education. When the store went up in the apocalyptic blaze, the young retailer gave up the merchant trade and headed back to the derricks. Tuckertown, like the South itself, would rise again.

Naamon was sixteen when he met a fun-loving fifteen-year-old "common country girl" named A. D. Cox, who lived across the Texas border in Hugo, Oklahoma. Two of her sisters were married to Powell Field roughnecks, and every year she and her mother would come down from Hugo to visit and pick cotton during the harvest season. Naamon fell for her during one of her lengthy stays. He never did learn what the initials A.D. stood for.

Naamon and A.D. courted long-distance for two years. It was an attraction of opposites. Naamon was full of bluster and given to surly moods, though he was perhaps less so around his young paramour. A.D. was lighthearted and cheery—always looking for an excuse to kick up her heels and laugh. They wrote to each other through the winter months, both looking forward to the cotton harvests, when they could be together. Naamon and his Oklahoma sweetheart finally decided to marry in the spring of 1926. They were not yet eighteen years old and had never kissed. Visiting his grandparents in Arkansas, Naamon told Plez of his plans before he took the leap. Plez took him out walking and gave him a pep talk that the nervous teenager never forgot. It was the last time Naamon saw his grandfather alive.

"He hadn't any objections," Naamon recalled, "but he told me what the fundamental rights was of marriage: 'Be sure you're right; study it over; talk about it; ask God above; make your decision; and when you've got it, and you know you're right, hold your head up and walk proud. Go straight ahead.' "

Naamon and A.D. walked straight and proud down the aisle of Corsicana's First Baptist Church on April 26, 1926. Shortly thereafter, the young groom quit his job driving horses and signed on to lay pipe for Gulf Oil. After a brief job hiatus, during which the newlyweds visited relatives, Naamon returned to the Powell Field to work for Pure Oil. He and A.D. moved into one of Tuckertown's shotgun shacks, and there in the long Texas night, between derrick tours, their first child was conceived. Nine months later, just before midnight on March 30, 1928, Dr. Dan Hamill was summoned to the Frizzell home.

The baby was late. The women kept the doctor waiting on the front porch till he was needed. Finally, at 12:35 A.M. on March 31, Naamon and A.D.'s son came squalling into the world "in an oil field behind an oil well." No one noticed which hand he favored. The proud parents named him William Orville Frizzell, but immediately took to calling him Sonny. The kinfolk called him Orville. Both nicknames proved useful three years later, when William's brother Bill was born.

Sonny had scarcely taken his first howling breath of oil-field dust when his father and grandfather were transferred back to El Dorado. Naamon and A.D. loaded their belongings onto an old Model T and headed across East Texas with their cumbersome baby — three months old and, according to Naamon, already weighing twenty-four pounds — squeezed in the front seat between them. They hit Arkansas's Red River lowlands in the July heat, Naamon driving hard and fast with the windows down to cool the boy while A.D. sang to him. They discovered to their pleasant surprise that her lilting melodies had a pronounced and immediate effect on Sonny's comfort. "He loved that music *so* much," Naamon said. "It would soothe him, or entertain him, or get him quieted down."

From the day his parents turned their backs on Corsicana, Sonny grew up on the move. The stock market crashed and the natural flow of the oil industry conspired with the ravages of the Depression to keep roughnecks chasing every rumor of black-gold riches gushing down the line. Naamon carried his family to an ever wider assortment of urbanized tristate cities: El Dorado, Arkansas; Kilgore, Cooper, and Sulphur Springs, Texas; Gandy and Rodessa, Louisiana.

Sonny was two and a half years old when the Joiner No. 3 Daisy Bradford opened the mighty East Texas oil field—"the Black Giant"—in the piney woods between Kilgore and Henderson. The Black Giant flooded the world with Lone Star crude, and the boomtown way of nightlife attained new heights of debauchery. Crapshooters tossed their dice till midnight, when the oil field musicians took over. Juke joint bands were everywhere. At Longview's Avalon Club, white singer Al Dexter and "His Colored Band" kept roughnecks and hustlers jukin' into the East Texas dawn, knocking down a mix of blues and electric hillbilly riffs. Their sound and all its like would one day be named for the honky-tonks where it happened.

Papa Naamon and his family made it to Kilgore in 1931, just in time to watch the glut oil prices plummet and the Black Giant jobs dry up. Industrious as ever, Naamon talked a black man who owned oil-rich land into letting him run a toll and concession stand. Naamon sold food to the roughnecks and moved bootleg whiskey that he hid in the high center of a rutted dirt road near the toll. His regular customers would pull up at a certain spot and Naamon would reach underneath their cars. Business went slack, though, when oil bottomed out at ten cents a barrel. Panicked corporate producers called for statewide production cutbacks and prorated pricing. Small independents kept right on pumping while their outraged neighbors—some maybe primed with Naamon's whiskey—promised to dynamite their tanks. The Governor of Texas declared martial law and sent the National Guard to "Proration Hill" in Kilgore. The Black Giant rigs were silenced. The Frizzells retreated to El Dorado.

Tough times or not, settled or moving, Naamon's family grew. Bill was born in Kilgore, followed by brother Lesley and sister Betty, both in El Dorado. A second sister, Johnnie Lee (rhymes with Connally), was born in Rodessa, while Ola Mae greeted the world from her aunt's house in Cooper, Texas. A close-knit bunch of rambunctious kids, they closed ranks around A.D., whose almost childlike love of laughter balanced Naamon's increasingly violent ways. With her husband working any seven-day job he could find to feed the family—and often drinking when he wasn't working—A.D. took responsibility for raising Sonny and his younger siblings, for nursing their wounds, and for sorting them out when they tangled in backyard scraps.

Hard times drove the family from house to house, from a quiet shack by the railroad tracks to a barn outside of El Dorado. Rats rustling among the corn shucks chased Sonny and his siblings out of the barn to a better home in the country. Meanwhile, though constantly moving from barn to cottage and from town to town, the oldest boy grew into what his father would describe as "a modern kid like any other." His parents' mobile lifestyle hindered his schooling, but when he did make it to class, he proved himself a better-than-average student. His favorite subjects were the creative ones. Sonny loved to draw line pencil por-traits and developed his own curving, minimalist style. His penmanship was florid. He constantly practiced signing his name in big, curlicued letters.

Sonny was short and slightly built. He carried what weight he did have on spindly legs that would embarrass him all his life, as would a giant birthmark—a goiter-like flap of skin that snaked down the right side of his neck. If too much dirt crawled under the useless flesh, the conspicuous birthmark would stand out red and ugly against his throat. A.D. would labor feverishly to clean her boy's unclean neck. She knew where the birthmark came from. Back in Tuckertown, late in her preg-nancy, she had rounded the corner behind the house and run headlong into a slaughtered hog hanging on a meat rack. Terrified, she had jumped back and stared into the murdered animal's vacant eyes. Weeks later, when Sonny was born with a mark on his flesh, A.D. blamed herself.

Birthmark or no, with his father's thick auburn curls and his mother's laughing disposition, Sonny was on his way to becoming the boyish charmer who would inspire country girls to abandon their Sun-day School morals for years to come. He was just as popular with the boys. Gregarious, funny, friendly, and physical, he developed early on a lifelong habit of grabbing or tapping his friends on their shoulders while speaking to them. He'd laugh and throw one of his buddies into a headlock, then drag him around the room while explaining some schoolboy point of order. He thrived on storytelling, often holding his brothers and sisters in terrified thrall as he ad-libbed spooky tales. But if Sonny made friends easily and picked up his mother's happy-go-lucky joy in life, he was not without his father's prickly temper. He wasn't big, and he never sought fights, but he was short-fused and fearless, and his fists were, according to every last person who knew him, lightning quick. Sonny wouldn't blink before decking any kid, of any size, fool enough to harass him. For instance, one day at recess in El Dorado, a schoolyard bully started taunting Sonny with a line drawn in sand. "I dare you. I dare you," the punk kept saying, sneering and pointing at the line he thought his skinny victim lacked the nerve to cross. Sonny's usual smile faded. The poor bully never saw the left hook coming. In the immortal words of his father, Sonny "hauled off and salivated the little boy."

Scrambling in the Arkansas dirt, the bully cried out: "You lefty devil! You took advantage of me!"

"Lefty devil" did not stick. Plain old "Lefty" did.

Chapter 2

NAAMON AND A.D. couldn't figure out why Lefty loved to visit his uncle Lawrence so much. A timber man, Naamon's brother lived in the country outside El Dorado. Most Sundays the family would go visit. The kids would crowd into Uncle Lawrence's house while Naamon and Lawrence talked trees. It was 1940. The Depression was ending. Naamon had started his own independent timber firm and would, for a brief time, prosper to the point of running forty-two employees. While he and his brother talked their Sunday talk, twelve-year-old Lefty would slip out the door and disappear.

One day, Lefty disappeared again. Lawrence went out looking for his nephew and found him at the edge of his property, visiting an old black farmer who lived there. Lefty was sitting rapt at the old man's side, his eyes glued to the farmer's fingers. Lawrence realized why Lefty took off every Sunday. The old man was teaching him to play guitar. "He'd be down there with that old guy, picking, knocking right on that old guitar," Naamon said. This time, Naamon recalled, when Lawrence showed up, the old man pointed at his guitar and said to Lefty's uncle, "I wanna give him that." Lefty's heart stopped. But his uncle wasn't about to take charity from a colored man. "Well, I'll buy it," Lawrence finally said. "What'll you take for it?"

The old man looked at Lefty, then back at Uncle Lawrence. "That boy wants it so bad," he said, "give me couple of dollars, you can have it."

Music was everywhere in young Lefty's life. His mother liked to sing, and Naamon had moonlighted in a western band that played Friday-night dances in Tuckertown. When Lefty was two months old, his mother's voice had soothed his infant nerves, the sound imprinted on his soul as he jounced across Texas in his father's Model T. Two years later he surely absorbed at some subconscious level the music that drifted twenty-four hours a day from the Black Giant gambling joints and honky-tonks of East Texas. As years went by, the sounds Lefty loved came to him across the airwaves. His father bought a crystal radio set, one of millions sold to American homes between the two world wars. In October 1935, when Lefty was seven years old, El Dorado's first radio station, KELD, took to the air with a hundred watts of startup power. Spinning the dial to KELD, he could pick up ephemeral acts like Pinto Pete, the Shillings Cowboys, and Singing Sam.

Beyond El Dorado, the airwaves grew richer and stranger as powerful local stations and national networks fought the intrusions of the Mexican border blasters. On Saturday nights, Nashville's WSM radio pitched the Grand Ole Opry across the entire South, while on any night, Villa Acuña, Mexico's, XERA pitched goat-gland transplant surgery (said to rejuvenate the "sexually weak") around the entire globe. In 1938, a weird gospel number called "The Great Speckled Bird" made an Opry superstar of Roy Acuff, one of Naamon's favorite singers. As Lefty passed through the fourth and fifth grade, Bob Wills and the Texas Playboys hawked Play Boy brand flour over Tulsa's 25,000-watt KVOO; when the wind blew right, Lefty could probably catch the Playboys' swinging amalgam of fiddle tunes, pop, blues, and gutbucket jazz. Lefty heard it all, but mostly had ears for the Playboys' smooth-voiced singer, Tommy Duncan. Sliding along through "Trouble in Mind," Duncan's casual phrasing made perfect control sound lazy. Lefty would not forget that lesson.

Sonny, as the family still called him, may have learned other lessons just by walking the streets of downtown El Dorado. "Automatic phonographs" (soon to be known as jukeboxes, thanks to one of white America's great co-optations of black vernacular) popped up in lunchrooms and roughneck hangouts throughout the Southwest, often loaded with so-called "race" and "hillbilly" music, the likes of which network radio tended to ignore. The jukebox industry exploded during the Depression, especially in 1934, after the repeal of prohibition. Wurlitzer sales escalated from a paltry 266 nationwide in 1933, to 45,000 in 1938 alone. When the record industry took a bath through the early part of the decade, the companies responded with thirty-five-cent budget lines oriented toward jukeboxes and poor folks. In 1933, Victor introduced their cheapo Bluebird label, while American Decca, likewise a budget imprint, went into business a year later. Battling for the race and hillbilly dollars, which they'd discovered were quite numerous — Bluebird and Decca both offered records by Shreveport's Jimmie Davis, the future Louisiana governor, who yodeled bluesy double entendres about a mysterious assailant known as the "bedbug stingaree." Though Davis's biggest smash of the 1930s was "Nobody's Darling but Mine," it was probably his mournful "It Makes No Difference Now," spinning scratchily on some downtown Wurlitzer, that really caught Lefty's attention. Written by Houston honky-tonker Floyd Tillman, the song was so ubiquitous that at least one man took a shotgun to his local jukebox rather than listen to it again.

Lefty had barely attained the age of reason, though, when one solitary, yodeling cry entered his father's house and changed his life forever. With Depression livestock prices dropping below the cost of feed, Naamon tethered the family's aging milk cow and took it to a neighbor's house to trade for something useful. He came back home with a windup Victrola and a stack of 78 rpm records by Jimmie Rodgers, the late, tubercular Mississippi native known far and wide as "The Singing Brakeman" and the "Famous Blue Yodeler." As the 78s spun, and the scratches crackled, the ethereal voice of a man "lonely and blue" poured from the tinny speakers, wreaking mortal havoc with Lefty's enraptured soul.

Nowadays routinely referred to as "The Father of Country Music," Jimmie Rodgers culled his musical influences from any sources available — mountain folk songs, pop puffery, blackface show tunes, black bottom blues — and fused them with an eerie, tumbling yodel that utterly enchanted Lefty. Rodgers would work as well with an Appalachian string band as with Louis Armstrong. A former railroad man, he sang country love songs with enough lugubrious grace to stoke any hillbilly parlor passion, but when passion got ugly, Rodgers in song would call on a pistol "long as I am tall."

Starting with the songs he recorded at Ralph Peer's famous "Bristol Sessions" of 1927 (during which the Carter Family was also discovered) Jimmie Rodgers sold millions of records over a five-and-a-half-year career, throughout which he was dogged by the devil TB. His ailing health inspired his hair-raising 1931 recording of "T.B. Blues," a Depression-era statement far more personal and every bit as fatalistically chilling as the famous plaint "Brother Can You Spare a Dime." In May 1933, as working men like Naamon Frizzell scratched out subsistence livings across the South, Jimmie Rodgers lay hemorrhaging in a New York City hotel a thousand miles from the streets of El Dorado. He died at age thirty-five, the single most important figure in the history of country music, arguably the most influential pop performer of his era, and indisputably the idol of Lefty Frizzell's youth.

For Lefty, Rodgers's voice was more than music he loved—it was the means of coping with an impoverished childhood begun in an oil field and half lived in the backseat of a Model T Ford. The uniqueness of the singing brakeman's yodel, its inarticulate sound—half howl, half river chant—afforded Lefty an escape from the harsh realities of his daily life. With his brothers and sisters laughing and screaming behind him, Lefty would listen to the Rodgers 78s with his head stuck all the way inside the Victrola cabinet. "I'd come in frustrated from school and it'd help me," he would say years later. "It has always helped me. I loved his voice and I'd yodel and harmonize with him and it gave me peace. I can truly say he was the biggest influence on my life."

When Uncle Lawrence bought Lefty his first guitar (actually, there's strong evidence it was A.D. who came up with the cash), the boy's precocious goal was nothing less than to learn every one of Jimmie Rodgers's songs. The black tenant farmer had shown him a couple of chords; another friend taught him more. Lefty automatically played right-handed, simply because that's the way he was shown. "I'd come in from work, and he'd be sittin' on the porch somewhere," Naamon said. "Plunk, pum, pum with that thing, tryin' to learn it. And he'd get in there and play on that old Victrola thing, Jimmie Rodgers records and stuff like that. He told everybody to get out of the way. Or he'd try to hum along or pick music like they was. And that was his ambition."

Naamon wasn't so keen on his oldest boy's ambition. He knew the bottom-line value of picking a guitar, having played in a Tuckertown dance band during good times, when the oil field workers were still flush. Even then, his loose-knit band had had to scrounge for Friday night work at the oil camp parties. They might walk out with five dollars per man, perhaps a little more if the roughnecks, having drunk enough to forget to go home, pooled their money to keep the band swinging after midnight. Naamon knew it was no way to make a living. Coming home from his timber work to find Lefty picking atonal dissonance on a two-dollar guitar, Naamon, annoyed, would tell his boy to get busy doing something useful. Schoolwork or chores or something. Lefty wouldn't budge. "How am I supposed to learn to play this guitar with you always wanting me to do something?" he'd demand.

To his friends, Lefty's front-porch work sounded better than the "plunk, pum, pum" that made Naamon wince. When a teacher at the Parker's Chapel Hill School outside of town started planning a school program, one of Lefty's pals tipped her that the oldest Frizzell boy wasn't a half-bad singer. A little short on talent, she invited Lefty on the show. Lefty was thrilled by the offer, but distraught over his lack of decent shoes to wear onstage. Much to his humiliation, he agreed to wear his mother's oversized laceup oxfords in lieu of manly footwear.

On the night of the program, Lefty's mother and his brothers, Bill and Lesley, sat down front in the school auditorium, watching proudly as bigfoot Sonny, accompanied by the teacher on piano, worked through Gene Autry's "South of the Border" from the 1940 movie of the same name. The song was written by a pair of Irishmen who had never seen America, let alone a cowboy. "He sang it pretty good," A.D. would later say. "Everybody just hollered and patted, you know . . . and he was just thrilled to death. Oh, he thought he'd really done something, you know. So then, we went home and he just kept talking about it . . . how good he done."

It was no accident that Lefty sang one of Autry's hits that night. He loved B-movie horse operas and horror flicks — Autry, Tom Mix, and "good old Frankenstein." Anytime money permitted (the family fortunes picked up when Naamon started the timber company) he'd head for the Saturday matinee. Like the cabinet of his father's Victrola, the movie theater was as much Lefty's school as his escape. Becoming a bit of a dandy himself, he was as entranced by Autry's Hollywood western fashion as by as the music. Lefty loved to wear bright bandanas around his neck — both to hide his birthmark and to better affect the cowboy style. He'd have his mother sew flashy buttons onto his shirts and sometimes ask her to dye them. Dressed the part, munching popcorn in a back row, Lefty could imagine himself the man in white, dispensing justice with a six-gun and six strings. It was an adjunct vision to fuse with his raw musical ambition, a fantasy any roughneck's kid could understand. The B westerns proffered Hollywood reality — a bizarre yet orderly world in which the cavalry outran armored tanks, even as Hitler's armored tanks were overrunning Europe.

Naamon's once-flourishing timber business had been pruned to one truck and two black hired hands when the news flashed over KELD that Japan had attacked Pearl Harbor. After the bombing, rootless roughnecks and mill hands enlisted in droves. For Naamon, the decision was not so easy. He was, after all, thirty-three years old with a wife and seven children to consider. But in the end, that only made him feel he had that much more to fight for. He couldn't live with himself sitting on his callused hands. Naamon fretted for nine months, then came to the only decision a red-blooded Union County working man could make. On September 26, 1942, a year to the day after his seventh child, David, was born, the thirty-three-year-old father volunteered for the Army Air Corps. His proud family waved goodbye as he left El Dorado to be inducted into the army in Little Rock. He abandoned acres and acres of standing timber that he never would reclaim. The day after his induction, Naamon was sent to an Army Air Corps training base in Greenville, Texas. His oldest boy, Sonny, was fourteen years old.

With Naamon gone to Texas and the first family allotment check not due for three months, Lefty proudly declared himself man of the house and quit school. He hit the El Dorado pavement looking for work and convinced a drugstore owner to give him a job delivering telegrams and medicine. The gig paid a dollar a day, plus tips, and Lefty took it seriously. To make his rounds, he literally ran from house to house, until his aunt Cara Mae, no doubt moved by his adult sense of responsibility, bought Lefty a bicycle. After that he made his deliveries on wheels, splashing through the muddy streets with his pants legs rolled to his knees.

Sometimes Lefty would take A.D. along on his rounds, letting her ride on the seat behind. A.D. and Lefty, laughing mother and earnest son, were never closer than during those early months after Naamon left. At night, coming in exhausted from work, Lefty would spin a couple of Jimmie Rodgers records, then jump up and tell A.D., "Mama, get on your coat right quick, and somethin' on your head, and let's go get the kids somethin' to eat." They'd spend Lefty's tips at a grocery store run by blacks, each night coming away with corn bread and maybe a gallon of milk. Afterward, as A.D. later recalled, Lefty would let his mother wash his mud-splattered calves. "Mama, don't laugh," he'd say. "We both got little legs, but we've stood up on 'em, ain't we?"

Chapter 3

T HE DEPRESSION struck many rural Texans as a Yankee banker's problem, a distant, esoteric crisis not to be confused with the daily immediacy of dust storms and drought that forced Lone Star farmers off the land. But the war was entirely different. Army and air bases like the one outside Greenville opened all over the state, and young men from Dallas, Tyler, Brownsville, and the rest of Texas gave up more than their fair share of blood. As one historian put it, "Texans tended to be combative. In the war years, Texan casualties were the clearest indication."

Defense money poured into Gulf Coast cities and North Texas cow towns. With it came displaced farmers, ranch hands, cotton pickers, fishermen, and Rosie the Riveters — all the Depression-era underemployed who did not make their way directly into the armed services. During the 1940s, Dallas's population grew from 294,000 to 434,000. Houston grew by 55 percent. Corpus Christi almost doubled. The trend was repeated all over Texas and throughout the South. Migratory paths from the dust-bedeviled farms to the crime-bedeviled cities — from the Mississippi Valley to the Northeast factories, from the Okie heartland to the California coast — sent the tenuous Christian mores of small-town America crashing into Babylon.

What drillers and roustabouts hadn't learned in Smackover's "Death Valley," machinists and soldiers picked up in Dallas taverns. Songs like Al Dexter's "Pistol Packin' Mama," inspired by a waitress in the East Texas oil field, drew crowds to Lone Star dance floors on Friday nights. Anxious farm boys watched jaded city women pass by their tables dressed in gingham, two-stepping to the fiddle jump and amplified steel of Bob Wills and Leon McAuliffe. Ted Daffan's "Born to Lose" broke nationwide, fueling the sorrow of heartbroke soldier boys while Daffan himself built B-24s in Houston. The war years, Texas-style.

When his first allotment check came through, Naamon sent for his impoverished family. A.D. and the kids rode the Cotton Belt rail line down to Sulphur Springs. They stayed there until Naamon found a four-room country cottage near the army base, seven miles out of Greenville. A rail crossroads nestled in among the lush, blackland hills east of Dallas, Greenville boasted the world record for a single day's cotton processing. The cotton record was the town's great claim to fame, but Greenville was also the site, in 1908, of the infamous lynching of a black man accused of raping a white girl. Screaming for blood, a Greenville mob dragged the prisoner by rope to the courthouse square and burned him alive at the stake. Refusing to condemn the lynching, the mayor later declared that "the penalty of death was administered by an orderly body of citizens from the city and country."

Greenville had quieted down considerably by the time the Frizzells moved there in 1943, despite a flurry of activity caused by the newly opened air base. The new Frizzell house, rented for twenty-five dollars a month, was owned by a childless couple who lived nearby. Looking kindly upon A.D. and her brood, the neighbors were generous with their milk cows and chickens. The Frizzells lived modestly but comfortably, their allotment income supplemented by seasonal work during cotton harvest time.

The whole family lived a Tom Sawyer idyll in the East Texas countryside—swimming, fishing, playing hide and seek in the tall grass—the spell only broken when the radio brought reports of the carnage in the Pacific. At night, the kids would gather at A.D.'s feet, all sitting quietly while she crocheted and told them stories of family lore, of picking cotton in Navarro County and children born behind an oil well.

Though Lefty was no longer burdened with feeding the family, he quit school after two days in the Greenville system, perhaps because he was so far behind. He never got past the sixth grade, a fact that would dog his self-confidence as years went by. Within the family, though, his brothers and sisters continued to look to Lefty as their leader. He entertained them with impromptu guitar performances, ghost stories, and extemporaneous speeches delivered from his bed. He already loved to play to an audience, his shows acted out in a world proscribed by the close walls of a four-room country house.

But fifteen-year-old Lefty was too ambitious to settle for his siblings' adoration. He had seen the life he wanted reflected in the upturned faces at the El Dorado school auditorium. He made friends with a Greenville kid named Gene Whitworth, who lived with his widowed mother on the far side of town. Gene, too, played guitar. He and Lefty started working their way into weekend parties and house dances, anywhere folks would give them attentive ears and space to swing their six-strings, anywhere Texas women gathered to forget about their missing boys while close-mouthed men passed a crumpled sack in the shadow of the trees out back. Lefty was developing as a singer, though not so much as a musician. On guitar, he had graduated from a mere two chords to three or four. But he could still slay the older dancers with his naively earnest approach and his lackadaisical imitation of Ernest Tubb, his voice sinking down low in his throat as he growled, "She's gonna trifle on you. . . ."

Ernest Tubb was Lefty's new hero. Born in a town not far from Corsicana, the lanky "E.T." had also idolized Jimmie Rodgers as a young man. He yodeled like Rodgers, befriended Rodgers's widow, played Rodgers's guitar, and debuted on record in 1936 with "The Death of Jimmie Rodgers." Then he got tonsilitis and his yodeling career went all to hell. Hitler was already in Poland before Tubb resurfaced on wax, this time with an urbanized sound built around electric guitar and a vocal style that dispensed with conventional worries about timing and pitch. The more flat Tubb sang, the more Texans loved him. As the first few Zeros closed in on Pearl Harbor, jukeboxes with Tubb's "Walking the Floor Over You" were swallowing nickels faster than roughnecks swallowed beer. A couple years later, his "Soldier's Last Letter" set a standard for maudlin hillbilly-in-the-trenches morbidity, a theme country fans have been suckers for ever since. Lefty learned every one of E.T.'s hits. He even dug back into Tubb's Jimmie Rodgers years to learn the ubiquitous "Mean Old Bed Bug Blues," though Tubb's song, unlike Jimmie Davis's "Bed Bug Blues," was a yodeling jailhouse downer that never mentioned the bedbug stingaree.

Without Naamon to rain practicality on his dreamy parade, Lefty was able to act on his musical ambitions. A.D. gladly acted the part of stage mother, a role she had relished since the El Dorado days. Her attitude toward Lefty's aspirations had always been the opposite of Naamon's. She encouraged her boy, pushed him even. Back in Arkansas, when KELD started an after-school children's talent show, A.D. had volunteered her two talented boys, Lefty and Bill. Lefty had already come through his stage debut with flying colors; he handled the radio pressure fine. But apparently Bill was a little young for show business.

"They asked Bill, 'What are you gonna sing?,'" Naamon explained. "He said, 'God Bless America.' He got up and sung 'The Airplane Song.' Yeah, 'Fly away, airplane . . .' I don't know what it was. And it was right different from what he said he was gonna sing. It was kind of comical."

In Greenville, A.D. would drive Lefty to his informal jobs at neighbors' dances and gauge the crowd response, nodding her head if he was going over well, shaking it if he was screwing up. Once, almost by accident, the two of them together milked the shoppers at the Treadway's grocery in downtown Greenville. Set up on the market patio, Lefty sang, A.D. Charlestoned, and the Treadway's manager collected twenty dollars passing the hat. Having conquered the grocery-store circuit, Lefty figured it was time to up the ante. His mother knew how. Sometime in 1944, at about the time of Lefty's sixteenth birthday, stage mama A.D. was proud to swing him a fifteen-minute slot on KPLT in Paris, about forty miles up the road from Greenville. At 250 watts, the station signal barely reached the Frizzell house. But it was strong enough for them to know the station was there. Lefty auditioned for a two-hour variety program broadcast at one o'clock on Sunday afternoons. The show, sponsored by the Lowrey's furniture store in Mt. Vernon, did not have the most stringent audition standards. "All you'd have to do is call and make a promise that you'd have your child there," Naamon said. Aside from occasional appearances by genuine talents like Hawkshaw Hawkins, who was stationed near Paris, KPLT was a revolving-door circus of freewheeling, seat-of-the-pants wartime staffers, three-chord pickers, and wannabe Andrews Sisters. "If you were breathing, you got on the air," says Dorothy Locke, who worked as the station's traffic manager.

Lefty's Sunday showcase in Paris was no high-profile gig, but it gave him his widest audience to date, and, just as important for his self-esteem, paid him a token fee. KPLT was the first genuine professional singing job of his life. No more passing the hat at Treadway's. Lefty was making real money doing what he loved most. KPLT's fifty-mile listening range carried his adolescent voice into Greenville, Sulphur Springs, Mt. Vernon, Mt. Pleasant, and on into the mighty Red River Valley. It was a question of identity. Not only neighbors and kinfolk but total strangers could hear him sing his beloved Rodgers and Tubb songs. Every Sunday, A.D. would drive Lefty to Paris, where he would sing and play his solo guitar. "His mother did that," Naamon said, "and she'd go out there and help him, you know, and tell him what to do, and what not to do, and so forth. And I remember one case . . . she told Sonny, she ate him up, you know, said, 'Boy, don't get in there and just stand still. Put a little twist to ya. Get the girls a-hollerin' for ya.' "

Evelyn was one of the first to holler. She was a casual girlfriend a few years older than Lefty (it was probably a compromise setup she endured because of the shortage of eligible eighteen-year-olds). One Sunday evening in the spring of 1944, she, Lefty, and A.D. passed through Sulphur Springs on their way to visit friends in Mt. Pleasant. The three of them stopped at a downtown Sulphur Springs hotel that had been converted into a soldiers' hostel by the American Rescue Workers, Inc. A.D. knew the hostel proprietor's wife, a woman named Ruby, and wanted to say hello. When they walked into the hostel lobby, Lefty immediately noticed a high-cheeked, dark-haired beauty who looked to be his age—and his size. She wore a pleated skirt and penny loafers. She had blue eyes and obvious Indian blood. Lefty knew he had seen her once before, walking through Mt. Pleasant. He had liked her legs. The second time they saw each other, in the hostel lobby, she noticed him staring. She stared back. Lefty was wearing his usual bandana and one of his fake cowboy shirts. He had moccasins on, and was carrying his guitar strapped across his 125-pound frame. His thick curls were plastered flat with an ocean of Brilliantine. The girl took one look at him and wrote him off. "I thought he was kind of sissy-lookin'," she said.

The girl, Alice Lee Harper, was a mere three months younger than Lefty. At least a quarter Cherokee, she was born July 1, 1928, in Winnsboro, Texas, the oldest child of Luther Thomas Harper and Mina Dickey Harper. She had one brother, Luther Thomas Harper Jr., who was almost exactly Bill Frizzell's age. Luther Sr. (or L.T., as most called him) spent the Depression moving from farm to farm between Mt. Pleasant and Sulphur Springs. When Alice was barely old enough to start school, her mother died of pneumonia. People say L.T. went crazy with grief and hit the road, leaving his children to be taken in by relatives. He eventually returned to Mt. Pleasant and married Maggie McCrary in 1934. When L.T. joined the seabees after Pearl Harbor, Alice and Luther Jr. were left to split time between their stepmother in Mt. Pleasant, an aunt in Sulphur Springs, and their grandmother in Winnsboro.

Alice responded to the movement and instability in her life by becoming an independent, self-sufficient teenager. She held down a soda job at a drugstore in Mt. Pleasant, but hardly had time to make any friends. Her autograph book boasted all of two signatures. Neither signee had much to say. Alice did have a boyfriend, but he dumped her and later regretted it. ("I feel like a *mule* to ask you to forgive me," he wrote to her.)

A carny handwriting analyst called teenage Alice self-conscious and sensitive but responsible and loyal to notions of right and wrong. "You do not seem to be in the habit of building air castles or daydreaming for you are given to thinking in a rather practical manner." The analyst also noted jealous tendencies. "There is a sign of distinct temper. . . ."

Alice Lee Harper was made for Lefty.

When A.D., Lefty, and Evelyn ran into Alice, in the lobby of the Service Men's Free Hotel, it was no more than a typical Sunday gathering of Texas friends and kinfolk. "Small world" was not an operative phrase. Evelyn, though, was nonetheless outraged to notice Lefty shamelessly staring at blue-eyed Alice Harper. "She got real jealous, and real mad at him," Alice recalled. "And pretty soon they left, and he told me later that she made him go. Well I said, 'Well, that's silly. How can anybody make you do anything?' "

But after their first brief encounter, Lefty started angling to see Alice again. His best chance arrived when he learned from his mother that one of Alice's many relatives was coming to Greenville to visit. Seizing the day, Lefty said to his mother, "Tell her . . . if she's coming up here, have her bring Alice, that girl. I wanna meet her."

A.D. put in Lefty's request and Alice's relative played along. Reluctantly, Alice agreed to make the trip to Greenville. The Frizzell and Harper parties met at Treadway's. Alice didn't know she'd been snookered. She was dumbfounded to find the sissy-lookin' kid with the eccentric fashion sense waiting for her at the market. She hadn't thought about him since the day she first saw his greasy curls. But she sensed something was up when someone suggested, "Why don't Son take Alice to the movie?"

"Hmm," Alice thought. "Oh, shoot."

Thirty miles away from home, she had no way to back out of the forced date. She and Lefty, and several of Lefty's brothers and sisters, headed to the theater to see some forgotten B western — "a Gene Autry movie, or Tom Mix or somethin'," Alice recalled — while Alice's relative went about her business. At the theater, Lefty tried to make a sly move. He put his arm around Alice in the dark but she pushed it away. "No!" she said, and stared at the screen. Undaunted, Lefty leaned over and kissed her on the cheek. Years later she would laugh about that first kiss from Lefty: "Oh, he was a Romeo. Yeah, Romeo," she said. "Even at that early age, he had an eye for the pretty girls."

A persistent eye, too. Despite Alice's cold response, after the movie let out Lefty asked her for a real date. She hesitated, but agreed. "Well, I guess so," Alice said. Two weeks later, Lefty borrowed his mother's '41 Ford, a car she'd bought with money from the harvest work, and drove to Sulphur Springs. He picked Alice up at her aunt's house and took her to a local café, where he bought her a "nice hamburger." Everything was going fine until it came time to pay. Alice, no upper-crust debutante, nevertheless watched in horror as Lefty emptied his pocket and counted out pennies to cover the check. ("Can you imagine . . . going with a boy that counted his pennies?") But Lefty wasn't the least bit embarrassed. In fact, he was happy to discover he had enough pennies left over to buy his new sweetheart a giant peppermint stick.

But then Lefty really blew it. He took Alice for a drive in the country to visit some Frizzell family friends who lived outside of town. The family had two girls, both of whom fancied him. He pulled off the road and started up toward their house. "Where are you going?" Alice said.

"Well, I'm gonna go out here and see these people."

"What people?"

"Well, it's these two girls."

The mere suggestion appalled Alice. "Listen here!" she said, her temper quick to rise. "Well, now, no. Now, I'm not going out there. . . . I do not want to meet anybody. I do not want to meet any girls."

Lefty paid her no heed.

"We got out there," Alice recalled, "and for protocol I had to save face, and I had to get out and say 'Hi.' And went inside for just one second only. Soon as their backs turned I went out the door, and I left, walking. And you talk about mad! I was angry! And I took that big old peppermint stick, and I threw it, and it broke into a jillion pieces."

Lefty, on the ball, hadn't even noticed that his date was missing. As Alice told the story:

Their little brother . . . he come in the house, and they said, "Where's Alice?" He said, "I don't know, but I seen a girl walking down the road, and she was mad. 'Cause she took this big old stick of peppermint candy, and she just throwed it and broke it everywhere."

And Sonny, he says to hisself probably, Uh oh. So he decides he'll get in the car and come and get me. And I said, "No, I'm not getting in the car with you. I do not want to see you anymore. Just forget it." The last of it. So he said, "Well all right, if that's the way you feel about it, okay." And he zoomed up the road. . . . And so I walked on, and pretty soon he backed around, and he come back, and he tried to get me to get back in the car again. "No!" And finally he begged. I thought, Good lord, there's people passing by, and some of 'em probably know me, and lived here, and so . . . I said, "All right, I'll get in."

So I got in, and he began to talk to me, and he said, "You shouldn't
done that . . . they didn't mean one thing to me. One thing. Mama just
said if I went down there to go in and say hello to 'em." 'Cause they was
good friends. And I thought, Well, hooey.

Having survived their crisis, the two made up and "went to sit somewhere where the locals parked." They talked and laughed, and made
plans for their next date, picking a night two weeks down the line.

The second date went about like the first, only in reverse. Lefty
threw a jealous fit over one of the soldiers at the hostel, a kid with
smelly feet and a disconcerting resemblance to Mickey Rooney. When
Lefty accused Alice of stepping out on him with the GI, prickly Alice set
him straight on that score. "First place, I do not go with soldiers. Never
have went with soldiers. And never do intend to." But once they got
that "little debate" out of the way, everything was fine. "And so we sit
somewhere," Alice said, "and then we were in a good mood. Laughing
and talking, and this and that, you know."

All told, it had taken a mere two dates for Lefty and Alice to set the
combative tone of a love that would last, however embattled, for thirty-
one years. "We always did fight stubborn and high-tempered," Alice
explained. "Since the time we met."

The spring of '44 became summer, and the summer, a long romantic
winter. The Frizzells' Tom Sawyer idyll played itself out with a new
twist as Alice and her brother joined in the fun, the hide-and-seek
games affording her and Lefty time for surreptitious kisses in the shadows. The teenage couple swam together, played in the fields together,
and joined their brothers and sisters at jacks and card games. (Lefty,
everyone discovered, "delighted" in cheating.) If Lefty or Alice had a
little money, they'd roller skate at the local rink and take cheek-to-
cheek snapshots in the photo booths. On Sundays, Lefty made his treks
to Paris, working his fifteen minutes on KPLT while Alice tried in vain
to hear him sing through the static. Lefty wrote her romantic notes and
sent them down to Sulphur Springs. He called her his "sweet darling"
and told her how much he wished they could be together all the time.

"I'd never gone with anybody like him," Alice said. " 'Cause he
was . . . he was different. And the fellows that I went with were like—
they were macho . . . they were men's men and boys' boys. Anything
that the boy was supposed to know how to do—repair a car or
anything—they did it. But [Lefty] wasn't that way. It wasn't his style.
God made him to write beautiful songs."

Lefty had indeed been writing songs, no doubt spurred on by his heroes, Rodgers and Tubb, both of whom wrote much of their own best work. Lefty's urge to write songs, as well as sing them, marked a subtle but critical development in his musical growth. It pointed to the organic view of music to which he already unknowingly subscribed. Songs, to him, were for more than singing. They were supposed to reveal the emotional substance of the man—or boy—behind the voice. At sixteen years of age, Lefty wrote with juvenile directness, chronicling his adolescent fears and heartaches in songs with titles like "My Sweetheart Marium," "Girl of My Songs," and "My Times with You." He wrote boyhood laments for his overseas father that included "Daddy's Song," "Hurry Home Daddy, We'll [Be] Waiting for You," and "Thinking of Daddy Tonight." The latter three numbers were probably treacly rip-offs of Rodgers's "Daddy and Home" or Autry's "That Silver Haired Daddy of Mine." "Thinking of Daddy Tonight" may have also borrowed from the Carter Family's "Thinking Tonight of My Blue Eyes."

Lefty's own blue-eyed first love, a rich girl he had fallen for before he met Alice, was probably the inspiration for "It's Too Late Now," "You Went Away and Changed Dear," "You'll Be Sorry You Went Away," "My Gal, She Left Me," and "I'm Glad We'll [sic] Through." She was certainly the femme fatale behind "Be Mine Blue Eyes" and "So Long Blue Eyes," both of which were among the eighteen "Songs By Lefty" the teenage troubadour had cataloged by the time he and Alice got serious.

Azure-irised herself, Alice never knew "Be Mine Blue Eyes" wasn't written for her. Lefty told her it was. He had discovered what a romantically utilitarian number the song could be when he won a five-dollar prize singing it at a Dallas talent contest called "Wayne Babb's Stage Show." The contest wound up a tie between Lefty and a scene-stealing youngster half his size. But when the audience was asked to break the tie with their applause, Lefty smiled for all the blue-eyed girls and women in the front row. The half-pint didn't have a chance.

Lefty stared into Alice's blue eyes a little too long one fateful night in March 1945, A.D.'s '41 Ford parked in the country outside Sulphur Springs. The hours passed quickly in the timeless still of teenage romance. Before either one knew what had happened, it was three o'clock in the morning, many hours later than sixteen-year-old Alice was ever allowed out. "Oh, am I in for it," she said, thinking of her father, just home from the war. "I'm gonna catch it. Catch it for sure."

Lefty, worried and protective, couldn't stand to think of his young love catching it. There had to be a way out. "Well," he said, the wheels turning, "I guess we could just—guess we could just go get married. Run off and get married."

Alice weighed the magnitude of such a decision against the horror of her predicament. "Well," she admitted, "I hate to go home. It's too late."

"Well, let's just go on over and see what Mama says," Lefty suggested.

The nervous pair drove straight to Greenville and woke A.D. Lefty said, "Mama, me and Alice are gonna have to get married. She can't go in this time of night."

A.D. scoffed at the very idea. "Oh, you're too young to get married. You're only sixteen."

"Well, my goodness, you and Daddy married when you were seventeen!" Lefty answered.

Mother and son argued for awhile, Lefty more and more scared that Alice's father would come knocking on the door any minute, until he finally talked A.D. into driving them across the border to Antlers, Oklahoma, where A.D.'s sister lived, to get married. They woke the other kids, rounded them up, and took off. The carload of Frizzells, and one Harper, pulled into Antlers in the dark predawn hours of March 12, Lefty and Alice asleep in the backseat with her head on his shoulder. A.D. and the other kids laid pallets on the floor of her sister's house. Several hours later, after a brief, cramped sleep—and while Alice's father had the sheriff out looking for his daughter in Sulphur Springs—Lefty borrowed a couple of dollars from his mother and tried to buy the marriage license. However, he discovered to his dismay that even in Oklahoma, he and Alice needed a parent's signature. It took another protracted mother/son argument, with Alice sobbing, scared the whole deal was off, for A.D. to agree to sign. A.D.'s sister signed for Alice, in place of her parents. On the way to the justice of the peace, Lefty and Alice—stubborn and high-tempered from day one—managed to get into one last prenuptial lovers' spat.

"I just think I'll just tear our license all up," Lefty threatened.

"Good!" Alice cried. "Just tear [it] up!"

As always, they made up as quickly as they had fought, and could not remember what the trouble had been in the first place. The justice of the peace married the sixteen-year-old couple—still just children at the peppermint-stick age—with his wife as witness. As she said her vows, Alice tried not to focus on having set her life's path in the same wrinkled dress she wore for a date the night before.

About two weeks later, a tornado touched down in Antlers and nearly blew the town right off the map. For the rest of their lives together, Lefty never let Alice forget that their marriage had angered the elements.

Chapter 4

ASSIGNED TO THE European theater, Naamon Frizzell fought bravely, though he almost never saw combat at all. While still in training he contracted pneumonia and his division shipped out without him. The army gave him a medical discharge, but Naamon didn't know it because they also lost his service records. A bureaucratically unrecognized soldier, he was sent overseas on the *Queen Mary* to catch up with his comrades. After marking time at a base in England, he crossed the channel on D+2 and survived the Normandy beachhead, only to come within inches of death when a German shell crushed a house near where he was fighting. The blast blew a two-by-four straight at his face. The rocketing timber pulverized his jaw and nearly took his head completely off. Shrapnel tore up his legs. He returned home via hospital ship in the summer of '45. Among his belongings, if he hung on to it, was a letter that told him his oldest boy had married.

The teenage couple's marriage was not going well. For one thing, Alice had got pregnant immediately, panicking Lefty into cruel retribution for what he perceived as enslavement to family responsibilities. "I wish to goodness I hadn't of never got married," he complained to his mother, with Alice listening. "I'm just now old enough to start going and looking at the girls." Alice couldn't stand to hear it. As A.D. related the incident, Lefty's bride threw some clothes in a paper sack, screamed that she was leaving, and ran out of the house. Instantly ashamed of his callous talk, Lefty chased her through the same fields where they had romped the summer before. Pleading and begging and apologizing, telling her how much he loved her, he talked Alice out of her hurt and rage. The newlyweds kissed, made up, and before long were laughing and talking again.

Even so, the simple life they had lived and loved was winding to a close. Things had to change. They had to grow up. Lefty went to work at the Service Men's Free Hotel and saved up several hundred dollars while they considered their next move. Naamon's return forced their hand. His first day home from the war, he saw A.D.'s car, saw the wild, carefree mood of her household, and saw his married son and the pregnant daughter-in-law about whom he had heard but whom he had never met. He was not pleased. "I am here to tell y'all, that the boom is over!" he thundered. "The boom is over!"

A.D. waited for Naamon to leave the room, then arched her eyebrows and asked the kids, "What boom is he talking about?"

Lefty and Alice knew what he meant. It was time to leave the roost and make their way in the world. Though Lefty didn't have a driver's license (a minor detail that had never curtailed his trips to Sulphur Springs), he spent $425, as Alice remembered, on a Model A two-seater with bad brakes. With car, guitar, and a hundred-dollar white and red embroidered cowboy singer's suit he had talked his mother into buying him, Lefty felt ready for the big time. That meant Dallas. "So, we headed for 'Big D,' " Alice said. "Alice Dallas. Headed for big old D to make our place."

Dallas founder John Neely Bryan beat them by just over a hundred years. In 1840, he traveled from Van Buren, Arkansas, to the banks of the three-pronged Trinity River to set up a trading post along the military route from Austin to the Red River. Four years and a land grant later, the Texas legislature formally recognized the fruits of his enterprise: Dallas County. The county's namesake town was platted that year. Bryan was named its first postmaster. Aside from distributing the mail, the ex–Arkansas trader sold what were, for many, the essentials of a Dallas homestead: tobacco, whiskey, powder, and lead. Had he dealt in Bibles, he would have had every frontier market cornered.

Bryan's vision of Dallas as the main stop on a major north-south commercial waterway never materialized. In the long run it didn't matter, for the blackland farming country east of the city made the Mississippi Delta look like the Mojave Desert. King Cotton expanded its imperial reign and Dallas developed as a prime railroad distribution center. As the years passed, though, cotton prices fell, and the natural movement of goods into town was accompanied by a natural movement of down-and-out tenant farmers. Black and white, they left their plows. On the move from a bad situation to a worse one, the migrant families held on to their music as a way to make sense of Depression madness. "I'm an eagle riding papa, from Tennessee," some sang, following the lead of blues singer Georgia Tom Dorsey, who would one day give them "Precious Lord, Take My Hand." On its way from Deep Ellum in Dallas to Fort Worth, Dorsey's "eagle ridin' papa" became an "easy ridin' papa." Fiddlin' white hipsters heard the song and the lyrics changed once again: "I'm an easy ridin' papa, from Tennessee" became "We're the Light Crust Doughboys, from Burrus Mill," and later, "We're the Texas Playboys, from the Lone Star State."

The song, and others just like it, sprang from the repertoires of the Light Crust Doughboys, Bob Wills and His Texas Playboys, Milton Brown and His Musical Brownies, and Cliff Bruner and His Texas Wanderers. Dance bands all, they overran Texas in the face of dust and Depression, their music drawn from ancient tradition and modern invention, from Italian violinists and Deep Ellum bottleneck guitarists, from polkas and waltzes and Tin Pan Alley. One or another of these bands' music popped up on radio in every major city in the state. In Dallas, Bill Boyd and His Cowboy Ramblers ruled the hillbilly airwaves on WRR. (Boyd's only serious Dallas competition came from his own pianist, Roy Newman, whose hard-hitting branch-off band played a badass version of Louis Armstrong's "Black and Blue.") Over in Fort Worth, the Light Crust Doughboys sold Burrus Mill flour by the ton, giving Burrus Mill magnate "Pappy" W. Lee O'Daniel enough exposure eventually to catapult him from the concert stage to the Texas governor's office.

In addition to the star radio cowboy bands, innumerable semipro and amateur dance bands raised on Bob Wills takeoffs and Fats Waller piano breaks were forming. On any Friday night, they'd set up at the nearest Dallas boneyard tavern where the patrons had a few extra dollars to toss in their cases. One of those clubs was the Old Top Rail, a tiny joint described by an old Dallas picker as "way out on the highway in no man's land," where not much happened except hillbilly music, Texas-style, and "a lot of fights and a lot of bad news." Lefty found the Old Top Rail during a jaunt in his Model A two-seater. He looked at the cramped stage and scuffed floorboards, the chairs and tables chipped and scratched from too many brawls to count, and must have thought he heard the ghost of Jimmie Rodgers singing "Treasure Untold."

With a hundred dollars between them, Lefty and Alice checked into a hotel on Ross Avenue in downtown Dallas. First off, they drove around looking for work for Alice. Opportunities were plentiful. Postwar prosperity was nowhere more evident than in Texas, and sure enough, Alice landed counter work at the Odd Penny Cafe, serving breakfast to a clientele too bleary-eyed to notice her growing belly. Every morning, Alice rode the bus to work while a cousin of Lefty's who lived in Dallas took him around to the Big D clubs. Lefty's expanding repertoire of cover tunes and fast maturing down-home voice won him a job at the Old Top Rail, where he was hired to front the house band. Hillbilly stardom seemed imminent.

"We thought we just had it made," Alice said. "He was working at the Old Top Rail, and making some money, and I was working at the café . . . and puttin' both our money together, and we done saved up enough money to buy us some nice outfit of clothes, and a watch, and the ring, and nice car, and done had all our chickens hatched."

Giddy over his instant fortune, Lefty took the stage each night and never noticed the cynical looks cast back and forth among the bored pickers behind him as he led the band from a second chord to a third, but rarely hit that fourth or minor seventh. All he saw was the audience, which one night included his mother, who arrived from Greenville to see him perform. That night, she and Alice took a center table and ordered home-cooked fried chicken, naturally assuming that dinner was on the house for the family of the star of the club. Between sets, Lefty sat with them, feeling important, like Jimmie Rodgers must have felt when the night was right and the coughing fits subsided.

It never crossed Lefty's mind that the job at the Old Top Rail, his first honky-tonk gig, would last all of three weeks. After that, the fed-up band members said they didn't care how good Lefty sang, they weren't gonna play down to his three-chord level anymore. The owner gave Lefty his last check and said he had to let him go. Already crushed, Lefty looked at the check and his heart sank as low as the honky-tonk hardwood beneath his feet. His mother's chicken dinner had been deducted. So had Alice's. Too discouraged to face his wife at the hotel, Lefty did something he had never done before—he drank. He bought one beer, then another and another, and suddenly it probably didn't matter so much. The corners of the hellish honky-tonk softened and it didn't matter that he was seventeen years old, jobless and broke, with a hotel tab waiting and a pregnant wife still slinging hash to help make ends meet. He drove back into town, stumbled into the hotel room, and lay across the bed. Alice leaned over him and said, "Sonny, what is the matter with you?"

The next thing they knew, they were back in Greenville and Naamon was talking about oil in southeast New Mexico. Naamon sold A.D.'s car and bought a station wagon instead. The whole family, including Lefty and pregnant Alice, piled into the wagon. They drove across Texas to Hagerman, New Mexico, chasing oil through the mighty, dry Permian Basin as if nothing had changed since 1928.

In Hagerman, Lefty picked alfalfa and cotton, all 125 pounds of him stooped in the fields from dusk to midnight, cutting and bailing and pulling, his tight brown curls plastered to his forehead as the hours wore on and the cotton bolls tore at his hands. He hated it. When one of his uncles, a Cox, came home from Japan and went on a tour of the kinfolk, Lefty and Alice hitched a ride as far as Oklahoma. They stopped in Dallas one more time, in late 1945, the baby due in less than two months and not a penny to pay for delivery, and then moved on to Waco. There, as Lefty would one day put it, "I got a job driving for my wife's half aunt's second husband"—the irrepressible Reverend Lewis E. Satterfield, National Commander of the American Rescue Workers, Inc.

Satterfield ran the Service Men's Free Hotel, the place where Alice first caught Lefty staring at her, and had since moved the enterprise from Sulphur Springs to Waco. At 404 Franklin, above a corner drugstore on the third floor of the Provident Building, the reverend and his organization honored their charter principles: to "stand for God, to uphold Americanism and help suffering humanity."

As in Sulphur Springs, the Waco hostel offered soldiers and veterans "a Home Away from Home" with a "Special Room for Hospital Patients." Lefty and Alice got a special room of their own as part of a deal that put Lefty behind the wheel of the American Rescue Workers' canvassing car, dressed in a blue Salvation Army–style suit. Down the streets of Waco, Lefty and his fellow servants would ride, singing stodgy church hymns. A genuine believer, Lefty never once questioned God's existence, mercy, or mysterious ways. But he knew what foolishness was. He had never felt so stupid in his life.

When the reverend felt Waco's charity had been exhausted, he sent his mission out on the road. Lefty and several others headed south toward San Antonio. Lefty took his cut of the canvass (less expenses, which he paid himself) and sent the money to Alice, five or ten dollars at a time. On February 3, 1946, Alice wrote to her "Darling Dearest Husband" care of San Antonio General Delivery. "Darling I do Love you so and miss you so much when you are gone, you'll never know. And I pray always that God may take care of you & bring you safely back home to me." She told him his family had just been to see her in a new car, an Oldsmobile. "They gave me the phone no. of the camp when I get sick so you can call them."

Poor Lefty never saw his wife's letter. The Rescue Workers had already sent their canvass crew north to Paducah, Texas, where Lefty mailed a note of his own: "Alice Darling I'll be in as soon as I can get in. You know I'd like to be in right now, with you. Darling I would have send [sic] this money sooner but I just didn't have it, it's all that I've got right now. [B]ut maybe I'll make some more today. [F]or I'll need it for I owe John expenses for every day we've been gone. I'll close now. With all my love. I love you. Sonny."

Happily, Lefty did make it back to Waco in time to be there when Alice got "sick." On February 16, she gave birth to Lois Aleta Frizzell at Hill Crest Hospital. Lefty's relentless road work had earned him enough to cover hospital costs, but he came up fifty bucks short for the doctor's fee. The doctor would just have to wait. Lois was barely settled into her bed in a cedar chest drawer, her features scarcely imprinted on Lefty's mind, before he was back on the highway, driving and singing for suffering humanity. Twelve days after their daughter was born, Lefty wrote to Alice again, this time from Lawton, Oklahoma.

> Alice Darling — I hate that I'm gone, but things will be better, when I get back home. "I know you hated to see me go away, but hon I'll be back in just a few days, I'll do all I can dear oh you understand, and I'll be true dear, I know I can, I'll love you darling, till the end, because I know hon your my only real friend."
>
> Well hon I hope you like this poem, I made up last night. I love you darling. I'll be seeing you real soon. Kiss the baby for me.
>   Leftie sonnie F.

Making the most of his loneliness, Lefty began writing songs and sending them to Alice. "First Year Gone Away" was written on their wedding anniversary in March; "I Cried While Writing to You" was scratched out on notebook paper somewhere west of Waco. "You mean the world to me," he wrote, "your all I've got, you see, I cried while writing to you." With Lois to support, money was tighter than ever. Lefty sent eight dollars from Denver and reminded Alice to put two of those dollars aside for the jeweler. "Darling I don't have but about $37.50 dollar now," he wrote. "I haven't made so much have I."

The American Rescue Workers hit Los Angeles in late June, by which time Alice had left Waco and returned to her relatives in Sulphur Springs. "Well I'm so happy tonight, darling," Lefty wrote from L.A., "because I think that I'm going to get to come back home, to you. I love you so. Sweetheart I'm a long ways from you tonight, I'll be so glad when I can get to love you some More. I don't think I'll ever leave you Any More."

Lewis Satterfield led the Lord's workers out of L.A. the next morning, and Alice met them in Waco. After the tour was over, Lewis and his wife, Ruby, decided to move out of the Service Men's Free Hotel into a regular house in the city, leaving the hotel to someone else's managerial care. Lefty, Alice, and the baby moved with them, but it was obvious from the start that the overcrowded situation wouldn't work. Alice could at least cook and clean house in exchange for room and board. But Lefty had no skills to barter. "Sonny . . . he had to find something else to do," Alice explained. " 'Cause it wasn't no good like that. Wasn't no money being made. I was just having a free place to stay while he went off to look for another place to start."

Like so many men before him, so many jobless young husbands and determined young fathers, Lefty hoped a better living lay somewhere in the great "out there." He had a cousin in Wichita Falls who he thought might be able to help him get up on his feet. If not, Lefty knew he could just continue west to his parents' home in New Mexico. One morning he pulled on his "old yellow-looking" boots and packed a few clothes in a battered suitcase. He scraped together all the money he could find in the house — $1.17. He threw his guitar over his shoulder and kissed Alice and Lois goodbye. "Now, I'll send for you and the baby," Lefty said.

"Okay, I'll be all right," Alice assured him.

Standing at the door in Waco, she watched her worried man walk off, a Tom Joad folk hero vision she never forgot. "Down the road. Guitar slung on his back. Only weighed a hundred and twenty-eight pounds, and that soaking wet."

Chapter 5

LEFTY THUMBED HIS WAY north to Wichita Falls, but the town was a total bust. His cousin did what little he could for Lefty—put him up and promised him work with a local medicine show run by a husband-and-wife team he knew. The job never materialized, so Lefty, guitar still hanging across his back, bailed out of Wichita Falls and headed west across the Texas flatland to Dexter, New Mexico, where his parents and a number of relatives were living. As before, he joined A.D. and the kids in the cotton fields. "He picked cotton, and he picked cotton, and he hated picking cotton," Alice said. "And he picked cotton." Lefty's only relief came on Saturday nights, when his uncle Johnnie Cox would chaperon him to the bars in downtown Dexter to sing hillbilly hits for tips.

In the fall of '46, after logging untold hours in the cotton fields and hillbilly watering holes, Lefty saved enough money to send for Alice and Lois. He wanted their reunion to be something special so he rented a motel room in Roswell, a larger town located fifteen miles up the highway from Dexter. He picked out a room he liked and paid a week's rent in advance, then sent Greyhound fare to Alice in Waco. But in his eagerness, he made one small miscalculation. "What he had forgotten," said Alice, "was how long it would take me to get there on a bus by the time I got the money." Mail was slow, buses slower. By the time Lefty met his wife and daughter at the station in Roswell, they only had one night left of their romantic week in the motel.

After a lone night of bliss, Lefty trudged back out to the cotton patch. With five dollars he had left over from the motel fiasco, he rented an unheated Airstream trailer, one of two that an older couple let behind their house in Roswell. As winter approached, the New Mexico nights turned chilly, the dry winds whistling in under the trailer door. Lefty and Alice would curl up under the blankets and tuck Lois tight between them to keep her warm. "We were just simple, simple little children," Alice said. "Simple children. Not out looking and searching for rainbows then." Alice found a café job near the bus station. Lefty sought music work in Roswell and neighboring towns, singing for tips at roadside inns. Not much came of his efforts at first, though he did befriend a number of local pickers and even cut a few primitive home disk recordings on a machine owned by musician Ray Patterson.

The first that many of the Roswell players heard of the new singer in town was at a stage show at the Chief Theater. The Callahan Brothers, an old-time duet with a national reputation, introduced Lefty as their opening act. For a time he also accompanied a woman and her trick horse, humming and whistling and singing cowboy songs. On opening night at the Yucca Theater, the horse, which knew how to see-saw, showed its ad-lib comic flare when it lifted its tail and "did its business," as Lefty put it, in front of the packed house. The woman was mortified until Lefty, who knew his movie cowboy trivia, assured her that Tom Mix used to pray for just such a finale.

The holidays never looked so bleak as they did that first winter in Roswell. "We didn't know what a Christmas present was, little less a good Christmas dinner," Alice said. When a musician friend of Lefty's who lived in the next trailer suggested stealing a neighbor's goose—a killing offense in those parts—Lefty "was kind of leery of the idea" but also intrigued. On Christmas Eve, the two hungry pickers clambered over the fence and corralled the goose, which made "the awfulest racket" as they hauled it away. They managed to kill the poor bird, though Lefty "didn't know about killing a chicken, little less a goose." While Alice and the other musician's wife prepared the Christmas meal, Lefty and his friend stuffed the doomed bird's feathers into a hole they had dug, destroying the evidence.

As the winter winds blew colder through the Pecos Valley, Lefty and Alice found a better-appointed, five-dollar-a-week, trailer—this one with heat. With Alice's café job paying the rent (and Lefty's little sister Betty often caring for Lois), Lefty made his music rounds. He approached Jud Roberts, station manager of KGFL ("Keep Good Folks Listening"), which was Roswell's oldest radio station. Located a block off the town square, on Richardson Avenue, the station had covered much of the Pecos Valley since 1931, but its programming was somewhat thin. Impressed with Lefty's drive and KPLT résumé, to say nothing of his talent, Roberts offered him fifteen minutes a day on the air and $3.75 a week as long as he could come up with sponsors. That was all the green light Lefty needed. He hit up every retailer in town. He'd walk in the door and announce to whoever was there, "My name's Lefty Frizzell, and I've got a radio show, and I would be glad if you would be one of my sponsors. I believe I could help you. And you could help me."

Several businesses, swayed by Lefty's enthusiasm, signed on. A shoe store, a paint store, the Roswell Pool Hall, and the Roswell Planing Mill all pitched in. With the merchants' support, Lefty went on the air in the spring of 1947. For material, he dug deep into his honky-tonk repertoire: Ernest Tubb songs, Floyd Tillman songs, Ted Daffan songs. And always Jimmie Rodgers. Lefty chose Tubb's "I Ain't Going Honky-Tonkin' Anymore" as his theme song. He sang "Drivin' Nails in My Coffin," a rip-roaring boozehound number favored by both Tubb and Tillman. He dredged up Tubb's "Mean Old Bed Bug Blues," with its images of jailhouse bedbugs the size of a whale. Usually Lefty performed by himself, but sometimes he brought in a fiddler, accordian player, or second guitarist.

As his show caught on and his local fame spread, Lefty decided he'd outgrown his two-dollar guitar. His shoe store sponsor, Pat Owens, cosigned the note on a $125 Martin D-18. Lefty's show moved a lot of boots. He took his new prize home and knocked on the trailer door. Striking a star pose on the stoop, he strummed his best Jimmie Rodgers lick. Alice opened the door and nearly fainted, certain he'd procured the lovely flattop the same way he had their Christmas dinner.

Singing from 1:45 to 2:00 every day, Lefty built a loyal following. People hired him to play Pecos Valley dances and private parties. Angling for a steadier gig, he introduced himself to the New Mexico Playboys, the house act at a local dancehall called the Cactus Garden. Lefty asked the band's leader, Pat Espinoza, if he could sit in for a night. Espinoza said sure. Lefty went over so well with both the crowd and the pickers that Espinoza hired him full-time, not only for their regular weekend job at the Cactus Garden, but also for road dates up and down the Pecos and Hondo Rivers. Working with the band, he sang his Tubb repertoire, took the Tommy Duncan part when the Playboys covered Bob Wills, and on occasion, threw in a song or two of his own. (Smiley Mauldin, fiddler with the New Mexico Playboys, says one of Lefty's that really got the cowboys in a lather was called "Why Do Gals Wear Britches.") Once Lefty had established himself, the owner of the Cactus Garden, likewise impressed, decided to help sponsor his radio show.

"Y'all come on out to the Cactus Garden and dance and have a good time," Lefty would say on the air. "I'll be there, and I'll be singing the latest numbers."

Lefty had found his element. Situated on the Dexter Highway south of Roswell, the Cactus Garden was built like a barn. On warm nights, the huge side doors would swing open to reveal the tumult inside. Besides the New Mexico Playboys, the hall booked out-of-town acts like the Maddox Brothers and Rose, "The Most Colorful Hillbilly Band in America," and T. Texas Tyler, "the man with a million friends." A better, more relaxed venue than the chicken-wire whiskey joints most of the headliners were used to, the Cactus Garden still attracted wild sons of bitches who "came there to drink and fight." The cowboys were the worst. One particularly obnoxious group of twenty or so would bring their bad moods and bottles down from the ranches every week. They'd set up a shit-kicking gauntlet by the dancehall exit, bumping roughnecks and making comments about their wives just to make something happen. "If they didn't have a fight, they didn't enjoy themselves," says one of the club's former patrons. From time to time, Lefty had to stand tough and fight like a lefty devil. He was small, but not afraid of anything. Recalled Smiley Mauldin, when a group of local toughs threatened to beat up the whole band, Lefty said to sit still, he'd take care of it. He did.

From the first night he sat in with the New Mexico Playboys, Lefty was a hit at the Cactus Garden. Roughnecks, cowboys, and cotton pickers marveled at his way with the songs of their jukebox heroes. But it wasn't just the mimicry that made the teenage singer popular. It was his infectious good humor and the whole modernist country style he tapped into. Lefty had an intimate sense of song, a one-on-one style that invited individual empathy. The Texas dance bands had carried an older generation through the dust bowl years, but pummeled by the chaos of the war and the nerve-wracking rigors of postwar industry, Lefty's listeners turned inward. What they saw inside themselves — pious or ravaged — was private and vague till a Floyd Tillman or an Ernest Tubb made music out of their fears. That's what honky-tonk was about. The sliding steel and electric guitars gave the sound a serrated emotional edge, but it was always the singer — and now that meant Lefty — who tore into their sorrowful Southwest hearts.

In many ways, Lefty lived that spring and summer of '47 in outgoing opposition to the isolated summer of love he had spent in the country with Alice the year they met. He'd hang out downtown, hang out at friends' houses, hang out at the Cactus Garden. On a typical night, he and his friends would find somebody to buy them beer and then drive out to the country to drink it. Other nights, they'd gather in somebody's living room, drinking six-packs while picking out tunes on their guitars and writing snatches of songs that might not turn up again for years. Lefty ran with his cousins, Jack and Junior Cox, and with a group of downtown buddies attracted by his growing local fame. He also met a more distant cousin, a Corsicana relative named Lucky Cook, a musician who was stationed at the Roswell Army Air Field. Cook played second guitar on Lefty's show and used his service connections to get Lefty work at the NCO and enlisted men's clubs. "He would go in there and play in the enlisted men's club," said Cook. "Just walk in there with his guitar and start playing. That's just the way old Lefty was—he liked to play for anybody."

Cook and Lefty would solicit sponsors together, or hit the local theaters to check the traveling cowboy shows like Jimmy Wakely's, or Monte Hale's. Lefty had grown cocky enough to criticize their work, especially the work of singers who imitated Roy Acuff. But he also felt the reflexive sting of his comments, his own bread and butter being hillbilly mimicry. Still, he had begun to experiment with his own personal style—a softer sound than Tubb's, more slurred and serene, more natural to his tristate Southwest accent. And he still had that cowboy fashion sense. He sported a new dippity-do ringlet over his forehead to go with his emergent vocal identity, and jokingly tried out a promo moniker: Lefty Frizzell, "a boy with a wave in his hair and a curl in his voice." At KGFL, he put both to use—style and sound—singing with the window blinds raised so the phone company women across the street could watch him work.

Lefty had never ridden such an emotional high. Suddenly his life was shaping up as he had envisioned it. No more singing on the family bed for Bill and Lesley and Betty. No more passing the hat at Treadway's. No more American Rescue Workers cap. No cotton. No alfalfa. No stolen goose. Just "singin' and pickin' on a guitar." Lefty had never been happy in quite this way—not when he married, not when Lois was born. Those were beautiful times, each irreducibly perfect in its own way. But this was a different happiness. Lefty hit the stage at the Cactus Garden and knew he was headed where he wanted to go. A few languid sweeps of his accented voice—"Please be mine, blue eyes, be mine"—and the Cactus Garden would roar.

"And then," said Alice, "that's where the little girls began to be so crazy about him."

Chapter 6

IN THE PARKING LOT by the Cactus Garden, in the sweet of the evening, Lefty did what he'd been doing all summer of '47: just leaning back on the hood of a Chevy or lying down in the grass, smelling the mesquite and cholla blossoms, happy as he'd ever been. Inside the dancehall, the Maddox Brothers and Rose, or some other band, raised the roof with manic chortles and a thumping bass that rocked roughnecks down to the floor. Outside, Lefty punched his buddies on their shoulders and chests and laughed for the teenage girls nearby. They always came calling at the Cactus Garden, and Lefty wasn't about to turn their attention aside. Just nineteen himself, he was making up for lost time, trying to reclaim the years of teenage flirtation and backseat tussles he had abandoned by marrying young. Lefty liked the forward type, the fast-action girls who would come after him, instead of vice versa. One group of five or six "wild gals," as Lefty's cousin Junior Cox called them, were especially notorious. Alice concurred. "They're like fourteen and fifteen. And they don't care," she said. Lucky Cook remembered a night several approached him and Lefty and suggested they all go out on the town. The cousins laughed and said they had no money. "Well, I got the money," said one of the wild gals. "Well, we got the time!" was Lefty's reply.

Fooling around was all a big lark to the dandy boy with the curl in his voice. None of it, he told himself, had anything to do with Alice. She didn't need to know, and if she did, she didn't need to worry. She was the one he loved; these others were just summer fun he had never had before. Much as their crushes did for his ego, his favorite times were the simple ones with Alice, the afternoons when she and him, and little

Lois, would spend their last couple dollars on a cowboy movie, daring fate to break them. But Lefty got careless with Alice, sometimes to the point of insult. Junior Cox recalled an incident in Roswell. He, Lefty, Alice, a couple more friends, and a fourteen-year-old local girl were hanging out on a Saturday afternoon. Someone suggested hide and seek, a game that Lefty should have outgrown back in the fields of Greenville. They decided to play anyway. The game had barely gotten underway, however, when Cox heard horrible screams in some nearby bushes. Alice was knocking the hell out of the girl. Seeking a hideout, she had found the girl making out with her husband and beat up the one she decided deserved it.

Of all the wild gals who hung out at the Cactus Garden, this fourteen-year-old was the one who, according to various accounts, really got hung up on Lefty. Apparently something of a honky-tonk Lolita, she was, as Alice indignantly put it, "everybody's gal in town." Maybe so, but that summer of '47 she only had eyes for the boy with the pretty curls and prettier voice. And Lefty saw no reason to spurn her adolescent affections. Maybe he knew she was only fourteen, maybe not. Married at sixteen himself, it's not certain he would have cared if he did know. But one warm night in July, while Alice was away visiting her family in Texas, the girl, a friend of hers, Lefty, and several of Lefty's friends all rode out toward the Pecos for one of their usual summer nights. The precise details of what happened in the car that night may never be known—how much coercion, if any; how much degrading intimidation, if any; how much of what, many years later, would be debated as "consensual sex." What could not be debated was age. The girls were fourteen. Lefty was nineteen. One of his friends was twenty-three, another twenty-two. Lefty may not have known how young the girl with him was, but he knew the law. He knew what men meant when they warned each other against "jailbait."

According to the worst account, after the men "slam-banged" the girl, "she walked back to town and turned 'em in." Others, mostly Lefty's friends, have said she fingered him out of sheer jealousy for his refusing to take her crush seriously. In Alice's version, the girl didn't "holler" about the incident until her parents got wind of what happened and threw a fit. "And I guess she was scared, you know. And so they said, 'Who were they? Who were they?' And naturally his name came up, 'cause he was popular." No arrest records are known to exist, but there was, in fact, a curious omission in newspaper reports of the charges. On July 13, just eight days after the alleged capture of a flying saucer made Roswell front-page news worldwide, a small blurb in the

Roswell Daily Record noted that "Four youths entered pleas of guilt to charges of statutory rape." Lefty was not among the four named. It wasn't until three weeks later, on August 8, that Lefty's own guilty plea was mentioned in the paper. However, on July 17, his name quietly disappeared from the KGFL logs; his celebrity reign ended in infamy. Fans unaware of what had transpired would have turned on their Zeniths at 1:45 and instead caught Riders of the Purple Sage — wondering, perhaps, why Lefty wasn't going honky-tonkin' anymore.

For several weeks, Lefty and his family fought to have the charges dropped. The owner of the Cactus Garden reportedly went to bat for him, and Naamon came up from the oil field where he was working to try to reason with the DA. Lefty had never been in trouble; he had a wife and a baby to look after; what were they gonna do? The prosecutor said tell it to the judge. Indignant to the end, Alice maintained that the DA was eager for a juicy case to "feather his cap," and she may have been right. "They made examples of about four," Alice said. "And [Lefty] got to be one of the unfortunates. I mean, there was no way that they were gonna let them off. It was statutory rape."

If the prosecutor was, in fact, looking for publicity, he miscalculated on the media end. Locally famous though Lefty was, his case never made it out of the court-record blurbs and into the headlines, probably because of the close ties between KGFL and the *Daily Record*.

On August 21, the district judge slammed his gavel and sentenced Lefty, and three others, to two to three years in the state pen. Not completely without heart, he suspended all but six months of the sentences. Those six months, he announced, were to be served in the Chaves County Jail, smack in the middle of town. It was almost more humiliating than getting shipped to the pen. Lefty was utterly devastated that he would actually do time for an act he considered to be more a crime against his marriage vows than against society. And Alice was far more forgiving of Lefty's transgressions than the court had been. She swore that if he'd been released she "would've just hugged [him] and said, 'Forget it. I love you.' But, no, no, that wasn't to be." Lefty was locked away in a cell seven miles west of the Pecos River, he and Alice both crying as they said goodbye. "And in there," said Alice, "he wrote his heart out."

He had to. Lefty was so wracked with guilt and grief that writing songs became his means of survival, his only way to communicate his anguish to his wife. He suffered nightmares, and even the good dreams seemed worse than nightmares once he woke up and discovered he was still in his cell. In one of his first letters from jail, he wrote, "Alice last night I dream[t] that I saw you & Bill come up to the window of the door, I heard you say you had come to get me out. [S]aid that the girl that got me in this trouble had drop[ped] everything against me. if I was giting out. What a <u>dream</u>."

When, to cheer Lefty up, Junior Cox wrote him a letter and inno-cently asked him to "sing 'Mean Old Bed Bug Blues' for me," Lefty thought that his friend was making fun of him. He read the letter and cried.

But what preyed on Lefty's nineteen-year-old conscience the most was not knowing what Alice would do, not knowing if at any given moment she might be on her way to the Greyhound station with a banged-up suitcase swinging at her side, their quiet little daughter cling-ing to her. Had the jailer not permitted Lefty a soft-leaded pencil, a tablet, and a stash of Chaves County Courthouse stationery, he might have broken all the way down.

Lefty wrote his first jail song to Alice on Friday, August 29, just one week after his sentencing. It was called "I Know You Couldn't Feel the Way I Do," and he dedicated it "To My Darling Wife." "I'm so sorry — little darling. I'm sad, I done you wrong, Please wait for me, I pray it won't be long." Six days later he wrote "I Had Two Angles [sic] at Home." On September 7, "Write Me a Letter & Say You're Still Mine," "A True Song to My Only Sweetheart & Wife Alice. I Love Her So Much. I Swear. Sonny." At the end of the song, Lefty added a P.S.: "Honey I do love you so much. I'm trying so hard to prove it to you. Please like my songs, for they are true from my heart — All my songs I write, will always be to you & Lois. I'll love you & her <u>for-ever & ever.</u> Sonny."

After that, the deluge. Between September 11 and October 11 he wrote nine more songs (original titles and spellings preserved here): "I Suppose Your As Blue As I Am Too," "You Loved Me All Along the Line," "I Tirfled on You, My Last Time" ("I'll always live up to this song, I swear.") "I Know You're Lonesome While Waiting for Me," "If I Loose You, I'll Loose My World," "I Caused Grief and Worry," "Three Hearts Broken Now," and "Those Simple Things." Every last lyric was a confession, a promise, a plea for absolution.

Yet none of the songs really nailed what he meant to say until, one September afternoon, he pulled out his small, wide-ruled notepad and wrote down the lyrics to a song he called "A Thousand Ways." It started with the line "I love you, I'll prove it in days to come." At the end of the song, on the bottom of the back side of the paper, he swept across the page with a flourish, "To My Only Darling & Sweetheart <u>Wife</u>/<u>Alice</u>, I love her <u>so</u>. By Lefty."

Dissatisfied with how it looked, he turned to a new page and started over. This time he called the song "I Love You, I'll Prove It a Thousand Ways." He wrote the lyrics down again, and added as a postscript, "Alice Darling I pray that you will believe me, when I say I will prove it <u>a thousand ways</u> a thousand times, that I do love you, — if you have really been true, & honest. [L]ike you say you have & will be. [F]or now I know in my lonely heart dear, that there's no one else in this wide world for me. I swear I love you. Sonny."

Lefty looked the letter over again. It still wasn't right. So he turned to his store of Chaves County Courthouse stationery and flipped a sheet over, turning the picture of the courthouse facedown. He straightedged a series of lines, giving the stationery the look of tablet paper, and wrote it all down, one more time:

> *I love you, I'll prove it in days to come, I swear it's*
> *true, Darling you're the only one, I think of you, — of*
> *the past and all our fun, I love you, I'll prove it*
> *in days to come.——*
> *You're my Darling, you've been true, I*
> *should have been good to you, you're the one that's*
> *in my heart, while we'll [sic] apart, — I'll be true,*
> *I'll prove it to you some-day, my love is for*
> *you, in my heart you'll always stay, I've been*
> *so blue, and Lonesome all these days, I love*
> *you, I'll prove it a thousand ways. ——*
> *I'll be nice and sweet to you, and no-more*
> *will you be blue, I'll prove I love you every day,*
> *all kinds of ways, — Darling please wait, please*
> *wait until I'm free, there'll be a change, a great*
> *change Made in Me, I'll be "true," there'll be no*
> *More blue days, I love you, I'll prove it a*
> *thousand ways, — When I'm Free.———*

> *The End By Lefty*

Lefty was not allowed his guitar in jail, but there's no question he had tunes in his head for each of the songs, including "I Love You, I'll Prove It a Thousand Ways." Melodies stuck, it was getting the words on paper that determined if Lefty would remember a song or not. Early in October, when Alice came to see him, he sang "If I Lose You, I'll Lose My World" to her a capella in the visiting room.

As the weeks crawled past, Lefty's remorseful terror that Alice might leave him mutated into an obsession with her fidelity and personal safety. "I had to move from the little trailer," Alice said, " 'cause he wanted me to, 'cause he was so afraid that somebody would hurt me." She found a one-room house in a better neighborhood across town and finagled a job at the Rainbow Drive-In, leaving Lois with Betty or a next-door neighbor whenever she had to work. With Lefty in jail, Alice also had what she called "my first, and only, talk with what they call human resources." The agency told her she didn't qualify for assistance. "Well who does qualify?" she wondered. "I have a baby; they took my husband away. . . ."

Alice scraped by, though, and grew more and more proud of being able to do so on her own. Nevertheless, Lefty kept picturing all sorts of horrible scenarios occurring in his absence. He finally convinced her to move in with his parents in Loco Hills, an oil field forty miles southeast of Roswell. "So there I was—oh Lord—sand dunes everywhere, my husband in jail. I loved him dearly."

Stuck in Loco Hills, Alice was nearly as miserable as Lefty. Naamon drank hard and physically terrorized his family—including his wife. For her part, A.D. played psychological games with defenseless Alice. Every two weeks, when Lefty's parents would drive her to Roswell to see Lefty, A.D. would recite to him a litany of Alice's shortcomings. Lefty never listened. "All he wanted was me and Lois, and to be out. And free, and independent, and just us together again, making our own way."

By November, the situation at home had grown unbearable. Alice begged Lefty to let her take Lois to Texas. "Sonny, just let me go back home," she said. "Let me go back to the folks. Maybe I can make it a little better."

"Well, honey, I hate to be away from you," he told her, "to not even see your face."

"I do, too," she said. "But it's just gotten so impossible for me and Lois, and I just can't hardly stand it."

With his own memories of Frizzell home life, Lefty understood her desperation and finally consented, though her departure only magnified his own desperate fears. Just before Thanksgiving, Lefty sent Alice a long letter illustrated by a cross drawn tattoo-style and inscribed, "True Love to My Wife."

"Alice Darling please keep waiting for me," he wrote, "I will make you so very happy honey, please—please believe me, I promise I will be good to you, I could never be mean to you again, for I see now you have always been so sweet & good, you have never done me wrong— that I know of. . . ."

Surprisingly, once Alice took off for Texas, instead of sweating the rest of his sentence Lefty shifted into smooth, time-marking gear. He responded to her leaving as if freed of the constant reminder of his guilt — Alice's watering eyes, and Lois's uncomprehending ones, before him every two weeks to scrape his raw conscience. He knew his family was in good hands, that Alice's brother Junior was seeing to their welfare. "Darling I'm sure proud of Junior . . . ," Lefty wrote. "Hug his neck for me. . . ." After they left, he spent less time atoning for his sins and turned back to focus on life inside the walls. Seasoned inmates taught Lefty important jailhouse survival tricks — like how to drain the stimulant from a Vicks inhaler into his coffee cup for an electric speed buzz. Bouncing off the bars and concrete wasn't good fun, but it beat sitting still and staring as the walls closed in. Lefty also learned to walk with one hand covering his ass to avoid getting goosed. It was no minor concern. For one swift pinch could send a prisoner jumping into the man in front of him in the food line, which was cause enough for a serious beating if the man in front was, shall we say, sensitive about his sexuality. Sometimes the guards would mess with Lefty's head, demolishing his neatly ordered writing area on the pretext of searching for contraband. But he may also have had an informal furlough or two, for he later told Junior Cox that on several occasions the sheriff snuck him out to play private parties, in each case returning Lefty to his cell just before the morning crew came in.

As the months passed, Lefty wrote less and doodled more. He drew crosses; hearts; portraits of Alice; portraits of Kilroy; a crossroads streetlight, with Roswell at one end and Waco at the other, a solitary oil well halfway in between. After viewing Lefty's artwork, one of his prison buddies scribbled on his tablet, "Lefty is indubitably an egotist." Even the songs Lefty did occasionally write were jauntier than the initial batch, braced with swagger instead of self-flagellation. "Country Jail House Blues" was straight-up Jimmie Rodgers blues fare: "I loved on all the women, the judge says it just won't do, for loving on all the women, the judge says it just won't do, he said listen my boy, it's the country jail for you."

As the end of his sentence approached, Lefty started making frenzied calendar notes: "41 days to go," "40 more days to go now," "39 days to go," "Lois Aleta Birthday," and, in the margin next to February 21, "A Happy Day If Alice Is Waiting." Past that, nothing. "Gone for good I pray," he wrote. By the beginning of February, Lefty knew that the twenty-first would indeed be "a happy day." Alice had returned from Texas. Despite her brother's caretaking, her two months had turned out to be "hell up one side and hell down the other" — a Dickensian flight from violent relatives that left her jobless in Waco, traipsing coatless through the winter streets as she looked for work that she never found. When little Lois took sick in Waco, the ubiquitous Ruby Satterfield had mercy on Alice and bought her a bus ticket to Loco Hills. Lefty was ecstatic. "Alice Darling I bet I can't even play a guitar when I get out," he told her. "I hope I can, because I want to play and sing to you & Lois, hon, I want to sing you all the songs I've wrote to you and Lois Aleta. . . ."

The morning of February 21 broke clear and cool. A.D. drove Alice up from Loco Hills to get her baby out of jail. "Oh, it was a beautiful day," Alice recalled, "beautiful, beautiful day when they turned him loose." Rejoicing in front of the Chaves County Jail, the young family hugged and clung to each other like embattled refugees, Alice biting her lip to hide her repulsion at Lefty's bloated physique, the pounds put on him by months of the jailhouse diet. When the moment passed, the reunited family turned away from the county jail and headed south to Loco Hills, Lefty hauling a handful of clothes and a head full of tunes for no one but Alice to hear.

GUSHER

Chapter 7

LEFTY LEANED BACK in the doorway of the shotgun shack, his knees pulled halfway in and his Martin laid across his lap. The sun bore down on the roof from due east, casting morning shadows across the green-tufted sand dunes undulating to the desert horizon. Loco Hills, New Mexico. Loco. As in crazy. As in anyone who wanted to live out there with the spiders and scorpions, the cattle skulls and carrion. Lefty hummed a lax refrain and picked a Jimmie Rodgers fill. His muscles ached. He was tired. Other than that he felt good.

He knew that any minute Naamon would pull around in the oil field truck, thrust his head out the window, and bellow up to the house, "Hey in there! Ain't you ready to go to work?" Had it been any other morning, Lefty would have kissed Alice and Lois goodbye and slid into the truck next to his father. They would have bounced and spun across the Loco Hills sand dunes, out to the derricks where Lefty had a job—part birthright, part penance—as a roustabout, "pulling tubing" for the Texas Trading Company. His father had scored him the job a few weeks after his release from jail. Now the manager of eighteen wells for the Texas Trading Company, Naamon had risen to the rank of superintendent while Lefty did time in the pokey. He led by example and had his underlings' total respect. They called him "Red."

Red used his clout to put his scrawny boy on the payroll. Lefty was "one of the best hands I ever had. He was very quick and active," Naamon said. He had to be. In those days, pulling tubing (raising the drill pipe and changing the bit) was some of the toughest, heaviest, dirtiest work on an oil rig, requiring the men who did it, the roustabouts, to deal with drilling-mud and oil splatter. In general, roustabouts were at the bottom of the derrick hierarchy, subject to the whims and demands and petty cruelties of tool pushers and roughnecks, superintendents and quisling company suits. Their job, as one roustabout has put it, required little more than "a strong back, a high tolerance for pain and subordination, few skills, and little education."

At least "little education" sounded like Lefty.

Once he put his son to work Naamon made a special point not to let his nepotistic indulgence extend to the job at hand. "I showed him no partiality whatsoever," he proudly stated. In fact, far from sugarcoating Lefty's job, Naamon took a lifer's gleeful pleasure in watching his fastidious son struggle with the roustabout's grimy duties. He'd see the kid take a hit from stray crude and tease Lefty mercilessly. One time, out on the rig, when Lefty wasn't paying close attention, a rush of straight crude caught him square in the face and drenched him head to foot. Seeing his son looking "as old and nasty as a dog," Naamon doubled over. "You better watch it!" he howled. "You better watch it, you're gonna get that oil on you!" The greasy muck and oily dust drove Lefty crazy. "He hated that old hot, slushy oil," Alice said. "He *de-spised* that stuff."

Lefty despised it, but he took it. Day after day through the spring of '48, he took it all — the grease, the teasing, the backbreaking work that was meant for a man twice his size. At night, "He'd be so worn out," Alice said, "he'd have to sit in a chair, and I would wash his face, and wash his arms, and wash his hands, and get his face real clean, and he would be too tired to eat. And I'd put the food in his mouth with a spoon and feed him. And he would eat, and just plunk out on the bed. Just deathly give out." Times he had a little energy left over, Lefty would take his Martin out to the vacant roughneck shacks where he'd sit and sing "I Love You, I'll Prove It a Thousand Ways" or "I'm Lonely and Blue," his voice echoing from the empty room into the silent desert night.

The next morning, Naamon would pull up in front of the company shack where they lived with his "Hey in there! Ain't you ready to go to work?" and it would start all over again.

Lefty and Alice could only think of escape. Recalled Alice, "We were determined we were gonna get away from there. That was our plans. Our high plans was to get away from Loco Hills, and get back into the stream of life and do something. Take his guitar, and zoom."

A broken-down auto stood dismantled in front of their house, an infuriating symbol of their dreary stasis. All they could do was wait. Lefty was grossing $225 a month, and the couple saved every penny that didn't go to groceries, or rent on their two-room house. "Every time he'd get paid," Alice said, "we'd get it in bills—eighty-five dollars, you know, in one dollars." Lefty and Alice would lay their stash on the bed and count it, putting a ritualistic hope in the stack of Washingtons as if each paltry dollar represented one more mile from the hated sand dunes. Finally, one night they counted their escape fund and it came to $320. "That's quite a bit of money," Alice said. Lefty thought so, too. He thought it sounded like quite enough money.

According to Betty Frizzell, the final push Lefty needed to get out of Loco Hills was a terrible fight with Naamon—one of the worst the family had ever witnessed. Lefty had always tried to protect his mother from Naamon's abuse. One night in Loco Hills, Lesley Frizzell ran next door to Lefty and Alice's house and told them that Naamon was going after A.D. again. Lefty ran back over with him and father and son knocked each other around the room until Naamon fell into a corner table. Lefty picked up a rock. Naamon went for a knife. When A.D., seeing the knife in Naamon's hand, fainted on the spot, the horrible battle finally ended.

The next morning, Lefty, Alice, and little Lois got up and ate breakfast like always. But instead of getting ready for work, Lefty lifted his guitar from the corner. He took the Martin and sat down with it outside in the doorway. "He had all them pretty songs and he started singin' 'em," Alice recalled. "And that old guitar sounded soooo pretty. Just real pretty. Beautiful sound." When Naamon brought the truck around, he found Lefty, who was due out in the field, strumming his guitar, as relaxed as if it were Saturday evening under benign western skies. "Ain't you ready to go to work?" Naamon asked.

"I ain't going," Lefty said.

"What? You ain't going?"

"No."

Naamon stepped down from the truck. "Why? What do you mean you ain't going?"

"I'm not going," Lefty repeated. "This is it. I've had it. Me and Alice has got some money saved. . . ." He shrugged. When Naamon realized what he meant, he exploded. He flew into the house, saw the couple's pile of one dollar bills, and yelled, "Sonny, what in the hell's wrong with you! That is not enough money to go anywhere on!," as if this were all about money. Naamon was understandably put out. For one thing, his superiors were bound to notice that the son he had been so quick to hire had been just as quick to retire without notice. He'd also seen where Lefty's musical aspirations had landed him—the Chaves County Jail—and the sight of his boy picking his guitar again when he should have been getting down to a day of real work infuriated Naamon. He argued some more with Lefty and tried to talk him into at least postponing the move. But Lefty was adamant. "No, Daddy. I'm going now."

Naamon had probably never been late for work in his life. He gave up and roared away in the company truck. Lefty stood up and stretched, and told Alice to start getting ready; they were leaving. Alice smiled to herself, knowing he meant back home to Texas. She played dumb, anyway. "Where we gonna go, Sonny?"

"Well, we'll see."

They packed a single suitcase and left the next day. On foot. It was seven miles to the bus stop in Loco Hills proper. "Seven miles in sand dunes is a long time," Alice said. They bought tickets and caught the next Greyhound, Alice carrying two-year-old Lois while Lefty hauled the suitcase, the Martin slung over his shoulder. "Thank the Lord we were gone from Loco Hills," Alice said with a sigh. "Me and him and Lois and his big old guitar. And all the pretty songs he'd wrote while he was in the Chaves County Jail."

In their short time together, Lefty and Alice had lived in Greenville, Dallas, Waco, Roswell, Loco Hills—and now Lubbock. Pushing toward 70,000 inhabitants by the summer of '48, Lubbock was Gotham incarnate compared to Loco Hills—or Roswell, for that matter. It was a city bursting its industrial seams, a South Plains distribution point where cotton met cattle, and cowboys met migrant Mexican labor. In one of the more ludicrous career moves of his life, Lefty signed on as a bellhop at a swanky downtown Lubbock hotel.

His job was twofold. Lefty's boss expected him to carry guests' bags to their rooms. The guests expected him to carry contraband to their rooms. Lubbock was bone dry, in legal theory, but positively Amazon-like in practice. "Somebody would hand you a card and you could have beer delivered to your house," remembered one former resident. "Bootleggers were well-known. They had souped-up, jacked-up cars."

An earnest employee, Lefty learned his way around the beer and whiskey underground to better serve his hotel clientele. Unfortunately, his professional zeal got him canned. One night he stepped into the hotel elevator, on his way to make a delivery. The hotel manager jumped in beside him and started giving him some kind of instructions. To emphasize his point, the boss man tapped the young bellhop on the chest. A bottle clanged under Lefty's brass buttons. That was the end of his brief tenure in the accommodations trade.

It was just as well, for Lefty was anxious to get back into music again. A full year had passed since he made any money "pickin' and singin' on a guitar." He'd been a bellhop, a roustabout, and a convict more recently than he'd been a professional singer. But instead of hanging out in Lubbock and scrounging for two-bit tip jar work, Lefty set his sights higher than he ever had. Adrift again, Lefty slung the Martin over his shoulder and made what, at the time, appeared to him and Alice as his "last ditch effort."

Back in early April of '48, no more than six weeks after Lefty's release from jail, Shreveport, Louisiana, station KWKH had taken to the airwaves with a Saturday-night country music program called the Louisiana Hayride. Broadcast live from Shreveport's Municipal Auditorium, the Hayride had an initial lineup of small-time local talent and a few transplanted veterans of the Grand Ole Opry. But from the first night of music, April 3, 1948, and for the next ten years thereafter, the Louisiana Hayride developed into a country music institution to rival the Opry itself for sheer hillbilly talent, if not for broad cultural impact. The Hayride signed many of country music's most legendary artists at points in their young careers when the conservative Opry wouldn't touch them. Hank Williams, George Jones, Webb Pierce, Faron Young, Jim Reeves, and scores of other top-notch singers would build their early audiences in Shreveport while the Opry waited to lure them away once they had proved their commercial mettle. (Memphis truck driver Elvis Presley, on the other hand, put in a full year on the Louisiana Hayride *after* his one-night stand at the Opry.)

But while Lefty was running whiskey in the halls of a Lubbock hotel, the Hayride was no more than an infant country radio show with a signal substantially stronger than its talent roster. KWKH beamed the Hayride due west across Texas and into New Mexico on a 50,000-watt channel, clear to Loco Hills and Lubbock. Lefty had been thinking about the program all summer. Naamon, in fact, insisted that Lefty bailed out of Loco Hills with the express purpose of trying out for the Hayride. He said that the two of them argued about the idea (which Naamon thought foolhardy) that last morning before Lefty and his family disappeared across the sand dunes. If so, whatever sidetracked Lefty to Lubbock no longer stood in his way. Without a job, and without much self-esteem, he didn't have much to lose. Lefty decided to audition for a spot on the Louisiana Hayride.

Once more, the Frizzells bought seats on a trusty Greyhound and trundled across Texas. Lefty dropped Alice and Lois at her grandmother's house in Winnsboro, then continued on to Shreveport. Alice's brother, Junior, whom Lefty liked immensely, joined him on the trip. They left on a Friday in late July or early August, and headed straight for KWKH, unannounced. Lefty sent Alice a postcard to let her know they had arrived safe and sound. ("Didn't have no money for phone calls," Alice said. "No phones, no way. Them's for rich people.") Someone at the radio station told Lefty he would have to wait till the following Wednesday for an audition. He and Junior took a motel room for the weekend, Lefty sweating the heat and the money he didn't have. On Monday, he wrote to Alice for the second time, his letter a catalog of devotion and anxiety:

> Hello Darling.
> Well, honey, here it is Monday evening. Hon, after I wrote you that card Friday, we went to the radio station WKKH [sic]. It's right here in town. And they told me to come back Wednesday morning for the Louisiana Hayride's audition. So we've been waiting for Wednesday to get here. I'm just about broke, too. But I'm sure we will make it. I sure hope I get on. If I do, I will write you right quick. But maybe you might want to listen in, I don't know. Darling I sure have missed you. I've been so lonesome and blue. Honey, how have you and Lois been getting along? Fine, I hope. Hon, I want you to write me. Darling, if I don't do any good here, I won't be back. I'm going to go someplace else until I do. Tell Lois I love her. Darling, I'm going to write Daddy and Mama today also. Alice, Honey, things sure are high here. It takes a lot of money to get by. I love you Darling. Well Darling, I guess I will close for today. It sure is hot here. Junior said hello to everyone. I hope I'm lucky Wednesday morning at ten o'clock. Don't you, Sweet darling? Well, tell everyone hello for me, Sugar. I hope to see you soon. Be good and think of me. With all my love.
>
>   With all my love, to my sweet
>   angels, Alice and Lois Aleta. I love
>   you. Your husband, Sonny.

Lefty wasn't done, though, for he turned the paper over and added a few more troubled thoughts.

> Darling, I'm not going to give up this time. I want something and I will go a long ways after it. I hope I get it here. For I would like to see you now. Well, so long, honey. With all my love.
>
>   Your husband, Sonny.
> P.S. I wish I didn't like music, don't you? I love you, hon.

That Wednesday afternoon, Lefty failed his Hayride audition. How he failed has, over the years, become a matter of Frizzell family legend. For supposedly the singer the Hayride did hire that day instead of Lefty was a pale, pencil-thin hillbilly genius named Hank Williams. As the often told story goes, Williams showed up that Wednesday afternoon with a three-piece band while Lefty had only himself and his guitar. The Hayride brass brought both singers into one room for a joint audition. After each had sung a song or two, Williams was hired. The station rep told Lefty, "If you had a band, I'd hire you."

That's the legend. Horace Logan and Tillman Franks, both of whom were involved in Williams's hiring, insisted that it never happened. "There wasn't any formal audition for Hank," said Logan, who was the Hayride's program director. "Hank called when we started advertising that the Hayride was going to start. *Billboard*, *Cashbox*, and other publications were running stories about it. Hank contacted KWKH and wanted to get on the show. Hank already had a reputation as a drunk, and we didn't need any drunks. And he was told that if he could stay sober for six months and prove it, that he'd be put on the show." By the time the Hayride went on the air, said Logan, Williams was calling every week from Montgomery, Alabama, and putting his own station manager on the line to confirm his continued sobriety. After six months, Logan invited him on the Hayride. "And he pulled into Shreveport in an old Chrysler, had his mattress and springs tied on top of it. And inside was his wife Audrey and her daughter by a former marriage. He walked in my office, said, 'Here I am, I'm ready to go.' " Franks, and others, tell somewhat different versions, but consensus is that Williams never had to audition for a spot on the show.

Lefty's only recorded reference to the botched audition is oblique. "They had so many guitar pickers, including Hank Williams and Zeke Clements from Grand Ole Opry I decided I didn't want to stay there," he said. Almost certainly, Lefty and Hank did cross paths that Wednesday afternoon in Shreveport, but in all likelihood, Lefty had thought he was auditioning, while Hank was actually getting his job rubber-stamped. In any case, Lefty made zero impression on the Hayride bosses, for Logan has no memory of Lefty approaching the show until he appeared as a guest star, two and a half years later. By then, he damn sure knew who Lefty was—perhaps the only honky-tonk singer on the planet able to match Hank Williams's jukebox appeal nickel for nickel and tear for tear.

Chapter 8

SIX YEARS HAD PASSED since Lefty's branch of the family left El Dorado, since he had spun through the streets on his drugstore rounds, A.D. laughing on the bicycle behind him. But after the disappointment in Shreveport he and Alice returned. Though Lefty was only twenty years old, the familiar porches and storefronts, the town square, and the old movie theater must have struck him as still-life backdrops to some other boy's life. So much had happened in between, so many miles had been logged. William and Velma Frizzell, Lefty's grandparents, still lived in El Dorado. But he and Alice found other quarters in the home of an elderly couple known simply as Mr. and Mizz Lauderdale. Mr. Lauderdale was a retired railroad man. Mizz Lauderdale sold second-hand furniture for money, and rescued stray dogs as a hobby. The kindly arthritic old woman kept a motley pack of them in a pen outside Lefty and Alice's window. The loud assortment of wayfaring puppies gave Lefty and Alice fits. "It wasn't so much the bark as the smell," Alice remembered. On weekends, Mizz Lauderdale would go to the market and gather all the leftover meat bones, many of them rank, and use them to stew up washtubfuls of homemade dogfood for her canine charges. Between the pen outside and the cauldrons inside, poor Lefty and Alice were trapped in their room like refugees between pockets of mustard and nerve gas. But they grew to love the eccentric Mizz Lauderdale and her ex-brakeman husband. Besides, the old railroader had a Victrola, and a stash of Jimmie Rodgers records.

Lefty and Alice quickly fell into their familiar routine. She found a job at a photography shop downtown, pushing Brownie prints for seventeen dollars a week—three of which she would turn over to

Grandma Frizzell in exchange for babysitting Lois. Lefty hit the clubs. Union County's two main honky-tonks were the Shady Grove and the Ace of Clubs, a pair of vicious little joints facing each other across the highway between El Dorado and Smackover. Lefty worked both before settling into a regular gig at the Ace of Clubs. The locals called it the Bloody Bucket. Alice called it "worse than any dive you ever saw." Lefty fronted the Bucket's house band, Jelly Elliot and the Knotheads, all the while watching lest some would-be Bob Feller test his pitching arm with a twelve-ounce fastball. Across the South, chicken wire was in vogue as the honky-tonk drapery of choice, management's protection for the sitting ducks on stage, but the Ace of Clubs had no such shield. When bottles, chairs, and tables started to fly, it was up to Lefty to hide his Martin and duck out of harm's way. One night, in the middle of a typical roughneck melee, he looked up to see a waitress about to bear down on the crown of his head with a pentagram-pointed glass ashtray. At the last second, she realized she was about to brain the club's entertainment. "Oh! Excuse me, Lefty!" she said, and wheeled around to sap some other sucker.

Though a night at the Ace of Clubs made the Cactus Garden look like cotillion, the Frizzells' life in El Dorado was little different from what it had been in Roswell before Lefty got in trouble. Relatives came and went; Junior Harper and Bill Frizzell often crashed at the foot of Lefty and Alice's bed. And Lefty returned to the radio, appearing with Jelly Elliot and the Knotheads on the show they hosted Saturday mornings on KELD, the same station that featured Lefty as a musically precocious twelve-year-old. As in Roswell, Lefty enjoyed a modicum of local celebrity, an aura accentuated by having played professionally "out west." The romance of Lefty's Pecos Valley pedigree impressed the Union County teens, many of whom would flock to hear him when he played low-rent concerts from a flatbed truck in the fields outside of town, the kids all leaning on their hoods much as Lefty had done at the Cactus Garden. Other nights, when Lefty wasn't dodging Jax empties at the Ace of Clubs, he would work intermission at the 7 Drive-In near Smackover, fighting solo for entangled couples' attention while the projectionist changed the reels.

But if admiring locals projected the romance of western hillbilly stardom onto Lefty's livelihood, he no longer felt much of that romance himself. With every ashtray that whizzed by his ear, with every yap from the homeless canines under his window, with every night he came home from the club to find his wife, daughter, brother, and brother-in-law all crowded into one tiny room in the Lauderdales' house, pickin' and singin' on a guitar seemed that much more absurd a living. The final insult hit him one night when he staggered home from the Ace of Clubs—"looped again," as Alice would say—and slammed into the hat rack in the Lauderdales' front hall. Reeling back, Lefty said, "Excuse me," then realized he was apologizing to a piece of furniture. It was too humiliating. Jimmie Rodgers would never have excused himself to a hat rack.

At that moment, Lefty decided his job at the Ace of Clubs just wasn't worth it anymore. "They probably'd a killed him anyway," Alice said. Lefty had grown so disillusioned that when his father wrote and told him he had a roustabout job waiting in Loco Hills, Lefty accepted.

Except there was no job. Naamon's higher ups nixed the deal while Lefty was en route to New Mexico. He was stranded again in Loco Hills, where a man's moral compass spins insanely in the blinding sun. Lefty's spun 360 degrees and pointed him back to his Martin. When he learned that a fiddle player lived in another section of the Loco Hills lease, Lefty walked two and a half miles across the cactus-tufted dunes to meet the fellow sandblasted musician.

Ray Olen Thurman was an oil field mechanic, a bit older than Lefty, who had learned fiddle tunes from a veteran of the Light Crust Doughboys and gutbucket blues from an anonymous black man out in East Texas. An accomplished bassist, as well as fiddler, Thurman anchored the Pecos Valley Ramblers, a western dance band headquartered in Artesia, New Mexico, a refinery town between Loco Hills and Roswell. After Lefty made his two-and-a-half-mile trek to meet Thurman, they wound up singing and playing for a couple of hours, each liking what he heard in the other's work. And Thurman had a car. Lefty liked that, too. With his new friend's blessing, Lefty started sitting in with the Pecos Valley Ramblers—fronting the band in their dancehall travels from Artesia to Lovington to Carlsbad. When the Ramblers fell apart, Lefty and Thurman hooked up with a guitarist named Raymond Branch and booked out as a trio. They covered the same southeast New Mexico turf the Ramblers had—the Ranch House, the Colonial Club, the Cottonwood Gym, the Cactus Garden, the Petroleum Club, the Red Barn, even a Carlsbad fat farm. Stripped down as they were, the trio made the most of Lefty's untrained musical dexterity. "He could play in any key," Thurman says. "If I wanted to play a tune, 'My Gal Sal,' or anything, *anything*, he could pitch his voice to most any of 'em." But stylistically, Lefty still hadn't eradicated his tendency to ape his heroes. "I told him not to do that," Thurman says. "I said, 'You sing your own style, you sound better.' "

Lefty was by no means afraid to do so. In between singing his ever-in-demand honky-tonk cover tunes, Lefty would get adventurous and try his own material on the Artesia roughnecks and Carlsbad cowboys. According to Thurman, he regularly sang "I Love You, I'll Prove It a Thousand Ways," and a bittersweet number called "I Want to Be with You Always" that recycled scattered lines from his other jailhouse tunes. "He wouldn't sing 'em to just everybody for a while," says Thurman. "He made 'em guarantee he had a copyright on 'em, you know."

As warm and selfless a soul as Lefty ever hooked up with, Thurman also helped him get back on the radio at Artesia's KSVP. The station manager knew of Lefty's bad rep in Chaves County and wasn't especially eager to take him on. A statutory rape conviction wasn't going to please too many sponsors. But Thurman made a trip to Roswell and asked some friends for the real Lefty lowdown. After hearing their stories, he reported back to KSVP that the whole Chaves County episode had been a frame-up. Lefty's moral character thus vindicated, at least to the station manager's satisfaction, he was given a regular slot on KSVP.

Back in the saddle again, Lefty sent for Alice and Lois. At first they lived in an old waterworks that had been converted to migrant workers' barracks, then the drifting family moved into a weekly rental motel in Artesia. Alice found counter work at a local drugstore soda fountain. Lefty slept by day and sang by night, and looked after little Lois when Alice was serving milk shakes. On weekend nights, Thurman would pick up Lefty (always having to wait while the dandy singer set his hair just so) and they'd hit the hardwood, knocking dancers dead with "My Gal Sal" and "I Want to Be with You Always."

"He was popular here," Thurman says. "We had so many out to the Ranch House, they didn't have standing room in there."

Lefty was stuck on the local fame treadmill again, but he handled it better than he had in Roswell or El Dorado. He took a relaxed approach to his life, working his weekend dates with Thurman and Branch, now and then thumbing to Carlsbad or Dexter for a solo shot of some kind. He once made it as far as Albuquerque, where the locals allowed him to sleep in the jail since he had nowhere to stay. Back in Artesia, he'd frequent the downtown bars with Thurman, the two of them playing for tips. Unlike in El Dorado, where Lefty sometimes got "looped" on the job, with Thurman he generally limited his intake to a glass or two of wine to loosen his vocal chords. And the Artesia joints weren't as rough as the Union County roadhouses anyway. When fights did break out, instead of ducking ashtrays Lefty and Thurman would squelch the trouble themselves. "We'd just keep playing, you know, and maybe go over and say, 'How about me giving you a beer?' You know, get his mind off

68   DANIEL COOPER

it," Thurman says. But even in Artesia, the boy with a wave in his hair
and a curl in his voice had to fight off the sweet young things in town.
"He was popular with the girls," Thurman affirms. "Too popular."

It might have gone on like that for months and months had a musician friend not called Lefty one day with an interesting job lead. The
musician (an unnamed bass player who Lefty said "knew me when he
didn't even play music") had been offered work in Big Spring, Texas, at
a beer joint called, ironically, the Ace of Clubs. The bassist couldn't
leave his day job in Artesia because his wife was "fixing to have a baby,"
so he told the club owners about Lefty. The unknown kid, twenty-one,
sounded all right for the Ace of Clubs. The owners offered Lefty the job,
sight unseen. The gig, they said, paid $42.50 a week, plus tips, for seven
nights and a matinee on Sundays. It was, far and away, the best music
money Lefty had ever heard of.

His only trouble was getting there. Big Spring was two hundred
miles away, and Lefty didn't have time to wait for the next Greyhound
out of Artesia. So he went to see Naamon, who, having reconciled
himself to his boy's chosen profession, put up money for a used
Studebaker. Lefty immediately drove the car to Olen Thurman's house
and tried to talk his buddy into making the trip to Big Spring with him.
The older man sadly shook his head and said he couldn't go; he had a
family to think about. But he assured Lefty, "When you get there, you'll
pick up more better musicians than I ever thought about." Disappointed, Lefty shyly asked Thurman if he thought he was ready. The
fiddler nodded, and said, "You've been ready years."

The two pickers said their goodbyes, and then the mechanic Thurman did one last favor for Lefty by tying the Studebaker into overdrive.
"I got under that thing and fixed it for him, and he took off," Thurman
says. "That's last time I seen him."

His first night on the Big Spring job, Lefty was late. The Studebaker
blew a tire on the West Texas plains, and Lefty, who was no grease
monkey, took forever getting it changed. The house band had already
hit the Ace of Clubs riser by the time he showed up. He found Stella
Simpson, one half of the husband-wife team who ran the joint, and told
her, "I'm the guy that's supposed to be here." She didn't waste her
breath chastising him for being late—not with a club full of cowboys
and soldiers. She just jerked her thumb and said, "Get your guitar and
get up onstage."

Big Spring, Texas, was founded in the 1880s at the juncture of the
Rolling and South Plains east of New Mexico. The town was settled by

white men when word got out that Jay Gould's Texas and Pacific Railroad was headed that way. The early speculators, mostly ranchers, were rewarded when Big Spring did, in fact, wind up a Texas and Pacific cowtown stopoff. But their children made out even better when oil spewed from the land in the 1920s. The year of the stock market crash, the Cosden Refinery was constructed on the northeast side of town. The somber Goliath of South Plains industry still dominates the local landscape. The Depression hit the city hard, but the economy turned around when the Big Spring Bombardier School opened in May 1942. By the time Lefty took the stage at the Ace of Clubs, in the spring of 1949, the Air Force and the refinery together determined the city's fortunes. Together they provided the bulk of the club's clientele, as well as that of the Ace's crosstown rival, Yale's Inn, where the swing-crazed band was led by two of Bob Wills's pals, Hoyle and Ben Nix.

The Ace of Clubs was run by Hugh and Stella Simpson, a likeable rough-and-tumble couple who had bought the Big Spring honky-tonk only a year before. Like Alice's, Stella's ancestors were Native American. Hugh had been a sailor, a truck driver, and had even driven a Caterpillar under Naamon Frizzell in the Kilgore oil field. Hugh and Stella probably saw a lot of themselves in Lefty and Alice, for they, too, tended to fight uproariously and make up quickly. Having gotten the worse end of his battles with Stella, Hugh would grumble, "I'd divorce that damn Indian. . . ." But for all their caustic veneer, the Simpsons were warm, good people. Lefty would one day refer to them as "wonderful friends, like my mother and dad."

It didn't take Lefty long to learn how wonderful they could be. A couple nights into his Ace of Clubs gig, the band started complaining about his limited musicianship, just as the Old Top Rail boys had complained in Dallas years before. "He didn't contribute much to the band," Alice explained, " 'cause he just stood there with the little chords he knew, and sang, with that beautiful voice." But Stella had a broader view of the situation. She had noted how quickly her patrons had taken to the new good-looking kid, three chords or not. She stared down her whining pickers and told them, "Well, if you all don't like it, you can quit. 'Cause that boy's staying."

With his job secured, Lefty brought Alice and Lois to Big Spring, where they moved into a motel room as usual. This one was just down the street from the club. "It was such a dinky, dinky, dinky little place," Alice said, "especially if two or three of our loved ones would show up. Where we gonna put 'em? On a nail?" Lefty's $42.50 a week was terrific money by his standards, but it wasn't enough to pay the rent and buy shoes for Lois. Alice thought long and hard, mulling over her career options. Drugstore? Diner? Drugstore? Diner? At first she settled for the bus station counter, but she didn't care for the atmosphere, so she found a diner where she could work the morning shift and wait for Lefty and Lois to meet her at lunch. With Alice working, the couple saved enough money to move to a better residential motel—one with room to house the constant influx of Frizzells and Coxes and Harpers. The drawback was that the new place had no private bath. The whole motel shared one shower. Lefty and Alice learned to take their turns in the afternoon when normal people were at nine-to-five jobs. "Oh, we kinda paid our dues," Alice said.

But not like they paid them in Roswell or El Dorado. Compared to the Ace of Clubs in El Dorado, the one in Big Spring looked like Carnegie Hall. Even if it wasn't much more than a bandstand by the front door, a pool table, and a stack of beer cases in back. The difference was bottles did not fly—or if they did it was not with impunity. "Man, they had some bouncers that would bounce you three bounces," Alice said. "They didn't put up with no rough stuff. I could go in there and sit, and nobody bothered me." And once the grumbling musicians got used to Lefty, the band started to click, giving the Nix boys at Yale's Inn—who had already cut a few records—a serious run for their money.

It was friendly competition, of course. As the year wore on, Lefty's band and the Nixes' worked back-to-back Saturday shows on Big Spring's KBYG, giving Howard County roughnecks a double dose of West Texas honky-tonk and swing firepower good enough for any major market in the country. Lefty Frizzell and His Westerners, as the Ace of Clubs band came to be called, were a five-piece unit led by Lefty and a piano player nicknamed Jelly. Steel guitar was a revolving door. Sometimes a guy named Upchurch sat in. He was famous in West Texas circles for making his lap string instrument sound like an organ. As always Lefty leaned heavily on cover tunes, taking pride in handling every audience request no matter how current the hit. He knew the tips came faster if he gave the refinery workers precisely what they wanted. Once a week he took a dollar down to The Record Store, a shop on Main Street, and if any of the big stars had a new release, Lefty would buy it. "Wasn't no new number that he didn't learn," Alice said. "If Ernest Tubb came out with one, he learned it. Tommy Duncan, he learned it. Jimmy Dickens, he learned it." The piano player, Jelly, had his own batch of feature tunes to supplement Lefty's. His favorite was Slim Willet's "Tool Pusher from Snyder," a honky-tonk oil field anthem

busting out of roadhouse jukeboxes all over West Texas that winter of
'49–50: "Oil is what I'm after, that's why I'm drillin' down. . . ."

But no matter how much he appreciated the tip dollars earned aping
Ernest Tubb and Little Jimmy Dickens, Lefty was too creative to content
himself so parasitically. Between Tubb's "Slippin' Around" (written
and also sung by Floyd Tillman) and Dickens's "A-Sleepin' at the Foot
of the Bed," Lefty would work in "I Love You, I'll Prove It a Thousand
Ways" and other originals from his Chaves County jailhouse repertoire.
At such moments, the slurred vowels and tumbling notes of the soul
style he was making his own would stop beer bottles still on their way
to soldiers' mouths. Asked if the Friday crowds responded to Lefty's
own songs, erstwhile Ace of Clubs bartender Grady Kilgore minced no
words in response: *They damn sure did.*

Kilgore (who says Lefty still owes him fourteen dollars) met the
singer after defecting from Yale's Inn to the Ace of Clubs. The scene at
the Ace suited Kilgore better—"everybody and their brother was
there"—though Stella made a habit of firing him nightly, for no particular reason, only to rehire him before opening the next day. It was how
she showed her affection. Always quick to make a new friend, Lefty
took to the droll barkeep whose refusal to fret small matters, like getting
fired every shift, appealed to his sense of perspective. "He was a damn
good friend of mine," Kilgore says of Lefty. "He was just there if I
needed him." Night owls both, Lefty and Kilgore fed each other's desire
to extend the evening well past closing. Sometimes they'd head to a
chicken shack called Charlie's for a post-midnight meal. Other times
they'd borrow from the Ace of Clubs beer stock to enjoy a little late-
night libation under the Rolling Plains sky. Like Olen Thurman, Kilgore
insists Lefty wasn't drinking to excess at that point in his life. "We'd get
a case of beer," he says, "and we might not drink a half dozen between
us." On the way home, they'd stop at the club and return the rest of the
case. Trouble was, sober or not they often stayed out to the light of
morning, by which time Alice would be due at work and Lois would
need looking after. Several times when Lefty and Kilgore parked the
Studebaker in front of the motel, Alice, boiling over in rage, pummeled
the car with rocks. She threw them at Kilgore, too, for keeping her man
out all night. And though Lefty may not have been drinking too much
in general, West Texas singer Don Walser, who as a teenager at the time
would sometimes accompany his father to the Ace of Clubs, recalls that
one night the band passed the hat to bail Lefty out of jail.

All through the winter of '49 and into the spring of '50, Lefty honed
his craft at the Ace of Clubs. His situation in Big Spring was the best

career setup he'd ever enjoyed, yet he still felt his small shoulders pressed against the low ceiling of local fame. When his voice started to go, his dry throat constricting from the West Texas dust and Ace of Clubs smoke, Lefty threatened to chuck the whole stupid business of pickin' and singin' on a guitar. Driving around with Alice and his brother Bill, he said, "I just oughta give it all up. Just oughta quit, it just bothers me."

Lefty knew where the serious action was: Big D. The Nixes had gone to Dallas and come back with their name on a real record. The owner of The Record Store in Big Spring acted as the town's main Dallas liaison, tipping independent Big D producers to the talent out west. Lefty's name was probably kicked around. In fact, Ben Nix says Lefty gave him permission to cut "I Love You, I'll Prove It a Thousand Ways," and that he would have done so had Lefty not made it to Dallas himself before the Nixes' next session. But when a jukebox operator heard Lefty sing "I Love You, I'll Prove It a Thousand Ways," he told him he ought to go to Dallas to record it, and suggested a studio run by a man named Jim Beck. Lefty contacted Beck and was invited to Dallas for an audition. Loyal and bighearted as ever, Ace of Clubs co-owner Hugh Simpson drove Lefty and the Westerners to Dallas in his own car. The Big Spring entourage arrived at Jim Beck's recording studio one morning in April 1950. As usual, a handful of Dallas musicians and songwriters were lounging around the office waiting to pitch tunes to Beck. When the studio owner walked in, the Big Spring boys were waiting. Once Lefty satisfied the terms of his audition—payment of one hundred dollars cash for the privilege of testing Jim Beck's ear—the session got under way.

Chapter 9

DALLAS HAD COME a long way in the five years since Lefty got canned at the Old Top Rail. A roaring western music scene since the 1930s, by 1950 the city was jumping with hillbilly swing bands like never before. Eight or ten major outfits gigged in the region — all making money, all blithely overstepping the obstacles to steel and gut-string renown. The booming Dallas scene revolved around station KRLD, host of the Saturday night "Big D Jamboree." Emceed by local deejays Johnny Hicks and Al Turner, the Jamboree was broadcast from the Sportatorium, a south side wrestling arena that boasted the "biggest seating capacity in the biggest state in the United States." The Sportatorium was home base for a coterie of hotshot Dallas pickers — men like fiddlers "Big Howdy" Forrester and Billy Jack Saucier; steel stalwart Jimmy Kelly; and a swinging lead guitarist named Leon Rhodes, who'd sneak away from gigs to sit in with the R&B bands stomping after midnight on South Ervay Street. The Big D Jamboree's rhythm guitarist was Alabama native Buddy Griffin, whose brother Rex Griffin penned numerous honky-tonk standards, among them "The Last Letter," the most desolate suicide number country music has ever produced. In addition, all of the big-time Hanks — Williams, Thompson, Snow, and Locklin — routinely appeared on the Big D Jamboree, as did Waco's Billy Walker, who called himself the "Traveling Texan" and performed his schtick in a Lone Ranger mask.

Besides their gig at the Sportatorium, the Jamboree pickers also mixed it up across the street at Bob's Barn, at Al Dexter's Bridgeport Club (till it burned to the ground), at Dewey Groom's Longhorn Ballroom, or at the Roundup Club on Ervay. Three blocks up from the

Roundup was another stop on the Big D hillbilly circuit, the Silver Spur, a beer joint run by a transplanted drugstore cowboy from Chicago. His afternoon matinees were the wild street's biggest draw, as salesmen and Bell telephone girls danced away the happy hour. The proprietor's name was Jack Ruby. By all accounts a "fidgety" guy, he loved to imitate Bob Wills, wave his .38 pistol, and threaten his musicians with a blustery rasp: "Sonofabitch, I'm gonna kill you!"

The pickers loved it. They thought he was quite a character.

Jim Beck was a character, too. An engineering prodigy from Fort Worth, he built his first studio in his bedroom—at the age of twelve. Before he was old enough to drive he was harassing his neighbors into buying airtime on his private schoolboy radio station. During World War II, the army learned of his remarkable way with wires and circuits and put him to work as a radio engineer. After breaking his legs in a truck accident, he moved to Dallas, where he was an announcer at KRLD. He built yet another studio in his garage on Main Street, and later moved the whole enterprise to 1101 Ross Avenue. Part of his KRLD gig involved covering the professional wrestling matches out at the Sportatorium, a felicitous arrangement that introduced him to the fabulous world of body-slam promotions. It also introduced him to the Big D Jamboree musicians and other country movers and shakers. In wrestling-business hustlers and hillbilly pickers, Jim Beck found a world tailor-made for independent recording. He started with custom transcriptions of weddings and commercials and such ("They Speak for Themselves") but soon progressed to actual records. Most sessions featured raw local country talent, released on such distant labels as Nashville's Bullet or L.A.'s Imperial. But as independent label heads began to realize the quality of his work, word spread through the decentralized postwar music industry that Jim Beck's was *the* studio in Dallas—if not the entire Southwest. All who worked with Beck were awed by his creative engineering skills. He was the best sort of sound man—always in the vanguard of studio technicians, yet secure enough in his expertise not to enslave himself to technology for technology's sake. Beck was the kind of engineer who could—and did—build a soundboard so complex that no one else could run it, yet he'd readily jettison a drummer's two-thousand-dollar kit if a cardboard box with a wallet on top sounded better. He could resuscitate a dying session by moving a microphone the correct six inches. As Beck's fame spread, the Big D musicians started gathering around his sound booth for days at a time—not only to watch the genius at work, though that was part of it, but also to see which hotshot record man might walk through his door offering contracts, whiskey, or a combination thereof. And yet, for all his brilliance and growing reputation, Beck had never made the big music industry score. He operated too far out on the hillbilly frontier, too far from the New York and Hollywood powers that were.

Not that the pickers necessarily liked Beck personally; many didn't. The line on him, at least in certain quarters, was "technical genius, lousy personality." Much of that lousiness had to do with money. Nobody remembers getting rich off Jim Beck's technical creativity or personal largesse. Quite the contrary. A less than gifted businessman, somewhat paranoid in his genius, he operated on the assumption that others would gladly rob him, thus he should rob them first to be safe. The old-timers say Beck was the kind of guy who could pat you on the back with one hand and have the other hand deep in your pocket. He was two different people—artist and grifter. When Lefty handed Beck a hundred dollars and prepared for his so-called "audition," the genius patted him on the back and set up the microphone. The grifter prepared to pick his pocket clean.

For openers, Lefty didn't exactly blow Jim Beck away with his Ernest Tubb imitation. "Son, you got something there," Beck reportedly said, "but you're gonna have to pull it out of the mud." That was his indirect way of telling Lefty what he thought of old gravel-voiced Ernie. After that, Lefty and the Westerners noodled around all afternoon, at some point trying "I Love You, I'll Prove It a Thousand Ways" on for size, and even reverting to the Lefty warhorse "Be Mine Blue Eyes." None of the ballads meant much to Beck. After he'd given Lefty close to a hundred dollars' worth of his time, he finally said, "Lefty, you need something uptempo."

"Well I don't write that kind of stuff," Lefty said. "I only write ballads. Love ballads."

"Well don't you have anything?"

Lefty searched his mental catalog for an upbeat original song—a "novelty," as the pickers would say—but all he could think of was a springy number he'd started a year before. He had never finished the song because a guitar-picking buddy of his didn't like it. Lefty agreed at the time, and literally threw the song out the window. Maybe it was worth retrieving. "I did have a couple lines," he told Beck. "Little old song: 'If You've Got the Money, I've Got the Time.' "

Lefty sang the discarded lines—"If you've got the money, I've got the time/We'll go honky-tonkin' and we'll have a time"—and Jim Beck flipped. "That's it! That's it! That's it!" he cried. "Finish it! We'll take it!"

With Beck excited, his studio pickers jumped to attention. They all tried tossing lyrics at the incomplete song. "I threw in a line," says singer-guitarist Clay Allen. "I said, 'Bring along your roller skates.' " It didn't make the cut. "Somebody else said, 'Let's paint the town tonight,' or something. But anyway, we stayed there till six, about six in the morning."

Lefty listened to their input, ignored most of it, and finished the song overnight in the back room at Jim Beck's studio. "I'm sure that Lefty put it together," says Allen, "because Jim Beck, by God, he could barely write his mother." (Beck's wife, Mary, disagreed, citing the copy he wrote as a radio announcer as evidence.) Lefty cut the song the next day, not with the Westerners but with the studio gang. Allen and Johnny Warden played the guitar parts, Bob Keller handled bass, George McCoy was on steel, and Jimmy Belkin, fiddle. Besides "If You've Got the Money, I've Got the Time," they recorded "I Love You a Thousand Ways" (shortening the original title), "Lost Love Blues," and one other song—either "Be Mine Blue Eyes" or "I'm Yours If You Want Me"—completing the standard four-song union session. Beck listened to the final playback of "If You've Got the Money, I've Got the Time" and said, "Damn, I'll bet I can get Jimmy Dickens to play this." That's not exactly what Lefty had in mind.

Lefty's first hundred-dollar lesson in the music business was a simple, straightforward one about studio economics. But from the moment Jim Beck got him on wax only to pitch his song to a star singer, the industry lessons taught to Lefty were complex and twisted. Lefty would learn all of it over time, and he would learn it well. But it would take smart guys teaching him the hard way. He had just met one guy—Jim Beck, who was smart enough to list himself as coauthor of "If You've Got the Money, I've Got the Time." For the next year, Lefty's life would be nothing but music, mayhem, and other smart guys looking to capitalize on the astronomical numbers that he was destined to put up.

Beck got things rolling right away. His pickers expected him to mail the demo of "If You've Got the Money, I've Got the Time" to Dickens's people in Nashville. They were astonished when he left Dallas to hand-deliver the record. According to most accounts, Beck showed up at a Nashville hotel room where Dickens and several industry bigwigs were sitting around listening to demos (or "dubs," as they're often called) of songs potentially to record. One of the honchos present was Don Law. "He was A&R man for Columbia Records," said Alice. "The Big Shot. The Man."

Don Law wasn't merely a smart guy; Don Law was truly brilliant. A barrel-chested expatriate Englishman, he'd fallen for the myth of the American West as a young man and made it to Texas in search of the cowboy dream. He found records instead. Based in Dallas through the 1920s and thirties, he rose through the ranks of record distribution and production to become, by 1950, one of the most powerful men in the country music industry. As a protégé of Columbia's legendary producer-executive "Uncle" Art Satherley, Law had been directly involved with the first recordings of, among others, Bob Wills, Al Dexter, and the mythical bluesman Robert Johnson. While his career took him to New York and Nashville, Law maintained strong ties to Dallas and knew Beck through Dallas connections. (They may in fact have worked together on a Columbia session the Big D Jamboree's Johnny Hicks cut that spring.) As for Beck, when he played Lefty's demo for Law and Dickens, he was simply hoping to get a song half-credited to him as writer recorded by a superstar. Dickens was Columbia's hottest country act at the time, and he had a knack for scorching the charts with breezy lightweight novelties. Beck's pitch was really just an unimaginative argument for the status quo in Dickens's career. But Don Law didn't listen like Beck.

"Don, he's real sharp," said Alice. "And he set there, and he's listening — and he's listening to the voice. And he said, 'Well, I'm not too much interested in the song. . . . Who is the kid singing?' And Beck said, 'Ah, some kid from out in West Texas.' Well Don made it a point to find out where in West Texas he was."

Except Jim Bulleit found Lefty first. Next lesson.

An ex–WSM announcer, Jim Bulleit had been among the first visionaries to sense the moneymaking possibilities in recording Grand Ole Opry artists on their turf. In 1945 he started his own Nashville record label, Bullet Records, and in between recording hillbilly and "sepia," or race, records, he lucked into one of the biggest pop smashes of the 1940s with Francis Craig's "Near You." In 1949, he sold out his interest in the label, but soon started another record label and distribution enterprise that brought him into contact with Beck. Radio men both, Beck and Bulleit grew to be good friends. But friendship was friendship and business was business.

Like everyone who has ever survived for more than six months in the record industry, Bulleit understood the number one secret of the business: no matter what the artists might think, the lasting money isn't in recording hit songs, it's in publishing hit songs — that is, in owning copyrights. A hit record might be over in a matter of months. But a hit song was damn near eternal. Bulleit knew that. When he got wind of the fact that Don Law was interested in a song by Lefty Frizzell, he shifted into cutthroat highjacking gear. He called Lefty from Nashville—most likely to ascertain if he had signed any papers yet—then brought his whole family to Big Spring, Texas, as if taking a casual summer vacation at the shores of the Cosden Refinery. "He come to see us," said Alice, "to our humble little one-room living quarters, clean, neat, curtains white, starched, and ironed. He came, and naturally he was after the songs."

And he got them. In his eagerness to exploit "If You've Got the Money, I've Got the Time," Beck, who for all his smarts was still a novice on the business end, had neglected to sew up the publishing rights to Lefty's songs. So there in Big Spring, Bulleit put a piece of paper in front of Lefty that, if signed, would give Jim Bulleit Music the copyright control of "If You've Got the Money, I've Got the Time," "I Love You a Thousand Ways," "Lost Love Blues," and "I'm Yours If You Want Me." He sold the deal to Lefty on the promise that he could "turn it over to Columbia Records." It was an old-fashioned industry gambit: swinging a lucrative deal by promising to do for an artist something he doesn't know has already been done. Lefty bought it. He signed away his publishing rights, not realizing that he didn't need Bulleit's help to interest Columbia Records.

From the moment Lefty signed with Bulleit, his recording career started to spin out of his control before it had even begun. When Beck heard what had happened, he panicked and brought in another player, Troy Martin, to help him deal with the situation. Martin worked for Peer-Southern, the American music publishing behemoth owned by Ralph Peer, who discovered Jimmie Rodgers. As Peer-Southern's country music song plugger, and unofficial talent scout, Martin was one of the unrecognized behind-the-scenes individuals who helped build the modern country industry from scratch. A dead ringer for Nikita Khrushchev, he had the ear of both Don Law and Decca's Paul Cohen. The man could make things happen in Nashville—or Dallas. Beck enlisted his help, and the two of them headed to Big Spring to see if they could solve their little publishing crisis and get Bulleit out of the picture. Beck gave Lefty a five-hundred-dollar advance ("which I could have used," Lefty later said, rather testily; "I guess anyone can use an extra five hundred dollars") and apparently had him sign a backdated letter intended to nullify the contract with Bulleit.

"Mr. Beck came after Mr. Bulleit had been there," Lefty later said, "and he was scared Bulleit had me tied up and he wanted to come in, but I didn't understand, so he brought Mr. Troy Martin and he made me

an advance and he said, 'This will be the only way.' You see, I made him
a deal to have half of 'If You Got the Money, I Got the Time.' In fact, I
had sent it to him way before Bulleit had been there and actually we
just wrote a letter about it that covered it, about six or seven songs."

With the backdated letter in hand, Beck and Martin brought Lefty to
Dallas. Beck put him up for a night at his own house on Mockingbird
Lane, then moved him into a motel across town in Oak Cliff. Several
days later, both of Columbia's big shots, Don Law and Uncle Art
Satherley, showed up to meet their young prospect. "Jim Beck played
them my songs," Lefty said, "and the next day they asked me if I could
stay there that night. I had been gone four or five days but they asked
me if I would stay over to talk to them the next day. I did. They gave me
a Columbia contract." Actually, they just shook hands. "That's your
contract until we get it to you," Law said.

Beside himself, Lefty rushed back to Big Spring and blurted the good
news to his wife. "Alice, just think! I'll see my name out on a record like
Jimmie Rodgers!" In the short time he had been away, the Simpsons
had leased the Ace of Clubs, and half of Lefty's band had taken a job in
Albuquerque. So Lefty headed over to Yale's Inn to find some musicians
to whom he could brag about his contract. The local pickers didn't buy
that handshake stuff. They wanted to see paper. Gearing up for his big
move, Lefty sent Alice and Lois to Sulphur Springs. He stuck around
Big Spring for another month or so, played a few gigs at Yale's, and
waited for Columbia to contact him again. When they did, he said his
goodbyes to the Simpsons and Grady Kilgore. Leaving for Dallas, he
talked steel guitarist Jimmie Curtis, who had defected from the Nixes'
band, into coming with him. Together they hocked a Fender amplifier
for gas money, then headed, as Alice would say, to Big Old D.

In Dallas, on June 15, 1950, Lefty Frizzell officially signed a two-year
contract with Columbia Records. It called for four sides per year, at a
royalty rate of 2 percent of 90 percent—which, at prevailing prices,
meant a little under one and a half cents per record. His first recording
session wasn't scheduled till late July, however, possibly because of the
Jim Bulleit mess. Instead of sitting on his hands, Lefty set to working his
way into good standing in the overwhelming Dallas nightclub scene.

He began by introducing himself to Morris "Steve" Stevens, the
pearl-handled-pistol-totin' owner of the Roundup Club. Stevens, in
turn, presented Lefty to his featured bandleader—the great Ted Daffan,
who was back on the Big D scene after having nearly lost his eyesight
in a chemical explosion. Lefty worked a few weeks at the club as

Daffan's vocalist. Daffan, in fact, says he liked Lefty's style so much he wanted to use him on his own records, but Lefty's contract situation didn't permit it.

Lefty also made friends with the Beck studio regulars, including Ray Price. Though he would eventually break out of Dallas to become one of the most important artists in the annals of country music, in 1950 Price was a somewhat comic figure best known for telling stories that didn't always line up with the facts as others understood them. Happy to show Lefty around, Price took him backstage at the Big D Jamboree and introduced him to Buddy Griffin and Billy Walker, the Traveling Texan. Lefty excitedly told Walker that he was due to have a record out on Columbia. But the Traveling Texan had a few records under his own belt, and knew how much they meant in the real world. He advised Lefty not to get too excited. Apparently Lefty played a few times on the Jamboree himself that summer. Beck probably pulled strings at KRLD to get him on the show, though Lefty hardly made an impression once booked. Unknown to the five thousand Sportatorium enthusiasts, "If You've Got the Money, I've Got the Time" was received warmly when Lefty debuted it. But their applause for the unreleased song grew weaker every week, down to where, as Clay Allen put it, "it sounded like *Laugh-In*."

As Lefty acquainted himself with Dallas, Jim Beck prepared to toss him out on the road. It had to do with politics — which in midcentury Texas was never too far removed from music. The state's democratic primary was coming up near the end of July. Among the twelve candidates running for lieutenant governor was one Pierce Brooks, a Dallas insurance man with a long, proud record of failed bids at public office. "Swept," as his supporters put it, into the race by a purported outpouring of popular demand, Brooks needed a gimmick to set his voice apart from the eleven other hopefuls. Like every Lone Star politico, Brooks had seen how Pappy O'Daniel turned hillbilly music into his link with the plain folks. He figured he could do the same. Brooks hooked up with Beck and one of Beck's cronies, an ex–wrestling promoter named Charley Wright. Together, Beck and Wright organized the Pierce Brooks Western Caravan, which featured Al Dexter, Ray Price, Billy Walker, the Texas Swingbillies, several Big D Jamboree pickers, "Master of Ceremonies" Jim Beck, and — with top billing, even over Al Dexter — "Columbia Recording Star Lefty Frizzell."

The Brooks Caravan hit the campaign trail in early July, stumping through North and East Texas towns like Paris, Gainesville, Stephenville, Tyler, Mineola, and Palestine. The band members rode on a flatbed pickup, taking their payment in small change and smaller meals doled out by Charley Wright. After the first couple of stops, Dexter and the Jamboree gang quit in disgust. Meanwhile, Brooks prattled on, promising no new taxes and a government run like a profitable business. The wealthy insurance man took a mendaciously populist tack. "He was gonna Ross Perot 'em," says Clay Allen, who joined the caravan after Dexter quit. Sweating outside with the common people, Brooks would berate the fat cats campaigning elsewhere in air-conditioned ballroom splendor. For his theatrical clincher, he'd bring the whole band up to sing "In the Garden." Lefty, Price, and all the others would join in the small-town confusion of religion and politics, the audience rocking on their heels as they reverently affirmed, "He walks with me, and He talks with me. . . ."

With Dexter and the Jamboree heavyweights out of the picture, Lefty stepped up from nominal to actual top man on the tour. He and Price would pull rank on Allen, suggesting he rest his voice whenever the crowd numbered in the thousands, complaining of their sore throats and offering Allen the lead when it dwindled to fifty. At times, the tour was an overblown comedy of errors. To help fill the void of pickers, Lefty brought in Jimmie Curtis, the Big Spring steel player. Lefty had always liked Curtis's work, but Allen says the first time Curtis tried to handle "In the Garden" was the last time the band tried to play it. Worse still, in Palestine, the whole show was taped for playback on local radio, but something went wrong with the recorder. When the boys stopped at a fire station to hear themselves on the air, they tried to slink away after three bars, humiliated by the warped sound of the replay. "Is that you guys?" the amused firemen asked. "No! No!" the pickers insisted. "That's that band with the politician."

The Brooks caravan limped home after three miserable weeks in the hinterland. On July 22, the populist insurance man received 22 percent of the primary vote — good enough to top the field and qualify for an August runoff, which Brooks would then lose after dumping the band and taking his show to the air-conditioned ballrooms. The people of Tyler spoke.

Three days after Brooks's initial victory, his star campaigner, Lefty Frizzell, was called into Jim Beck's recording studio to fulfill the terms of his Columbia contract. After five years, the wildcat days of dry holes and dusters were about to end. Lefty would drill a gusher.

Chapter 10

A S LEFTY PREPARED for his Columbia session, the remarkable thing was how much trouble the different players were taking to keep him under wing. Unknown and unheard beyond a few Southwest oil fields and army bases, he had industry mavens and fringe dwellers fighting over him like a proven million-seller up for grabs. Jim Bulleit drove his family a thousand miles and undercut a close friend to get publishing rights to an unreleased song half-written overnight in a studio in the industry provinces. Jim Beck had been willing to throw ethics to the wind by having Lefty sign a backdated letter to retrieve that same song, and to hang on to an artist in whom he had initially shown no interest. Strangest of all, Columbia Records waged their own battle to retain the untested singer, even after Bulleit weaseled his way into the deal. And Bulleit still wasn't out of the way, for on July 7 he filed his copyright claim on "If You've Got the Money, I've Got the Time" with the U.S. copyright office. Yet Don Law honored his handshake with Lefty, when it would have been much easier to have thrown up his hands and left the newcomer to Bulleit, letting the Nashville indie producer hit or miss with Lefty on his own. In 1950, with hillbilly singers a dime a dozen, there was no reason to assume that Lefty Frizzell was worth the annoyance.

On the other hand, all of them — Beck, Bulleit, and Law — had well-tuned professional ears. Beck had knocked back a bottle or two in his time and knew what would play on the streets of Dallas. The exuberant drive of "If You've Got the Money, I've Got the Time" made for a natural jukebox hit, a sure thing among men and women who came to town looking for fun, not to have their morals judged. With Lefty squeezing terse double meaning from the lines "we'll go to the park where it's dark/we won't fool around," the song was as straight to the point as a country song could be in 1950. In fact, one of the first orders of business at the July session was to tone the song down. They changed the lines "Ain't no use in marrying or having those love pains/ we'll spread joy oh boy oh boy without that ball and chain" (which was as honest a sentiment as Lefty ever wrote) to the far less hardy "Ain't no use to tarry, we'll go out tonight/we'll spread joy oh boy oh boy and we'll do it right." But with or without the "ball and chain" line, the song stood out for its gender ambiguities; it satisfied the male-bonding world of the Cactus Garden parking lot, and spoke of illicit sex, yet Lefty's unapologetic willingness to let the woman pay his way gave his honky-tonk romp a gender-role-crushing whammy.

Don Law, however, was taken not so much by the song as by the strangely slurred inarticulation of Lefty's voice. His throaty drops and sudden rises were like nothing Law's jaded, veteran ears had ever heard. When Lefty sang "leave my old wreck behind," it came out as "leave maold wreck behind"—and sounded all the more kinetically tense for the sliding, muddied vowels.

Nor was Law unimpressed with "I Love You a Thousand Ways." Lefty's delivery of the Chaves County Jail ballad, particularly his overpronunciation of the long "a" throughout the song ("I'll prove it in dayees to come . . ."), was indisputably unique. In 1950, all country singers, whether of the smooth-voiced Eddy Arnold school or the harsh Hank Williams style, adhered to basic, unquestioned musical rules. A note, once hit, had to be held true. A wild, yodeling throwback like Hank's "Lovesick Blues," rooted in a decades-old rendition of that song, was the spectacular exception that proved those rules. But Lefty, not content merely to resurrect the blue yodel, completely modernized its impact by internalizing the sound within his own *ballad*—not blues—lyrics. It was a deceptively simple maneuver, yet revolutionary for country music. By liberating himself from the old ways of singing, by gliding up and down on any given syllable, Lefty was able to invest the song with a deep, everyman sincerity that the words, traditionally sung, could not have conveyed.

In standard union fashion, the Columbia crew cut four sides that day at Beck's studio: "I Love You a Thousand Ways," "If You've Got the Money, I've Got the Time," and a pair of recent tunes "co-written" by Lefty and Beck. (Further extending the range of his interests, Beck brought in a song by his barber as the basis for one of the co-writes.) The demo musicians assumed they'd get first dibs on the master session, but as it happened, they were eased out and replaced by several of the Big D Jamboree players. Unswervingly loyal to his friends, Lefty insisted on Jimmie Curtis for steel guitar, but it appears that Curtis may have had to sit out the session due to last-minute illness. The one non-Dallas ringer who definitely was on the session was Madge Suttee, a pianist whom Beck called in from Wichita Falls. Her high-register honky-tonk keyboard carried the bridge in "If You've Got the Money, I've Got the Time," thereby deflecting attention from the song's structural monotony and adding a justifiably famous layer to Lefty's overall sound. As she told Charles Wolfe, when Don Law listened to the playback he instructed Beck, "Change anything on the record but the piano; leave it there." Meanwhile, Beck worked his engineering genius to the hilt. Listening to the record, one can almost see him furiously working the soundboard, manipulating the levels as the various instruments move in and out of the mono mix.

The trouble with a three-hour union session circa 1950 was that once it was over, the singer had to go home and wait, with no idea what was to become of his material. For a first-timer, the ensuing void was unendurable. In Lefty's case, poverty compounded the usual post-production letdown. His savings ran out about the same time he cut his session. It didn't take him long to find out what Billy Walker meant when he warned Lefty not to get too excited about cutting a record. In musician-filled Dallas, a Columbia contract was weak collateral. Beck had already fronted him five hundred dollars, and from Beck's worldview, that was like underwriting a thirty-year mortgage. Once the session was in the can, the best he would do for Lefty was dole out a few dollars a day—barely enough to buy Lois and Alice a hot dog apiece. In exchange, Lefty sang studio demos for Beck.

Literally homeless, Lefty and Alice would sometimes stay all night at the Roundup Club, if only to have a roof over their heads. The Roundup's owner, Morris Stevens, who had hooked Lefty up with Daffan, offered to book Lefty himself for ten dollars a night. But Beck wouldn't let him play anywhere until after the record appeared, so that he could up his performance fee. When Lefty showed up at the Roundup one day looking to hock his watch, Stevens couldn't take it anymore. Though he toted a pair of pearl-handled pistols on the job, he was far from heartless, and couldn't help feeling sorry for the struggling singer and homeless father. He told Lefty to keep his watch and loaned him ten dollars. He also said he had an empty club with a sleeping loft over in one of the Hispanic sections of town, and that Lefty and his family were welcome to stay there rent-free if they'd keep an eye on the place. Lefty said, "Well, if you'll give me the address, I'll be there yesterday." After moving into the club, he discovered a little bonus: a working jukebox stocked with race records. Lefty figured out how to trip the jukebox so it would play for free. He spent months with his life and career on hold, making himself sick on hot dogs and spinning the likes of Ivory Joe Hunter's "I Almost Lost My Mind."

Finally, near the end of August or in early September, the moment arrived for which every singer lives, the moment when the radio transmitter sends out an electric rush of legitimacy. When Lefty heard "If You've Got the Money, I've Got the Time" drifting from a nearby root beer stand, though, he nearly cried on the spot. It wasn't him singing.

Bulleit had messed him up again. Still retaining rights to the song, Bulleit had placed "If You've Got the Money, I've Got the Time" with a singer named John Talley. Alice said that after she and Lefty heard Talley's version on the radio, "our hearts just sunk. Oh, our little hearts just went plunk."

But just as quickly as Talley's version hit the airwaves, Columbia rushed out Lefty's. On September 2, the trade magazine *Billboard* quietly listed "I Love You a Thousand Ways" and "If You've Got the Money, I've Got the Time" among the week's "Advance Rhythm & Blues Record Releases." For Lefty, sequestered in Dallas with a jukebox full of rollicking R&B records, the inclusion of his debut among their like was oddly appropriate. Two days later, on September 4, Columbia dispatched Lefty's record to radio stations and stores. Its immediate competition included Hank Williams's double-sided hit "Why Don't You Love Me" and "Long Gone Lonesome Blues," and Hank Snow's "I'm Moving On," the hard-charging unsentimental classic that rejuvenated the Singing Ranger's journeyman career. Times were tough on newcomers. The proliferation of independent labels allowed wide latitude for regional breakthrough hits, but the national scene favored the tried and true—acts whose voices could sell any song on reputation alone, and whose country successes functioned as proving grounds for pop covers. The week Lefty's record hit the streets, every artist on the charts was a veteran with a solid record of hillbilly sales.

It didn't matter. "If You've Got the Money, I've Got the Time" blew deejays out of their sound booths and roughnecks out of their Rocket 88s. It was a bona fide instantaneous smash hit record. "It just went all over the U.S.," Alice marveled, "and all over everywhere, and you didn't hear John Talley's no more."

The song's impact was immediate and awesome. Deejays and small-time bandleaders were waylaid by requests for the new hit. Everywhere

Lefty's record played, professional entertainers and men on the street were startled to attention by his delivery—not just the stylistic nuances of his slurred vowels and "ayees" but the resonant quality of his inimitable tone. It was so unusual, so unlike the harsh wail of Hank Williams or the crooning lugubriousness of Red Foley, that other singers, songwriters, and musicians never forgot their first encounters with his music. Doodle Owens, an aspiring songwriter in Waco, Texas, was leading a nightclub band when "If You've Got the Money, I've Got the Time" broke. He remembers a drunk woman demanding he sing it "about fifteen hundred times" in the course of one night. He almost had to fight her husband. Abe Mulkey was an Oklahoma singer just starting out on his own career when he heard the B-side, "I Love You a Thousand Ways," on a drive-in jukebox in Paris, Texas. He asked his wife to go see who was singing. He had never heard a voice like that in his life. No one had.

But Lefty didn't know at first. Though he heard "If You've Got the Money, I've Got the Time" on radios and jukeboxes here and there in Dallas, he had no idea the song had struck nationwide. Beck sure didn't tell him. Unconcerned with Lefty's financial plight, Beck told his credulous charge he still wanted to hold off booking club dates till they could demand better money. "Wait till they want you," Beck advised.

Fine. Except the repo man couldn't wait.

Never one to stick with the same car for long, Lefty had gotten rid of his Studebaker and picked up an old Model A that he was embarrassed to drive. Though his hit record was breaking, Lefty couldn't make a sixty-dollar payment, and he could not afford to lose the car. Desperate, he drove Alice and Lois to Alice's relatives in Sulphur Springs, then turned around and headed for Snyder, Texas, where Naamon was working in the oil field. Lefty showed up at his parents' house and explained the situation to his father. Naamon, who'd heard the song enough times to know Lefty had a hit on his hands, was dumbfounded by Beck's logic and not a little annoyed with his son for putting up with it. "Wait till they want you? How long do you gotta wait for them to want you?" he scoffed.

Lefty spent the night in Snyder, unable to eat breakfast the next morning because his hot dog diet had given him ulcers. When Naamon got off work, he and Lefty spruced themselves up and drove to Big Spring to find work for Lefty. As usual, they disagreed on how best to proceed. Naamon wanted Lefty to hold out for a single big money bash at the City Auditorium. But Lefty, not quite so sure of his stature, said, "Let me handle this." He insisted they drive over to Yale's Inn, where he knew his friends would be hanging out. Sliding into a booth, not wanting to tip his hand that he needed a gig, Lefty acted the soul of nonchalance. Just a budding star visiting his old stomping grounds while taking care of family business. Elliot Yale, cash registers ringing in his head, sidled up and just as nonchalantly inquired whether Lefty might be willing to sing that night. Lefty said he didn't know. He had to get back to Dallas and all, but maybe. . . . Yale offered $125 and a free phone call to Dallas if he'd take the job. After biting his tongue throughout the negotiation, Naamon finally blurted out, "For one night?" "No," Yale answered. "Two nights."

Lefty agreed to a two-night stand for $250. Yale called in every swinging West Texas musician he could afford to back the conquering local hero. Among the witnesses to the impromptu honky-tonk gala was barkeep Grady Kilgore. "Old Elliot Yale got him out there, and he had about twenty, twenty-five guys up there in the band," Kilgore says. When Yale extended the two-night stand to include a Sunday matinee, Lefty made off with almost four hundred dollars for a weekend's work. He paid off the money he owed on his car, sent grocery money to Alice, and started to wonder if Jim Beck's management skills were perhaps less refined than his engineering ones.

But Beck wasn't wasting time either. Not entirely. And neither was Columbia Records. A mere three weeks after its release, "If You've Got the Money, I've Got the Time" was flying out the warehouse door so fast that Law and Satherley called for another session at Beck's studio. This turn of events was so unprecedented that even the *Dallas Times-Herald*, which like most big-town dailies thought hillbillies totally unnewsworthy, made special mention of the imminent arrival of the "Two Vice Presidents of Columbia Records. . . ." The paper reported, "This will be the second plane trip Mr. Law has made to Dallas within three weeks to record Frizzell, whom he calls Columbia's find of the year." All this based on three weeks' worth of sales reports.

With Law at the helm, and Beck on the boards, Lefty and a crew from the Big D Jamboree cut four more sides on September 21. Two were throwaways, weak material that Beck just happened to have published. Of the remaining songs, one of them, "My Baby's Just Like Money"—again ostensibly "co-written" by Lefty and Beck—was a hard-driving, bass-slapping, three-minute spate of cynicism influenced by the R&B Lefty had listened to while he kept an eye on Morris Stevens's club. The fourth song was a complete about-face, a scintillating, lovelorn ballad called "Look What Thoughts Will Do." Lefty had put it together in the nightclub loft with co-writer Dub Dickerson, a good old boy from Waco who was one of Jack Ruby's favorite carousers to flag from his club. (Though Dickerson never earned wide acclaim as a country music performer, he obtained fabulous local notoriety for biting off a hunk of Jack Ruby's forefinger.) Of course, Jim Beck's name also wound up on "Look What Thoughts Will Do." But what the hell— another songwriter says Dub took it from him.

By October, Lefty's furious retail action was reflected on the charts. On the fourteenth, both "I Love You a Thousand Ways" and "If You've Got the Money, I've Got the Time" popped up on *Billboard's* informal "Country & Western Disk Jockeys Pick" list. Two weeks later—the same week the Seeburg jukebox firm unveiled the first 45-rpm jukebox in history—Lefty made his no less historic debut on the *Billboard* charts when "If You've Got the Money, I've Got the Time" slipped in at number ten among the "Best-Selling Retail Folk (Country & Western) Records." (In those days, *Billboard* divided its charts into separate Sales, Deejay, and Jukebox lists.) Directly across the magazine fold, a full-page Columbia ad showed Lefty holding his trusty Martin and wearing his standard knotted bandana. The vigorous copy plugged his Columbia debut as "a double-header that's a runaway!" On November 4, "I Love You a Thousand Ways" cracked the disc jockey's poll at number six, and a week later "If You've Got the Money, I've Got the Time" broke onto the jukebox chart. And that's when the covers all started showing up.

Cutting hit records in the postwar country field was, in many ways, nothing but a crapshoot. Nobody was ever too certain what would score, although under certain circumstances—Lefty's, for instance— the pros could make pretty good guesses. But even their best prospects, their most explosive numbers, could slip through their fingers if stronger rivals were fast on the cover. Thanks to the era's quick recording and quicker pressing procedures, it was not unusual for a label to see a song breaking big in one region and to rush one of its contracted singers into the studio to cover it. The idea, especially if the cover was by a bigger star, was to blow the original out of the air. It was a parasitic, unimaginative way to do business, but nearly everybody tried it. Just as prevalent a trend was for pop singers to cut velvet-tone versions of hillbilly hits. Bing Crosby perfected the pop/country cover with a slew of 1940s smashes including his droll rendering of "Pistol Packin' Mama." Two of the biggest crossover monsters in American music history—"Goodnight Irene" and "Chattanoogie Shoe Shine Boy"— dominated radio that summer of 1950, while the biggest of them all, Patti Page's immortal version of "The Tennessee Waltz," was shattering songbook sales records throughout the fall. This sort of thing drove

Yankees insane. As a *New York Times* journalist put it, "New York's writers of pop tunes look in envy and calculation at the 'country' songsmiths now outsmarting the city slickers."

Besides John Talley, whose premature version didn't quite qualify as a cover, Ernie Lee, Wayne Raney, Texas Jim Robertson, Kenny Roberts, and a Mr. H. Dalton and the Buckeye Boys all tried to leapfrog Lefty with country takes on "If You've Got the Money, I've Got the Time." On the city-slicker side, the "thrush" Joan Shaw and Jo Stafford both punched in with vanilla versions. "Miss Stafford tries for another 'Timtayshun' with this likely honky tonker," *Billboard* wrote. "Her tongue-in-cheek hillbilly approach could start this one rolling in the pop field."

Miss Stafford's version did start rolling down Main Street America, though it was more like a lopsided rumble. Her record was backed by a cover of "The Tennessee Waltz," which—despite the fact that Miss Page's version was selling at a million-copy pace—did well for Stafford. Though she only took "If You've Got the Money, I've Got the Time" as high as number fourteen, Stafford's added clout was sufficient to place Lefty's song on *Billboard*'s all-purpose crossover list of "Songs with Greatest Radio Audiences." When airplay estimates were tabulated, "If You've Got the Money, I've Got the Time" hung right in there with such heady company as "Harbor Lights," "La Vie en Rose," "Rudolph the Red-Nosed Reindeer," "Frosty the Snow Man," and "the beautiful Tennessee Waltz." In the same issue of *Billboard*, two days before Christmas, Lefty's "If You've Got the Money, I've Got the Time" finally hit number one. But his and Miss Stafford's weren't the only versions of note. On November 6, Southern Music sent Don Law a cryptic memo: "This is to inform you that Decca has made a race record of 'If You've Got the Money, I've Got the Time.' " As if to acknowledge the song's extraordinary success, on November 8, less than five months into his original contract, Lefty's deal with Columbia Records was completely overhauled.

Chapter 11

U NCLE ART SATHERLEY had long been known in the record business as a very smart guy. A native of Bristol, England, and graduate of Queen Elizabeth College, Uncle Art wore pince-nez, spoke an aristocratic brand of the King's tongue, detested the term "hillbilly," and called his Stetsoned cowboy stars "m'lad." Along with Ralph Peer and a few others, Satherley was of the pioneer generation of hillbilly hunters who roamed the South with mobile recording equipment throughout the 1920s and thirties. Traveling 70,000 miles per year, Uncle Art arranged field sessions in hotel rooms and prison wards. Uncomprehending provincial pickers earned twenty-five dollars per recorded side. For a star, Uncle Art might spring for a half-cent royalty.

One of the great record men of all time, Satherley discovered scores of famous blues and cowboy singers, most notably (and lucratively) Gene Autry. And when Depression-era buyouts consolidated the record industry, Uncle Art discovered Don Law. Satherley took the Dallas bean counter and fellow Englishman under his wing and provided Law entry into the creative end of the business. Law, of course, made good, bringing to Satherley's attention Bob Wills, Al Dexter, and Ted Daffan, among others. Columbia's eventual decision to split their country sector (east of El Paso, west of El Paso) between Law and Satherley was a way of acknowledging Law's contributions. In 1950, Satherley's main jurisdiction, Hollywood, still looked like the juicier turf. But Law was making things happen east of the Rio Grande. So why, then, did Uncle Art Satherley fly to Big D for Lefty's second session?

Well, for one thing, Satherley was, as Lefty would sourly put it, "Mr. Columbia Records." As such, he probably had a hand in sorting out the

Jim Bulleit fiasco. Ultimately, Bulleit sold his Lefty copyrights to Peer-Southern, with Columbia acting as intermediary. Southern filed its copyright claims in December, though the "race record" memo to Law would indicate they had control of "If You've Got the Money, I've Got the Time" at least a month before that.

Most likely, Satherley also played some sort of role in the November renegotiation of Lefty's Columbia contract—or at least gave his tacit approval of terms agreed to by Don Law. Instead of two years with two separate one-year options, Lefty's new pact hooked him for one year with four one-year options. The initial paperwork indicated the royalty held at 2 percent, but Don Law's records show the "2" scratched out and replaced by a "3"—which was also to be the royalty for Lefty's first two option years. The last two option years would pay him 4 percent. These were not insignificant changes. On a hit record, single percentage points translated into thousands of dollars.

But that didn't address Lefty's more immediate business needs. As his career took off, Lefty had no real manager, no booking agent, no one to look after his interests except for Jim Beck. And Beck had cut himself into Lefty's income at every turn even *before* Lefty was making money. With royalties stacking up and ready to be disbursed, the stakes had risen astronomically higher. So Beck and Satherley got together—most likely at or around the time of the September session—and drew up a contract giving themselves joint control of Lefty's career. The agreement called for a nice even split of his earnings. All the money Lefty made from his songs and records for the next three years was to be divided three ways: one third to Jim Beck, one third to Uncle Art Satherley, and—almost as an afterthought—one third to Lefty. In exchange for dividing the royalties three ways, Beck and Satherley promised to find good songs for Lefty to record. Helluva trade. Lefty didn't quite get it. "Uncle Art was to kind of lead things—I didn't understand," he later said. " Just kind of be head man of it, I guess, in a way."

The day they approached him, Lefty was on his way to a gig and in too much of a hurry to read the large print, let alone the fine. Trusting the big shots implicitly, he signed the foul contract. "Later, I was surprised . . . ," he said. "I just glanced over it whenever I should have gotten it down and took it home and spent maybe a year with it." Alice was even more surprised. When Lefty showed her his contract with Beck and Satherley, she moaned, "Oh, Sonny, why in the world did you sign such a silly thing? It's awful."

Beck's behavior, if not excusable, was at least understandable—and not all that uncommon for an independent producer in those days. As poorly as he was handling Lefty, he was operating out of ignorance and his own paranoid form of industry naïveté. He had been building studios since he was twelve, not managing star singers. He took as wide and immediate a slice of Lefty's income as he could because deep down he feared that someone better positioned, and more experienced, would nab Lefty later on. Dealing Satherley in was the perfect solution. It gave him additional security. No one, Beck surely assumed, would be so well positioned as to mess with Uncle Art.

But Satherley himself did not have fearful inexperience as an excuse for his role in the three-way split. His double role as agent and label executive was a bold conflict of interest, tough to countenance for "Mr. Columbia Records." No hard copy of the infamous contract is known to have survived, so the precise date it was signed is uncertain. Two years later, Lefty could pin it down no closer than "after I had made about two recording sessions." But if the contract was signed on or near September 21, the date of the second session, the one that brought Satherley back to Dallas, then all of Columbia's moves that season—the full-page ad in *Billboard* urging retailers, "Order Today—Keep It In Play," and (especially if the 3 percent royalty kicked in right away) Lefty's renegotiated Columbia contract—appear tainted by Satherley's desire for personal profit. What's more, in terms of internal corporate politics, Lefty wasn't Satherley's act. If Don Law knew of the deal, he could not have been happy about it.

Ironically, the long-term raw deal helped Lefty in the short term. It gave Beck a much more sizable stake in his earnings—enough to drop his "wait till they want you" booking strategy. As "If You've Got the Money, I've Got the Time" and "I Love You a Thousand Ways" chased each other up the charts, Beck invested in his own two-inch *Billboard* ad alerting talent buyers to his address and phone number should they want to "book Lefty Frizzell for personal appearances." Then, on December 16, a clever little lie appeared in the press that would stick to Lefty for the next thirty-five years. "The 22 year-old warbler earned his nickname, Lefty, while an amateur boxer."

Up to that point, Lefty had been booking his own shows—traveling alone, or with Billy, his soft-spoken younger brother, who also had musical aspirations. In early December the two brothers made a mini-tour through Lefty's old West Texas/Southeast New Mexico stomping grounds. They played through Hobbs and up to Roswell, where Lefty made a triumphant return to the scene of his disgrace, riding into town in a brand-new 1950 Mercury convertible. From Roswell, Lefty and Billy cruised down to Artesia and sold out the local skating rink, then

Lefty continued on to Carlsbad. Apparently, he and Billy got their wires crossed between Artesia and Carlsbad, for Billy was sitting in the living room of Artesia musician Jesse Ezell, listening to a Carlsbad radio show, when Lefty suddenly came on the air. "Well, here comes Lefty Frizzell, just now walking in the studio," the deejay announced.

"Yes," Lefty answered, "and I've got a brother Billy out there somewhere that's already due down here in Carlsbad. If you're listening in, you better get yourself down here. We're supposed to start playing."

While barnstorming the Permian Basin skating rinks, Lefty got a phone call from Blackie Crawford, an acquaintance from the South Ervay scene in Dallas. Crawford had since joined Pee Wee Reid's group, which was due to start a new base of operations at Paris station KFTV. They were hoping Lefty might help them make a big initial splash. "They said my records were hot and how wonderful it would be if I'd come down and start them off," Lefty recalled. Not averse to helping a friend, Lefty and Billy drove overnight to make it to Paris in time. They stayed several days. As Lefty explained:

> I wanted to help them — even went out to the clubs and they played one of my records. It was real hot and they always got me to sing. I had nothing in it, just thought I would go down and start them off. I asked them how much money they had made — I don't know how many boys he had. He said, well — he hadn't made too much money because of the deal they had, so I said — well, I said, "I tell you what. You just count me as one of the boys and we will divide it up." He said, "No, Lefty, that wouldn't be right. You really helped us — helped us pull in a lot of people — got us started on this radio station — it wouldn't be right." I told him — it came to ten dollars apiece or eleven dollars and I said, "Give me twelve dollars" and I grabbed the twelve dollars and said, "So long."

With the aid of his *Billboard* ad, Beck started getting Lefty road work with a full band to back him up. Starting in mid-December 1950, a two-car caravan — Lefty's Mercury and another — broke out of Dallas for a haphazard series of one-night stands in North and West Texas, never roaming too far since the band, comprised of Big D Jamboree players, had to get back to the Sportatorium on Saturday nights. Tapping into the Jamboree talent pool, Beck allied his neophyte star with front man Buddy Griffin, and with the Callahan Brothers, the act Lefty had opened for years before at the Chief Theater in Roswell. During the golden era of Jimmie Rodgers and the Carter Family, Bill and Joe Callahan had reportedly sold millions of copies of their yodeling duos. While their rube comedy and Appalachian harmonies were precisely the old-time style of country entertainment young Lefty had rejected, the "Crazy Callahans" (as they were known in 1950) nevertheless brought much needed professional showmanship to Lefty's instinctive, road-house mien. The young comer Lefty and the veteran Callahans hit it off right away. Bill Callahan remembers his tenure with Lefty as "just absolutely fabulous pleasure. Wonderful. He was great. You did your business, he didn't try to tell you what to do, he'd just [say], 'Do what you do, and do it your best.' "

Lefty would ride in his own car with Jamboree jock Al Turner, whom Beck had talked into acting the part of road manager. The other car trailed behind, loaded down with pickers and their instruments, the neck of the bass lying across a front-seat passenger's shoulder as they watched the West Texas snow swirl across the highway. "We traveled hundreds of miles that way," says Jimmy Kelly, steel guitarist on the tour. Separate cars or not, the emerging superstar was not exactly play-ing high and mighty. He'd often buy the boys dinner and let them ride in his own car to alleviate the crowding—though at times the players may have preferred the sardine conditions in back; Lefty's nervous habit of poking people while talking to them was enough to have his best friends diving out the door. In the musician underground, Lefty immediately grew so famous for his punchy tick that some colleagues would flat refuse to get near him. Singing cowboy Tex Ritter, whom Lefty adored, once turned down a cross-country junket with Lefty with the words: "If I ride with you, I'll be black and blue."

As hot as Lefty's songs were, he was dogged by low name recogni-tion. Nobody knew who he was. Deejays didn't help much, as they were given to rather gross mispronunciations of his last name. "Frizzle" was common, "Frazzle," a little less so. "Pretzel" was not unheard of. Most places they toured that winter advertised the songs, not Lefty. But that's all it took. "He always drew a good crowd, a big crowd," Buddy Griffin said of those early dates, "as soon as his first record come out." Lefty was grossing two or three hundred dollars a night, but out of that he was paying the band (and paying them well, according to Callahan) *and* footing the bill for his own gas, food, and lodging. Furthermore, as Lefty's booking agent, Beck was claiming 25 percent of his nightly fee. Apparently half the writer's credit on Lefty's songs, and one third of his overall income, wasn't a fair enough take. "Beck was always calling for something," Lefty dryly said. Beck's managerial inexperience cost Lefty in other ways, too. He got Lefty in trouble with several union locals by failing to file a contract properly. But the winter's worst blow was not

Beck's fault. In Amarillo, Lefty was buying his boys their lunch one day when somebody busted into his Mercury and stole his precious cowboy suit. That was hitting Lefty Frizzell where he lived. "It was sad, man," says Bill Callahan.

On the plus side, Beck pulled off a major coup for Lefty to close out the year: a guest spot on the Prince Albert network portion of the Grand Ole Opry in Nashville. In 1950, the country music industry was so decentralized that a Nashville base of operations was not critical to a singer's success. Lefty was proof of that. But there was no denying the broadcast power of the Opry. It had grown from being one of countless "barn dances" to emerge from the Depression and war years as the most potent force in country radio. Run by a tough, tightfisted bunch of conservative businessmen who liked union scale and didn't like drums, the Opry exacted a brutal toll on its staff performers. The working conditions were miserable. Herded into two cattle-stall dressing rooms backstage at the Ryman Auditorium, a converted tabernacle, the singers and pickers were forced to elbow their way past friends and rivals en route to the microphone, pouring sweat through their yoked shirts as the non-air-conditioned Ryman grew steamier and raunchier than a West Texas honky-tonk. It took a stolid hillbilly soul to survive a night at the Ryman, yet anyone who worked there will tell you they felt magic as they sang to the upturned faces cheering in the pews. Lefty may not have needed Nashville to hit number one on the charts, but the Opry's prestige and the NBC hookup couldn't help but boost his profile as a breakout artist.

Beck took Lefty to Nashville without the boys. During the trip, Beck made a point of introducing him around town, but kept him close at his side lest any Nashville industry vultures attempt to spirit Lefty away. They made an important stop at station WKDA to meet Hugh Cherry, one of Nashville's top country deejays. Cherry had been plugging "If You've Got the Money, I've Got the Time" from the get-go and knew his listeners were interested in the youngster from Texas. But to Cherry's great discomfort, the normally talkative Lefty clammed up and uttered nothing but " 'yes,' 'no,' and some indistinguishable grunts" in response to his questions. And what little initiative Lefty might have shown, Beck intended to smother. "He always seemed afraid for Lefty to speak for himself," Cherry told Charles Wolfe. "He had great confidence in Lefty's commercial potential, little in his ability to articulate. And he was, probably at that time, right. Jim and Lefty drank together. Lefty had a small tolerance for booze; Jim's was great."

Confident but still somewhat awed, Lefty squeezed into the Ryman that night of December 30 and came face to face with many of his heroes. Ernest Tubb was one of the Opry's shining stars, and to Lefty's boundless delight Tubb greeted the young fellow Texan warmly. Less impressed, according to Naamon Frizzell, was Roy Acuff, who saw Lefty roaming backstage and asked who he was. "That's Lefty Frizzell," somebody answered. "You know, the kid that's got that song 'If You've Got the Money, I've Got the Time.' " "Oh," Acuff said, then allegedly turned his back on Lefty and walked off.

The Prince Albert segment aired from 9:30 to 10:00 and was hosted by Red Foley. Minnie Pearl, Rod Brasfield, the Jordanaires, and the Old Hickory Singers were also on the show, while Lefty was the designated special guest. After a Foley song, a few Brasfield jokes, and the requisite plugs for Prince Albert pipe tobacco, Lefty's moment arrived.

"For those of you who may not have seen tonight's guest on his personal appearances, or heard his fine recordin's," Foley intoned, "let me say that he's twenty-two years old, he stands about five eight, he hails from Corsicana, Texas, he's a self-taught musician who started playin' barn dances when he was fourteen, and he's got a record now that's way up among the first ten. Folks, for the first time on Prince Albert—and we sure hope it's the start of many more appearances— Lefty Frizzell!"

"Red, this has always been my ambition, appearin' with you and the gang on Prince Albert's Grand Ole Opry," Lefty announced.

"Well, now that you're here, I know the folks are mighty anxious to hear you sing and play that big song o' yours."

"Well, we sure ain't aimin' to keep 'em waitin', Red. Here we go."

Lefty jumped into "If You've Got the Money, I've Got the Time," and returned later to sing "I Love You a Thousand Ways." When his Opry debut was over, he and Beck lit out of Nashville in time for the New Year in Texas.

Lefty celebrated the changing of the calendar with his recording career building toward a critical mass of propulsive energy. On January 2, Columbia released his second single, "Look What Thoughts Will Do" and "Shine, Shave, Shower (It's Saturday)," and nine days later scheduled his third session at Beck's studio. A week after Lefty played the Opry, "I Love You a Thousand Ways" hit number one on the deejay chart. Overshadowed by the meteoric popularity of "If You've Got the Money, I've Got the Time" the flip side had trailed with tortoise-like tenacity. As the novelty gloss of the A-side wore off, the sublime luster of "I Love You a Thousand Ways" shone that much steadier. Lefty's songs were always about his style as much as his lyrics, and in "I Love

You a Thousand Ways," that style was an intimate entrée into his listener's blood.

"His voice [was] the most outstanding thing," says Bill Callahan. "His voice was absolutely wonderful, and he had them breaks in his voice. It was absolutely great."

Lefty brought those breaks to bear on the key song of his third session: "I Want to Be with You Always." After a short fiddle and steel intro, he eased in near the top of his range and glided down through the lines "I lose my blue-ue-ue-ue-ues/Honey when I'm with you-ou," establishing an undefinable sad tension by following his polysyllabic reading of "blues" with a clipped take on the word "Honey." He had pushed the envelope with his elongated vowels on "I Love You a Thousand Ways," but nearly every other note of "I Want to Be with You Always" was broken up, played with somehow. It was a beautiful, disquieting performance, and when Lefty hit with the lines "Then we'd travel far/To some big shining star/Just you and my guitar," there was no question that he meant the song for Alice — not the Alice of 1950, but of their traveling days when all Lefty had to offer was a song and a guitar with a strap frayed thinner every year. And yet, at that same January session, Lefty recorded his second version of "My Baby's Just Like Money," the uptempo surge of hardboiled cynicism driven by Bill Callahan's plunging bass. Back-to-back on the same single, the two songs made for yet another double-sided Lefty classic. And both songs again listed Jim Beck as co-writer — even though Olen Thurman remembered Lefty singing "I Want to Be with You Always" with the Pecos Valley Ramblers in 1949.

Immediately after the January session, Beck sent Lefty out on the road with Buddy Griffin and the Crazy Callahans, this time with wrestling promoter Charley Wright protecting his interests. The tour headed through Oklahoma and over to New Mexico, then back out to Kilgore in East Texas, where Beck himself showed up. It was, according to Lefty, the only road trip Beck made with his client other than the one to Nashville.

For the most part Beck sat tight in Dallas, at 1101 Ross Avenue, toying with his gadgets and collecting his money. Which is where Beck was when he answered a call from a woman named Neva Starnes. She ran a nightclub in Beaumont, down on the Gulf Coast, and wondered if Lefty Frizzell might be available to play there. Beck said sure. After the usual dickering over price, Beck agreed to send "Lefty Frizzell and His Famous Television-Radio and Recording Band" to Neva's Club in Beaumont for a show on Saturday night, January 20, 1951.

In hindsight, it was probably the worst business decision of Jim

Beck's career. But for Lefty, it was the opening gig of the fastest, wildest, richest tear through the swingin' doors of American music any hillbilly singer had likely ever known, a year in which he would claim unrivaled dominion over jukeboxes and record spinners, sweat-soured beer joints and angel-sweetened honky-tonks.

Of course, it would nearly destroy him. And of course, it would all start with oil.

BOOM

Chapter 12

THROUGHOUT THE LATTER decades of the nineteenth century, ever since George Bissell grew obsessed with the idea that oil seeping up through the rocks of western Pennsylvania might be useful as a means of illumination, the gathering of petroleum products was an unspectacular venture. Wells were drilled with cable tool rigs. Once discovered, oil had to be pumped from the subterranean crevasses where it lay. Early tycoons like John D. Rockefeller didn't even bother finding the stuff; they made their fortunes hoarding, moving, and selling it.

But all of that changed on Spindletop, a grassy salt dome raised above the coastal plain four miles south of Beaumont, Texas. On January 10, 1901, a wildcat well drilled by Anthony F. Lucas changed the world's destiny when it regurgitated six tons of drill pipe from the depths of the Texas soil. The piping demolished the top of the derrick and flew apart in midair as workers fled in terror. Moments later, a second deafening roar of mud, gas, and green crude oil followed, shooting up twice the height of the derrick like a two-hundred-foot black geyser of scum. Fixated, Anthony Lucas could only murmur to himself, "A geyser of oil. A geyser of oil."

The Lucas Gusher not only changed the petroleum industry's balance of power, it changed its identity and aesthetic. The Spindletop "geyser of oil," a phallic hail of dark, earthen slime, was the perfect image for the new industry, and Beaumont set the paradigm for all future booms. The city was a blueprint for swindles, gunfire, gambling, mud, sex on the cheap, and leases traded on the basis of rumor and speculation. No wonder that for a time Beaumont accounted for half the whiskey drunk in Texas. And no wonder that when a lake of oil caught fire on the hill at Spindletop preachers prophesied the apocalyptic burning wells "would submerge the entire coast under a sea of oil which would ignite and destroy all living beings."

Like all later booms, the one in Beaumont eventually quieted, though not before the usual dancehalls had begun to appear. In the late 1930s, western swing star Cliff Bruner built his own club, complete with a moveable bandstand, out on the Port Arthur Road. Several years later he sold it to some people who ran it as the Bluejean Club, which is what the locals knew it as in 1950 when Neva Starnes took it over.

Neva was better half to Jack Starnes Jr., a bespectacled schemer known in past life as "a drifter and an oilman." Jack and Neva married in Oklahoma in 1933 and moved to Beaumont with their three children seven years later. Their marriage was a rocky one; Neva sued for divorce in 1941, charging her husband with drinking and fooling around. Apparently they patched things up, for a year and a half later the Starneses together bought an acre plot in Voth, just north of Beaumont, and went into the restaurant business. Out there by the highway, Neva's Chicken Dinners did a thriving turnaround in fried chicken, seafood, steak, hot biscuits, and "your favorite beer." It didn't hurt Neva that her tin-roofed business had a license to serve your favorite beer on Sundays—or that the restaurant was blessed with a row of your favorite slot machines.

Though he lacked his wife's flair for Southern home cooking, Jack Starnes was no idle partner in their enterprise. Not long after the restaurant opened, he bought an adjacent plot to house a nightclub and a motel; in effect, giving the Starneses a self-contained all-night entertainment complex to serve the oil men, drifters, and soldiers who passed through Beaumont after the war. By 1950, they had done so well that Jack and Neva were driving his-and-hers Caddys. After she acquired the Bluejean Club on the Port Arthur Road, Neva changed the name to Neva's Club. Initially, her idea was to turn Cliff Bruner's erstwhile headquarters into a hoity-toity dinner club showcasing out-of-town black tie acts. Her first major booking was Ray Anthony—formerly Glen Miller's trumpet player. It took Neva one night of empty seats to figure out how candlelight and "Moonlight Serenade" would play on the Port Arthur Road. So she cut her losses and called Ken Ritter, a star country deejay at Beaumont's KTRC, to find out what kind of hillbillies might be worth booking. Ritter told her "the hottest guy going" was a singer in Dallas named Lefty Frizzell.

After being contacted by Neva, Beck put Charley Wright to work organizing a full-scale Gulf Coast tour, hoping to give Lefty maximum exposure in a promising region he had not already overworked. Wright called on one of his wrestling contacts, a Louisiana promoter who lined up a weeklong series of dates from Lake Charles to Corpus Christi to follow the one in Beaumont. Though he was daily more upset with Beck for taking his 25 percent without paying the band or his expenses, Lefty was excited about the Beaumont show scheduled for January 20. He had played there once early on, when no one knew who he was, and had been particularly well received. "Everybody was nice to me and I wanted to come back," Lefty said. "I even mentioned to Jim Beck that I always wanted to come back to Beaumont because everybody was great."

Beaumont was Lefty's kind of town—earthy and urban all at once. The sulphur smell hanging over the Port Arthur Road was as familiar to him as a trail of Greyhound exhaust. Before his show, Lefty and his boys checked into Spindletop Courts, a motel near Neva's Club, and Lefty perhaps started drinking the bourbon whiskey for which he was starting to show a dangerously steady thirst. That night, according to deejay Ken Ritter, the concert at Neva's was "just bedlam." Lefty hit the stage in the same room where Cliff Bruner used to swing down on the oil men with "Beaumont Rag" and tore it up with "If You've Got the Money, I've Got the Time." Backing him were the Callahans, Griffin, and several other Dallas players, including a horn blower who doubled on trumpet and sax. "I had a western band," Lefty said of that group, "pretty good pieces."

Backstage, Lefty was introduced to some of the luminaries of the Beaumont music scene—Ritter, KTRM deejay Boyd Whitney, and Neva's husband, Jack. Lefty said he met Jack Starnes "on the bandstand or behind the bandstand or under the roof somewhere." He thought little of the introduction until after the show, when Whitney suggested the three of them—he, Lefty, and Starnes—should drive downtown to get something to eat. Whitney said he wanted to talk to Lefty, said it had something to do with Lefty's career. They piled into one car, Lefty and Whitney side by side on the moonlit Port Arthur Road, a picture of false affability and thwarted innocence. After the usual pleasantries, Whitney got down to business. "I don't think you are making the money you should make," he told Lefty. "How much are you making?"

Caught by surprise, Lefty exaggerated. "I am making around five hundred dollars a week," he said, though three or four hundred was closer to the truth.

"I don't think you are making the money you should make," Whitney repeated. "You should tie in with someone who could help you, someone who could do you some good."

Lefty gazed out the window at the night-lit Beaumont skyline. He thought about Jim Beck and his Dallas studio, how he'd be calling for his 25 percent. He thought about the three-year contract with Beck and Satherley, then dismissed it as a simple annoyance. They had never lived up to it anyway. Here was this Beaumont deejay who thought Lefty should tie in with someone who could help him, someone who could do him some good.

"It sounds all right to me," Lefty said.

The someone Whitney had in mind was Jack Starnes. Unbeknownst to Lefty, Whitney (whose motivation remains obscure) had been at Starnes's ear about trying to manage Lefty since the minute he heard the new hillbilly hero was coming to town. Whitney set up an appointment for Lefty to meet with Starnes the next morning at Neva's restaurant. The Callahans and Buddy Griffin rode over with him, but when it came time to talk, Lefty and Starnes sat at a separate table. Lefty ordered Neva's chicken and listened while Starnes opened his pitch by asking what kind of deal he would like to make.

"I would like to get a thousand dollars a week and I am yours," Lefty said.

Starnes blanched. "That is too much!" he cried. "I would like to talk but that is too much money."

So Lefty brought Whitney's name into the discussion, but Starnes cut him off. "Mr. Whitney ain't got no money no way. It is me that has the money. I got the money to do the backing."

Lefty shrugged and said, "Well, if you are the one got the money, it's you and I will do the talking—makes me no difference."

As Lefty later said of the discussion, "It rocked on for another day." Finally, Starnes came to him with an offer of six hundred dollars a week, guaranteed, and a split between them of anything above that amount. Lefty said he would "study about it." While Lefty was studying the offer, Starnes embarked on a crash course in entertainment management. Specifically, he made a mysterious trip to Houston "to talk to somebody who knew something that he didn't," as Lefty put it, probably Harold "Pappy" Daily, a jack of all country music trades who had built an independent recording and distribution empire there. Whoever it was that Starnes talked to had a sophisticated grasp of how to put a stranglehold on an aspiring country singer. Starnes roared back into Beaumont and went hunting for Lefty. He wanted to drop the six-hundred-dollar offer and take their negotiations to the next level. They met at Neva's Club. "I am much smarter," Lefty recalled Starnes saying. "I know a few things more about it than I did before."

"The way it is here," he further explained, "is I would like to come in, see, and make a contract for a year. Now, if I could get half of your royalties for that year, in case I lost a batch of money on you, I would at least have something coming back. Maybe I wouldn't lose too hard or something."

"No," Lefty answered, "I don't want to ever give anybody any of my royalties. I am in a deal over it now. I am trying to get away from a guy who was trying to cut in on all my royalties. Mr. Beck."

At that point, Lefty gave Starnes the bad news that he was already spoken for. He outlined the oppressive pact with Beck and Satherley, but Starnes, the ex-oilman and drifter, was not intimidated. He picked right up on Satherley's questionable involvement and saw it as a potential out. "I am sure that Mr. Art Satherley will not want his name brought out," Starnes said. "I believe that I can get that out of the way for you. I am sure I can." Starnes didn't say how he could get it out of the way, but more or less hinted he had lawyers who could take care of it.

Nothing was decided right there. They left the talks hanging. But that night, Starnes went with Lefty to a gig in Lake Charles, the first of his dates booked through the Louisiana wrestling promoter. The show was trouble from the start. The tiny joint held a packed house of Lefty fans who weren't going to hear a thing because the wrestling guy hadn't thought to provide a microphone. Starnes came right to the rescue and helped hustle a PA system from a local radio station. Lefty was impressed—and that much less enchanted with Jim Beck, Charley Wright, and all their wrestling connections. In a foul mood, he bitched to Starnes about his deal with Beck and Satherley. Starnes couldn't have agreed more; the three-way deal was no good. He again promised Lefty that he could have the Beck-Satherley contract "put away" if Lefty would sign with him on a fifty-fifty basis. In other words, Starnes was offering to improve Lefty's take from one third to one half of his own earnings.

Lefty made it through the sloppy gig in Lake Charles, then canceled the rest of the appearances the wrestling promoter had booked. Though he and Starnes hadn't signed any papers, from that point forward Lefty considered himself in Starnes's managerial care. Debating whether to keep the band or not, they decided not only to keep it, but to put more pizzazz in its appearance. Lefty bought himself a new sixty-dollar western suit to replace the one stolen in Amarillo, then he and Starnes drove to Houston to order matching suits for the boys. They agreed that Starnes would pay for the outfits and deduct the cost over time from the band's wages. Starnes also paid off the boys' motel tab at Spindletop Courts, where they'd been stranded since Lefty canceled his week's worth of shows. These were small money matters. They'd work themselves out over time.

On Thursday night, less than a week after the show at Neva's, Lefty called Beck in Dallas. "I told him I was through, that twenty-five percent was too much and everything and Mr. Starnes had told me how hard he would work and how much he could help me." The next day, January 26, Lefty, Starnes, the Callahans, and Buddy Griffin were downtown near Starnes's lawyer's office when Starnes said, "Well, we might as well get it over with." The lawyer was well prepared. He had a contract drawn up. Remembering what had happened to him last time, Lefty sat down and read it, start to finish. Then he gave it to the boys and had them read it. The agreement called for Starnes "to give his full time, best effort, skill and ability to the advance work in procuring engagements" for Lefty, and to do his best to secure him radio, televison, and movie work. It also required Starnes "to furnish and maintain a motor vehicle for the transportation of the band or orchestra." For his efforts, Jack Starnes would receive half the royalties from any of Lefty's Columbia recordings made or released during the life of the contract; half the royalties due for covers of Lefty's songs by other artists; half the royalties derived from sheet music sales of Lefty's songs; half the money Lefty made through personal appearances; and half the money made from those same radio, TV, and movie spots that Starnes was going to try so hard to secure. Just in case that half-and-half stuff wasn't clear enough, a separate clause stated that "all royalty checks shall be made payable to Jack Starnes Jr. and William O. Frizzell, jointly." Life of the contract was one year, with, as it later appeared, a two-year renewal option—though Lefty Frizzell would go to his grave denying that there had been an option clause in the contract he actually signed.

To no one's surprise, Jim Beck was waiting at the motel when Lefty and the others got back to Spindletop Courts. After a sleepless night in Dallas, during which he saw his every industry fear coming true, he had rushed three hundred miles to Beaumont to change Lefty's mind.

"Well, we got out to the courts and Mr. Beck was there," Lefty recalled. "I had done had this telephone call, so I knew he was going to start crying and talking and talk me into staying and I knew if I had the contract on me, he would want to look at it and we would argue and talk and he would want to look at it and so I said, 'Here, keep the contract.' "

With his signature barely dry, Lefty put the contract in Starnes's glove compartment and told him to take it home and lock it in his safe. Lefty wouldn't see the contract again for almost a year.

In the motel room, Beck asked Lefty if he had made a deal with Starnes. "I have," Lefty said.

"You ain't gave me a chance," Beck protested. "You never gave me a chance."

"I told you twenty-five percent was too much," Lefty said.

They argued and talked, and talked and argued, round and round the same old issues. Lefty defiant, Beck trying every strategy he could think of to bring his prodigal property back into line. Beck said Lefty owed him money. Lefty said that wasn't true. The band owed Beck, but that wasn't Lefty's problem. The argument went cold and broke off when Beck told Lefty, "You better take a good look at that contract. I've got you and I'm going to keep you."

That night, Lefty played his first gig under Jack Starnes at a Port Arthur honky-tonk called the Lighthouse. Beck and a couple of his Dallas cohorts showed up too, but stuck to themselves on the fringe of the action, not ready to confront Starnes in his own neck of the woods. That was on a Friday night. On Saturday, the Louisiana Hayride pulled into town.

Chapter 13

FIVE SATURDAY NIGHTS a year, KWKH had to give up use of Shreveport's Municipal Auditorium and send the Louisiana Hayride out on the road. Making the most of a difficult situation, they would bring the cumbersome caravan of soon-to-be stars to Southwest hillbilly meccas like Little Rock, Oklahoma City, or Corpus Christi, always rolling into town behind a week's worth of advance advertisements. Ads for the Hayride's January 27 show at Beaumont's City Auditorium had been running the whole week Lefty and Starnes were courting. When the Shreveport convoy showed up, Lefty and his manager of twenty-four hours approached the top guys—Horace Logan, and possibly his new man in charge of finding talent, good ol' Jim Bulleit. Bearing no grudge for the snub of two and a half years before, Lefty still wanted to sing on the Hayride.

"They showed up at the show and wanted to know if Lefty could go on the show as a guest," Logan says. "Well, we were certainly familiar with Lefty. Lefty was the only artist who was already quite— very prominent before he went on the Hayride. Everybody else was basically unknown except regionally. But Lefty was doing well with records at that point. We damn well—we was glad to have him on the show."

Though he'd played Neva's just a week before, and Port Arthur's Lighthouse the night before, Lefty still brought the house down at the City Auditorium. "Lefty was already on the jukeboxes everywhere, and on the radio. So he got a tremendous reception," Logan says.

Alice came down from Sulphur Springs in time to catch Lefty's Hayride debut. With Lefty burning up the highways and shifting his base operation to Beaumont, the couple would see each other infrequently for the next nine months. Alice and Lois stayed in Sulphur Springs, except on occasion when Lefty would take them along to a show here and there.

As a freshman manager with a 50 percent stake, Starnes was intent on putting his man on the road nearly full-time. The Hayride appearance kicked off a year of relentless touring that started with a ten-night stand at the Show Boat in Louisiana, directly across the Sabine River from Orange, Texas. From there Lefty made another stop at Neva's, one more in Port Arthur, then stormed down the Gulf Coast to Galveston, Victoria, and Corpus Christi. His band, now called the Tune Toppers, trailed behind his Mercury (soon to be replaced by a Cadillac) in a paneled station wagon hauling an equipment trailer. Lefty's new single, "Look What Thoughts Will Do" and "Shine, Shave, Shower (It's Saturday)" broke out by February, though "If You've Got the Money, I've Got the Time" and especially "I Love You a Thousand Ways" were still holding strong near the top of the charts. *Billboard* reviewed both new songs. They guessed wrong that the bigger hit would be "Shine, Shave, Shower," which was pegged as a "bright novelty bouncer" likely to "attract sprightly play." The reviewer dismissed "Look What Thoughts Will Do" as "a lesser effort by Frizzell on a ballad which he does in backwoods fashion."

Backwoods or in the city, Lefty and the band rocked the house harder every show. Buddy Griffin had returned to Dallas, but the Crazy Callahans stuck with Lefty, still billed as a separate act with their own drawing power. Lefty had Charley White on steel guitar and Norman Stevens on lead, both from Fort Smith, Arkansas, by way of Jim Beck's studio. In Beaumont, Lefty picked up Cajun pianist Jerry Desamoreaux and drummer Jimmy Dennis. Dennis was a tall, skinny goofball who wore bow ties and a derby and whose specialty schtick was to lip-synch—or rather body-synch—to Spike Jones records. The shows would open with the Callahans working their own repertoire. Then, while Joe Callahan sang a couple of solo numbers, Bill Callahan would disappear backstage and change into his comedy outfit. After ten or fifteen minutes of cornball jokes and pratfalls, Joe Callahan would introduce Lefty, who would jog onstage with a little boxing weave that always slew the audience. "Oh, we had a helluva show, man," Bill Callahan says. "In fact we didn't have buildings big enough half the time to take care of the crowds."

Surprisingly, Lefty's fame hadn't gone to his head—at least not in the sense of putting on superstar airs. "He was a wonderful person to work with," Callahan emphasizes. "He was just—you couldn't beat him, really. He was just great. Kind, nice, good to people."

And very funny. Sometimes unintentionally. For instance, Lefty kept Callahan in stitches with his handling of the bankroll whenever he got paid. "Bless his heart, I loved that boy," Callahan laughs. "He'd stick it in his pocket and [it would] look like knots sticking out here. He didn't let nobody handle his money. Yeah. First time it ever happened to him, big money like that."

"He didn't act like a star," Logan concurs. "He was just an ordinary, down-to-earth fellow. He didn't seem too impressed with his popularity. He was very quiet about it . . . none of the stardom, none of the moods, none of the 'I want it my way'–type crap that you get from some stars. Lefty was a very down-to-earth fellow. He was more interested in girls than he was fame."

Women and liquor. Many a hillbilly before Lefty had thrown away riches on wine, women, and three-chord song, but few had done so with quite his hedonistic abandon. As his career took off, Lefty's appetites kept pace. There had already been one possible indiscretion the night of the Hayride show in Beaumont—practically under Alice's nose—and it would come back to haunt Lefty. As for the liquor, the steady supply of whiskey he carried made even his drinking buddies nervous. Most enjoyed a good backstage party, but Lefty never wanted the party to end.

Judy Burkhart, a pretty, cherubic brunette whom Lefty met in Corpus Christi, didn't want it to end either. Raised in Johnstown, Pennsylvania, she had migrated to Texas by way of Michigan because she heard that San Antonio was a beautiful city. She found that Corpus Christi was even prettier. A registered nurse by profession, she was, on her own time, what she liked to call "a party girl." Always laughing and having fun, she loved country music. Her house at Quaile and Villa Drives was a favorite hangout for singers passing through Corpus Christi on their Southwest sojourns. She'd go nuts with the Polaroid camera, and often set a reel-to-reel tape recorder in the middle of her living room floor, preserving informal guitar pulls and singing sessions. Hank Williams, Hank Snow, and Roy Acuff had all picked a lick or two under Judy's roof, and she loved their music one and all. But none of them had ever moved her like Lefty Frizzell, whose "I Love You a Thousand Ways" had been spinning nonstop on Judy's record player from the moment she first heard the jailhouse plea. The day she saw a poster in the window of Moore's Grocery Store in Corpus Christi announcing that Lefty was coming to the Old Mexico Restaurant Lounge,

Judy rushed home from the grocery store and called the restaurant to reserve a table front and center.

Lefty's gang rambled into Corpus Christi on Saturday, February 24, and stopped off at the local radio station. A Cajun fiddler named Abe Manuel was holding the fort there. Manuel did a little plug for Lefty, and put him on the air to chat briefly, but couldn't get him to sing. Starnes told Manuel that Lefty's contract wouldn't allow it. "They gave me some song and dance," says Manuel. Nevertheless, Lefty liked the Cajun's fiddle work so much he offered him a job with the Tune Toppers on the spot. Manuel said no thanks, he was doing pretty good on his own. They wrapped up the little promo visit and got ready for the show. But neither Lefty nor Starnes would soon forget Abe Manuel.

The Old Mexico Restaurant Lounge filled up early with Gulf Coast country fans. Seated with a couple of friends at her front table, Judy Burkhart bought drinks for Lefty and the band and called her request for "I Love You a Thousand Ways." Four years older than Lefty, and by no means shy, she invited him to her table at intermission and out to her house after the show. Earlier that day, she had painted palm trees and water scenes on her den walls—hoping to make the room look wider—and stenciled a fluorescent moon and stars on the ceiling. She told Lefty she painted the room for him. He said he just had to see it.

Starnes came with Lefty to Burkhart's house, along with a friend of Judy's, and her friend's brother. After the show, the small party sat around Judy's den, singing and laughing and talking into the late hours about whatever came to mind. For Lefty, that meant his fast-escalating career. "He'd talk about coming back as soon as he could, and how his songs were doing so great, and all the crowds, you know, were just so big at all the places that he went, and he was just all excited about his whole tour that he was on. And he knew that Texas never disappointed him. In Texas they come out in droves."

There was, recalls Judy, "so much chemistry going on between us, I just felt like that we both just fell in love there, I don't know why, or how, or anything, but we both felt the same way, and it was real crazy." It got crazier when the brother of Judy's friend got jealous of Lefty. "I had just met the little young fellow that afternoon, but when he saw the chemistry going on between Lefty and I, he took a swing at him. Well, I grabbed the fellow so he wouldn't hurt Lefty, and his sister grabbed Lefty so he wouldn't hurt her brother." The two women held the men in a weird, gender-twisted version of a Mexican standoff till the sister broke the spell. "She reached down and bit Lefty's leg," Judy says. "We've been laughing about it ever since."

"Well, anyway, he and the sister, they left. So [Starnes] and Lefty and I, we sat around for a little while longer and talked and carried on and had a few drinks and some snacks. And then Lefty says, well, he had to go, and that he'd be back, and he would always come to visit anytime he would come to town. So I told him, I said, 'Well, the key's gonna be in the mailbox.' " Before leaving, Lefty gave her a promo glossy showing him all gussied up in his embroidered white western suit. He signed it "I Love You a Thousand Ways." Typically, he added a P.S.: "Thanks For A Real Night."

On the surface, the whole evening looked like one more casual road encounter between Lefty and one of the many women, in every port, he so easily charmed with his talent and humor. But this was different. Judy was right—there *was* chemistry between them, stronger than the simple, direct passion of a one-night liaison under artificial fluorescent stars. Lefty would stop to see her whenever he could, pulling the key from under her mail for many years to come. (One of the last times they would be together was on a snow-packed ridge in central Pennsylvania, six months before Lefty was dead.) Judy would see Lefty in Corpus Christi again a mere six weeks after the first time. Yet even during that brief span, Lefty's astonishing career would have risen to another level.

Keeping up with Lefty's signature exhausted Don Law. As soon as Lefty inked the deal with Starnes, he called Law and confessed that he'd "done somethin' I shouldn't ortera done." Law, in Dallas for the entire month of February, sucked in his breath and told Lefty to bring all his contracts to his place and they would sort them out. With all the paper in front of them, they figured out that Lefty had signed away more than 100 percent of his earnings. Law advised him there wasn't much he could do except hire a good lawyer and buy up some of the contracts. Namely the Beck/Satherley one. From Law's standpoint, it was a colossal headache but had to be dealt with. Lefty was far and away the hottest country act Columbia had found in years; they couldn't afford to put his development on hold no matter who claimed to be running his show—even "Mr. Columbia Records." Lefty's first single was still raking in jukebox nickels, his second was heading up the charts, and his third, the exquisite "I Want to Be with You Always," was to be released in March. The first week of February, Columbia took out another full-page ad in *Billboard* declaring that Lefty was "stepping out!"

Beck did not give up his property without a struggle. He made several more trips to Beaumont to deal directly with Starnes, but finally stepped aside by early March. It appears that Starnes, not Lefty, paid

Beck and Satherley a token five hundred dollars apiece to get rid of them. However, Lefty later said he thought Satherley's five hundred had something to do with a Hill & Range publishing deal signed later that month. "I don't know whether it was to get rid of him or not," Lefty said, "but he gave him five hundred dollars for something. I thought it was concerning the Hill & Range contract if I recall."

Beck may have stepped aside, but his and Satherley's contract with Lefty had not been officially "put away," as Starnes had promised it would be. Lefty had to settle that nasty little detail out of court a couple of years later. Over the years, a tantalizing but wholly unsubstantiated rumor has circulated among Dallas musicians that Beck stepped out of the Lefty picture at the point of a gun. Few deny that Jack Starnes was capable of such a tactic, but no one has been found to corroborate the rumor. Never in his life did Lefty hint at such a confrontation to family or friends, and when asked about it many years later, Jim Beck's widow was plainly dumbfounded to hear of the alleged showdown. Most likely, the rumor has as much substance as those inspired by the ugly birthmark on Lefty's neck. (Some said he'd been scarred in a terrible car wreck. The more imaginative said a jealous husband had slit his throat.)

However he wrested control of Lefty's career, Starnes felt confident enough by March to go public with his claim. He openly advertised that Lefty and his Tune Toppers were touring the nation under management of Jack Starnes Jr.: "Write or wire for open dates." *Billboard* reported that "Lefty Frizzell (Columbia) has inked a management pact with Jack Starnes, Beaumont promoter," and blandly mentioned that Lefty had not signed an exclusive writer's deal with any publishing firm. Let the games begin.

Through one of Starnes's more inspired bits of promotional dissembling, it was also announced that "Lefty Frizzell's brother, Rightie, who works with the Columbia recorder's ork, will enter service soon." Unfortunately, Bill Frizzell was not the only orchestra member Lefty lost to Uncle Sam that winter. With America sinking deeper into the Korean morass, Charley White and Norman Stevens were also drafted, and by March, Jack Starnes was scrambling to put together a new bunch of Tune Toppers. Blackie Crawford's band took care of that. "They called me up after I was with Starnes," Lefty said. "The band—they were just some boys you couldn't hardly trust and he said he couldn't tell about them. They were giving him a lot of trouble and Crawford was calling me two or three times a week. In fact, I got two or three calls out here at Neva's to tell me 'Your worries will be over if you hire us.' So, I told Mr.

Starnes about that. He thought they would be great and I said, 'That's something I don't want to have anything to do with.' "

Despite Lefty's less than enthusiastic endorsement, Starnes was intrigued. He drove to Paris, checked out Crawford's act, and hired the nucleus of the band — guitarist Crawford, bassist Pee Wee Reid, and a phenomenal eighteen-year-old steel player named Curly Chalker. They started working with Lefty that March, just in time to back him at a series of Hayride dates that Starnes — again to Horace Logan's happy astonishment — requested Lefty be permitted to join. "I told him, heck, yes, he could join!" says Logan. "And Jack, Neva, and Jack and Neva's son started coming up with Lefty every Saturday night."

Lefty's crew hit Shreveport in fine style — a big swinging band, matching Cadillacs, and a Tune Toppers tour bus that Starnes had talked Lefty into buying with him, fifty-fifty. By now, royalties were pouring in, and Lefty spent accordingly. He bought a personalized ring, the letters "LF" encrusted in diamonds, that motivated him to wave his hands a bit more than he used to while talking to friends. He ordered a custom-built Gibson SJ-200 — a whopper of a flattop with "Lefty Frizzell" emblazoned across the top pick guard. (Scuffed and scratched, its burnished recesses showing every mile Lefty ever traveled, the Gibson now hangs in a display case at the Country Music Hall of Fame in Nashville.)

On March 8, Lefty Frizzell, alternately known as the "Singing Sensation of the Nation" and the "Beaumont Flash," was back in the East Texas oil field. He worked that night at the Palm Isle Club, in Longview, where "Look What Thoughts Will Do" was the number one hillbilly hit at Jimmie's Music and Cigarette Service. A week later, Lefty held a personal homecoming concert at the High School Auditorium in El Dorado. He worked the Hayride on Saturday night, March 24, and again on the thirty-first, the day he turned all of twenty-three years old. It proved to be quite a birthday. Lefty celebrated by signing a brand-new two-year publishing contract with Hill & Range, a song firm run by Jean and Julian Aberbach, a pair of Viennese immigrant brothers who had made a killing off country tunes (and would make a bigger killing off Elvis Presley). Starnes swung the deal for Lefty at the annual jukebox convention in Chicago. "He went on his own," Lefty explained. "He said it was worth it to learn something." Law attended the convention as well, and probably Satherley. If five hundred dollars did pass from Starnes to Satherley, it could have happened in Chicago.

The new publishing deal gave the Aberbachs rights to nine of Lefty's songs, including the soon to be extremely lucrative "I Want to Be with

You Always" and an unrecorded song called "Mom and Dad's Waltz." It also required Lefty to write a minimum of eight songs per year, and stipulated that three out of every four sides he cut for Columbia Records had to be Hill & Range songs written or co-written by him. For his efforts, Lefty would be paid the standard royalty rates. Again, the contract stated emphatically that all checks would be made out jointly to Lefty and Jack Starnes Jr. As a one-time signing bonus—*not* an advance against royalties—Hill & Range paid Lefty $7,000.

Some portion of that money was bulging the pockets of his western suit when he departed from Shreveport for an April Fools' Day matinee in Little Rock. The Arkansas gig opened a six-day run of one-nighters that would take Lefty down through the Southland and on to New Orleans. He would have plenty of company that tour, including his father, whom Lefty had liberated from the oil fields and hired to drive his bus. Also heading to the Gulf Coast with Lefty was none other than the Hillbilly Shakespeare himself, Hank Williams.

Neither Hank nor Lefty was the same man he had been that summer day in 1948 when they crossed paths at KWKH. Since then, the Louisiana Hayride stage had turned out to be Hank's launching pad for the ultra-smash "Lovesick Blues." And from there it had been a quick and easy jump to the Grand Ole Opry and a stratospheric level of hillbilly fame that Lefty was only just reaching. While "I Want to Be with You Always" was spinning into the top ten, Williams was already there with "Cold, Cold Heart," which, better than any other performance, showcased the redemptive quality of his spirit-sundering despair when wedded to song. In 1948, only a few more pickers on Hank's side had separated the two singers, or so Lefty believed. Well, now everything was different. Lefty had a band, too.

Chapter 14

ONE WEEK is precious little time in the glorious scope of a music with roots sunk a thousand years deep in history. Six days on the road. Hardly time enough for defining a musical essence. And yet, if one wanted to point to honky-tonk's apex, the instant that symbolized the genre's zenith, such an instant could be the six-day stretch in April 1951 when Hank and Lefty shared the two-lanes from Little Rock south toward sawdust and oil, leaving in their wake a trail of hearts grown cold and love a thousand ways tried.

Promoter A. V. Bamford organized the unprecedented package. Both singers brought their own bands. Lefty hit the tour with spirits high and pockets jingling from the Hill & Range signing bonus. Hank hit the tour sober and singing well. Though Lefty was nominally second billed, and though Hank was secretly unimpressed with Lefty's style (perhaps because it departed so radically from his own), Williams had no problem treating Lefty as an equal onstage. The two would flip a coin to see who would open for whom, billing be damned. Offstage, the pair would talk shop, with Hank apparently trying to convince Lefty to join the Opry. They also kicked song ideas around, and Naamon recalled that in one of the towns they played, Hank walked into Lefty's hotel room and asked, "Lefty, did you ever write a song that you just hate?" Lefty said he did. So Hank suggested,"I'll give you one I hate, you give me one you hate." Lefty agreed to the trade. There is no clue what Lefty might have taken from Williams, but a good guess as to what he might have given up is "I Ain't Got Nothing but Time," one of the nine songs listed on his Hill & Range contract a few days before. Lefty never in his life cut a song by that title. Hank did, though only as a demo. It's pure speculation, but while Williams is credited as the writer of "I Ain't Got Nothing but Time," the song's theme—time, joy, casual romance, and no wife waiting—has Lefty written all over it.

The Little Rock show, a day/night twin bill at the Robinson Memorial Auditorium, kicked off the tour. The matinee was scheduled for three o'clock, with the second show slated for eight. Both bands stayed at the Hotel Marion. Hank got there first and picked out rooms for himself and Lefty, side by side. Before the first show, Williams and Bill Lister, Hank's front man, joined Lefty for an informal Jimmie Rodgers guitar pull in his room. Between shows, everybody returned to the Marion. The pickers stood around in the hallway, doors open, just shooting the bull. The two stars had again repaired to Lefty's room, perhaps swapping songs or trying out co-writing ideas. Lefty wrote the lyrics to a song called "What Good Did You Get Out of Breaking My Heart" on the hotel stationery and tucked it away.

Into the hotel corridor came a teenage girl. She materialized from nowhere and walked down the hall to Lefty's door. She knocked. Lefty opened. To the pickers watching, it didn't look like Lefty had any idea who she was. But he talked to her for a moment, then let her inside. The door closed. It immediately opened again and Hank walked out of Lefty's room. No one saw Lefty again for quite a while. The musicians took mental note of what had transpired—that the girl approached and entered Lefty's room unsolicited—but gave it little more thought until several months later. Says Don Helms, the Drifting Cowboys' legendary steel guitar man, "It didn't look like an upcoming problem; it just looked like something I had seen a thousand times."

From Little Rock, the tour headed south to Monroe, Louisiana; Baton Rouge; Shreveport; Corpus Christi; and finally New Orleans, where a crazed female fan tore the fringe off of Williams's shirt. For that little expression of ardor, Hank gave her what one observer called "the worst cussin' a woman ever got." Otherwise, Hank was in control of himself that tour. In Corpus Christi, he and Lefty were getting set to take the stage when Lefty broke out the bourbon. "Hey, I'm gonna have a shot," Lefty said. "How about it, would you like to have a little shot?" Hank declined. "No," he said, "if I had just what you are fixing to take, if I had that, I'd want another, and the first thing you know, I'd be gone."

True to his word, Lefty looked up Judy Burkhart before the show in Corpus Christi. She knew Williams, too, but wasn't interested in seeing him. "I was mad at Hank Williams," she says. "He made a couple of passes at me when he and Hank Snow came to the house. I didn't appreciate his crudeness, you know. I had all eyes for Lefty anyway."

The concert was outdoors at the Schepps Palms Baseball Park, about five blocks from Judy's house. Taking turns with Lefty's customized Gibson, the two stars blistered the band shell with a two-fisted act that was, says Judy, "just like battle dances." During Hank's set, Lefty stayed to the side with Judy, lifting her up on the ballpark railing so she could better see the show. "I remember the light orchid dress, it was like a ballerina dress I wore that night," she says. "Yeah, the way he grabbed my waist and picked me up, put me on the railing. Yeah. And Hank Williams kept looking over there, and he was sorry he acted the way he did the last time he was in town."

After the concert, Lefty and Judy went back to her house while Naamon drove Hank to New Orleans. When the unprecedented tour closed out on Friday night at the Municipal Auditorium, one of the most remarkable weeks in the history of country music was over. In later years, Lefty would speak of Williams as the lonesomest man he had ever known.

A week after Hank and Lefty parted, and almost exactly one year after Lefty showed up at Jim Beck's studio, Columbia Records' "discovery of the year" saw all three of his singles in *Billboard*'s top ten at one time. "I Want to Be with You Always" broke in at number ten; "Look What Thoughts Will Do" was at number five (a notch below Williams's "Cold, Cold Heart") and at number six, logging its twenty-third week on the charts, was the iridescent "I Love You a Thousand Ways." Three songs in the top ten simultaneously. Surely Lefty would never beat that.

Jack Starnes had liked what he saw when Lefty played the Palm Isle Club in Longview, Texas, in early March. In fact, he so admired the big airy joint, he wanted to buy it. Starnes's taste was impeccable. One of the most venerated honky-tonks in all of America, the Palm Isle (later the Reo Palm Isle) opened in 1935. The club was 200 feet long by 80 feet wide—built to hold 1,800 drillers, angels, and crosseyed married men. Legend has it that in the old days, bootleg liquor was served through a trapdoor in the bandstand floor. Thirsty roustabouts would order their drinks from the musicians, who would stomp their feet on the offbeat to alert the subterranean bartenders that a round was needed up top. During World War II, a good old girl from the oil town of Borger, Mattie Castleberry, took over managing the Palm Isle and later bought it outright. Sadly, her health failed her and by 1951 she was looking to unload the club. Jack Starnes bailed her out. He bought the Palm Isle on April 10 for $18,900. Besides the 200 by 80-foot building itself, he also took over 907 chairs, 276 tables, 61 double benches, 27 electric fans, 6 fire extinguishers, a PA system with two speakers, a baby grand piano, a ticket booth, a desk, a cash register, a 27-foot zero plate Frigidaire (with a 72-case capacity), an air-cooled Frigidaire icebox, a back bar, two Coca-Cola boxes, a kitchen range, and, presumably, the kitchen sink.

The Palm Isle gave Starnes a second professional base for Lefty and the Tune Toppers—one just an hour's drive from Shreveport and the Louisiana Hayride. Starnes was already negotiating with Jim Bulleit to get his boy a permanent slot at KWKH, but nothing had materialized. Nevertheless, the Tune Toppers relocated to Longview, where they came up with a new name for themselves: the Western Cherokees. Lefty kept working his Hayride guest spots—wowing the fans, charming management types like Logan and Tillman Franks, and setting a star example for the young staff singers. Among those signed to the overachieving program were Faron Young, Red Sovine, the Wilburn Brothers, Van Howard, and the best-known Sears & Roebuck salesman in all of Shreveport, Louisiana: Webb Pierce. With Lefty working so many Hayride dates, Horace Logan thought up a cute little promotion scheme to please Jax Beer, a show sponsor. One of the phrases Lefty sang in "If You've Got the Money, I've Got the Time" was "dance, drink beer and wine." But Logan suggested he change it to "dance, drink Jax, it's fine."

"They would love it," he told Lefty. "Their guys will eat it up."

But Lefty had done the song so many hundreds of times that without fail he forgot the promo gimmick and sang the line as written. Says Logan, "It finally got to where he'd say, 'dance, drink beer and wine— oh, Mr. Logan, I missed it again!' Right in the middle of the song."

One of those especially impressed with the superstar character's glittery facade was a wide-eyed teen at the time. Merle Kilgore, who would grow up to be a country star in his own right and Hank Williams Jr.'s manager, would hang around Lefty's dressing room and bring him Cokes, later watching in youthful wonder as Lefty turned the Hayride upside down. "It was just like when Elvis [appeared]," he says. "I was there when Elvis came on, too, see." One night, while working the Hayride, Lefty told Kilgore (who still does a primo Lefty accent): "Now listen, I'm gonna be in Longview, Texas, and I want yew to be theyah to-morrow night."

Kilgore promised he would be there. The next evening, he and a friend drove over to Longview to see Lefty at the Palm Isle. Kilgore waited around with the boisterous East Texas crowd, all 1,800 of them packed in among the 907 chairs, 276 tables, and 61 benches. As the evening wore on and the audience got antsy, Kilgore started to get worried. He hunted around behind the club and found Lefty relaxing in his Cadillac, knocking back some whiskey. Alarmed, Kilgore said, "Lefty, it's time to go!"

"Merle, it's time to go!" Lefty agreed, and took off running for the stage.

He never made it there. Sprinting full tilt, with the gangly Kilgore running behind, Lefty whacked his head against one of the Palm Isle's infamously low ceiling beams and knocked himself out cold. "They liked to riot!" Kilgore marvels. "They tore up seats; they started throwing 'em and everything when they said, 'Lefty can't go on, he knocked himself out.' Well, people in the back — hell! — they didn't believe that. People down front saw it!"

Lefty, knocked out cold, was taken to a hospital while 907 chairs caromed off the Palm Isle walls. The accident didn't slow him down, however, for his touring schedule only intensified as summer approached. Starnes sent him all over the South and Southwest, often with little thought for geography. Lefty would be in Atlanta one minute, Arizona the next. Early in May, or thereabouts, he was headed toward Shreveport when his Cadillac, supposedly with the Western Cherokees' bus trailing, hit a detour. A guy selling cigarettes at a roadside general store told Naamon the road ahead was clear. It wasn't. Lefty and the band drove into the wilderness between two cotton fields spreading out on either side of the highway. With no warning, the blacktop disappeared. End of the road. The band realized they would have to back the bus up and return thirty miles to the detour. Lefty had a few words with his daddy, who had insisted on believing the cigarette man. Someone said something about Lefty being always late. Blackie Crawford, who was riding in the car, said that sounded like a good idea for a song.

Lefty agreed. He told Crawford to pull out the tablet he kept in his glove box. By the time they showed up late in Shreveport (another version of the episode has them headed to a gig in Pharr, Texas), Lefty had a new song in his repertoire, Blackie Crawford had co-writer's credit, and Naamon Frizzell had bragging rights to a piece of the heaviest action his family would ever see.

The big action started the last week of May, in a tense return to the studio after the mania of the Beaumont spring. Don Law scheduled Lefty for a recording session on the twenty-fourth in Dallas — at Jim Beck's studio. Regardless of the bad blood between Lefty and Starnes on the one hand and Beck on the other, Law was now so reliant on Beck and his electronic wizardry that he had no intention of cutting

Lefty elsewhere. As per his Hill & Range contract, Lefty brought four of his own songs to the session, including the new one, "Always Late (With Your Kisses)," and the sentimental ballad "Mom and Dad's Waltz." The latter classic has uncertain, almost mythic origins. Lefty always claimed he wrote it while holed up and homesick in the Dallas nightclub the summer before. But his sister Betty vividly recalls Lefty sitting on the hood of his car back in Big Spring, writing the song to just their mother. "I guess I ought to put the old man in there, too," Lefty decided, and fleshed out the song accordingly. And finally, Buddy Griffin says Lefty wrote it in a hotel room in San Antonio after his first record was already out, and then took it straight to a local radio station and sang it on the air.

If the session was tense because of the people involved, arbitrary circumstances only made it worse. Billy Walker, newly signed to Columbia himself, was at the session and recalls that at one point the musicians were trying to lay down tracks when a car horn started bleating outside, disrupting their work. A considerably annoyed Don Law asked Walker to step outside and see whose car was the culprit. He discovered his own horn had shorted out and was raising the curbside ruckus. The Traveling Texan opened his hood and nervously yanked the wires free, praying that Law wouldn't hold it against him and annul his fresh new contract.

As Walker recalls, the session grew even more strained when it came time to record "Always Late." Lefty, the band, and Law settled on an arrangement that opened with Curly Chalker's Texas steel spiraling to an entry point from which Lefty would descend with his now legendary "Ah-al-ways lay-ee-ate. . . ." They ran through the intro several times, but Lefty couldn't pinpoint his takeoff. "Lefty could never get the timing on it," Walker said. "And Curly Chalker . . . said, 'Hey Don, Lefty thinks that meter's something you put a nickel in.' And Lefty reached over there and got ahold of him, and Don had to go in there and separate 'em."

Chalker, on the other hand, says that no such confrontation occurred between him and Lefty at the Columbia "Always Late" session, but that there was some minor trouble at a navy recruitment session held around the same time. Either way, Lefty and Chalker would quickly forgive each other, and the quavering steel intro to "Always Late" — incredibly, struck by Chalker on the first recording session of his life — would go down in history as the most famous instrumental lick ever played on a Lefty Frizzell record. After the session, Lefty walked out of Beck's with two songs in the can that combined back-to-back would cap off his terrifying success with his biggest record yet.

Almost as a reward, Law returned Lefty to Beck's just one week later for the dream session of his life: an eight-song set of Jimmie Rodgers covers that Columbia intended to release as an LP. Someone—Chalker says it was not him—outdid himself sliding bluesy licks behind Lefty on dobro, an acoustic instrument favored by the old school but used less and less in commercial country productions of that steel guitar age. As for Lefty, recording Jimmie Rodgers tunes was almost more than he could bear. His yodels came out quaintly ineffectual, as if he were still a twelve-year-old child trying them out with only his family listening. But his sincerity was palpable, and on at least one cut—the agonizingly romantic "Treasure Untold"—Lefty's version of the song completely outclassed Rodgers's original. Lefty, of course, would never have presumed to think so.

Results aside, there was no denying the turbulent May sessions augured trouble in Lefty's camp. Crawford and the Callahans were old hands, but Lefty and the rest of the crew were far too green to maintain a professional grip in the midst of the pressure his nonstop, accelerating career was generating. For one thing, Lefty's way with women didn't endear him to boyfriends or husbands. Fights like the one at Judy Burkhart's house were too funny to bother anybody, but others were far more heated and vicious. At a gig in Port Arthur, Lefty had to be escorted onstage by a pair of bodyguards. Bassist Pee Wee Reid remembers a stop in Louisiana where some admirer's would-be boyfriend kept following Lefty around, pointing at the singer's precious western suit and calling him a monkey. In a restaurant over lunch, Lefty decided he had had enough and, according to Reid, broke the guy's jaw and one of his legs.

And then Lefty got tired of the band. He had no problem with the Western Cherokees as people or musicians. They were a crack western unit, as lively and tight as any Lefty could have hoped to work with, and he liked them individually. Nevertheless, Lefty, as he put it, had grown weary of listening to them "argue among themselves" and let them go. But Starnes then put the Western Cherokees under separate contract to Neva and sent them back on the road with Lefty. Not a good faith management move, but Starnes was a family man who liked to keep business close to his doorstep. Besides turning the Cherokees over to his wife, Neva, he assigned Lefty Frizzell fan club duty to his daughter and pulled his son, Bill Starnes, out of military school to take over as Lefty's road manager. The boy was fourteen years old. Though he held his own and made a few key managerial moves—not the least of which was convincing the reluctant Corpus Christi fiddler Abe Manuel to come aboard with Lefty after all—he was absurdly young to be put in charge of such a carefree spirit as Lefty on the road.

The Starnes family might have been lousy managers, but Lefty was also becoming an unmanageable act. Bill Starnes was forever having to pull him out of movie theaters to make his club dates. In one famous incident, Lefty was driving down a Louisiana highway, en route to meet some of Columbia's front office heavyweights, when he plowed through a picket fence straight into the local magistrate's yard. The lawman ran out of the house, saw the wreckage, and moaned, "I can't believe it, that's the third time that's happened to me." Lefty pondered his plight, then reportedly drawled, "My advice to you is to move."

In a less famous but more destructive incident that June, Lefty's Cadillac was clobbered at an intersection in Jasper, Texas. Some accounts had Lefty driving drunk himself, others had him in the backseat with his girlfriend of the moment while Jack Starnes or Crawford drove. The crew had just been to a Jasper rodeo—possibly to see Hank Williams perform—and none of them were any more drunk than half the cowboys in town. They got creamed by a driver as bad off as Lefty was. "The two damn fools met at a corner," said the doctor who treated them both. The collision spun the Cadillac completely around, and the other driver sustained head injuries, though nothing too severe. Lefty and Neva were thrown from the car. Neva was banged up pretty bad, but Lefty got off with minor injuries and an insurance lawsuit settled out of court. At his first show after the accident, however, he was still so shaky he had to be helped onto the stage.

For months, Starnes had tried to land Lefty a regular spot on radio. No doubt he demanded too much money, for even KWKH, much as they loved Lefty, never signed him to the Hayride. Ken Ritter recalled that in Beaumont, Neva Starnes pitched one of the local stations on a package deal for Lefty and the Western Cherokees' soon-to-be front man—Ray Price. Lefty's pal from the Beck studio scene had been signed by Don Law in March, and his debut Columbia record was a gorgeous Lefty composition called "If You're Ever Lonely Darling." In July, Price, filling in for Bob Wills at Wills's Ranchhouse in Dallas, was listed as being under management contract to Beck. But somehow, at some point, Neva seems to have lured him away to Beaumont. Jim Beck must have been apoplectic. To persuade the Beaumont radio man of the two singers' pull, Neva promised that with Lefty and Price sharing the microphone, "The post office is gonna have to put on another truck to bring the fan mail over."

Meanwhile, though wary of an Opry contract, Jack Starnes made a couple of trips to Nashville to negotiate with WSM on Lefty's behalf. On June 16, Lefty himself returned to Nashville. He performed that evening at the grand opening of Hank and Audrey Williams's new clothing store, then a couple of hours later he returned for his second guest appearance on the Prince Albert segment of the Opry. The Western Cherokees made the trip with Lefty, though true to form, the Opry brass wouldn't allow Jimmy Dennis's drums onstage. "It broke his heart," said Chalker. Red Foley reintroduced Lefty as a "fine singer of homey songs" and casually mentioned that he'd received word Lefty would be joining the Opry as an official cast member. Lefty sang "I Love You a Thousand Ways," a song composed in the homey surroundings of the Chaves County Jail, and his new smash, "I Want to Be with You Always."

Reinforcing his reputation for scattershot routing, Starnes then sent Lefty into the Midwest and from there to the Riverside Rancho in Los Angeles, where the Aberbach brothers of Hill & Range threw him a party and gave him a gold horse statuette. The Riverside Rancho was a major hillbilly venue and was run by Marty Landau, a heavyweight West Coast country promoter. In addition to booking the Riverside Rancho date, Landau arranged a follow-up tour for Lefty and the Western Cherokees up the coast and into the great Northwest. In Bakersfield, California, Lefty worked the Rainbow Gardens, where he sang "Always Late" and "Mom and Dad's Waltz" for what he said was the first time before a live audience. Of the three thousand frantic Bakersfield fans lucky enough to hear the twin debut, one was a worldly juvenile delinquent who'd been told he could sing like Lefty Frizzell. Merle Haggard described that wondrous event—one of the most momentous of his young life—in his autobiography, *Sing Me Back Home*:

> Lefty bounced out on the stage and the crowd was so thick again that I could hardly see him. I pushed myself through the crowd trying to get closer. I looked up as someone passed a chair above my head.
>
> "Stand on this so we can see you, Lefty," a voice called out as the chair was handed onto the stage. And that's what he did. He climbed up on the chair and did his entire show as we stood watching him—me for one—in absolute wonder.
>
> There is really no way I can describe the effect Lefty had on audiences back in those days. He had the soul of Hank Williams, the appeal of Johnny Cash, and the charisma of Elvis Presley. He had it all—brilliance and clarity. He was dressed in white—heroes usually are—and he was

truly an inspiration to me that night. I believe the impact he made on country music, and on *me*, at that time was not even measurable.

Behind the scenes, though, the West Coast tour was somewhat difficult, what with tensions on the bus and promoters refusing to pay. One deadbeat in particular, intent on hanging on to Lefty's share of the receipts, tried to pretend that he was passed out drunk after the show. Naamon told Lefty to step back, then nearly took their payment out of the method actor in flesh.

Besides playing enforcer, Naamon was also still driving the tour bus — which all agree was an adventure unto itself. On a mountain outside Portland, Oregon, the brakes gave out and Naamon, downshifting, stripped the gears, plunging the Cherokees into a breakneck death descent. With the cross street below coming up fast, Chalker coolly directed Naamon to hug the curb to stop the bus. "If it hadn't of stopped completely, we'd have killed a bunch of pedestrians," Chalker said.

"It wore the tires out on both the front and the back, a-stoppin' it," added Bill Callahan. "Nobody got hurt. Everybody got out smelling like a rose."

But later in the tour, when Naamon nearly backed the same bus over a ridge in New Mexico, the band mutinied. No more of Naamon driving. It was just as well, for A.D. had recently given birth to their last son, Allen, and Naamon wanted to stay home to look after the two of them. Sick at birth, the baby needed a complete blood transfusion, which Lefty paid for.

While Lefty's professional life grew fractious on the inside, on the outside it continued to steamroll. In mid-June, as he made his second Opry appearance, "I Want to Be with You Always" was number one on two of the three *Billboard* charts. "I Love You a Thousand Ways" hung in for its thirty-third week in the top ten. On July 21, Lefty Frizzell officially joined the Grand Ole Opry, a move that united him with old heroes like Ernest Tubb and new friends like Hank Williams. Hank, in fact, had played the Palm Isle in Longview the night before, and he and Lefty may have returned to Nashville together.

Lefty's next Opry performance was slated for August 11. An otherwise typical night at the Ryman, it included a most unusual backstage visit from two policemen. They found the curly-haired Opry rookie, and after letting him do his part of the show, served him with a fugitive warrant. For the second time in his life, Lefty Frizzell was under arrest for what he might have called carryin' on.

Chapter 15

THE CHARGE AGAINST LEFTY stemmed from his April Fools' Day interlude at the Hotel Marion in Little Rock. The girl who had showed up and knocked on his door had been a minor, though mercifully not as minor as the one in Roswell. Instead of statutory rape, Lefty was taken downtown and charged with "contributory delinquency," a misdemeanor. He posted a thousand-dollar bond, courtesy of Jack Starnes, and tried his best not to panic. He signed over his power of attorney, either directly to Starnes or to Starnes's lawyer, and waited to see how high the scandal would blow. "I didn't know whether I had done anything wrong or not," Lefty said, "but sure I wanted it kept down."

He needn't have worried. The Little Rock papers were silent, while *The Tennessean* reported Lefty's arrest in the Sunday paper—but only in a three-sentence blurb on page seven of the metro section. "Fugitive Charge Faces Opry Star." Harder copy on the same page reported on "thirty-three Texas cowboys, wearing 10-gallon hats and high-heeled western boots" who attended the Opry on the audience side.

Starnes advised his boy to skip the next week's Opry appearance, then he set about settling the matter as most any artist's manager in Texas would have done. Via payoff. Who he paid may never be known. But after Starnes called Lefty in Nashville and told him everything had been taken care of, Lefty reimbursed him for twenty-five hundred dollars and the case was dismissed several months later "for want of prosecution."

In the end, the only publicity Lefty's troubles may have generated was indirect, courtesy of his Little Rock buddy Hank Williams. On August 10, the night before Johnny Law came for Lefty at the Ryman,

Hank recorded a never-found version of "I'm Sorry for You My Friend," a song directed at a man forced to answer for his infidelity. The lyrics make no explicit mention of jail, but the song is laden with pregnant lines like "Today's the day you start to pay. . . ." Lefty himself said Williams "wrote it for me when I was having trouble with my better half." What sort of trouble, Lefty did not say. It could easily have been pure coincidence, for there is no ignoring the fact that the song was recorded the night *before* Lefty's arrest, not after.

Any threat Lefty's arrest may have posed to his career was nothing compared to the threat to his marriage. Lefty really was having trouble with his better half. Big trouble. Alice had nearly been forgotten in the spectacle of her husband's sudden fame. Throughout the year she had mostly stayed in Sulphur Springs, caring for Lois and spending time with Lefty as his schedule and volition permitted. If Alice suspected her Sonny of cheating on the road, she chose to put up with it, torn as always between her fierce love for him and fury at his philandering. But the Little Rock episode was different. It threw Lefty's behavior in her face, humiliating her and shaming him before her. It wasn't just that Lefty had trifled on her again, and been caught again—although that was plenty. The worst thing, if she was inclined to think that way, was that he had fooled around on her within weeks—perhaps days—of their conceiving their second child. For at the point the cops eased Lefty out the back door of the Ryman Auditorium, Alice was four and a half months pregnant.

For Lefty, the Arkansas crisis felt like a moral cold shower. He suddenly understood how tired he'd grown of the road games, of the Ancient Age hangovers and hotel trysts that his overnight fame encouraged. As he had in Roswell, he determined to make it up to Alice and to devote more time to her and Lois—not out of guilt or pity, though that was part of it, but because he genuinely, deeply missed them. He decided to take them on his tours more than he had before. And in October, the reconciling couple did what was, for the nomadic likes of them, unthinkable. They purchased a comfortable home at 2214 East Drive in the wealthy Calder Highlands of Beaumont, Texas. It was a modest two-story house with a good-sized front yard and a goldfish pond in back. Their next-door neighbor was a doctor who Lois Frizzell says looked down on them as "get-rich-quick white trash." Alice immediately furnished her new home with all the amenities of 1950s suburbia—new furniture, fancy curtains, a vacuum cleaner, a maid to push it.

For his part, Lefty bought a $50,000 life insurance policy from Cliff Bruner, who had temporarily set his fiddle aside. A roughneck descendent, Lefty luxuriated in the stability of home ownership, in the space it provided him to wind down during the brief respite between tours. Speaking of those autumn months of 1951, Lefty would wax warm and nostalgic. "I was on tour and when I got in town I was pretty busy, and I loved home cooking and I stayed at home to eat beans and go to a movie ever now and then, carried my wife and little girl because I didn't have much chance to stay at home."

Yet as Lefty settled in and patched things up with his beloved Alice, he was having serious misgivings about his manager. He had to credit Starnes with knowing how to squash a scandal, but he was rapidly losing confidence in Starnes's ability to direct his activities — at least well enough to justify his 50 percent take. For one thing, Lefty continued to chafe at the Starnes-knotted rope connecting him to the Western Cherokees. After a year on the fast-action highways, Lefty had decided that he didn't want the attachment to a band. He much preferred to travel light. Abe Manuel, who had taken the stage name Sandy Austin, was the only musician Lefty actually kept on his own payroll.

And the Opry gig, once Lefty returned to it, proved a scheduling nightmare. Operating out of Beaumont or Longview during the week, Lefty would be expected in Nashville on Saturday night and booked anyplace Starnes found him work on Friday and Sunday. To further complicate matters, signed to the Opry, Lefty had to participate in its out-of-town package shows, some of which were organized without his knowledge. Apprised of an impending date, Lefty would look to Starnes for guidance and/or explanation, but the manager wouldn't know anything about it. Lefty had a fit one night when he closed out the late segment of the Opry, only to be told by Little Jimmy Dickens that he was due for a show on the Atlantic Coast the following afternoon. Another time, according to Manuel, after Lefty and Hank Williams both missed a scheduled Ryman appearance, they arrived the next Saturday and were turned away at the door by show security. What a sight. Hank Williams and Lefty Frizzell, locked out of the Grand Ole Opry.

Starnes figured out a way to turn Lefty's discomfort to his own use. Rather than pay stricter attention to potential scheduling conflicts, he suggested to Lefty that the two of them go in together on a private airplane to make the long jumps workable. With their own plane and pilot at their beck and call, the distances between stops would be irrelevant. Of course, for a kid who a year and a half before had been driving a bald-tired secondhand Studebaker, the idea of half-owning a twin-engine eight-passenger Cessna was irresistible. Lefty fell hook, line, sinker, wings, and tail for Starnes's proposal. The two of them bought the Cessna in September and first made use of it on an October tour back to California. At 20,000 feet above every hillbilly Cadillac in Texas, above the Red River Valley and the East Texas oil wells, the bloody buckets and the Chaves County Jail, Lefty felt the thrill of his career at its peak.

Not that it took the spinning propellers to tell him so. Lefty's shows broke attendance records all over the country. He played to 3,000 people at the Circle A Ranch in Deer Park, New Jersey, and joined Ernest Tubb, Moon Mullican, and several other Opry acts at a two-day festival in Washington's 38,000-seat Griffith Stadium. In Fayetteville, Arkansas, 1,000 fans including the mayor congregated at the airport, waiting to greet Lefty before a scheduled show at a local tobacco warehouse. Two hours later, 650 of the fans were still waiting, a witty few singing "Always Late." That was nothing. In Stillwater, Oklahoma, Lefty and Manuel never made it off the runway. Lefty's admirers stormed the airplane as it taxied to a halt. Manuel said he and Lefty did their entire show from the wing of the Cessna.

North, south, east, west—it made no difference, the response was always the same. "He was so hot that it was unbelievable," said Manuel. "Everything he did was encore, encore, encore. They couldn't hear what we was doin', so it didn't matter if we played good or not." At an auditorium show in Los Angeles, the fans went berserk when Lefty's limo pulled up. Manuel stepped out first and the crowd tore into his fancy western suit, bought for him by Lefty, before they'd even seen his face. "People just went crazy, man. They started pulling my fringes. They pulled my shirt plumb off, thinking I was Lefty."

Clothes were very much on their minds anyway. Since he'd made enough money to afford them, Lefty had been designing his own western outfits—heavy on the leather fringe angle. But out in California that fall, Marty Landau, owner of the Riverside Rancho, took him to meet the rising star of cowboy glitz: Nudie the Rodeo Tailor. Lefty may have pitched Nudie his own fashion ideas. "Detachable fringe" was not the least of Lefty's concepts. But Nudie, an ex–G-string manufacturer, had his own plans for Columbia's Discovery of the Year. Asking Lefty to be his guinea pig, he designed a white cowboy shirt with an "L" and an "F" scripted on the yoke. He then filled the two letters with blue rhinestones. According to Nudie's wife, that shirt of Lefty's marked the first time Nudie the Rodeo Tailor ever put rhinestones on a country singer's clothes.

Lefty's autumn West Coast tour ended three days before the October 13 issue of *Billboard* hit the stands. "Always Late" had been poised at number one since mid-September. When Lefty returned with his Nudie shirt, it was still number one. But in addition, the B-side, "Mom and Dad's Waltz," was number two, while "I Want to Be with You Always" held down the fifth spot. Lefty had three songs in the top ten way back in April, but this time, jumping in at number seven, along with the other three was Lefty's rendition of "Travellin' Blues," one of the Jimmie Rodgers covers recorded in June. One, two, five, and seven. Four songs by one man in the country top ten all at once. Country music would not see anything like it again — except, of course, for the following two weeks, when Lefty repeated the feat. (For many years, it's been widely publicized that Lefty Frizzell was the only country singer to ever place four songs in the top ten at the same time. In fact, in August 1948, the week he resigned from the Grand Ole Opry, Eddy Arnold had *five* songs in the top ten all at once.)

The excitement over the airplane deal briefly deflected Lefty's unhappiness with Starnes but didn't solve anything. With a new home in Beaumont, fatigued and eager to spend more time with Alice and Lois, Lefty was trying to reprioritize his life for the first time since "If You've Got the Money, I've Got the Time" hit radio. Starnes's hard-squeeze management style didn't fit with Lefty's new priorities. Later that October, while Lefty was up in Longview, he called Alice and asked her to retrieve his copy of the contract with Starnes — the one forgotten since the moment Lefty put it in Starnes's glove compartment to keep Jim Beck from seeing it. Shortly thereafter, back in Beaumont himself, Lefty reread the document. He felt his blood run cold as he came upon a clause he had no recollection of reading in the lawyer's office in January. On page three of the contract, directly under the bit about the agreement covering a one-year period, Lefty read: "SECOND PARTY [Lefty] agrees to give FIRST PARTY [Starnes] an option for his services in a similar capacity for two years, the term of which option is to immediately follow the term of this contract."

Livid, Lefty told his manager to meet him downtown. They were going to take a little walk, Lefty said, over to the office of Starnes's attorney to look at the original in his safe. As it turned out, the lawyer was conveniently absent from the office that day, so Lefty didn't get to view his copy. Lefty and Starnes, now genuinely wary of each other, discussed the option clause — which violated Lefty's perception of the agreement he thought he had signed. Stalemated for the time being, they decided to defer any further argument. "We talked about it and finally we said let it go to some other time," Lefty later testified. "I said, 'Sure,' so I just went ahead and kept on working. I had jobs to do and couldn't cancel out—no use to cancel out—I just kept working."

On the nineteenth of October, Lefty was in the studio again—this time in Houston, not at Beck's in Dallas. The session went so poorly that Don Law never released any of the four takes cut that day. Afterward, Lefty took to the road once more with his fiddle player and ever-closer friend Abe Manuel. Pared down to a two-man traveling team, they worked with house bands in the boondocks, and with the staff musicians at the Opry. "Back then it was real hectic, man," Manuel says of the Opry shows. "We'd have to get outside, and no dressing room, and run upstairs, and meet somebody coming down . . . it was something else. We'd just get up there, and he'd hit a separate chord and start playing. We'd never have a program. Just whatever come to mind, he'd just play his A chord or whatever he was gonna do it in and start singing, and we'd jump right in there with him." Sometimes Ernest Tubb would introduce Lefty, other times Red Foley or Minnie Pearl. "Of course everybody loved him," Manuel added. "He was such a fantastic writer. He was always writing. Always."

As the miles disappeared and the towns grew blurrier, Lefty grew to depend on Manuel to take care of his arrangements on the road. Always a generous boss, Lefty repaid him with a piece of his concert concession action. (In those days, for a country star, the songbook and photo sales were often more profitable than the gate receipts or royalties.) The more the Cajun fiddler learned about Lefty's income and organization, the less use he had for Starnes. "I was keeping books for [Lefty] on the road, taking care of his money," he says. "Jack didn't like that at all because I knew too much about Jack." Deep as he had his own claws in Lefty, Starnes resented the extra income Manuel made as the singer's sideman and unofficial road manager. But he was more than happy, Manuel says, to hold him accountable for Lefty's highway transgressions. "Lefty'd do things, and then Jack would blame me for that. 'Hey, I'm just a peon,'" Abe would protest, "'just a fiddle player.'" Moreover, so far as Manuel was concerned, there was an element of hypocrisy in Starnes's taking him to task for Lefty's erratic behavior. "I know a lot of times, Jack wanted Lefty to drink. Oh yeah. When Lefty was drunk he was kindhearted."

All the bad blood that had been simmering for months boiled over during the holidays. It started when Starnes arranged a two-week tour for Lefty through Canada. In the dead of winter. Lefty and Abe flew into

St. John, New Brunswick, on November 19. Manuel has never forgotten the shock upon deplaning. "It was eighty-five degrees in Beaumont, Texas, when we left that morning, and it was twenty-four below when we landed in New Brunswick." At customs, Lefty declared a seventy-dollar value on his customized Gibson, and another ten dollars for Abe's fiddle. Three days later, Lefty applied for a permit, via the Prince Edward Island Temperance Act, to purchase twenty-two quarts of liquor to see him through the tour.

The Canadian promoter with whom Starnes had contracted greeted the duo when they arrived. He handed them a four-figure check as their guarantee. Again the tour was arranged to feature Lefty, his fiddler, and whichever hired guns the promoter could find to fill out the band at each stop. "Hal Lone Pine" Breau, a Canadian star of modest stateside fame, also joined as Lefty's opening act. It took but a couple days in the Canadian snow and ice—with Starnes home basking in the Gulf Coast sun—for Lefty to realize he was being taken advantage of. For one thing, the gigs the promoter booked were outrageous. Manuel recalls the worst of them all was at an ice-skating rink. "They got us in there, of course we went in through the back, and we didn't know that it was an ice skating arena. We got in through the back and only went into the dressing room; the nice steam heat. It was nice and warm back there. And every once in a while we'd see some people walk around there in skating uniforms. We didn't know what it was going on."

What it was going on was an ice show preceding the concert. When Lefty's turn came, he and Manuel found themselves on a stage in the middle of the rink, on four feet of ice. "And we didn't have no jacket on, where we needed an overcoat, what we needed. I think we did two songs and started on a third, and we had to quit because nobody would play no more." Their fingers too frozen to feel their instruments, Lefty and Abe gave up and stepped off the stage. Manuel's toes went one way and his fiddle the other. He crawled out of the rink on his hands and knees while a kid on skates breezed by to pick up the fiddle and bow.

The next gig was booked halfway to the North Pole. It didn't even happen. "Man," says Manuel, "we drove and drove and drove and nothing but white. And when we finally came to the place, it was this priest and a bunch of boys playing basketball. Nobody. I found all the posters in a little bitty hallway there by the bathroom. They had never put up the posters, nobody knew he was supposed to be there. No radio advertising. No newspaper. Nothing. Nobody showed up. So the guy, he was gonna dock Lefty for that weekend. I told him, heck, no, man, this your problem. You the one didn't advertise, not us."

From there, the Canadian tour improved, but not by much. Lefty took sick (no surprise, considering the working conditions and the twenty-two quarts of booze he brought with him), but still made the rest of the dates, including one at Toronto's famed Massey Hall, and the last few shows were planned well enough actually to make money. But out of all the misery and cold, what angered Lefty the most was having to charter a plane to make it to one of the poorly routed venues. He could stand Starnes's 50 percent cut, though he didn't like it, and he could stand the tours he had to make with Crawford's band, though he wanted independence. But the one thing he could not stand was freezing to death in a foreign country, with no means of transportation, while his manager relaxed in dear old Texas with the Cessna sitting idle. "We got over there," Lefty said, "and had to charter a plane to get over the snow and ice and here we had a plane here and I was having to charter a plane over there. It just wasn't any good and I got to feeling bad and I was sick and I called Mr. Starnes and told him I was through."

Lefty telephoned Starnes from his hotel room in Canada at one o'clock in the morning. He had already spoken to Alice earlier to get her support for his decision to split with Starnes. When he reached Starnes at home, Lefty was in a foul mood and fully resolved to sever their relationship. The conversation was long and heated. Lefty told Starnes to tear up their contract. (In a particular fit of pique, he told him to ram it.) Starnes tried to talk Lefty's temper down, but Lefty fell asleep, right in the middle of his manager's smooth-talking cajolery. Manuel had to wake Lefty to finish the conversation. He called Alice one more time before the night was up, then finally went to sleep. In the morning, says Manuel, Lefty had to fork over $125 to cover his hotel phone bill. They took their final payment from the Canadian promoter — in cash, since Manuel was highly suspicious of the guarantee check — and the tour ended with Lefty and Abe crossing the border to catch a midnight train out of Buffalo. "We were starving to death," Manuel says. "Man, I offered a woman ten dollars for a cracker."

For the next two weeks, Lefty went underground. Completely incommunicado. Starnes had no idea where he was. Defiant and fed up, Lefty contracted with Oklahoma booking agent Lucky Moeller for a six-day, four-thousand-dollar run through his trusted West Texas and Southeast New Mexico haunts. Working with a band that featured Red Garrett and star harmonica wizard Wayne Raney, whom Lefty had met at the Opry, Lefty halted the wildcat tour in Clovis, New Mexico. A bit less sure of where he stood, once he'd blown off some steam, he called

Starnes to try to feel him out. Starnes immediately hit Lefty with his lowest managerial blow yet.

"I think I asked him what he was doing on something," Lefty testified, "and he said he was seeing what all he could do about that contract and that he had a girl, a pregnant girl, and her mother and dad and [the] sheriff were waiting on me at the airport when I came back in."

That was barely a week before Christmas. Alice was due any day.

Chapter 16

STARNES'S PLOY WORKED. Lefty returned to Beaumont in a somewhat conciliatory mood. Whether Starnes's paternity threat had any substance or not, there was no sheriff waiting at the airport. Lefty and Starnes regrouped. Jack told Lefty about two prime tours he had lined up for the coming spring. The first would take him to New York in March and would include a guest appearance on Perry Como's TV show. Immediately afterward, he would flip-flop coasts to work a lucrative eight-week tour through California and the Northwest. Lefty could hardly turn down such prospects. Still assuming that his one-year contract with Starnes would be up at the end of January, he agreed, in principle, to stay with his manager and extend the terms of their agreement through the duration of the two coastal tours. After that, they would talk again and see if they could possibly renegotiate a more reasonable deal.

The Frizzells and Starneses spent Christmas Day together in Beaumont, three days before Rickey Rodger Frizzell was born. Thinking ahead, Starnes and Lefty had arranged to have the holidays off to devote to Alice and the baby. Always excited and happy around Christmas, Lefty lounged in the living room of his new home on East Drive, coo-cooing over his son and singing carols with his delighted daughter. He surrounded the tinseled tree with presents, enjoyed his family's laughter, and peacefully reflected on the unpeaceful year coming to a close. The last twelve months had put Lefty through more emotional changes than many artists undergo in twenty years, yet the bottom line was that of the thirty bestselling country songs of 1951, Lefty Frizzell, alone, accounted for seven. He had leapfrogged Hank Williams, Hank

Snow, Eddy Arnold, Ernest Tubb, Red Foley, and all the other veteran acts whose stardom he had always wanted to emulate. *Billboard* listed "I Want to Be with You Always" as the year's number one record on hillbilly jukeboxes across America. "Always Late" weighed in at number three for the year. Had jukeboxes not been exempted from copyright law, a situation bitterly contested in the halls of Congress, Lefty probably could have lived off his Wurlitzer action alone.

A singer's life goes on anyway. A week after the New Year's champagne bottles were emptied, Lefty headed to Dallas to recut three of the four songs botched in October in Houston. A new lineup, including West Coast steel guitarist Pee Wee Whitewing and ex–Texas Playboy fiddler Johnny Gimble, backed Lefty as he added "Don't Stay Away (Till Love Grows Cold)" to his already lengthy list of sorrowfully romantic country ballads. Meanwhile, the incomparable "Always Late" and "Mom and Dad's Waltz" were still slaying listeners, and his newest hit, "Give Me More, More, More (Of Your Kisses)," was also lighting up the jukeboxes. Ray Price wrote the latter song with Lefty a year before at the "I Want to Be with You Always" session. That night, Lefty had run out of decent songs and asked his friend Ray, who was just hanging around the Beck studio, and who didn't consider himself a songwriter, to "get on back there and write one" for him. But Don Law, not even convinced of Price's worth as a singer, didn't consider him a songwriter either. He left the off-the-cuff number in the can for almost a year before finally releasing it. Neither Law nor Lefty nor Price could have guessed that the insipid novelty "Give Me More, More, More (Of Your Kisses)" would turn out to be the fifth number one hit of Lefty's year-and-a-half-old recording career, and that it would be his last chart-topper for over a decade to come.

Gearing up for the springtime onslaught of coast-to-coast dates, Lefty worked the easy Southwest turf from Kilgore to San Antonio, and on up to Oklahoma. He continued to make his Opry jumps and package shows, joining Ernest Tubb and Cowboy Copas for a Birmingham blowout that drew 5,000. Such figures did not excite Starnes. He figured that Lefty had outgrown the Grand Ole Opry and didn't need to waste his Saturday-night fees warming to the WSM microphone. The notoriously low-paying Nashville institution offered "little more than prestige," as the trade press put it, and country radio in general was perceived by progressive entertainers as a technological dinosaur. Television was the future. The entire country music industry appeared to be moving toward Hollywood, which by 1952 was being hailed in the press as "Hillbilly H.Q." Starnes and his client talked the situation over. Though

Lefty considered the Opry one of the "best deals," they agreed that the spring tours would end his affiliation with the program. Ray Price told Lefty the Opry hated to see him go, and over time, other people would talk about Lefty's quitting the show as one of the worst decisions of his career. But Lefty, whose brief Opry career had been checkered to say the least, had every bit as much reason to leave the Opry as stay.

In February, Starnes flew out to California to finalize the details of the impending West Coast tour. Instead of booking through Marty Landau, his usual California contact, Starnes negotiated the deal with the Americana Corporation, a hillbilly booking behemoth run by a stogie-chomping ex-cop named Steve Stebbins. The tour was to run for April through June, and would guarantee Lefty approximately $500 to $750 per night—*after* expenses, and *after* Starnes's 50 percent cut. Had Lefty been under more advantageous managerial care, those two months' worth of dates could have netted him $50,000 or more. Peanuts by 1990s standards, but an astronomical sum for a country singer in 1952.

Lefty and Abe Manuel took off on the eastern tour in early March to work the Ohio Valley, the Great Lakes industrial belt, and upstate New York. They played a one-nighter in Hannibal, Missouri, that drew 17,000 to the local armory. The Western Cherokees joined Lefty and Abe for a number of dates, but apparently not for the March 19 appearance on Perry Como's variety show. Like most of the pop singers of the day, Como was tuned in to the popularity of country music, and had already featured the Hanks (Williams and Snow) on the small-screen show he hosted. But Como may not have understood the threat to his own stage dominion that Lefty Frizzell would pose when he invited "the Beaumont Flash" to New York. Manuel remembers it well.

> It was unbelievable! Perry was such a fantastic showman. . . .We went up there and I don't remember who was with us, backing us. But just walking on that stage, we had thought that the crowd that Perry Como had up there would have been a Perry Como crowd. But it was unbelievable the reaction people gave us. When we got on the stage, they just, they just went wild! Oh, God, just like every other stage we'd go on, they'd go wild. [Lefty] did "Mom and Dad's Waltz," and "I Love You a Thousand Ways," and "If You've Got the Money," and after he'd gotten them three there done he could hardly do anything else. Perry had a good reception, but nothing in comparison to what Lefty [got].

After the Como show, Lefty worked his way back to Beaumont, riding with Starnes in Neva's Cadillac. Along the way, they picked up a pair of Chryslers that Jack had ordered as transportation for the Western

Cherokees and a couple of other singers he and Neva were pushing, Johnny Rector and Danny Brown. At the time, Lefty didn't think much of Starnes's auto purchase. But to tell the truth, he didn't much care what Jack did. Though he had paid lip service to the idea of renegotiating a deal with Starnes, Lefty was really just playing out his contract. The two pulled into Beaumont on Lefty's birthday, caught their breath, and drove to Dallas for an April 4 session at Beck's. Lefty was running thin on material. Working with the Gimble and Whitewing lineup again, the four songs he recorded included a dreadful "answer song" to his debut smash called "If You Can Spare the Time (I Won't Miss the Money)," a fair take on a Bob Wills ballad, and the five-year-old Chaves County Jail composition "I Know You're Lonesome (While Waiting for Me)." Only the third song cut that day, "Forever (and Always)," ranks with the best of Lefty's work. As in "I Love You a Thousand Ways" and "I Want to Be with You Always," the theme of enduring, embattled romance pushed Lefty to the limits of his soul-searching delivery.

The West Coast tour started five days after the "Forever (and Always)" session, beginning with a couple of Los Angeles shows at which Hank Williams also appeared. Lefty and the Cherokees drew a crazed four thousand to "Hometown Jamboree" in El Monte. From there, they worked a grueling string of one-nighters that took them south to San Diego, then all the way back up the coast. After a month of screaming fans, erratic sound systems, and nightly encores at joints like Yuba City's Moonlight Ballroom, where the roof folded out for starlit dancing, Lefty's voice completely gave out. He told himself that this was the end, that he would never again take to the road nonstop the way he had been doing for the last three months. Speaking in a hoarse, drawling whisper, he called Starnes, who had returned to Beaumont after the initial leg of the tour, and said, "I'm through. I've made up my mind and I'm through. I've been on the road too hard." Lefty told Jack that after completing the West Coast trip, he was going to start booking himself as a solo artist through independent agents, guys who would take their 15 percent commissions and leave him alone. He wanted nothing to do with a band. He wanted to stay home more. He wanted to be able to talk again. Starnes listened, but said little.

With his voice growing hoarser every day, Lefty started to consult doctors wherever he worked. There wasn't much they could do for him. One gave Lefty a shot of penicillin and sent him on his way. By the end of May, it was obvious he wasn't going to be able to complete the tour. Lefty and the band had exhausted themselves singing and picking almost nightly for three solid months. They wrecked one of the Chryslers, and they lost their steel guitarist before a show at the Garden of Allah Club in Niles, California. Homesick, the steel man hopped on a bus and headed back east. (The Cherokees replaced him with Pee Wee Whitewing, who had returned to the coast and was there that night.) "I played about seven days when I could hardly talk—much less sing," Lefty said, "and I would have to do two or three numbers and it was rough."

Even Al Flores, the agent Americana put on the road to handle the business end of the tour, agreed it was pointless to continue. With three weeks' worth of dates left to play, Lefty called Starnes again, this time from Potlatch, Idaho, and told him to cancel everything. The boys were exhausted. His voice was shot. He was coming home.

Lefty took advantage of the unscheduled down time to rest his vocal cords and his wiped-out, highway-battered body. On the way back to Beaumont, he stopped in Hobbs and Sulphur Springs to visit kinfolk, and generally to do as little as possible. He finally arrived in Beaumont in time to spend Memorial Day with Alice and Lois, and with his five-month-old son Rickey, whom he had scarcely had a chance to get to know. But his R and R didn't last. Lefty began to get nervous when his midyear Columbia and Hill & Range royalty checks failed to arrive. Sensing something was up, he knew he had to face Starnes to find out what had happened.

On Friday, June 13, Lefty and Blackie Crawford drove to Starnes's house, ostensibly to see if they couldn't renegotiate some kind of deal with Jack that would be more to Lefty's liking. Something closer to a straight 15 percent booking arrangement. The afternoon started out friendly enough. Jack, Neva, and their younger children sat around while Lefty sang a new song he had written. Then Lefty stood up, stretched, and laid the Gibson down by the couch. He and Jack excused themselves and stepped outside to talk about what they both knew was the real reason for Lefty's visit. Lefty asked what had happened to his royalties. Starnes said they had been delayed because he thought half the money was his.

"Well," Lefty said, "we will see if we can get them anyway and we will work the deal out among ourselves." Starnes then mentioned something about a lawyer. Startled, Lefty asked Jack if he had brought a suit against him. "No," Lefty said Starnes answered, "I would never throw dirt or something at you in any way unless them lawyers did." Lefty didn't know what that meant.

He found out four days later. "Them lawyers," hired by Starnes, filed an injunctive suit against Lefty in the Jefferson County District Court. Starnes's petition detailed the terms of his original contract and overall business relationship with Lefty. Among the so-called "facts" set forth was the following claim:

> That prior to January 26, 1951, the defendant had attempted to engage in the writing and publishing of songs for profit, as well as that of a musician presenting and singing such songs at various places of entertainment where he might procure employment; that nevertheless the said defendant had not acquired sufficient publicity and reputation whereby he was able, with profit to himself, to follow such composing, selling, and producing of said music, nor the vending of his services as a musician and entertainer.

The petition also included the positively outrageous contention that prior to hooking up with Starnes, "the defendant herein had not developed a reputation as a composer or entertainer beyond the immediate area of this county. . . ." Never mind that at the point Lefty signed with Starnes, he already had two nationwide number one hits under his belt, and an appearance on the national network portion of the Grand Ole Opry.

Though the lawyers took great pains to prove how important Starnes's promotional efforts had been to the growth of Lefty's career — a by no means unfair claim, for Starnes had kept Lefty's name out there — the crux of the matter was Starnes's insistence that Lefty was still under contract to him, and would be through January 1954. To support his position, Starnes produced a copy of the contract, complete with the two-year option clause that had shocked Lefty when he first noticed it in October. Starnes also provided a copy of a letter dated January 11, 1952, the original of which allegedly had been sent to Lefty to notify him that Starnes was exercising the option. The lawsuit papers further itemized every claim Starnes had against Lefty's unaccounted-for earnings. They included $250 for one of the post-Canada underground dates, $10,000 for the twenty shows Lefty told Starnes to cancel when his voice gave out in Idaho, and, most important, half the $12,000 and $18,000 royalty checks that were due Lefty from Columbia and Hill & Range, respectively. Altogether, Starnes's claim against his superstar country client amounted to $25,250. He also asked that Lefty be enjoined from collecting any further personal performance fees or royalty payments as long as the suit was pending. Jack Starnes meant to put Lefty out of business until he got his cut.

He was only partially successful. Lefty's lawyer filed the defendant's answer to the suit two weeks later. After discussing the case with both sides, the judge postponed a hearing on the injunction. Starnes's lawyers did effectively tie up the joint royalty checks, but the judge would not stop Lefty from recording or working on the road. While his counsel prepared his legal defense, Lefty made an after-midnight phone call to J. D. Miller, a friend of his who lived a hundred miles away in Crowley, Louisiana. Lefty woke his groggy friend up and said, "Look, I'm not gonna mess around with Jack anymore. I want you to handle me."

Then, as now, J. D. Miller—one of the most fascinating characters ever to settle behind a soundboard—ran a tiny recording studio deep in the heart of Louisiana Cajun country. Before World War II, idolizing Cliff Bruner, Miller had worked in a series of bayou western swing outfits. But as much as he loved the Gulf Coast bandstands, he had noted the fatality rate of dancehall musicians' marriages, and gave it all up on the day he said "I do." From that point on, he focused his attention on the recording end of the business. Miller built a series of studios and started a pair of specialized independent labels—Fais Do Do and Feature—for which he produced local country singers and hardcore Cajun talent. Through the 1950s and sixties, Miller would amass a boundless catalog of incisive blues and rockabilly records by some of the era's most engaging obscurities. He would write a pocketful of country standards, in part thanks to Lefty, and by the 1980s would be such a legendary record man that Paul Simon would use Miller's Crowley studio for one of the tracks on the *Graceland* LP. But long before that, J. D. Miller would have to survive a stint as the manager of Lefty Frizzell, a premium high-octane country act whose career was approaching chaos.

Abe Manuel had known Miller since they were kids in rival Cajun bands, squaring off in battle dances in and around Lake Charles. It was Abe who first introduced Lefty to Miller, at a show in Lafayette a few months before the lawsuit. Typically, Lefty and the down-home Louisiana producer hit it off right away, and they later got together in Crowley to fool around writing songs together. Impressed with Miller's work, Lefty introduced him to the ubiquitous Troy Martin over the phone, and urged the Peer rep to make a trip to Crowley to check out Miller's songs. Martin shocked Miller by doing exactly that. Martin's journey to bayou country led directly to what was undoubtably the most memorable cut of Miller's young career. After hearing "It Wasn't God Who Made Honky Tonk Angels," a Miller-written gender-bent answer to

Hank Thompson's "The Wild Side of Life" sung by one of the Feature label's no-name artists, Martin took the song back to Nashville and placed it with Kitty Wells. She promptly turned it into one of the most famous recordings in the history of country music.

With only a few slapdash collaborations tying him to Lefty, Miller was more than a little surprised when the prodigal singer woke him up at two-thirty in the morning and made his mind-blowing business proposition. In fact, Miller was nearly struck dumb. He had sworn off the music highway life when he married, but how could he turn down one of the hottest acts in country music—and a good friend to boot— when offered 25 percent of the singer's earnings? "Lefty, I don't want to leave home, man," Miller protested, feebly, knowing he was doomed to accept.

Like everyone else who worked with Lefty, Miller was immediately awestricken by his friend's talent and charisma. "I had never met a guy that could put the people in the palm of their hand like that . . . no question." As manager, Miller quickly formed a band of sympathetic Louisiana musicians, led by ace front man Lou Millet, to travel with Lefty. An outgoing, rambunctious gang of bayou boys, they had no trouble keeping up with their leader's late hours and wild antics. One of the pickers, says Miller, routinely had to be leaned against the piano, just to keep him upright through the shows. Lefty couldn't have been more pleased. "He believed in partying," Miller affirms.

Miller lost hours and hours of sleep, rooming with Lefty wherever they played. The Crowley producer loved his friend for his almost child-like devotion to laughter and fun, but not the unreliability that accompanied it. Night after night, Lefty showed up late for gigs and blew whatever money he made. Sometimes he blew money he didn't make. Driving through Dallas one time, he and Miller passed a car dealership with a nine-thousand-dollar Cadillac stretch limo gleaming in the showroom window. Lefty (who it seemed had already demolished a fleet of Caddys in two years' time) insisted on looking at the black beauty right then and there. "Man, we ain't got enough money to buy a damn Cadillac," Miller snorted. But Lefty was insistent. "Yeah, let's go!" he said.

Miller took a U-turn. He and Lefty, grimy from the road, walked into the dealership and headed straight for the Cadillac, Lefty running his admiring hands over the chrome while Miller waited for a salesman. None came. Offended, Miller sauntered over to the mechanics' station and said, "Guys, let me ask you something. Is that black Cadillac limo for sale?"

"You better believe it is," someone said. "They've been having it a long time."

"Well they don't act like it," Miller said. "We've been out there looking at it; nobody's ever come to wait on us or ask us if they can help. You see the guy over there with the striped pants and the pretty cowboy boots? You know who that is?"

"No."

"Lefty Frizzell."

Two minutes later, the head of the dealership himself was on the showroom floor, directing four lackeys to wipe down the limo and urging Lefty to take it for a spin. Lefty needed no urging. After one time around the block, pecking and punching, he started worrying Miller to death about how bad he wanted the car. Exasperated, Lefty's manager devised a plan. Knowing that Lefty's Hill & Range contract would be up in a few months, Miller called one of the Aberbachs ("to this day I don't know which of the brothers I was talking to") and fooled him into wiring a ten-thousand-dollar bonus for Lefty to renew his contract. Miller simply fabricated an alleged counteroffer from one of Hill & Range's rivals, and Hill & Range sent the money. "I went back and bought that Cadillac for seventy-five hundred dollars," Miller says, "and we had twenty-five hundred dollars to play with."

The next morning, Lefty had a breakfast date lined up at which he intended to show off his four-wheeled prize. The boys beat him out of bed, though, and snuck downstairs to mess with the Caddy. They jacked up one of the rear wheels just enough so that it would spin without traction. Later that morning, having all put up with Lefty's whoopie cushions and toy store gags, they busted their guts by the hotel windows, watching as Lefty, horrified, couldn't get his new baby to move.

After several months managing Lefty, J. D. Miller lost as much weight as he did sleep. Though he could never stay mad for long, Miller knew, for the sake of his nerves, that he couldn't keep at it much longer. His tenure with Lefty ended at a concert in New Orleans. Lefty and the band had been out on tour and were just heading back into Louisiana. They played New Iberia, down in bayou country, with the next night's gig scheduled for eight o'clock at the Crescent City's Municipal Auditorium. The New Iberia date brought them so close to Crowley that Miller hoped to spend the night at home. He asked Lefty if he could stay behind, then hook up with them back in New Orleans in time for the show. Lefty had no problem with that. "Oh, yeah, go on," he said. Lefty assured Miller that he would take care of everything in New Orleans—hiring a ticket taker, having change ready, all the preparatory details Miller usually handled himself. "I gave him forty-two hundred dollars," Miller says. "Gonna have plenty of change. And I said, 'Be sure that the boys are straight, and that everything clicks off at eight o'clock like it's supposed to.'"

The next night, Miller left Crowley around six o'clock, and by the time he hit New Orleans there was a line three blocks long waiting to see the show. "Gee, we've got a crowd," he said to himself. "Boy, this is it!" But then he realized why the line was so long. The auditorium was locked. There was no ticket taker out front. The boys were at the auditorium waiting for him—straight, too—but Lefty was nowhere in sight. Miller sweated bullets opening the place and selling tickets with the hundred dollars in change he had on his own person. At nine o'clock, and still no Lefty, he sent the band out to hold the fort on their own. They did as well as could be expected, but after an hour outside, an hour before an empty stage, and an hour of Lefty's band without Lefty, the crowd turned unruly. With Miller tearing his hair out, the star finally appeared. "He showed up at ten o'clock," Miller says, "him and a little gal from Bourbon Street. No money, he'd spent it all. Forty-two hundred dollars. I said, 'Well, this is it. I quit.'"

As for the show that night in New Orleans? "Oh, they loved him," Miller says with a laugh. "In spite of him getting there late, they loved him."

Chapter 17

WITH THE STARNES LAWSUIT hanging over his head, Lefty played as hard as an instant millionaire oil man ignoring the encroachment of Texaco. He had no manager, and it was his own fault. This time he had chased off a friend, not some smooth-talking promoter who saw him as a walking dollar sign. Though Lefty continued to tour hard and earn good money—working every audience into a frenzy—he also acted as if none of it could ever end, as if the fun times and riches and fan adulation were as limitless as the mineral bounty of the state in which he was born.

He did not notice, for instance, that for all of August 1952, he did not have a single song on the *Billboard* charts. Nor did he seem to know or care that as soon as the Starnes lawsuit hit the trade papers, his name disappeared from the columnists' print. All of a sudden, Lefty's career activities were less newsworthy than an injury Jack Starnes suffered while drilling for oil in Oklahoma. And his behavior was encroaching on his home life again. The tortured cycle of guilt and forgiveness that had entered the Frizzell marriage in Roswell had, by Beaumont, turned permanent. Lefty still had little time to spend at home, and he had quit taking high-tempered Alice out on tour after she beat up one too many of his too-amorous fans. Nor did Alice mind giving Lefty the same sort of treatment. Under normal circumstances she was a kind, reserved, generous woman well liked by all of Lefty's friends. But she also had a snapping point, to which Lefty's antics often pushed her. Their heated exchanges sometimes turned into rollicking carpet tussles, even fistfights, which Lefty invariably lost. "He never abused her," their daughter, Lois, emphasizes. "She would hit him, I would say. . . . She was strong as an ox, and Daddy was kinda thin, you know? And she, man, she'd belt him. She'd stand up and fight the devil. She didn't care." At times, Alice would belt him with whatever nearby object was handy, leaving Lefty marks to remember her by on the road. If friends saw his scars, Lefty would say—not without admiration—"I tell you that woman is *mean* when she gets mad!"

"Oh, man, they loved it," Lois says. "That's how they communicated . . . that's how they rationalized things, and worked things out. They'd fight about it. And then they'd unwind, and then they'd mellow out, and then they'd discuss it, and then everything was cool. You know, they'd make up, 'cause they *dearly* loved each other. I mean love that goes beyond the physical and emotional. It was more than that. It was something else, that most people look for all their lives and never recognize. . . . They must have been soul mates. I think they're still together."

But Lefty could only ignore the lawsuit for so long. On October 10, his attorney, Harry Rovenger, accompanied him to the office of Starnes's attorneys for the deposition. Representing the plaintiff, John G. Tucker questioned Lefty slowly, methodically, and very capably about his life, career, finances, drinking, arrests, and allegations of mismanagement on Starnes's part. After several hours, when all was said and done, the grueling deposition ran to 146 pages of testimony, the sum total of which only proved how thin Lefty's defense really was.

Lefty entered the offices in a confident mood, almost cocky as he sat back and drew from his memory the early years of his marriage and financial arrangements at long-forgotten clubs like the Old Top Rail.

"Were you making those contracts on your own at that time?" Tucker asked.

"I hope to tell you," Lefty affirmed, almost visibly smirking.

At times, his testimony was hilarious. Asked if he was claiming to have been drunk when he signed the contract with Starnes, Lefty answered, "I swear I wasn't drunk. I wish I had been, I would have had some reason for signing probably." And talking about the Louisiana promoter who had previously booked wrestling matches, Lefty more or less laid to rest the promo myth that he had boxed in Golden Gloves competition. "That guy had booked wrestlers—fooled with wrestling," Lefty said. "I remember because I had a lot of talk about it. I used to love the same kind of business. I kind of started out in a way wrestling, boxing or something."

His mood blackened, however, and his longstanding resentments surfaced when questioned about his early encounters with Jim Beck. It was not the size of Beck's cut that rankled him so much as knowing that for the rest of his life he would have to look at his own records, his *own* songs, and see Jim Beck's name next to his as co-writer. "All this time I wrote songs all my life," Lefty said, " — well, I thought they were songs — I was writing something — and I got an audition with Jim Beck at Dallas, Texas, and I carried my band and we went to Dallas for an audition. I paid him one hundred dollars and he guaranteed to get me on the company."

"You mean a recording company?"

"Singing the songs I wrote with no help from no one."

But if Lefty felt confident coming in, his self-assurance didn't last. He made a few serious blunders in his testimony early on. When asked about the length of his contract with Beck and Satherley, Lefty answered: "I think it was three years maybe with an option thrown in. They usually ride along with the contract most of the time." Considering his denial that the original Starnes contract had an option clause, he needn't have volunteered that such options were typical. As the day wore on, Tucker did a clean, professional job of grilling Lefty about his varied contracts, always circling back to his previous testimony. Lefty's resolve broke down before the slow but steady legal assault. At certain points, he claimed memory loss and/or a debilitating confusion. And when pressured to acknowledge that he had signed a backdated letter to falsely annul his publishing contract with Jim Bulleit, Lefty uttered his bitterest statement of the day: "I was just a hillbilly. I didn't know what to do."

On the other hand, while testifying under oath, Lefty wavered slightly but never backed down from his assertion that the signed contract Starnes presented in court read differently than it had when he had signed it himself. ("He knew something true, he wouldn't back down," Alice said.)

"My question was," Tucker asked, "the contract you just read — will you swear this is not the contract you signed there on January twenty-sixth before Morris Smith, a notary public?"

"I would not swear because I will not swear a lie," Lefty hedged. "I could be wrong but I think there has been something extra put in there; otherwise, like I say, I would never have talked or called for an appointment with him."

"Would you swear something has been put in that contract since you signed it?"

"I would be willing to swear it is not the same."

"It is not the same?"

"Something has been put into it."

"What has been put in it?"

"Two-year option."

From a strict feasibility angle, Lefty's assertion fell within the realm of possibility. The option clause appeared two thirds of the way down page three of the contract, whereas Lefty signed at the top of page four. A rewritten page three could, theoretically, have been substituted. But in the end it came down to Lefty's word against Starnes's, and Starnes had the paper to back him up. Sensing the futility of the option clause defense, or of alleging mismanagement by Starnes, Rovenger cross-examined his client with the intention of denying the deal with Starnes had been binding in the first place, given that Starnes never officially "put away" the earlier contract with Beck and Satherley. Lefty's counsel made that defense explicit several months after the deposition when he filed a counteraction asserting that far from owing Starnes money, Lefty was actually *due* $50,000 *from* Starnes for fees collected under the invalid contract.

Bristling, Starnes and his camp came right back with their own amended complaint, demanding the original twenty-five grand, plus another $13,000 in royalties from Columbia (the uncollected sum had grown from $12,000 to $38,000 in a year) and half of Lefty's estimated earnings through January 26, 1954. With Starnes's claim against Lefty now at roughly $100,000, the opposing sides prepared for a mid-June trial date.

Three days before his October deposition, Lefty cut yet another ribald, good-time-Charlie honky-tonk hit called "I'm an Old Old Man (Tryin' to Live While I Can)." Though the song sounded suspiciously autobiographical, Lefty actually wrote it as a wry, affectionate portrait of J. D. Miller's father. ("My daddy was kind of a rounder," the Crowley producer says.) The single never reached number one, but did ride high on the charts through the early months of 1953, giving Lefty plenty of jukebox exposure at a time when he needed it most. His holidays were relatively quiet, but after the New Year, Don Law put him in the studio three separate times in February and March. During the March session, on which he was joined by his new guitarist, Bakersfield hotshot Roy Nichols, he reached back into his childhood memories and put a lifetime's veneration into yet another cover of a favorite Jimmie Rodgers tune, "(I'm) Lonely and Blue." The Law/Beck production opened with a superb harmonica introduction by a man fast becoming Lefty's best new buddy: Wayne Raney.

Born "in an oil field behind an oil well." William Orville "Sonny" Frizzell, better known as Lefty, with his parents, Naamon and A. D. Frizzell.

Lefty, described by Naamon as "a modern kid, like any other."

Portrait of the artist as a young dandy.

Seventeen-year-old father Lefty with daughter Lois Aleta, 1946.

Sixteen-year-old newly-weds: Lefty and Alice Harper Frizzell, March 1945.

Lefty, the proud new owner of a $125 Martin guitar, in front of a car advertising the Cactus Garden, the dancehall where he often played, in Roswell, New Mexico, 1947.

Lefty Frizzell and His Westerners, at the Ace of Clubs, Big Spring, Texas, 1950.
Left to right: unidentified, Lefty, "Jelly," Bill Madrig, Charlie Stewart, Slim Agnew.

Linking arms with Blackie Crawford (black shirt) and unidentified musicians,
possibly members of the Western Cherokees, circa 1951.

Trouble in mind. Lefty seated in Bob Wills's lap, with unidentified woman.

On June 16, 1951, two months after touring with Hank Williams and just hours before playing the Grand Ole Opry for the second time, Lefty joined Williams at the WSM microphone for a live broadcast from the grand opening of Hank and Audrey's Corral, the Williams's western clothing store.

Honky-tonkin' and havin' a time with Abe Manuel, fiddle, and Pee Wee Whitewing, steel guitar (seated far right). Others unidentified. Sacramento, California, 1952.

"My Little Her and Him."
At home in Beaumont
with Lois and Rickey
Frizzell, 1952.

Lefty's 1954 touring band,
the Drifting Playboys, in
Clovis, New Mexico. Left
to right: D. J. Fontana,
Floyd Cramer, Jimmy Day,
Chuck Wiginton, Bill
Peters, Van Howard.

Courtesy of Van Howard

Hillbilly firepower. "Town Hall Party," circa 1955–6. Lefty, Joe Maphis, and Freddie Hart (on guitar, at left), with Merle Travis (obscured), steel player Marion Hall (likewise obscured), and Les "Carrottop" Anderson (right). (Thanks to Rose Lee Maphis for her keen-eyed identifications.)

Wonderful times in Northridge, 1957. Lefty with (clockwise from right) Lois, Rickey, Alice, and eight-month-old Marlon.

Lefty in Northridge.

Dang 'em, all for one.
Lefty with Roger Miller
(right) and Faron Young
(left), others unidentified,
Juarez, New Mexico,
probably early 1960s.

Above, left: Lois in Vietnam, 1968, a year before Lefty went over.

Above: Lefty in Vietnam, 1969, where the GIs said he was God.

Left: Forever and always. The last known shot of Lefty in concert.

A country star in his own right, Raney was a multifaceted talent—
singer, songwriter, and musician—whose instrumental specialty was a
tiny "4-hole" harmonica that fit inside his mouth when he played it. He
could literally make it talk. Born and reared on Wolf Bayou in central
Arkansas, Raney was playing professionally by his early teens, and had
even done a Depression-era stint on station XERA, the border-blasting,
goat-gland-dealing wonder of Mexican radio. He held a variety of music and deejay jobs through the1940s, until he eventually hooked up
with the Delmore Brothers in Memphis and laid down the oscillating
harp track on their monumental "Blues Stay Away from Me." Signed to
King Records as a solo act in 1949, he struck instant gold with "Why
Don't You Haul Off and Love Me." The record reportedly sold a million
copies and earned Raney (referred to as "a splinter whose grin is
broader than his accent") the media designation of a "swoonster." He
was also one of the bright boys who had covered "If You've Got the
Money, I've Got the Time" during the heady days of 1950. Lefty forgave
his friend for having tried to jump his claim.

After the two of them met at the Opry, Lefty often hired the lanky
harpist as an opening act on various tours, including the six-day wildcat-
ter that followed the Canada fiasco. An eccentric himself, Lefty could
appreciate Raney's idiosyncrasies, including his half-swallowed harp
and the fact that he had no phone on his bayou property but carried a
shortwave radio with him on tour. (To communicate with his wife from
the road, Raney would send radio messages through the Cleburne
County, Arkansas, sheriff.) Lefty and Raney became fast friends and co-
wrote a number of songs that Raney's contract obligations forced him
to file under pseudonyms. One of those songs was "Don't Stay Away
(Till Love Grows Cold)," an exquisitely desolate ballad Lefty recorded
upon his return from the Canada tour.

It was also through Raney, indirectly, that Lefty met talented singer-
songwriter Freddie Hart that winter. An Alabama native, Hart was a
fourth-degree black belt with one George Morgan cut to his credit. He
was living in Phoenix, working at a cottonseed oil mill that was on
strike, when Lefty passed through town for a gig at the Riverside Ballroom, probably in early December. Hart knew Raney and called the
Adams Hotel, where Lefty was staying. Eager to make Lefty's acquaintance, he dropped Wayne's name. "Any friend of Wayne Raney's is a
friend of mine," Lefty said, and invited Hart to the hotel. Hart raced over
so fast he arrived as Lefty was getting out of the shower. Steve Stebbins
of the Americana Corporation was in the room too, puffing on a stogie.
Standing there wrapped in a towel, Lefty encouraged the nervous
singer to have a seat and play him a song or two. Lefty was impressed.

After the show that night, Lefty asked Hart if he could go on tour with him. "You can help me with my guitar and things," Lefty said, "and maybe help me carry some of my stuff around."

Hart about fell through the floor. "God knows I'd love to go on the road with you," he said. By May that year, Hart had his own record deal with Capitol Records, a five-year booking contract with the Americana Corporation, and an unwavering lifelong devotion to Lefty Frizzell.

Don Law released "(I'm) Lonely and Blue," on May 1. On the twenty-sixth of that month, with the Rodgers cover earning no more than modest airplay, Lefty arrived in Meridian, Mississippi, the Singing Brakeman's hometown, to participate in the most hyped country music event of the era: the first annual Rodgers Memorial Day. Organized by Ernest Tubb, Hank Snow, and various Meridian movers and shakers, the daylong spectacle—originally conceived as a simple tribute to dead railroad men—took place in sweltering ninety-four-degree heat on the twentieth anniversary of Rodgers's death. The Deep South had never seen anything like it. WSM sent a team to broadcast live from the town's Hotel Lamar. Accommodations at the Lamar and any other hotel within fifty miles of Meridian were sold out a month in advance. Latecomers camped on the grass where they could. The festivities brought in a reported 35,000 spectators, the governors of Mississippi and Tennessee, Mrs. Jimmie Rodgers, Mrs. Casey Jones, and Jones's fireman, Sim Webb (who only lived to tell of the wreck because Jones had ordered him to jump to safety).

Throughout the momentous day, the celebration's dual purpose gave it a strange yet appropriate sense of historic juncture. A memorial train loaded with old railroad men rode a spur to the park where a veiled Jimmie Rodgers statue awaited. Governors' speeches melded with Hank Snow's comments about how hillbillies felt about the dapper Rodgers. Floor plaques beneath a flagpole in the park were dedicated by an RCA record man, a politician, a union railroad man, and the great hillbilly publisher himself, Ralph S. Peer. Hank Snow's son, Jimmie Rodgers Snow, received Rodgers's first guitar as a gift. Ernest Tubb's son, Justin Tubb, unveiled the Rodgers statue. (Having been ill since returning from a tour of Korea, poor E.T. himself had to miss the very party he had worked so hard to organize.) Lefty, who brought Alice with him to share in the day, rode the memorial train in his white western suit, the two of them laughing and carrying on while a home movie camera rolled.

By nightfall, Rodgers Memorial Day had merged with National Hillbilly Music Day. The proceedings in Meridian climaxed at the junior college stadium, where a country concert called "the greatest assemblage of hillbilly talent ever seen in one show" rocked on under the stars. "It was just like one big giant jam session," Hank Snow recalled. Performing in honor of the Father of Country Music that muggy Mississippi night were at least fifty country artists, including a full roster of Opry stars, and at least one Opry prodigal — Lefty Frizzell. His brief spot in the lineup was hardly a payback for all the untold treasures he had received from his hero, but it was a fitting close to the time in his life when his career most resembled Rodgers's.

Lefty stood on the stadium stage that night, the feintest touch lonely and blue perhaps, but in some sense fulfilled. He had changed in three years' time, and so had the wide world of hillbilly music. His friend Hank Williams was already dead, a desperate man gone down. Red Foley, who first introduced Lefty on the Opry, had just quit his high-profile WSM gig after seven turbulent years. Lefty himself was as good as broke, just making ends meet from gig to gig. The airwaves had been overtaken by a new crop of stars — brash young comers like Faron Young and Webb Pierce, guys whom Lefty had known when they were covering his own tunes on the Louisiana Hayride. With the lawsuit going to court in two weeks, Lefty stood on a stage in his idol's hometown. If he had thought about it at all, he would have known that nothing Starnes could take from him would change what he had accomplished the past three years — a full-fledged chapter of music history, written in a timeless artistic style that Jimmie Rodgers, had he lived, might have stood up to honor.

One week after the Meridian tribute, Lefty dragged himself back to Beck's to cut four sides that may have been the least inspired of his career to date. Exhausted, emotionally more than physically, he had also retreated to Raney's phoneless rural Arkansas spread for a week's attempted relaxation. He hunted and fished in the bayou waters and tried to ignore the imminent trial. Finally, on either June 10 or 11, with the judge waiting and the jury already selected, Lefty and Starnes reached a last-minute settlement out of court. The lawsuit was never tried. Starnes got cash and Lefty got his release from the disputed two-year option. The precise amount Starnes received was not disclosed, though Alice said it was "over twenty-five thousand dollars." The deal gave Lefty his freedom, but it also cleaned him out. "He didn't have a dime left," Alice said.

As far as Lefty's role was concerned, the Frizzell/Starnes mini-drama ended that second week of June. However, there would be one final act that would dramatically affect the history of country music. For Jack Starnes wasted no time putting Lefty's earnings to use. He had hired singers, and managed singers; now, thoroughly bitten by the music bug, he intended to record singers. Starnes met with his smart man in Houston, the jukebox operator and record distributor Pappy Daily. They worked out (or had already worked out in advance) a deal to start an independent record label called Starday Records—"Star" for Starnes, "Day" for Daily. The company would operate out of Beaumont, initially, but make ample use of Daily's production and distribution resources in Houston. Starnes bought a Magnecord Recorder, a piece of equipment popular with radio stations in those days, and after considerable technical difficulty he set up the recorder in his house in Voth. On June 20, less than two weeks after the lawsuit was settled, the trade press announced the creation of Starday Records in Beaumont. The label's first two singles were on jukeboxes by the first week of July, the third and fourth by August. The maiden single, Starday 101, was "Catfishing," by kiddie singer Mary Joe Chelette. Her flipside was "Gee, It's Tough to Be Thirteen," the yowling complaint of a pubescent girl "in the mood to expand my views." Lefty would not have been amused. Starday's second release was by none other than Blackie Crawford, while the fourth single, Arlie Duff's boisterous party shout "You All Come," gave Starnes and Daily their first top-ten smash. That quick. Duff's nationwide hit helped see the Beaumont label to the launch of Starday 130, "No Money in This Deal," the wildfire debut recording by a local boy named George Jones. Starnes and Daily knew the buzz-cut ex-marine had talent, but before they could get his career off the ground, Daily had to break him of the habit of imitating other singers— notably Lefty Frizzell, the man whose lost riches helped build the makeshift studio in which George Jones first recorded.

GLUT

Chapter 18

JOHN WAYNE couldn't sing. Nor could Ken Maynard. At least Maynard *tried* to sing, unlike the Duke, who as "Singing Sandy" had lip-synched to the vocal strains of a Hollywood big band warbler. It was 1934, and with talkies talking and B westerns running the same stage-coach chase scenes over and over, some added element was needed to jar cowboys from their celluloid doldrums. Some thought singing would do it.

Except Ken Maynard couldn't sing.

So Hollywood suit Nat Levine arrived one day in Chicago, where young Gene Autry had built quite a radio following with a "home on the range" schtick forced down his throat by the savvy Art Satherley. When Levine hired Autry for a barn-dance scene in an upcoming Maynard feature, the Oklahoma plowboy and ex–railroad dispatcher rode on Hollywood. After Autry made his first cameo, in *In Old Santa Fe*, hillbillies took Beverly by dust bowl sandstorm.

The marriage of country music to Hollywood glitz would seem, at a glance, to have been one of the least likely pop culture phenomenons ever to mess with America's mind. Yet both Sunset Boulevard and the Grand Ole Opry subscribed to a reductionist view of drama in which issues were raised and resolved in a populist fantasy of a just universe. And justice looked great decked out in fringe. The Hollywood horse operas helped the country through its back-to-back traumas of depression and war.

But when TV hit Hollywood, nothing fell as fast or hard as the singing cowboy from his steed. And no one better understood the reasons why than Autry. It wasn't, as has often been suggested, the post-Nagasaki end of innocence that ruined the cowboy matinees so much as simple broad-cast economics. B westerns were cheap fantasies; cheap first, fantasy second. As such, they lent themselves to small-screen production and back catalog buyout. The studios made their killing rerunning Hopalong Cassidy shorts, and moving Roy Rogers from the silver screen to the idiot box. As Autry himself commented in his autobiography, "Hollywood started turning out a new type of Western and half of the B theaters that had carried my films, and others like them, closed down. The other half started showing porno flicks."

The progression from Saturday afternoon at the theater to Saturday night at home was natural enough. But squeezed out of the picture tube was cowboy music. The TV horse operas kept the horse but dropped the opera. That opened the market to hillbilly variety shows. As television sales skyrocketed, music programming proved reliable at keeping the new audience watching. In New York, that meant Perry Como. In California, that meant cowboys. By 1952, fifteen separate country music television shows were airing in the Los Angeles region alone. They included everything from the Hoffman Hayride, hosted by Spade Cooley, the pop swing fiddler who would one day literally stomp his wife to death, to the low-rent "Cal's Corral," the boob-tube province of Dodge dealer Cal Worthington. But the daddy of all those early L.A. hillbilly shows was "Hometown Jamboree," an hourlong program put together in nearby El Monte by future Country Music Hall of Fame member Cliffie Stone. With a constant influx of top-rank stars, and a house band built around the hillbilly boogie chops of lead guitarist Jimmy Bryant and steel man Speedy West, "Hometown Jamboree" made your average network barn dance program sound like a 4-H square dance.

In those days, Cliffie Stone was a one-man music industry whirl-wind. A singer, bassist, deejay, producer, manager, and record execu-tive, he played a more multifarious role in West Coast country music than possibly any man of his time. His father was a country comedian, and Cliffie himself had graced a few stages and earned a few laughs before World War II broke out. In 1943, he started "Wake Up Ranch" on L.A.'s KFVD, a radio show that brought western tunes to the hud-dled masses gathering their strength over coffee each morning before eight more hours at the bearings plant. Stone was seated at the KFVD mike one day, when a big, jolly cop strolled in holding a carton of coffee and smoking a fat cigar. The cop offered Stone some coffee and said, "I'm Lieutenant Stebbins with the LAPD, and whenever I can, I listen to you in the morning and I really enjoy your show."

Thus began a friendship that would have a profound impact on Lefty Frizzell's career direction. Due to retire from the police force, Stebbins was looking for a new life in the fertile L.A. entertainment field, specifically in country music, which was his first love. Stebbins talked his deejay friend into letting him try to book personal appearances for him. When their first gig at a Ventura barn dance drew 700 eager "Wake Up Ranch" listeners and netted $300, Cliffie Stone was hooked. He and Stebbins started working together regularly and made their mutual commitment official by opening a joint booking agency called the Americana Corporation, with which Lefty would first work in the spring of '52. Stone had also been hired to head up the "Folk Music" department of the young independent label Capitol Records, and from that position he produced a fascinating mix of crossover pop fluff and sensational honky-tonk swing. A tireless hillbilly plugger, Stone moved his deejay gig to Pasadena's KXLA for an hour of country five days a week. And in 1949, Cliffie Stone got in on the ground floor of the latest media craze when he started producing and hosting "Hometown Jamboree" over KLAC-TV.

The Jamboree aired every Saturday night from seven to eight P.M. on the CBS affiliate, just before the hour allotted the infamous Spade Cooley, then, after a half-hour break to clear the chairs from the dance floor, continued off the air until one in the morning. Stone produced the show live from El Monte's Legion Stadium. The "stadium" was actually a converted high school gym that had survived condemnation after an earthquake took care of the rest of the school. Equipped with a full balcony, theater seats, and a restaurant under the backstage area, the Legion Stadium held boxing matches on Thursday nights and "Hometown Jamboree" on Saturday. The site's only drawback was the Southern Pacific railroad track that ran alongside the gym. Every Saturday night, the 7:20 train would rumble by and shake the cameras. Inevitably, Stone would smile and tell the audience at home, "Well, folks, there goes the old seven-twenty. Well, it's a little early tonight."

Built to hold 2,600 patrons legally, the Legion Stadium pulled in roughly that amount every Saturday — more or less, depending on the Jamboree lineup. On April 12, 1952, with a lineup that included Tennessee Ernie Ford, the Dinning Sisters, Blackie Crawford and the Western Cherokees, and, especially, Lefty Frizzell, the 2,600-seat "Hometown Jamboree" sold a house record 4,053 tickets.

"The first time that Lefty appeared on 'Hometown Jamboree,' I was amazed," Stone says. "I really was, you know? We always did very well. We were just like the Grand Ole Opry, or Renfro Valley Barn

Dance, or WLS, or WSM; we always had a pretty good crowd. And then I booked Lefty in there, and I think I got him for a hundred dollars. And that night, the people were crawling out of the woodwork. They begin to pour in at nine o'clock and it just never stopped." Six months later, Lefty drew over six thousand to the El Monte venue. "It was absolutely an amazing thing to me," Stone marvels, "because I had no idea that Lefty had, at that point in his career, so much power."

Lefty had that power and more, in Southern California no less than West Texas. The dust bowl Okie migration gave Lefty a natural audience in the oil and cotton district around Bakersfield. But the immediate L.A. vicinity was every bit Lefty's turf as well. The mechanics and soldiers who arrived from the hinterland during World War II stayed when the war ended. Metropolitan Los Angeles held four and a half million people in 1952, almost two million more potential country music fans than it had in 1940. Another two and a half million souls made their homes in the former orange groves transformed into suburbs. When Lefty first appeared on "Hometown Jamboree," Southern California ranked first in the nation for production of aircraft and pumps and compressors, and second in auto assembly, tire production, and oil field equipment. Nearly three million passenger vehicles drove the endless Southern California highways, and 70 percent of them had radios. Civic boosters boasted proudly that three quarters of L.A.'s commuting population used their own cars for the daily journey, while only 19.8 percent took the market-stifling public transportation.

Ironically, despite his radio-ready modernist country sound, Lefty had once very nearly found himself astride an Old Paint with the cameras rolling, his fringe flying and his guitar in hand as the B genre rattled its last. At the close of one of his 1951 West Coast trips, he had been offered a contract through booking agent Marty Landau (who was Americana's chief competition) to film eight movie shorts for a bulk sum of four or five thousand dollars. Landau had a screen test all set up. For Lefty, it would have been a boyhood dream come true. But Jack Starnes, for reasons he kept to himself, nixed the deal. That little episode raised a few legal eyebrows come lawsuit time, for Starnes's contract with Lefty specifically required him to "exert his best efforts" in securing TV and movie work for the singer.

A movie deal never happened, but Lefty had noted the impact he had on the California market in general. Indeed, the last inadvertent favor Jack Starnes ever did for Lefty was to book his final California tour—the one they had to cut short because of Lefty's laryngitis—through Steve Stebbins of the Americana Corporation, instead of through Marty Landau. Despite the length and unpleasantness of the tour, and despite the twenty canceled dates, Lefty and Stebbins liked working with each other. They came to be good friends as well as business associates. After Lefty broke off with Starnes, and after a frazzled J. D. Miller threw in the towel, Stebbins immediately took up the slack by arranging tours for Lefty on a straight commission basis, the two of them scrupulously avoiding the word "manager." It was precisely the setup Lefty had told Starnes he wanted to arrange. The relationship did, however, permit Stebbins to buy a few full-page *Billboard* ads for Lefty in early 1953, including one during the week of the Jimmie Rodgers festival that trumpeted "(I'm) Lonely and Blue." Columbia Records, caught up in the buzz around Carl Smith and Ray Price, had not seen fit to hype Lefty's timely Rodgers tribute at all.

When the lawsuit was settled in June, Stebbins came to Lefty's rescue and immediately whisked him away for what Americana called an "unlimited engagement" on "Hometown Jamboree." If Columbia was losing confidence in their former Discovery of the Year, Stebbins, with access to Lefty's nightly receipts, saw no cause for concern. Nor did Cliffie Stone, who never saw less than a turnaway crowd when Lefty played his show.

With his flashy clothes and down-home demeanor, Lefty was a natural for TV. "I can see him in a bright red outfit made at Nudie's . . . ," says Stone, referring to the rhinestone fashion kingpin. "Oh, yeah, a lot of fringe down underneath of the arm, which when he played the guitar—that looked crazy."

Just as Horace Logan had discovered while working with Lefty on the Louisiana Hayride, Cliffie Stone found the famous singer immune to superstar ego problems: "He never ever missed a show, and whatever I asked him to do, he always would do it." Stone and the Jamboree band would rehearse a couple of Lefty's hits in the afternoon and then back him up that night. They usually stuck with his softer fare—"Mom and Dad's Waltz" in particular—because Stone had to monitor what sort of sentiments entered suburban homes from his stage.

Lefty's run on "Hometown Jamboree" was a huge success and, according to Stone, a major contributing factor in the show's ongoing popularity. Lefty enjoyed the novel medium and the crowds never tired of seeing him. "I tell you, the crowds not only held up, they got bigger every time he showed up," Stone says.

But the TV show, like the Opry, did much for Lefty's exposure, and less for his bottom line. It didn't really affect his living or personal well-being. Losing the lawsuit leveled Lefty financially, and devastated him spiritually. "It hurt him real bad, all that stuff," Alice said. "You know, because it just—it hurts you. And so, you can't trust nobody." Here he was, still a major star, still a surefire full-house draw in dancehalls anywhere in the country, yet his life lacked focus, and it showed in his work. His first recorded performances after the lawsuit lacked the critical mass of energy and creativity that made him such an explosive force in 1951. His records always made noise with his devoted fans. But even some of the Lefty faithful were dismayed by a couple of duets he cut with Wayne Raney in November during his first post-lawsuit sessions. The tandem vocals with Raney downplayed Lefty's talent as he pinched his unique drawling style to match his friend's more nasal tone. The Raney duets went nowhere. More alarming was that of eight songs Lefty recorded that November, the only one that *would* hit the charts was the only one he had no hand in composing—Onie Wheeler and (credited pseudonymously) Troy Martin's "Run 'Em Off." Even as a songwriter, Lefty's creative juices appeared to have been played out.

A terrible malaise descended on Lefty those long months of 1953. For the first time, his drinking affected his live performance. Lefty had played countless gigs juiced in the past. But he had always known his capacity. He knew when to cut himself off in order to put on the show that his fans had paid to see and hear. But now things were different. Come curtain time, he sometimes had to ask Freddie Hart to fill in and sing a few songs while he showered and gulped down coffee backstage. If the night's bill called for two shows, the second was not a sure thing. Lefty quit playing the customized Gibson (it was allegedly warped beyond tunability) and started using the case to hold his bottle and shot glasses. At a show in Bakersfield, when a wide-eyed young Merle Haggard asked guitarist Roy Nichols how it was working for Lefty, Nichols answered, "Not worth a shit."

"He just went from bad to worse," Alice lamented. As troubled as their marriage had been at times, it hurt Alice to see her Sonny betrayed by music, the one thing he loved as much as he loved his family. The downturn in their fortunes brought the two of them closer together. Lefty and Alice had a deep-seated joint survival instinct based on years of suffering together. Just twenty-five years old, and married less than nine years, Lefty and Alice had paid more dues, and given more to each other than many couples looking back from a silver anniversary. Two people powerfully connected, by upbringing as much as by marriage, Lefty and Alice were closest under extreme hardship. Times would never be as hard as they'd been in Waco or El Dorado—or especially Roswell. But they were certainly harder than any Lefty and Alice had known since bedding down in an empty Dallas nightclub. And to make matters worse, with Lefty still reeling from the lawsuit, the IRS wolves came knocking on his door, as if they could smell the open wound in his soul. Lefty and Alice chomped down on the bullet. They put their Beaumont house on the market and moved to a rental in Sulphur Springs, forever turning their backs on Spindletop. The house sold in February 1954. When little Lois celebrated her eighth birthday, in Sulphur Springs, in a rented house just blocks from where Lefty and Alice first met in the Service Men's Free Hotel, the bitter irony of it all was not lost on her parents. "It was like we were finished," Alice said.

Losing the only house they had ever owned was, for Lefty and Alice, the end of a long, surreal dream. But it also offered Lefty a catharsis, a symbolic purging of the wreck his life had become in Beaumont and a chance to rethink his direction. And that direction was west. In January, just a month before he and Alice sold the house in Beaumont, Lefty broke the attendance record at yet another Southern California TV program. Almost four thousand of the country faithful poured out to watch him swivel his hips and waltz for his mom and dad on a new show called "Town Hall Party." Lefty's fans were perhaps even more rabid in the San Joaquin Valley. His shows at the Fresno Barn, backed by his friend Dave Stogner's airtight swinging outfit, were routine sellouts. But it wasn't just Lefty's popularity beyond the Pecos River, and it wasn't just his reliance on Stebbins that pointed his wagons west. More than anything, it was the simple need to move, to seek that better life he and Alice had known since the day they left Greenville was always waiting somewhere down the highway.

Yet before he could make the move, Lefty had to deal with his immediate financial crisis. Malaise or no, he was never a quitter. He was determined to sing his way back into the black. Again, Steve Stebbins came to his aid. He organized an exhaustive western tour for Lefty that was to begin in March and continue into July. The relentless schedule obligated Lefty to make 120 one-nighters in thirteen Southwest, coastal, and mountain states. Five or six gigs per week for four months straight. (Stebbins arranged the schedule so pious Lefty would have the Sabbath off.) Lefty knew that a tour that long and intensive could destroy his voice. But it would also guarantee him $72,000 in take-home pay. For that kind of money, Lefty would have played ice rinks again. He left his family in Sulphur Springs and packed his guitar for his western jaunt. It was 1954. Out in the East Texas oil fields, some tawdry, broken down B theater was showing Gene Autry's final film. Columbia Pictures called it *Last of the Pony Riders*. It would not be held over.

Chapter 19

THE TOUR DIDN'T START until a light blew out over Lefty's head in Longview. Horsing around in the dressing room at the Palm Isle (which Starnes no longer owned), Lefty slammed his forehead against a low-hung ceiling bulb and shattered it. He peered into the sudden darkness and said to his shocked, blinking band members, "I've done that before."

The musicians gathered at the Palm Isle were a crack outfit of staff musicians from the Louisiana Hayride. The main man was Floyd Cramer, a piano stylist with chops solid enough to keep baby-faced Jerry Lee Lewis from landing a spot on the Shreveport show. Cramer, strictly an instrumentalist, had his own recording contract with Abbot and was riding a modest hit called "Fancy Pants." Lefty hired him for the impending four-month tour and gave him the go-ahead to pick the other musicians. Cramer called on Hayride drummer D. J. Fontana, bassist Chuck Wiginton, fiddler Bill Peters, and steel guitarist Jimmy Day, one of the adventurous young men experimenting with pedals. As front man and rhythm guitarist, Cramer selected Van Howard, a three-year Hayride veteran from Clovis, New Mexico, who had cut a few fabulous records on Imperial. The players all knew each other well, and they all knew Lefty's songs well. As a unit, they gave him the most vigorous, cohesive musical support he'd enjoyed since parting with the Western Cherokees.

Lefty Frizzell and His Drifting Playboys, as the band was rather unfortunately named, pulled out of Longview in March and headed across Texas. Once again, the star rode in a limousine. Road manager Al Flores drove, while a sidekick of Lefty's, known only as "Curly," kept him company as he drank his backseat whiskey and munched on cheese and crackers. The Drifting Playboys tailed the limo with all six players crammed into Van Howard's 1953 De Soto, the equipment trailer bumping along behind. They spent a month in Texas alone, playing one-nighters in every Lone Star dancehall and honky-tonk they could find. They hit Dallas, Fort Worth, Waco, Austin, San Antonio. It was like 1950 all over again—Lefty plugging away like he was hellbent on reclaiming his glory in every inch of the state. He packed houses wherever he played, the crowds leaving satisfied every time. The show was multilayered, suited to any fan's taste. The Drifting Playboys would open with a tight, fast-swinging dance set broken up by a handful of pop ballads—"Harbor Lights" or "Secret Love"—for which Van Howard's pristine tenor was ideally suited. Cramer would then knock off a couple of instrumentals, followed by Lefty, who would take the stage to thunderous applause as the band kicked into "If You've Got the Money, I've Got the Time." Lefty's appeal had not diminished one iota. Neither had his showmanship. "What he did, he wore those suits," Howard recalls, "and he had that long fringe on his sleeves. And every time he'd make a move, of course those things'd just go crazy. And the girls in the audience'd just go crazy."

After a month on the road, Lefty's limo and Howard's DeSoto thundered into tiny Robstown, Texas, about thirty-five miles west of Corpus Christi, for a Saturday-night dancehall gig at Rob's Place. It was the usual spillover crowd, standing room only even on the patio outside. Lefty's old friend Judy Baker (née Burkhart) showed up with a dashing sailor she had recently married (and who would later leave her while she was six months pregnant with their only child). Judy and her handsome husband invited Lefty out to their house in Corpus Christi after the dance. He said he couldn't go, the boys were tired, but he would come the next day. Sure enough, Lefty, Flores, and Curly showed up for a Sunday spaghetti dinner and stuck around afterward to shoot the bull. Judy turned on the reel-to-reel, capturing Lefty in a moment of offstage relaxation as he charmed and teased a couple of her girlfriends who had gathered at the house.

"I understand you were feelin' pretty good last night," Judy said to one of her friends.

"Yes, I was."

Lefty piped in, "She was feelin' mighty fine last night. She walked up to me, and she said, 'Lefty, it's good—it's wonderful to see you again.' And shook hands with my piano player [much laughter]. So I understood, you know, that one eye was looking that way and one the other way. I understood. So I patted her on the back, and told her it was nice to have her there."

Judy and her friends wondered who the boys were. Not entirely sure himself, Lefty asked Al Flores to tell them. Flores rattled off their names and singled out Van Howard as a hit with the lady fans.

"I'll bet Lefty fired him," said one of the women present.

"No," Flores said, "Lefty keeps him along as insurance so they won't follow him all over."

Added Lefty, "We was talking this morning earlier about Van Howard. He is a nice guy. And a good-looking guy."

"Is he married?"

"No, he's pretty smart," Lefty said, laughing. "Anyway. No, he's a fine guy."

Lefty cracked a few more jokes, and talked a bit about where they had played. Hearing their itinerary, Judy said, "You've been following Billy Walker." Soon thereafter, Lefty confessed he had to be leaving soon to get to San Antonio for an interview with deejay Charlie Walker. "I swear, it's been wonderful," he said, "and I wish we had more time. I wish we had a day or two off so we could all get together and go fishin'."

"Wouldn't it be wonderful?"

"It sure would."

"I'm gonna get the guitar," Judy announced. "Maybe you'll sing us a song?"

"Get the guitar and I'll yodel some," Lefty agreed. "Odelaydeehee. Hah hah!"

Judy hauled out her flattop and started to tune it. Lefty stopped her. "Hey, now don't kill ya," he warned. "Because I'll never do nothing if it's in tune."

Lefty grabbed the guitar, picked a fill or two, then broke into the only music he ever wanted to sing when he was truly enjoying himself. Jimmie Rodgers. "I'm going to California, where they sleep out every night. . . ."

The days rolled into weeks and the weeks into months as they went to California, passing first through Tucson and Phoenix. The Lefty crew played "Hometown Jamboree" and impressed the hell out of Cliffie Stone, who had not expected Lefty to show up with such a sharp bunch of boys. From there, the Frizzell mini-caravan picked up Tex Ritter and headed north, the old cowboy determined not to ride with Lefty and thereby suffer the exasperating pecks and punches that were Lefty's signs of undying friendship. No chance. Lefty liked Ritter too much. It may, in fact, have been that very tour that Lefty further endeared himself to the Texas cowboy by filling his boots with gasoline. Ritter was crashed in the backseat when the limo ran out of gas. No can in the car . . . Tex asleep. . . . Nothing to use but the boots.

Oakland, Portland, Seattle. Oregon, Idaho, Montana. Cody, Wyoming. Salt Lake City. Lamar, Colorado. Week after week, the traveling troupe played five or six nights, rarely in the same town two nights in a row. Lefty held up well under the strain, his high spirits taking a dive only now and then. The band could tell the times he was down, or when the desert miles had afforded him time for one too many backseat shots, by a missing edge on his intimate vocals. But the crowds, who could barely hear him above their own screams, never knew. Lefty only really blew it one time—at the San Antonio gig. He mixed up "If You've Got the Money, I've Got the Time" with its answer song, "If You Can Spare the Time (I Won't Miss the Money)," ultimately getting so tongue-tied the show never got past the opening number. After nights like that, Lefty would wake up in the morning, pour himself an orange juice glass full of whiskey, and gulp it straight down.

Not surprisingly, after months of shoulder-to-shoulder all-night drives across the American West, the Drifting Playboys' nerves began to fray. Floyd Cramer tossed Van Howard's beatup straw hat out the car window in the middle of the desert. "I'm tired of looking at that crazy thing," he said. A couple of nights, D. J. Fontana threatened not to play. The others had to talk him out of his funk so the show could go on. Finally, mercifully, the tour ended in Missouri during the first week of July. But Lefty got no chance to rest. He immediately peeled off from the band for an eleven-day stint in Hawaii. The Drifting Playboys were offered their own stationary two-week gig at a club in San Francisco. The fiddler, Bill Peters, and the bassist, Chuck Wiginton, both said no thanks; they missed their wives. Everyone else took the job.

Within a year and a half of the '54 tour, Van Howard, Floyd Cramer, and Jimmy Day would be reunited in Nashville for a Ray Price recording session that would result in his immortal "Crazy Arms," the creative impact of which would reverberate through country music production into the 1990s. Cramer and D. J. Fontana would achieve separate notoriety working with a Memphis kid whose first record would hit radio stations that same July of '54. A fan of Lefty's, he, too, would leave a lasting mark on the country music industry. The same kind of mark Sherman left on Dixie.

As the Playboys split apart and drifted toward their dates with destiny, Lefty made official the decision his whole career had pointed him toward since he bottomed out in Beaumont. He and Alice agreed it was time to pack up and move to California. Alice put their belongings in storage in Sulphur Springs, then she and the kids drove to Los Angeles, where they were reunited with Lefty at the Sunset Boulevard office of Americana. "I think we come up the interstate to the office," Alice said. "And I believe we had one dime. One dime. 'Cause we were broke. Well I mean broke."

Broke, yes, but no longer in debt. More than an artistic and spiritual triumph, Lefty's four-month Western tour had also fulfilled its primary purpose of clearing his books. The Frizzells were back to square one. First, they rented a duplex in Pasadena, then a cottage in the middle of a lemon grove in Grenada Hills in the San Fernando Valley.

The transition was not entirely smooth. Waking up in the middle of a lemon grove can be disorienting to anyone, let alone somebody born in an oil field behind an oil well. Poor Lois was so nervous attending her new school that she threw up every day for weeks. Lefty's own discomfort with the foreign environment revealed itself more subtly, most often through a heightened protectiveness toward Lois and Rickey. After one of her first days in the local third grade, Lois stopped at a classmate's house on the way home and became engrossed in her new friend's bubblegum trinkets. By the time she got back to the lemon grove, two hours late, her nervous daddy had the police out searching for her. And when another girlfriend invited Lois to spend the night at her house, it took two weeks of pleading before Lefty and Alice would let her stay over. In the end, Lois came home early anyway, more upset than if she hadn't been allowed to spend the night at all. Wide-eyed and disturbed, she relayed to Lefty and Alice the strange way her friend's family lived: all of them were seated together at one time for dinner, no TV, no TV trays, no absent father calling collect from a motel in Billings, Montana.

Past the initial shock, the family adjusted fairly quickly, thanks in part to Lefty's many West Coast music ties, and also thanks to his proximity to close relatives. His brother Billy lived nearby, and his New Mexico cousin, Junior Cox, had moved to Tipton, where he was on his way to becoming one of the top-rated pool hustlers in all of California.

After several more months of road shows, TV work, and dwindling royalty payments, Lefty and Alice saved enough money to buy another house. In February 1955, they picked out a two-story affair, this one with the obligatory backyard swimming pool, on Superior Street in Northridge, hailed as the "horse capitol of California."

As he had hoped it would, the move out west rejuvenated Lefty. He enjoyed his television work and general proximity to the tinsel-town stars of his youth. He met the likes of Johnny Weissmuller, his white-hat hero Gene Autry, and became the first country singer to get his own star on the Hollywood Walk of Fame. As usual, gregarious Lefty made quick friends with the Hollywood hillbilly crowd. By late 1954, he had shifted his TV focus from "Hometown Jamboree" to the younger, though similarly formatted, "Town Hall Party." The show drew from the same West Coast talent pool that fed the Jamboree—Lefty, the Maddox Brothers and Rose, Freddie Hart—but threw the audience a few unexpected curves. The rock-boppin' Collins Kids, Larry and Lorrie, were frequent guests, while the Party's emcee was future "Let's Make a Deal" announcer Jay Stewart. Lightning-fingered picker Joe Maphis, Larry Collins's guitar mentor, headed the Town Hall band. A bona fide legend in his own right, Maphis could—and did—play everything from mournful Appalachian fiddle tunes to double-neck-guitar boogie heroics to hired gun handiwork for Hollywood soundtracks. (His picking set the mood for Robert Mitchum's fatal bootlegger's run in the movie *Thunder Road*.) Maphis was the perfect musician to straddle both moods "Town Hall Party" tried to convey—that of a folksy Shenandoah Valley gathering on the one hand, and a Bakersfield honky-tonk blaze on the other.

With a new bunch of friends to entertain, the house on Superior Street was never empty. The "Town Hall Party" crowd continually made merry under Lefty's roof. The three-hour show, broadcast straight out of Compton on Saturday nights, was a good hour and a half drive from Northridge. But many a weekend, after the show, Lefty would lead a Cadillac caravan of Nudie-suited country pickers to his hospitable home in the Valley. "I think every hanger-on would follow us in, knowing there'd be something good cooked on the grill," Alice said.

Hands on her hips, Alice would watch and sigh as the singers and pickers overran her patio and Lefty fired up the grill, or more accurately, subjected the charcoal to architectural planning worthy of the Egyptian pyramids. It was at those impromptu parties that Lefty's idiosyncratic eating habits became the stuff of country legend. He would only drink beer from a frozen mug, and only if an olive were dropped in the brew; he regularly ingested raw eggs; and no one who ever saw him meticulously build and bear down on one of his salted tomato, cheese, and cracker sculptures ever forgot the spectacle.

The party at the Frizzells' would regularly continue long past midnight. Come Sunday morning, Lefty's TV suit and all his greenback dollars would be hanging from the clothesline, his fringe and money both drying after an inevitable moonlit plunge into the swimming pool.

The uncomprehending neighbors were continually treated to surrealistic visions in Lefty's backyard, often involving pigtailed Lois and the pet horse Lefty had bought for her. Once, the poor animal mistook the dust-covered tarpaulin protecting the Frizzell swimming pool for solid ground and, breaking through to the water below, started paddling aimlessly with the tarp over its head. Another time Lois rode her pet straight into the kitchen to raid the refrigerator. The horse got stuck in the doorway on the way out and left a Tom Mix finale for Lefty on the kitchen floor. Still other times, the neighbors would peer out their windows and see a gang of good old boys laughing and waving golf clubs, testing their handicaps on the putting green that Lefty had created on his lawn.

In moments of gleeful reflection, Lefty and his family would laugh about their ridiculous backyard scenes and their neighbors' predicament, imagining how the Northridge townspeople must have grumbled, "God, I wish those hillbillies didn't live there."

Chapter 20

LEFTY WAS SWILLING whiskey and munching cheese and crackers, a couple of crumbs dropping in his lap as his limo sped through the rain-drenched forests of the Pacific Northwest. His great Drifting Playboys tour of '54 was in full swing, cutting him off from trade news and music industry jabber. Too tired and busy to have much time to read, he probably didn't notice a series of interesting though seemingly unrelated articles that appeared in *Billboard* that April and May. One reported that 1953 had been the most successful year in the history of country music. Record sales, publishing, and personal appearances brought in $70 million worth of hillbilly revenue. On the other hand, rhythm and blues record sales had also reached an all-time high of $15 million. The press noted that teenage buyers had started to "demand music with a beat." While Lefty was selling out 2,000-seat auditoriums in Oregon, Cleveland disc jockey Alan "Moondog" Freed was bringing his R&B road show to the East Coast. His "Moondog Coronation Ball" attracted 10,000 near-fanatical kids to the armory in Newark. Thousands more screamed in the streets outside. Something was up.

Whatever that "something" was went back a long, long way. No one knows when the first white farm boy picked a tune with his fiddling black buddy across the field. But whatever miscegenational undercurrent of American music was spilling over the surface in 1954 was already flowing strong and steady when twelve-year-old Lefty bought his first guitar from a black Arkansas farmer and when young Hank Williams learned to play guitar from a black street singer in Montgomery, Alabama. It was already there when Al Dexter broke meter with a veteran of Louis Jordan's band in the East Texas oil fields, and when a drunken Bob Wills hired a black trumpeter one night only to fire him the next morning after sobering up. It was there as young Pop Staples listened to Wills's "Ida Red" on the radio, and as Aaron Neville learned his falsetto flutter from the cowboy singers at home on the silver screen range. It was a Southern thing, but the North was quick to understand. So was the West. By 1952, Los Angeles record stores were noticing an alarming increase in R&B sales to white customers. Across the continent, the Moondog shows only made the trend visible.

But none of what came before—not Al Dexter's "all-nigro" band, nor Lefty's first guitar—provided the synthesis that was present in Elvis Presley's first Sun Records release, "That's All Right" backed with "Blue Moon of Kentucky." Breaking out of Memphis in July 1954, Presley's debut was not the first time a white man sang black music on record, not by a long shot. But it had never happened with transistor radios available, and with jukebox record purchases reaching eight figures. It had never been something for teens to hear and demand. Presley was nineteen years old when his first record hit, three years younger than Lefty had been when Don Law wondered who "that kid" was singing on Jim Beck's demo. In 1951, teenage girls had ripped Lefty's clothes and knocked on his hotel doors. Well, now it was little sister's turn with Elvis.

Within a year of his debut, Elvis had conquered the world that once belonged to Lefty. A month out of the chutes, he was already opening hillbilly shows in West Texas oil towns and stealing bandstand thunder from the likes of Lefty's old friend Billy Walker. He made his infamous one-night stand at the Grand Ole Opry in October, and a month later signed with the Louisiana Hayride. He shook his hips on the Big D Jamboree and pouted at the City Auditorium in Beaumont. He even played the 1955 Jimmie Rodgers festival in Meridian, a moment that, in its oblique way, defined country's biracial continuum better than any instant before or since. By the summer of '55, still releasing singles on distribution-poor Sun Records, the Hillbilly Cat had scorched so much Southern turf that the pandemonium he inevitably caused had started to look routine. Filing concert dispatches from the provinces, hillbilly deejays would tell *Billboard*, "As usual, Elvis Presley stole the show. . . ."

The oil town dancehalls that had once belonged to Lefty became rock and roll roadhouses. The real gone revolution Presley catalyzed had the Oedipal feel of sons attacking fathers, even if Laius was only twenty-six years old himself. At every whistle-stop Elvis rocked, some blue-collar kid who had grown up trying to sing like Lefty was converted and baptized in the good rockin' fire. Some, like West Texas warbler Roy Orbison, would one day understand how much they lost when they turned their backs on their honky-tonk heroes. Others caught the rockabilly fever and never recovered. The late Bob Luman saw pink-shirted, green-coated, nineteen-year-old Elvis shake his stuff in Kilgore, Texas—the honky-tonk center of the universe. The Memphis kid's sneering, gyrating act, and all the screaming, fainting girls, sent chills up Luman's back. "That's the last time I tried to sing like Webb Pierce or Lefty Frizzell," he told Paul Hemphill.

None of Lefty's territory was safe. Journalist Gordon Baxter was a Beaumont deejay, tight with Jack Starnes, when he introduced Elvis at a gig in Port Arthur, probably in January 1956. He described what he witnessed that night in his lyrical memoir, *Village Creek*:

> One by one the musicians slouched out, not looking up, and set up their equipment. More silence. The packed house holding its breath was a long tide pulling out. Then Elvis came on from left. Peg tops and shirt open; nobody was wearing cowboy stuff. And he was dragging a Martin flattop by its sling. Dragging it. A big, orchestra-model Martin. Enough right there to send him to hell for me.
>
> He put an arm out to the standing mike and I swear every woman in the house felt it slide round the small of her back. Then he hit "Blue Suede Shoes," or "Hound Dog," I'm not sure. It was one of those jiggety ones. And Elvis could have had every woman in Port Arthur. The waves of sound broke over the walls, every seat was wired to his voltage.

The rockabilly voltage blew hillbilly deejays against the back walls of their small-town sound booths. Southern jocks came under intense pressure from young listeners to program more of the phenomenon people were calling rock and roll. Some refused, espousing Jim Crow theories of country music purity that defied everything Jimmie Rodgers had ever stood for. Others grudgingly spun the "jiggety" stuff, hoping that the fad would blow over and they could all go back to plugging Webb Pierce. (Gordon Baxter liked to annoy his listeners by suggesting that Elvis hang on to his money.) Everything came to a head as 1955 came to a close. On September 21, no less than the Ryman Auditorium, the Mother Church of Country Music, trembled upon its evangelical foundation as the "Top Ten Review of 1955" brought Bo Diddley, Big Joe Turner, Etta James, and several other top-shelf R&B acts to the home of WSM's Grand Ole Opry. Six weeks later, WSM hosted the annual deejay convention at the Andrew Jackson Hotel in Nashville. There, among hundreds of stone country jocks, singers, and backslapping record men, Elvis Presley was the premier attraction. RCA executive Steve Sholes bought out Elvis's Sun contract a few days later.

As for the Hillbilly Cat himself, he found the whole convention setup rather bewildering. Searching for a sympathetic, familiar face in the hard-partying industry crowd, Elvis ran into always friendly Lefty Frizzell. Presley, so the story goes, as told by Lefty's family, brightened and asked the sage honky-tonker a question he'd be asking, one way or another, for the rest of his troubled life. "Hey Lefty, how are you supposed to act at one of these things?"

"Just stand around like you're having a good time," Lefty advised him. "Then leave as soon as you can."

Riding a three-month high of his own, Lefty hit the convention having taken a different sort of shot at the flimsy stylistic barriers dividing American music in 1955. On August 6, while Elvis was touring Florida as an opening act for Andy Griffith, Lefty and Hank Snow were the honored headliners at the Hollywood Bowl's so-called "Western Night." The first country program ever booked into that hallowed venue, the concert was part of the summerlong "Hollywood Bowl Pops" series of "Symphonies Under the Stars." Besides Snow and Lefty, the lineup included, among others, Freddie Hart, the Collins Kids, and cowboy singer Eddie Dean. Country deejay Jolly Joe Nixon, one of Southern California's favorite broadcast personalities, emceed the show. The house, of course, provided a backup band—the Los Angeles Philharmonic Orchestra, conducted by Robert Armbruster.

Well hyped in advance, the unprecedented high/low cultural affair attracted a full house of 12,000 patrons on a balmy August night. Many were proud hillbilly fans. A healthy percentage, however, were series ticket holders just as likely to have come out for Beethoven's Fifth. Though the concert planners were eager to see how the down-home program would play to their high-toned subscribers, they were also somewhat leery of the rhinestone-suited monster they had created. Said Jolly Joe Nixon, their attitude was basically, "We'll let you folks come in for three hours, but don't stay too long, and get your ass out real quick after the show's over 'cause we don't wanna be embarrassed." For their part, the country contingent, including Lefty, felt honored by the invitation and glad of the opportunity to open some doors into the black-tie community that had never paid them much heed. Not that they had any intention of acting the role of humble sharecroppers before the Hollywood elite. "We just made a big party out of it," says Nixon. "Hired a limo and zipped down Hollywood Boulevard."

The program was strangely syncopated, as the hillbilly numbers collided with the pop-classical segments, and vice versa. The Y-Knot Twirlers demonstrated square dances. Tuxedo-clad Robert Armbruster conducted a version of "Turkey in the Straw" that had been "transcribed for orchestra." A selection from Grofe's *Grand Canyon Suite* was sandwiched between Freddie Hart's "Loose Talk" and the Collins Kids' "Dance with Me Henry." And no telling what the Beverly Hills matrons thought when pint-size picker Larry Collins tore into "Shake, Rattle and Roll."

Lefty's slot in the fustian hoedown came just before "Turkey in the Straw." His flashy fringe and glistening boots made for an unusual sight as he tapped his foot and led the Los Angeles Philharmonic through "Always Late" and "If You've Got the Money, I've Got the Time." As Lefty sang on the rotating stage ("A fella could get drunk this way," he told Freddie Hart. "Be one of the cheapest drunks I ever had"), the longhair subscribers fanned themselves with the program notes in which they found edifying explanations of the difference between "Western" and "Country" music. "One of the wonderful things about Country Music is that it is a 'natural,' instinctive, untrained kind of music," the program read. "The songs are handed down more than they are written down. Most of the performers—probably around 80%—do not even read music."

Lefty followed his first two numbers with "Making Believe" (a superb single that had been overrun on the radio by Kitty Wells's less engrossing version) and his latest release, a frank meditation on cheating called "I'm Lost Between Right and Wrong."

All told, it was a revealing set. The first two songs had made Lefty rich. The latter two never made the charts. The cultural ground he helped break that night in front of 12,000 Angelenos had proven how scared—or at least aware—the tuxedo set was of their yoked-shirt competition in the San Fernando Valley. But it also pointed to how precarious Lefty's position was even before Elvis Presley came along. Lefty still rated headlining a high-gloss honky-tonk like the Hollywood Bowl, but he couldn't buy a hit.

Lefty himself was not to blame. In the first three sessions he cut after moving to California, he attacked his material with more revelatory vigor than he'd shown since the break with Jack Starnes. His emotional investment in "Making Believe" and "I Love You Mostly," both recorded after the move, nearly matched his best work from '51. It wasn't just the effort Lefty put into the vocals that carried the songs, it was an added quality to his voice itself. Jim Beck's ever more complex soundboard had started to capture a throaty resonance in Lefty's lower register that had only been hinted at before. Less inclined to fall back on his signature "ay-ays," which threatened to turn gimmicky, he was, instead, perfecting a textured sound that would one day define the very essence of soul country singing. Incredibly, the best country vocalist of his time was getting better.

Lefty's problem wasn't with his records, but with how he pushed them—or more accurately, with how he failed to push them. Getting along without a full-time manager was, for Lefty, a matter of self-respect and self-preservation. He had promised himself he would never get burned again. But to maintain his autonomy, Lefty sacrificed the watchful promotional eye that a manager would have provided. He had no one to seek out that lucrative slot on Perry Como's show; no one to bargain with Steve Stebbins by reminding him what kind of deal Marty Landau could swing; no one to make sure that he stayed sober and said hello to his deejay friends at the back-country thousand-watters. On record, Lefty's work could stand next to that of any of his peers. But the guys making money were the ones with good promotion. Stebbins couldn't do the job, at least away from the West Coast, for his quasi-managerial role was limited by design and more so by personality. "Steve Stebbins was a good man and a wonderful person," Freddie Hart says, "but he didn't like Nashville. He couldn't associate with people in Nashville." While the Hollywood Bowl was one of Lefty's proudest moments, in the end it was an isolated show that did little to further his career. The post-concert trade talk was all about Hank Snow's role and his follow-up appearance on, of all things, "Town Hall Party." Lefty's participation wasn't mentioned. It was all moot, of course, for with Bo Diddley and Big Joe Turner closing in on the Ryman Auditorium, the hillbilly conquest of the Hollywood Bowl was a mere sideshow. Afterward, Lefty departed Hollywood and the Town Hall for yet another Stebbins-booked Northwest tour. Back east, Elvis zeroed in on Nashville.

True to his generous character, Lefty did not feel the least bit threatened by Elvis. In fact, he rather enjoyed the furor Presley generated, no doubt recognizing a bit of his former self in the simultaneous exultation and panic that Presley's pout betrayed. Lefty liked an artist with his own look and sound, his own emotional credibility. "Elvis, he'd go out and shake his leg. Well Lefty got a kick out of that," says David Frizzell, who was starting to spend a great deal of time with his older brother. "And Jerry Lee's antics—he just *loved* that. Yeah, he did. I never ever seen him be in awe of anybody." Nevertheless, Lefty did feel some of the heat burning country singers all over the South. In Enid, Oklahoma, he was upstaged by a rockabilly booked into town the same night. Lefty was not surprisingly upset when his crowd abandoned him.

As for the business end of the crisis, rock and roll's real threat, or so it seemed at first, was to Nashville, not Dallas or Hollywood. Once Elvis started shaking radio transmitters beyond the South, outright panic hit Music City as country record sales plunged and pop stars switched their cover-tune priorities from hillbilly music to blues. Patti Page's "Tennessee Waltz" gave way to Pat Boone's "Ain't That a Shame." Before long, it seemed like every major-league honky-tonker in sight was getting saddled with a doo-wah chorus and desperate ersatz teen material. By the spring of 1956, Presley's "Heartbreak Hotel," recorded in Nashville, and Carl Perkins's "Blue Suede Shoes" were chasing each other to the top of every record chart in America—country, pop, and R&B. Roughnecks had found a new place to dwell. Hillbillies huddled on Lonely Street.

And when Jim Beck died suddenly in May of '56, it was as if a final nail had been driven into the coffin of Dallas honky-tonk. It was a horrid accident, as absurd as it was tragic. A friend had given Beck a piece of malfunctioning radio equipment to fix and sell if he could. Glad to make an easy buck, Beck took the radio back into his studio echo chamber and proceeded to clean it with carbon tetrachloride, an over-the-counter fluid commonly used for dry cleaning. At one point, his assistant and studio guitarist, Jimmy Rollins, poked his head in the ventless echo chamber and mentioned that the chemical smelled pretty strong. Engrossed in his work, Beck ignored him. Later that night, he and his wife, Mary, delivered the retooled radio to a buyer across town in Oak Cliff. After they came home, Beck had a drink, and something to eat, and went to bed. He woke up feeling sick. Twenty-four hours later, he felt sicker. His wife called the doctor, who immediately ordered Beck to a hospital, though he didn't know what was wrong with him. Beck was laid up three or four days, his sickness undiagnosed, until his wife recalled a story she had read about a woman prominent in the Dallas theater community who had cleaned her rug one night with carbon tetrachloride, gone to sleep on it, and never woke up. When Mary Beck told the doctor that her husband had been working with that same deadly chemical, he instantly confirmed the symptoms. Hearing the diagnosis, Beck asked the doctor how long he had. The doctor said not to talk that way; the worst was over. That night, Jim Beck slipped into a coma. He never came to.

For Lefty, Beck's death was disorienting. The two had their differences, and Lefty never would get used to seeing the studio engineer's name attached to his own on record. But bad blood aside, Beck had taken Lefty's native talent and showcased it as no other sound man could have. For six years, Lefty cut nearly every one of his records at Beck's studio, largely because Don Law, who knew how to make records, felt that no one else could get Lefty's intimate sound right. Law had a deep respect for Beck's abilities and restless talent, for the way he was always improving his studio and experimenting with new techniques. The echo chamber where Jim Beck had poisoned himself was one of the first ones ever built. And unlike Lefty, Law liked Jim Beck personally.

Beck's death forced Lefty back into the middle of the country music crisis he had been so ready to ignore. A few weeks after the accident, and just after appearing at the fourth Jimmie Rodgers Festival, he cut his first-ever session in Nashville. Law backed him with several former members of Hank Williams's Drifting Cowboys, and the results were strong. On "The Waltz of the Angels" and "Heart's Highway" (the latter co-written by Eddie Miller and the highly dubious "A.," as in Alice, "Harper") Lefty proved that he could bring off his uncompromising ballad style in any studio in America. What's more, surrounded by a creative community with their backs to the wall, Lefty also cut a song that was, for him, both straightforward autobiography and a comment on his ability to keep up with the rockabillies. He called it "Just Can't Live That Fast (Anymore)."

Chapter 21

WHETHER HE COULD have or not, Lefty didn't want to live that fast anymore. He enjoyed the slower pace of his life out west. Working mostly weekend dates and various TV shows near home, he could relax and spend time with his family and friends to a degree he had never managed in Beaumont. Once again, the Frizzell household became a revolving door and a crash pad for the likes of Wayne Raney, teenage David Frizzell, and Lefty's latest best friend—a talented Okie songwriter named Eddie Miller.

Best known for having co-written the country/pop perennial "Release Me," three different versions of which all hit the top ten in 1954, Miller was an ex–railroad man and western swing bandleader who wrote for 4-Star Music, a rather notorious independent publishing firm. Like Raney and Ray Price, Miller had lived briefly at Lefty's house in Beaumont. There he had earned his keep by serving as a drinking buddy, and by taking little Lois to her dance lessons. Though Miller, as one friend put it, "mistreated himself" as badly as Lefty did, he was always an affable, easygoing houseguest. The Frizzells loved him. In Northridge, Miller took over the bed on the family's screened-in back porch, where he weathered the daily intrusions of Lois and her tap dance routines. Miller's worst nemesis, though, was Lefty's pet boxer, Duke, a friendly overgrown beast who reserved his flatulence for the porch on which Miller slept. (Duke was also Lefty's main confidant. Many a laid-back evening, Lefty would pop a beer, settle into his armchair, and tell ol' Duke his troubles.) Whenever Miller was away from Northridge on tour, he'd send Lefty telegrams with questions pertaining to the matter that weighed heaviest on his mind: "Lefty, what will you do with the dog?"

The Frizzell family unit was completed in December 1956 with the birth of their youngest son, Marlon. Naamon, A.D., and the younger children had also just moved to the San Fernando Valley and were staying with Lefty when Marlon was born. Baby Marlon would soon grow up to replace Duke as the scourge of Eddie Miller's back-porch bedroom. He especially liked to wake poor mistreated Eddie by clobbering him on the head with a thick-plastic toy baseball bat.

As for Lefty and Alice's marriage, it endured in turmoil as it always had. One minute, the couple would be mooning over each other like teenage Greenville sweethearts, the next they'd be slamming doors and busting chairs. Typically, a raging Lefty would pack Marlon's diaper bag and tell Alice this was it; he and the baby were leaving. Alice would stand in the doorway and watch them go. Before long, they'd come strolling back. "Well, we just went down to the Dairy Queen," Lefty would say.

Sometimes the communal poolside frolics would turn into three A.M. battles between Lefty and Alice. One night, a houseful of honky-tonk revelers woke up to hear Lefty, roaring drunk, yelling at his wife: "You don't love me anymore, Alice, so I'm just gonna drown myself!" The grinning guests knew Lefty too well. They all poured out of the house to watch what they knew was going to be big fun. Peering into the bottom-lit pool, all they could see were Lefty's boxer shorts flapping on the surface. After holding his breath a good long while (it was one of Lefty's talents) he looked up and realized how ridiculous he looked. Sputtering to the surface, he told them, "I just thought it would be a good night for a swim."

What it came down to was that Lefty was drinking harder than ever, and it affected every aspect of his life. He put on considerable weight, all of it showing up in his upper body and face, making him look like he had aged ten years between 1950 and '55. He switched his primary allegiance from whiskey to vodka because the hangovers weren't so bad, and because it was easier on his breath. And while Alice knew how to handle him when he was in a drunken black humor, those moods could be traumatic for his children.

Most of the time, Lefty went out of his way to entertain his kids. Childlike himself, he'd join their games, take them to the zoo, take them fishing, ride Lois's horse, or ride a bicycle backwards to get a laugh out of them. When sober, he was the most loving—and fun-loving—daddy a kid could have. "I always thought other kids had stuffy parents," Lois says. "His sense of humor was so overwhelming. When he showed his love, it was always such a free, funny thing." Lefty had no problem communicating with his young children either; quite the contrary. "He got down to my level," Lois adds. "Not patronizing, he got into it. If I was eight years old, he got down to an eight-year-old level. He was my buddy, I could talk to him. If he wanted to get down on the floor and play jacks with me, well he'd do it. Just get down, boots and all. He was open-minded about listening to kids' ideas. We had *wonderful* times."

Lenient and supportive, Lefty allowed his children to act as they pleased and say what they thought. "Down to the bone honest" himself, Lefty valued their emotional sincerity and straightforwardness. The only thing never permitted was for the children to talk back, or in any way show disrespect for their parents. If they did, says Lois, they quickly found themselves picking themselves up off the floor. "It only happened a few times, but we learned not to do it."

But that was Lefty when sober, or only drinking beer, which was his form of moderation. That was even Lefty with a pretty good buzz on. He was a different father, though, when on the occasional bad drunk. "He was Jekyll and Hyde, literally," Lois says. Over time, as kids will do, Lefty's children learned to read the signs, to sense when he had had that one drink too many, the one that changed his circuits. Then they knew their best strategy would be to stay out of his way. If not, things could get ugly in an instant. "You knew not to cross a certain line. As much as he could show love, he'd show that much anger." One of the worst fights, Lois recalls, happened when Lefty returned to the house three days late from an out-of-town gig:

Mama and Uncle Bill was there, and me and of course the boys. And we were in the living room, and he got to griping at Mama, 'cause he was drunk, and accusing her of all kinds of things, and I got mad, 'cause I wanted to protect Mama. You know, I was a kid. And I jumped up and there was a big, giant glass ashtray on the coffee table. And I busted him in the head with it. Yeah. I picked it up, and I mean it cracked, you could hear it crack. And blood started running down his face, and it freaked him out so much, 'cause it was just a reaction, I guess. And he grabbed me around the throat, and strangled the life out of me till I blacked out, and Mama said Uncle Bill got him off of me. It enraged him so much that I cracked his skull open with that ashtray, 'cause he was onto Mama . . . [not beating her, but] screaming and talking like insane, crazy talk. And I didn't like it 'cause she didn't deserve it. She was Mama, you know. And so when I came to, they were—him and Bill were wrestling—'cause Bill was trying to keep him out, away from me. And then Mama was

screaming, and there was a big brawl, and so I came to enough to jump
up and run, and I hid in the closet for hours.

The road, alone, could sometimes put Lefty into that kind of state.
Though he made occasional forays into the South and Midwest (he
returned to the Big D Jamboree for a night in October 1956, one week
before "Roy Orbison and the Teen Kings" were due in Dallas), his
weekend TV appearances kept him working close to home. Often as
not, Stebbins would have him booked into some Bakersfield honky-
tonk or Ventura dancehall where the fans, though enthusiastic, had
started to take Lefty's appearances for granted. He'd work with house
bands that, on good nights, actually knew his music, while traveling
nearly solo. Maybe Eddie Miller would ride along; maybe his brother
David, who was in high school when Lefty started taking him to shows.
"I'd go with him, help him drive to 'em, and make sure he'd get back,"
David Frizzell says. "With Eddie Miller and people like Eddie, you
know, they'd always wanna drink a little bit, and stuff. So it was nice to
have me around, because I'd always make sure he'd get back." Lefty
preferred to pull into town a day or two early and check into a cheap
roadside motel. There he would hole up, like a B-movie gangster on the
lam, sending David out for cheese and crackers as needed. On the night
of the gig, the two brothers would hide out near the club till the usual
extra hour had passed. Finally, Lefty would tell David, "Okay. Let 'em
know I'm here so they can let me in the back."

Now and then, Stebbins would put together an out-of-state tour
for Lefty, though again it was too often through the far too familiar
Northwest circuit. On one summer tour, David Frizzell's attentiveness
to his brother paid off when the aspiring teen singer was added to
the bill as "Little David (Rock and Roll Sensation)," with a repertoire
of Elvis, Little Richard, and Fats Domino covers. Freddie Hart was
also part of the package, as was Hurshel Clothier, whose Oklahoma
Travelers provided everybody's backup, and whose unconverted bus
provided transportation. For Lefty, it was one more barnstorming
string of one-nighters at joints like the Community Building in
Coquille, Oregon; the Belfair Barn in Belfair, Washington; and the
Copeco Ballroom in Grand Junction, Colorado. (Klamath Falls, Oregon, seems to have been a particular hotbed of Lefty fanaticism.) But
for his little brother David, the tour was the first major step toward a
lifelong career in music.

"It was a lot of fun," he says, "and it certainly was an experience for
a young kid, to be out there with the professionals like Lefty and Fred-

die and Hurshel. And just to be around those kind of people, and playing music, was incredible."

Lefty taught David the subtleties of the country music concert business; in particular, the value of concessions. The rock and roll sensation was lucky to get ten bucks a day for his act. He made a lot more money hawking eight-by-ten glossy photos of Lefty and Hart. The pictures cost fifty cents apiece, of which the teen concessionaire's cut was a dime. But much more important than business tips were the intangible lessons about showmanship that David learned just watching his brother work. Lefty taught him that "when you walk on stage, dominate the stage. When you walk on it, you gotta take it. . . . He would just do it. He'd walk up, and I don't care who was there, *he* was the center of that attention. But he was the same way if he walked into this room. He had such a tremendous personality, and such a presence about him, that it was overwhelming. It absolutely stopped conversations."

One of the few examples of that presence in action to have survived over the years is an early 1958 appearance Lefty made on "Western Ranch Party," a TV spinoff of "Town Hall Party." Hosted by Tex Ritter, the Ranch Party also relied on the irrepressible bandleader Joe Maphis, as well as other Town Hall veterans, including the Collins Kids, Maphis's wife, Rose Lee, and Carrottop Anderson, whose personal Nudie special was a suit festooned with pistol-packin' carrots. On the show that featured Lefty, seventeen-year-old Lorrie Collins (who had, by then, smitten Ricky Nelson) sang the honky-tonk standard "Love Me to Pieces," leaning especially hard on the line, "I want to be your *slave*!" Wanda Jackson then preceded the star of the day with a fallen angel's lament about not being "half as good a girl as my mother thinks I am." Ed Sullivan this wasn't.

Standing a safe distance from Lefty's jabbing finger, the stately Ritter introduced his young friend with warm sincerity and grammatical ingenuity. "Not too many years ago, a young singer came out of South Texas that kind of set the record industry on its respective ear. . . . Lefty Free-zell!"

Lefty strode out from the wings in his fringed suit, and without so much as a "how are y'all this evening" hit the first couple notes of "Mom and Dad's Waltz." He sang directly into the cameras — "Western Ranch Party" had no live audience — and his sentimental honesty was so gripping it must have had Naamon and A.D., and any other moms and dads at home, reaching for their hankies by the fourth line. His performance seemed drawn from some spot in his heart that most singers never find, let alone tap into. Then it was over and he was gone without another word.

It was a wonderful experience for fans in 1958 to hear Lefty singing his seven-year-old hits with untempered conviction. But it was hardly a sign of a healthy career. For no amount of living room TV exposure could compensate for the street-level, jukebox charge of a current hit single. And Lefty hadn't landed one of those since February 1955. Nor could he blame rock and roll (to his credit, he never did) because his downhill slide on radio playlists started long before Elvis ever sang on the Opry. From the day Columbia released "If You've Got the Money, I've Got the Time," to the day Jack Starnes sued him, Lefty's songs spent a combined 196 weeks on the various *Billboard* top-ten lists, 32 of those weeks at number one. On the other hand, from the date of the June 1952 lawsuit through October 1958, Lefty logged but 24 sporadic weeks on the charts, none at number one. By the summer of '56, even his chipper fan club president was urging members to "request Lefty's records on the radio and see if we can't get him back on top where he belongs."

Don Law was certainly at a loss about what to do with his superstar in decline. He had fought the front office to ensure renewal of Lefty's Columbia contract in 1955, but since then, nothing he and Lefty had tried in the studio had made any serious waves on radio. He cut Lefty in Nashville; he cut him in Hollywood. He tried him in a duet with Johnny Bond; with Shirley Caddell; with the near-obligatory vocal chorus. Lefty sang his own songs, J. D. Miller's songs, Freddie Hart's songs, Eddie Miller's songs, Hank Williams's songs, and any number of Nashville workaday songwriters' songs. Some were admittedly lame efforts. At one point, he rerecorded several of his early hits with soft pop arrangements that were gallingly saccharine, even by the standards of the day. Don Law had the good sense to bury them. But other numbers from Lefty's dry years—the duet with Caddell on "No One to Talk to (But the Blues)" for instance—were positively exhilarating. None of them sold.

The Hollywood sessions were the worst. A free spirit, Lefty could not stomach the cold, corporate L.A. recording studio atmosphere. To him it represented the artistically corrupt antithesis of the creative, hands-on ambience of Jim Beck's in Dallas. Law was none too fond of recording in Hollywood either. Whenever economics demanded that he record Columbia's West Coast artists—Lefty, Joe Maphis, and Johnny Bond, for instance—in their own backyard, he and the singers would rush through their work to leave time for leisurely fishing, or maybe a little putting contest at Lefty's house.

The monthlong tour with Little David, the Rock and Roll Sensation, ran from mid-July to mid-August 1958. A month later Law brought Lefty to Owen Bradley's famous "Quonset Hut" studio on 16th Avenue in Nashville for one more try at breaking his mysterious commercial impasse. He hired the top musicians in town, a crew of closet jazz players to whom Music City referred as the "A team." They included guitarists Grady Martin, Hank "Sugarfoot" Garland, and Harold Bradley. Law paid for all of them. The rhythm section consisted of Bob Moore on bass and Buddy Harman on drums, while Floyd Cramer, who had come a long way since tossing Van Howard's hat out the car window, sat in on piano. The session was rounded out with saxophonist Jack Gregory — Lefty had never recorded with a horn player before — and steel guitarist Gene O'Neal.

The first song they knocked back that afternoon was a J. D. Miller co-write called "You're Humbuggin' Me." Pitched harder than country and softer than rockabilly, the uptempo arrangement opened full tilt with a raunchy blast from Gregory's horn. Probably for the sake of grounding more than anything else, the crew followed "You're Humbuggin' Me" with "She's Gone," a traditional country number by straight-up country songwriter Wayne Walker. Then it was back to some hopped-up honky-tonk for the third number, "Cigarettes and Coffee Blues."

A nicotine-fueled tune spun off of the old "walkin' the floor" theme, it was written by Marty Robbins, one of the few country singers halfway to succeed at the future King of Rock and Roll's own game. Robbins was hip to Elvis as early as September 1954, and, like white boy supreme Pat Boone, also had the temerity to cover Little Richard's "Long Tall Sally." He scored sizable hits with "Singin' the Blues," and "Knee Deep in the Blues," but by the time he wrote "Cigarettes and Coffee Blues," Robbins had moved on to headier stuff than blues and Little Richard covers; namely, New York sessions with Mitch Miller. A loyal Columbia artist, Robbins pitched his new song to Don Law and Lefty, both of whom liked it enough to record it. Swinging more casually than on the forced "You're Humbuggin' Me," Lefty (who hated cigarette smoke) nailed "Cigarettes and Coffee Blues." And for the first time in over three years, people responded. The song took off in Louisiana first, and by the end of November Lefty was singing it live on the dear old Louisiana Hayride. It broke across the rest of the country during the holidays, giving Lefty the best Christmas present he could have hoped for — a hit record. "Lefty's new one," wrote the trade press, "is spreading smoke signals of success."

Law was quick to try to capitalize on those signals, though his methods were none too inspired. In early December he rushed Lefty back into the Bradley studio to rerecord, yet again, his hits from the salad days of 1951. Though less horrible than the Hollywood studio remakes, the Nashville productions were less than captivating. The one substantial effort was a superb, loping version of "If You're Ever Lonely Darling," a song Lefty gave up to Ray Price for Price's first Columbia single in '51. Lefty reclaimed the song, but did it in an upbeat, swinging style that owed much to Price's own late-fifties work.

Law took the entire seven-song session, added a few tracks left over from California, and put them together for a full-length twelve-inch LP: *The One and Only Lefty Frizzell*. Columbia's art department, searching for the defining image for Lefty and his music, arranged for a California photo shoot with him and a coopful of chickens. Lefty, whose lone experience with barnyard fowl was stealing Christmas dinner in Roswell, posed seated on a wooden fence, prepared for an assault from his cackling fellow models. Lois was given the honor of tossing the birds at Lefty. As she picked up the first one, Lefty warned her, "Now don't throw and hit me with it. When you throw that damned rooster, you be careful."

"I will, Daddy, I will," Lois said, and promptly whomped him in the chest with the bird.

"Daddamn! I told you!" Lefty yelled.

"Daddy, please, Daddy!" Lois cried. "I don't wanna do this anymore. 'Cause it got doo-doo all over me!"

The unfortunate rooster finally settled down long enough for the photographer to get a clear shot. The album was released with a ridiculous cover photo showing Lefty, wearing a red and white fringed suit, smiling on a fence with his trusty Gibson in hand, the rooster at his side. Lois laughs, "I have a flashback every time I see [the album], of throwin' that damn rooster and hittin' Daddy with it—and shit goin' everywhere."

From a sales standpoint, the fact that the album did not contain Lefty's then-current hit, "Cigarettes and Coffee Blues," was more regrettable than the cover, though in those days, the labels treated LPs and singles as separate entities anyway. Nevertheless, had Law waited a few more months to package the record, instead of dull remakes of the early hits he could have included a fresh performance by Lefty that was as great, and enduring, as any he recorded in his life.

Chapter 22

I N LATE 1956, as American deejays nearly broke their wrists trying to keep up with the flip-flop action on Presley's "Don't Be Cruel" and "Hound Dog," thirty-year-old Webb Pierce sunk to the rockabilly challenge with his never to be forgotten "Teenage Boogie." That single cut may have represented the absolute nadir of the rock and roll crisis in Nashville, proving how pathetically unsuited most of the era's top country stars were for shaking their Nudie-cushioned tail feathers. Realizing they could not hope to run with the rockers, the Nashville community jumped to a different playing field. Bringing to bear all the soft-edge lessons they had learned from hearing pop singers cover their three-minute hillbilly gems, they started cutting pop music of their own. A year after "Heartbreak Hotel" nearly bankrupted half the city, the famed cushion-production "Nashville Sound" was born as Ferlin Husky's "Gone" and Jim Reeves's "Four Walls" both swelled near the top of the *pop* "Hot 100."

Regaining their confidence, Nashville producers became aggressive. While some settled for stale, patchwork applications of vocal chorus and strings, Don Law, usually aided by mercurial guitarist Grady Martin, turned out records built around ever more inventive arrangements. Fiddles and steel guitars were often shoved aside to make room for percussive banjos and tambourines. Instead of humming "oooh-ahhh-oooh," the Jordanaires jazzed things up with lines like "We fired our guns and the British kept a-coming." The last was from a Columbia Johnny Horton session in January 1959, a marathon date that had Music City buzzing as reports hit the streets of the wild production that Martin, standing in for Law, had put on "The Battle of New Orleans."

One week later, Law and company cut Stonewall Jackson's "Waterloo"; and two months after that it was Marty Robbins's immortal "El Paso." Within the span of ten weeks, Don Law's crew had produced, in Nashville, three top-five country/pop crossover hits. "The Battle of New Orleans" and "El Paso" would both sell a million copies. Which makes it all the more incredible that during the same ten-week stretch, Law would also preside over two of the most enduring pure country classics of the era. One of them, recorded two days after "The Battle of New Orleans," was Ray Price's "Heartaches by the Number." The other was Lefty Frizzell's "The Long Black Veil."

"Cigarettes and Coffee Blues" had just faded from earshot when Lefty hit Nashville for the March 1959 session. He brought David with him, and also a tough little honky-tonk number that he and Eddie Miller co-wrote called "Sin Will Be the Chaser for the Wine." That left three tunes to find to complete the standard four-song session. Law and Lefty set up an informal listening room in Law's suite in the James Robertson Hotel, then put the word on the street that they were looking for songs. Before long, Law's living room chairs and couch were shoulder-to-shoulder with Music City pickers and song pluggers. With no more than a couple of hours left before the start of Lefty's session, a songwriter-pianist named Marijohn Wilkin showed up at Law's door. A former Oklahoma English teacher, and a newcomer to Nashville, she had, in just six months' time, been signed to the sizzling Cedarwood publishing company and hired as their resident song plugger. One of the sharpest minds and most brilliant songwriting talents ever to grace the streets of Music City, Wilkin had already impressed Law once with "Waterloo," which she co-wrote with John D. Loudermilk. But this time she was representing Cedarwood's interests in general, not just her own tunes. She listened patiently while the resident old boys strummed their guitars, growing antsier with each dull tune they tried to get Law and Lefty to take. Finally, unable to contain herself any longer, Wilkin pulled Don Law aside and whispered, "Danny Dill and I have a better song than any of these."

The song she had in mind was "The Long Black Veil." The lyrics, written by Opry veteran Danny Dill, tell the story of a man wrongfully convicted of murder who goes to the gallows rather than compromise his lover—his best friend's wife—in whose arms he'd been lying when the crime was committed. The song's central Gothic image is of the grieving adultress walking the hills "in a long black veil," returning over and over to her hanged lover's grave. Dill drew the simple tale from several sources, including stories he had read of a woman who supposedly haunted Rudolph Valentino's grave. But what gives the lyrics their subtle power is the unspoken conceit—the same ploy used in the movie *Sunset Boulevard*—of having the story narrated from beyond the vale of tears. The voice you hear singing "The Long Black Veil" is that of a ghost.

Instead of putting his own music to the words, Dill took the song to Wilkin at Cedarwood and literally slung the lyric sheet across her desk. "I wrote this thing last night," he said. "I don't know if it's any good or not. If you like it, why, put a tune to it. If you don't, why, throw it in the wastebasket."

Wilkin read the eerie lyrics and got cold chills from head to foot. "I just put that sheet of music up on the piano and started playing, and just sang that thing out. And it just rolled right out."

That was in the morning. By late afternoon, Wilkin was pitching "The Long Black Veil" to Lefty and Law at Law's suite. "Well, swee-tie," the producer said, his eyebrows arched and his English accent rolling off his tongue, "play us a tape."

"We don't have one," Wilkin admitted. "We just wrote it."

"Well, how's it go?"

"Well, I'll just have to stand here and sing it to you."

While the other pluggers shifted in their seats, guitars inert, Wilkin followed Law and Lefty into the kitchen and sang "The Long Black Veil" to them a cappella. "Mr. Law and Lefty both just flipped over it," she says. "And they said, 'That's the best song we've got.' "

There was just one problem. With no demo tape, there was no way to teach the song to the studio band that night. Law solved the problem by hiring Wilkin to play piano at the session. Following her even-tempoed lead, and in direct opposition to the era's cluttered trends, Law and the studio players worked out an arrangement stripped bare as the bones of the fictional hero unjustly hanged. The subdued acoustic guitars carried the song forward while Don Helms's steel guitar slid in and out of the upper register, giving the whole spare arrangement an ethereal tone. The brilliantly understated production was nothing, though, compared to Lefty's brilliantly understated vocal. Always an intimate stylist, his hard country phrasing was so perfectly metered, his breath so close to the surface, you could practically hear the dead man's spirit whistling over the graveyard grass when Lefty sang the simple word "hills."

"Magic happened that night," says David Frizzell, who, watching in the studio, was completely stunned by his brother's work. "The magic was so intense on that. His voice just fit the lyric so perfect."

Lefty's magic hit the streets in late April and instantly took off. "The

Battle of New Orleans" was already the number one song in the country, and "Waterloo" was rising fast behind. But when "The Long Black
Veil" started to break out on pop stations in Atlanta — the main proving
ground for the era's crossover smashes — Columbia's overtaxed New
York office begged mercy from their Southern Midas, Don Law. "I was
again in Mr. Law's suite," Wilkin recalls, "when he received a telegram
from the head of Columbia, saying, 'For god's sakes, stop cutting hits.
We can't promote them all.' "

Forced to prioritize their plugging, Columbia's field promo men ral-
lied behind the Salvation Army rhythms of "Waterloo" and pushed the
song to number two on the pop charts. While "The Long Black Veil"
was Lefty's biggest hit record since the Jack Starnes era, the moody
country masterpiece never crossed over. With Columbia's operational
backing pulled, even given the sublimity of the production and of
Lefty's phenomenal vocals, "The Long Black Veil" was doomed among
mainstream deejays atuned to the martial beat of "The Battle of New
Orleans." And Lefty still had no manager to pressure Columbia into
following through on the song's initial heavy action, no one to explain
to the tin-eared pop jocks that "The Long Black Veil" was every bit as
viable as its loud, punchy labelmates.

Pop failures aside, the back-to-back country success of "Cigarettes
and Coffee Blues" and "The Long Black Veil" would have completely
revived the career of a well-managed artist. The higher profile his new
hits gave him would have heightened demand for his live appearances,
thereby increasing his talent fee. That's where "The Long Black Veil,"
crossover hit or not, should have really paid off. But Lefty stuck by his
long-standing vow and refused to sign with a manager. He would rather
be poor than robbed.

And as for increasing his talent fee, Lefty wrecked that angle by
himself. Steve Stebbins said he had to practically hold Lefty's hand to
get him to gigs. Lefty's chronic unreliability had long since sabotaged
his reputation among promoters and club owners. They all remembered the nights he showed up an hour late for his first set and the
nights he disappeared before the second. Many could recall some hair-
raising episode when he mixed a new screwdriver every thirty minutes
throughout the evening, his optimum performance pace calling instead
for at most one every hour. Hit records alone, they knew, would not
discourage such behavior. Right after "Cigarettes and Coffee Blues"
started sending its "smoke signals of success," Lefty and David were
booked into a Fort Worth venue. When Lefty hadn't appeared by
showtime, club management was forced to lie to the grumbling audi-

ence that his plane from Oklahoma City had been delayed. In reality, says a friend who was there, they had found Lefty holed up at his hotel, drunker than usual, and with several "kissin' cousins" about. Tracked down, he apologized and made it to the show, but was still so loaded that he botched his brand-new hit. Instead of singing "I've got those smoking cigarettes and drinking coffee blues," he twisted it into, "I've got those drinking cigarettes and smoking coffee blues." After the show, Lefty's followers fought him for the car keys but he wouldn't give them up. He disappeared into the dark streets of Dallas, remembering, perhaps, a mean drive he took years ago from a joint called the Old Top Rail.

As "The Long Black Veil" fell from the charts and the 1950s came to a close, Lefty was unable to sustain his return to heavy rotation airplay. It wasn't entirely his fault. In a rare show of professional poor judgment, Don Law saddled him with a copycat Horton-esque history lesson, "Ballad of the Blue and Gray," as a follow-up single to "The Long Black Veil." Written by young songwriter Harlan Howard, whom Lefty had met while Howard was a West Coast factory hand hanging out nights at "Town Hall Party," the chintzy record bombed deservedly and wrecked Lefty's chart momentum. "It taught me a lesson . . . ," Howard says. "What I learned was that I was following a trend. I got in on the very tail end of it, and so did Lefty."

By the turn of the decade, Lefty's career had returned to the status quo pre–"Cigarettes and Coffee Blues." He and David (who recorded a few Columbia sides of his own in 1959, including one written by Lefty that was not released) continued their run of San Joaquin and San Fernando one-night stands. "He was only pulling $300 or $350 a night in those little clubs," David told Patrick Carr. "He'd just book a million of them. He didn't have a band or anything. We'd use whatever local band was there, and that was so hard on him. Nine times out of ten they didn't know his songs, and we'd be playing some run-down club somewhere, or out in a pasture with the cows doing background for us."

When David joined the air force in August 1960, Lefty once again lacked the close traveling partner he needed. To fill the void, he looked no farther than his living room. Lois was all of fourteen years old in February 1960, so Lefty brought her along on a Canadian tour with Freddie Hart and a couple other Stebbins acts. As songbook and photo concessionaire, Lois was a natural, here and there making more money selling the glossies than Lefty made singing. "Sometimes I ended up feeding everybody," she says with a laugh. As he had with David, Lefty took his school-age daughter with him on short-hop one-nighters. He drove her one summer weekend to a job at a resort spot an hour outside of Phoenix. During the show, Lefty got tanked up and afterward passed out in the driver's seat of his pink Cadillac. Unable to drive, but with no other option, Lois pulled her daddy over to the passenger side and propped his head up on some pillows. She then slid in behind the wheel and inched her way back to the motel in Phoenix. The one-hour drive took her five hours. "By then I knew how to drive that sucker," she says. When Lefty came to and realized where he was, he started beating on the motel door in the middle of the night.

"How did we get home?" he demanded.

"I drove us," Lois said.

"You don't know how."

"I do now."

For Lefty, the saddest thing was that at that point in his life the resort job was a good one. A year after "The Long Black Veil" put him back in the top ten, his career bottomed out again. He was playing furniture store showrooms in the suburbs of L.A. The paltry $300 David remembered him making would have looked like decent money in 1961. That September, a four-day run at the Chestnut Inn in Kansas City earned Lefty all of $675—less than $175 per show, before expenses. In California, fiddler Gib Gilbeau, later a member of the Burrito Brothers, backed Lefty at Barstow's Hinkley Valley Grange Hall and watched in horror as the once and future country legend took home $35 for his efforts, just $15 more than Gilbeau earned as house picker. Lefty was so overexposed in the San Joaquin Valley that according to Junior Cox, deejays stopped plugging his appearances, and clubs he had once routinely sold out wouldn't bring in fifteen people. And that was Lefty's home turf. "People back in Maryland, and back north," said Alice, "they didn't know he was alive." Lefty must have been thinking in precisely those terms. On August 3, 1961, just ten days after receiving notification of his depressing Kansas City gig, he made out his last will and testament in Beverly Hills. He left everything to Alice and the kids.

Lefty knew something had to change. And in his life, change always meant movement. His instincts had sent him to California; his instincts had been wrong. His gamble that television would turn Hollywood into hillbilly music central had been a poor call. Nashville emerged from the rock and roll crisis stronger than ever while the great West Coast country TV shows were in their death throes by 1960. Lefty figured he could just pack up and go where twenty-twenty hindsight told him he should have been all along: Music City, USA.

Lefty had broached the subject of moving to Nashville five years earlier, after enjoying his first recording session there. Only partially concerned with the business angle, he had also taken the time to look around the city and check out the fishing on Old Hickory Lake in Hendersonville, a northern suburb popular with the Opry crowd. "You'll love it," he told Alice. "It's pretty there." His wife was skeptical, however. "Sonny, I don't know if I like Nashville or not," she said.

But now, when the subject of moving to Nashville came up again, Alice had no doubt it was the right decision. "I knew it wasn't being good for him, working them old clubs around and around."

Lefty's California blues officially ended in August 1962. He and Alice stuffed as much of their baggage and belongings as they could into two cars—the pink Cadillac and a maroon and white Buick—leaving room for three children, a Siamese cat with kittens, a lapdog, and Lefty's talking parakeet, Tino. Heartbroken, Lefty had to leave his drinking buddy Duke with Naamon and A.D. He and Alice put everything else they owned in storage and leased the house in Northridge.

The Frizzells left the San Fernando Valley and made for Nashville in the heat of summer. Lefty and Lois rode with Tino in the Caddy; Alice, the boys, and all the other pets trailed in the Buick. Along the way, they detoured to one of the seedy Mexican border towns and spent the day in the streets and markets feasting on the local cuisine. When they got back to their cars, poor Tino was lying on the floor of his cage with his tongue hanging out the side of his mouth. They had left the car windows cracked, but in August, in Mexico, it didn't much matter. The bird was near dead. Scared but cool-headed, Lefty grabbed a towel, drenched it in water from inside the ice chest, and draped it over Tino's cage. The tough little parakeet revived.

"Well, we finally got past Mexico . . . ," Alice said. A couple days later, the Frizzells rolled into Music City, pulled over on West End Avenue, and got out of their cars. It was August in Nashville, which probably meant ninety degrees and 90 percent humidity. All of Alice's justification for moving to Nashville melted on the sidewalk. "Oh, my goodness, Sonny, this is horrible," she said. "If we hadn't done leased the house out, I'd just take the children, and take the other car, and just head back out there and go home."

Lefty and Alice had no plans, no house waiting, not even a friend to put them up for the night. They drove to the southeast side of the city and checked into the Drake Motel. The five Frizzells, along with their dog, cat, kittens, and bird, all moved into one tiny room at the Drake. Miles away from the Ryman Auditorium, the Drake's orchid neon flashed in the night, outshining the stars over Nashville.

PRORATION

Chapter 23

LEFTY'S GREAT-GREAT-GRANDFATHER, John Wiley Frizzell, was still a Tennessee farmboy when a collection of hymns and vocal instructions called *Western Harmony* first appeared on music stands in Nashville, Tennessee. Considered the birth of the city's music publishing industry, *Western Harmony* was printed on the press of the *Nashville Republican* near a tiny cobblestone street known as Printers Alley. Though named for its high concentration of Fourth Estate enterprises, Printers Alley was, by the turn of the century, far more famous as the back-door entrance to Nashville's so-called "men's quarter" — a downtown district rich in grand hotels, barber shops, gambling joints, and prostitutes.

The delight of gentlemen boozers and outlaw gamblers, the Alley was also the focus of Christian fury, and in 1916, enforcement of the state's prohibition laws wrecked the Alley's preferred enterprise and drove one of the town's most prominent saloon keepers to suicide. Nevertheless, the shadowy street was soon humming again, and after World War II it became a popular hangout for Nashville's small but growing music community. Throughout the 1950s, A-team musicians like guitarist Hank Garland and drummer Buddy Harman would exit the hillbilly studios at night and set up chairs on the Alley bandstands. There, in a dim-lit corner of Jimmy Hyde's Carousel Club, they'd play straight-up jazz into the early-morning hours while unhinged singers, deejays, and politicos drank in the Alley darkness. Lefty hung with Hank Williams in the Alley. Marijohn Wilkin, fresh out of an Oklahoma schoolroom, sang piano pop at the Alley's Voodoo Club when she first hit Music City. And long before he headed for West Coast fame, deejay

Joe Nixon hosted "Breakfast at the Maxwell House," a morning interview program broadcast from around the corner at the regal Maxwell House Hotel, a monument to the Nashville monied elite nevertheless known to be crawling with hookers.

Back at the turn of the century, a couple of blocks south of the Alley the acoustically pure Union Gospel Tabernacle had resonated with the fire and brimstone excoriations of the Reverend Sam Jones. An itinerant preacher with a populist bent, his combative ministry had made a God-fearing Christian of riverboat captain Tom Ryman. Born again at a Jones revival, the captain dumped his whiskey into the Cumberland River, turned his saloon into a House of God, and set to building a new, majestic downtown church for the evangelist wonder who showed him the Way. In 1889, the foundation was laid for the Union Gospel Tabernacle, a non-Sectarian entity with the declared purpose of "promoting religion, morality and the elevation of humanity to a higher plane and more usefulness." Fifteen years later, when the good captain passed away, local humanity (feeling ever more useful and elevated) changed the stately building's name to the Ryman Auditorium.

As time passed, all manner of entertainers passed through the doors of the ever more secularized Ryman Auditorium. Enrico Caruso, John McCormack, Victor Herbert and the Pittsburgh Symphony Orchestra, the New York Philharmonic Orchestra, Isadora Duncan, Sarah Bernhardt, the Sousa Band, even Blackstone the Magician. And in 1943, WSM radio moved the Grand Ole Opry to the Ryman stage to preach to a Saturday-night congregation.

One year before the move, Opry star Roy Acuff approached versatile songwriter Fred Rose about starting a song publishing company. Acuff promised to put up the money if Rose, a pop writer well connected in New York and Hollywood, would promise to run the show. Their humble little company, Acuff-Rose Publications, went into business in 1942—exactly 117 years after *Western Harmony* rolled off the presses near Printers Alley. Nashville, a snooty city far more proud of its mock Parthenon than the Grand Ole Opry, was on its way to becoming the hillbilly capitol of the world.

Twenty years later, when Lefty checked into the Drake Motel, Nashville, a Southern crossroads dominated by banks, insurance firms, and produce dealers, was also a town with an ever more legitimate claim on the title "Music City." In just four years' time, the infant Country Music Association had done a superb job of convincing the world that Nashville meant country music, and country music meant big bucks for advertisers. With remarkable foresight, the CMA had proposed the spinoff Country Music Foundation to preserve the music's heritage, and had already chosen the first inductees to the Country Music Hall of Fame—Jimmie Rodgers, Hank Williams, and Fred Rose. Former Tennessee governor Frank Clement, many a country singer's lawyer, was running for office again, this time supported by a battery of singers who all remembered his mid-fifties stances on behalf of the hillbilly trade. A number of major labels had set up permanent offices in town, and even Starday Records, in which Jack Starnes had long since sold out his interest, had moved from Beaumont to Nashville.

Yet it wasn't just country music, or even country/pop crossover, that was turning Nashville into Music City. In 1962, the Nashville scene was wide open. For every honky-tonk classic like George Jones's "She Thinks I Still Care" or Ray Price's "Pride," the town offered a pure pop radio smash like Brenda Lee's "Break It to Me Gently" or Roy Orbison's "Dream Baby." Producers ignored the old rules. Saxophone riffs were as common as steel guitar. Grady Martin had just accidentally invented fuzztone. Even the color line, broken in Printers Alley when drummer Buddy Harman invited bassist W. O. Smith up on the bandstand and shattered in mainstream Nashville when scores of black students sat at the Woolworth's and other luncheon counters, was now under heavy stress in the studios. Mercury Records brought R&B giant Clyde McPhatter to town to record on Music Row. The million-selling soul groove "Snap Your Fingers," produced and co-written by Grady Martin, was sung by a former member of Nashville's Fairfield Four gospel quartet named Joe Henderson. Henderson's future roommate, Arthur Alexander, arrived that summer of 1962 on the strength of his chilling soul/pop hit "You Better Move On." Working with the Nashville studio pickers, Alexander knocked out "Anna" and "Soldier of Love," a pair of timeless singles that crossed the Atlantic and utterly enchanted some soon-to-be-famous boys in Liverpool.

And it all came down to publishing. Song publishers had built the town that Lefty was moving to—or at least the offices that would matter to him. By the time he arrived there were over a hundred publishing firms. As early as the 1920s, before discovering Jimmie Rodgers and the Carter Family, Ralph Peer had understood that the surest way to make money in the hillbilly business was to publish popular songs, earning royalties off the works of singers who could churn out new hits every day, or at least every few months. Roy Acuff understood that when he went into business with Fred Rose, despite his disingenuous claim that the two of them "were like blind pigs searching for acorns." And once Acuff-Rose set the precedent for linking the copyright office to the Ryman stage, the whole fabric of Nashville publishing got wrapped around the Opry microphone. Throughout the post–World War II growth years, a serpentine network of lucrative interests connected the Grand Ole Opry to the local publishing firms. Besides Acuff-Rose, the town's two other leading publishers, Cedarwood and Tree, were started by WSM executives, men in a position to influence singers' choices of songs.

Of the latter executives, the most audacious and commercially astute was Cedarwood chief Jim Denny. A self-made country boy with a fourth-grade education, Denny had worked his way up from the mailroom at WSM to become, by the early fifties, head of the Opry's Artist Service Bureau. He started Cedarwood Publishing in 1953 with Webb Pierce as his partner, staff writer, and ready mouth-piece for Cedarwood songs. Three years later, in-house conflicts and jealousies, as well as complaints about Denny's outside interests, led to his dismissal from the Opry. (Roy Acuff, for one, did not appreciate the logic of having his bookings set by a man who was his publishing rival.)

By no means amicable, Denny's departure split Music City in two. But it also further vitalized Nashville by creating a second country empire as powerful as the Opry. Popular with most of the artists he handled, Denny immediately stole several Opry stars and signed them to his fledgling Jim Denny Artist Bureau. With limitless power over the quality and number of his artists' bookings, Denny was able to subtly — and sometimes flagrantly — pressure them into recording Cedarwood songs.

Denny was tough, but he was also sharp. He knew who to sign, and why. He recognized that stars came into the business with pen and guitar but lost the pen on the endless road. Full-time writers were needed to take up the slack. With Marijohn Wilkin, Danny Dill, Wayne Walker, and Nashville newcomer Mel Tillis on staff, Cedarwood boasted one of the deepest pools of songwriting talent ever assembled in Nashville. Lefty had been drawing from that pool since 1956, when he recorded a Wayne Walker number called "Now That You Are Gone." Though the Wilkin-Dill composition "The Long Black Veil" was Lefty's most notable Cedarwood success, he had developed an artistic affinity for Walker's fertile pen in particular. A hard-drinking, transplanted Louisiana honky-tonker, Walker had provided Lefty with "No One to Talk To (But the Blues)," and in May of '62, during Lefty's last session while living in California, he recorded a mournful, dazzling Walker–Irene Stanton ballad called "Stranger." That it bombed in the marketplace was only proof that Lefty's career troubles had nothing to do with slack performance in the studio.

In 1961, Denny further revolutionized songwriting in Nashville by moving Cedarwood's offices to a building on 16th Avenue across the street from Owen Bradley's Quonset Hut studio. According to Wilkin, each of Denny's writers was given "a little cubicle and a desk and a pencil." Other music businesses followed Cedarwood to 16th Avenue, and just months before Lefty arrived in town, Columbia Records bought the Quonset Hut and opened a Nashville office. No more song plugging in Don Law's apartment. Music Row was open for business. The song factory system had arrived.

And with the factory came factory workers, an entire underclass of blue-collar tunesmiths who churned out hillbilly standards, changing the town's musical identity from Opry glitz to 16th Avenue sweat. Besides Cedarwood and its unbeatable crew, Tree Publishing had Roger Miller; Pamper Music, based in the suburbs, had Willie Nelson and Hank Cochran; Acuff-Rose had Felice and Boudleaux Bryant, John D. Loudermilk, and, for six months, the former real life factory hand Harlan Howard. The songs they wrote or later would write were the stuff of the country canon, the pop canon, the rock-and-roll canon: "Hey Joe," "Wake Up Little Susie," "All I Have to Do Is Dream," "Rocky Top," "Cut Across Shorty," "One Day at a Time," "Detroit City," "Ruby, Don't Take Your Love to Town," "Tobacco Road," "King of the Road," "Invitation to the Blues," "Hello Walls," "Crazy," "Funny How Time Slips Away," "Make the World Go Away," "I Fall to Pieces," "Too Many Rivers," "Busted."

"I think we invented some'n' for Nashville that kind of was a repeat of earlier times up in Tin Pan Alley," says Harlan Howard, thinking about those heady days. "There's an old saying, which I think of quite often, it says, 'When the pupil is ready, the master appears.' It was kind of like maybe the Left Bank of Paris was, or the old Brill Building in New York," Howard adds. "I mean it was too damn exciting. And the music was too good."

In 1962, the year Lefty arrived, every success was within reach of the Music Row crowd. But to the very end, they would, like Lefty, say they were songwriters first. Anything else, glory or wealth, was just God's way of blessing their three-minute struggles with truth.

Chapter 24

LEFTY COULD HARDLY believe it. Saturday night, standing in the wings at the Ryman Auditorium, two weeks in from California and still not sure if he should have come, he was watching the Opry crowd call Merle Kilgore out on stage for three full encores. Merle Kilgore. The Shreveport kid who used to bring him Cokes at the Louisiana Hayride, who ran after him at the Palm Isle the night he knocked himself out. The fans rose to their feet, their cheers ascending from the pews down low to the balcony thundering overhead. They were screaming for Kilgore to sing "Wolverton Mountain," a two-minute story about a hillbilly daddy named Clifton Clowers who wouldn't let no man touch his gorgeous daughter and whose redneck nature boy ways put him in tune with the bears and the birds, all of whom would sound the alarm if a randy stranger climbed Wolverton Mountain.

Dazed by the applause, Kilgore ran into Lefty on his way off the stage.

"Good gracious," Lefty said, shaking his head, "I gotta follow you!"

It was a rough close to a rough two weeks. Lefty and Alice had spent several depressing days house-hunting in East Nashville, a blue-collar Southern Democrat stronghold far removed from the old money mansions of Belle Meade. Lois looked after her younger brothers while Lefty and Alice toured the available tract housing. With their shallow savings about dried up, they settled on a tiny three-bedroom bungalow that felt the size of their Northridge living room. The furnished rental was located in Donelson, a suburban community laid out farther east than East Nashville. Rent was $125 a month. The house had no air conditioning. The parakeet Tino feared for its feathered life.

Once they paid rent and deposit on their cheap little cottage, Lefty

and Alice hardly had money left over to buy groceries. But Lefty was
never one to cower before the wolf at his door. He approached the Opry
about making a guest appearance on Saturday night, knowing they
would only pay him union scale, which amounted to less than thirty
dollars after taxes. Still, twenty-eight dollars would at least see his
family through the week. The Opry, of course, was more than happy to
have Lefty Frizzell freelance for a night at union scale. They gave him
two slots on the September 1 bill—one during the Stephens work
clothes half hour (Patsy Cline was also plugging overalls that night) and
one in the closeout slot for SSS Tonic.

He returned a week later, September 8, and this time the Opry upped
his profile with a spot in the Martha White Flour half hour. Lefty
appreciated the exposure, but he would have really appreciated more
money. He and Alice had sent for the rest of their belongings and had no
way to cover their outstanding bills. The Opry gig would feed the kids
for another week, but he figured he'd have to swallow his pride and hit
up Webb Pierce, who had made a mint buying radio stations and as a
partner in Cedarwood, for a loan to pay the bills coming due. Such
were his thoughts until the moment he watched in amazement as
Merle Kilgore brought down the house with "Wolverton Mountain."
As Kilgore later told the story, the two got reacquainted backstage.

"Good gracious, Merle," Lefty said, "didn't I used to know you—
didn't you used to hang around the Hayride when I was a kid, you was
a kid?"

"Yeah, that's right," Kilgore said.

"I thought you was a performer," Lefty said.

"Naw, I was just hanging around."

Kilgore hung around again to catch Lefty's number—which went
over well, if not as spectacularly as "Wolverton Mountain." Afterward,
Kilgore suggested the two of them go have a drink between shows. "I'd
love to," Lefty said.

Lefty and his long-lost Louisiana friend took a short walk across one
of the most famous informal footpaths in America—the stretch of concrete leading from the back door of the Ryman Auditorium to the back
door of Tootsie's Orchid Lounge. They found a vacant table in the dingy
rear room and sat down. Seeing past Lefty's good-time facade, Kilgore
abruptly said, "Something tells me you need five hundred dollars. I got
ESP."

Lefty, says Kilgore, nearly dropped his drink. Without saying a word,
he reached into his shirt pocket and pulled out a piece of paper. Lefty
handed it to Kilgore. It was a bill for $487.

"Listen, Lefty, I don't have five hundred dollars," Kilgore admitted. "But I will call my publisher tonight, and I'll get it in here, and we'll have it in here by Tuesday."

"You will?"

"Sure I will."

Come next Tuesday, Kilgore made good on his promise. With Claude King's version of "Wolverton Mountain" selling at a million-copy pace, Kilgore, the writer, had little trouble convincing his publisher to front him five hundred bucks, which he promptly turned over to Lefty. Not knowing how precarious the Frizzell finances really were, Kilgore figured the loan was no big deal. But those five hundred dollars saw Lefty through one of the most difficult transitions of his adult life. He never forgot Kilgore's no-strings-attached kindness. Several months later, when he repaid the loan, he sent Kilgore the money along with a sentimental poem he had written called "A Friend in the Night."

"There'll always be Miracles, Prayers & Sin," Lefty wrote. "My Prayer is you'll always be My Friend."

Kilgore's advance and the two Opry dates kept Lefty's head above water. Meanwhile, he was methodically putting the word on the street that he was in town, available, and eager to work as many jobs as he could. But finding takers was more of a struggle than he had anticipated. He spent hours in a Donelson phone booth, trying to scare up gigs, and made daily treks to the Music Row office of the Jim Denny Artist Bureau, where his friend Lucky Moeller, an ex–Oklahoma banker, was Denny's top booking agent. Lefty and Moeller had done handshake business for years. In the early 1950s, Moeller had managed the Trianon Ballroom in Oklahoma City, and it was he who had booked Lefty's infamous disappearing act when Lefty returned from Canada in 1951. Now, as the number two man in what was unquestionably the world's premier country talent agency, Moeller was in the best possible position to book his anxious friend. Yet by the time Lefty arrived on Music Row, his profile had sunk so low that even the Denny Bureau had trouble finding him work. Every day, Lefty showed up at Moeller's 16th Avenue office and nervously waited for calls to come through, for any sign that his music career had not completely ground to a halt. "Seem like it was a repeat of sittin' at Jim Beck's office every day," Alice recalled. "Nobody knew him."

As the first couple weeks of September passed, a few isolated dates in the hinterland started to trickle in. Moeller and his fellow Denny Bureau agents, doing their level best for Lefty, scored him an afternoon spot on Sunday the sixteenth at a highway venue near Charlotte, North Carolina. "I could only get $250.00 for you to play this date," Moeller's son Larry wrote Lefty in a memo. "This is a little bit under what I wanted to set you for but I didn't want to pass it up for I figured you would want to go ahead and take it."

He figured right. Lefty took the job, though the elder Moeller warned him it "won't hardly pay expenses." For the rest of the season, throughout the Indian summer of '62, Lefty took any job that came his way, no matter how bad the wages. A date all the way north to the Palace Pier in Toronto was worth $450. The Wil-Helm Agency, promoters of the "Bootheel Jamboree" in Risco, Missouri, paid $200 for the privilege of booking Lefty Frizzell the first week of October. Three weeks later, a pair of package shows, one in Minneapolis and one in Des Moines, earned Lefty $250 each, barely a quarter the fee Lefty's chum Ray Price commanded as headliner.

Then, as if a lack of money and caring for three kids, a dog, a cat, kittens, and a parakeet weren't enough to crowd Lefty's worried mind, his friends and kinfolk started showing up.

This time, it was relatives on the Harper side, who had also lived in California. They followed Lefty and Alice to Nashville, arriving a few weeks later. With them was a gifted picker and singer named Abe Mulkey, whom Lefty had met briefly toward the end of his tenure on the West Coast. Close to Lefty's age, Mulkey hailed from Cox and Harper country along the Texas-Oklahoma border. In 1950, while Lefty's first single was saturating the Southwest airwaves, Mulkey was singing for a tiny Oklahoma station with a signal that reached, he joked, "about as far as you could holler." He knew the Blackie Crawford bunch back then, but had never met Lefty. Still, he never forgot the first time he heard Lefty's lilting vowels on "I Love You a Thousand Ways" ascending from a Paris, Texas, jukebox. Nor did he forget the first time he saw Lefty onstage, at the Wills Point dancehall in Sacramento, with Billy Jack Wills and his maniacal swing band tearing up the bandstand behind him.

That was after Mulkey moved out west and joined in the feverish Bakersfield club scene, working for a while down the street from a club where babyfaced Merle Haggard played each night. Mulkey's club travels took him to Pismo Beach. There, in 1959, he and his band backed Lefty for an evening. After that, their paths didn't cross again for three years. When Mulkey learned that Alice's California relatives, whom he also knew well, would be traveling to Oklahoma and then to Nashville to see the Frizzells, he decided to ride along. Several weeks later, the whole crowd pulled into Donelson and went looking for Lefty. They couldn't find him. They tried to catch his children at school, but that didn't work either. They hit every schoolhouse except the one at which the kids were enrolled. After driving around the neighborhood, they finally saw Lefty standing in a corner phone booth, calling the Denny Bureau to see if any gigs had come through. Hard times in Donelson. Lefty didn't let it bother him. Not with company coming. He hung up the phone and greeted his visitors. "Follow me on out to the house here," he said.

So many people, so little space, they couldn't help but have fun. The Harpers caught up on family news while Lefty and Mulkey picked and pulled guitars into the night. An ace honky-tonk guitarist, Mulkey also had a golden ear for high harmony vocals. Lefty was impressed. He was also impulsive. As Abe Manuel and Freddie Hart had both learned, Lefty didn't believe in drawn-out courtship dances. Before the night was up he told Mulkey, "Go back and get your stuff, and come back and you can work for me." Taking Lefty at his word, Mulkey headed back to Oklahoma, packed his belongings, and moved his family to Nashville. For the next ten years, no one, except for Alice and the kids, would spend more time with Lefty than Abe Mulkey. He'd be Lefty's sober traveling partner, his front man, lead guitarist, harmony vocalist, songwriting collaborator, close friend, and—on the occasions when things were at their worst between Lefty and Alice—overnight host.

Nevertheless, however glamorous a job with the great Lefty Frizzell sounded in theory, in practice, Lefty had little to offer Mulkey. A lone spot in Alexandria, Indiana, at the end of November. A three-day run in Washington, D.C., the first week of December. A night in Columbia, South Carolina, the eighth of December. After three months in Music City, the Frizzells were so broke that with the fourth month's rent coming due they could barely raise the couple of dollars their merciless landlady demanded for a lamp that Alice had accidentally broken, let alone the $125 rent. As Lefty and Abe hit the road for one gig, Alice and Mulkey's wife, Joanne, prepared themselves for the imminent belt-tightening on the home front. "I've only got four dollars," Alice said to Joanne. "But you can have half."

Lefty Frizzell, thirty-four years old, already recognized as one of the greatest practitioners of his chosen art, was unable to make a single month's rent on a tract house the size of a camper.

So he bought a house.

Desperate to move, Lefty and Alice had already settled on a location twenty miles north of Nashville. Hendersonville, a quiet Middle Tennessee town grown up along the edge of Old Hickory Lake, was the popular fishing outpost Lefty had told his wife about when he first thought of moving in '56. Lefty, Alice, and the Mulkeys all took a Sunday drive to the lake and stumbled upon a wooded, virgin subdivision called Harbor Hills. Platted along a narrow inlet off the lake, Harbor Hills offered many homes with backyard access to the water. The house they zeroed in on was a split-level, pale brick affair on a long, downward slope from the street. The yards, back and front, were enormous. A deck and a boat dock were both provided. Inside, the house had a sizable kitchen and living room, a large downstairs den, and a huge basement. Better still, the rooms that would be the children's bedrooms were all bunched in close around the master bedroom. "Sonny liked it 'cause . . . he was funny about that," Alice explained. "Some people like to put their kids away up on the other part of the house. But he was kinda spooky about that."

They wanted the house badly, but they needed close to three thousand dollars for the down payment. Incredibly, considering the kind of life they led, their credit was in good shape. They found a bank willing to loan them the down payment against Lefty's life insurance (probably the policy Cliff Bruner sold him in 1951), and on December 10 they closed on the house in Hendersonville. Lefty, Alice, the kids, Tino, and all the other pets moved out of Donelson, leaving their landlady screaming about the broken lease and lamp. "She was gonna sue us and everything else," Alice said. "Well, we couldn't help that, 'cause we didn't have the money to pay her."

Money was tight, but life was good. The Christmas approaching would be a white one, a rarity in Middle Tennessee, with flakes coming down, as Lefty put it, "like silver dollars." Alice blessed their new house by planting a waist-high baby pine tree in the front yard. The first Saturday night in the new home, the kids likely gathered in the den for their favorite new TV show. The smash hit series told "the story of a man named Jed," an Arkansas hillbilly who made a million dollars off the oil beneath his land and moved his family to Beverly Hills. The program's theme song was performed by Lester Flatt and Earl Scruggs, a bluegrass duo who happened to be Lefty's labelmates. Released to radio, their novelty banjo breakdown hit the charts the same week Lefty bought his new house. Both show and song—the weird admixture of cartoon stereotype and oil boom fantasy—rocketed to the top of the ratings while Lefty Frizzell, born in an oil field behind an oil well, headed to Abilene, Texas, for a $250 date at the Key City Sportatorium.

Chapter 25

THE DAY AFTER his Abilene gig, Lefty pressed on to the Southern Club in Lawton, Oklahoma. It was important for him to do well there, for Buck Owens had just passed through, and two weeks before cheering for Buck, the same crowd had descended on the Southern Club to check out George Jones, the one man alive who anyone thought could sing country music as well as Lefty. Nearly a decade after imitating Lefty in Jack Starnes's home recording studio, Jones had come into his own with an instantly recognizable catch in his throat and a voice known to make Texas oil men weep. The Southern Club's talent buyer deserved credit for his taste—and for his courage. A betting man wouldn't have touched the action on which of the two, Lefty or George, might actually show up in Lawton, let alone show up on time. But Lefty knew he could not afford to mess up any gigs. He and Abe made their date at the Southern—ahead of time, no less, if Mulkey's memory of playing Lawton with Lefty refers to the December '62 gig. As Mulkey recalls, they drove into town and headed straight to a motel. There, upon learning they were country singers, management promptly turned them away. Seems that some hillbilly—no telling who, of course—had recently trashed one of their rooms.

Lefty and Abe found other lodgings and hauled their guitars to the club. During a break in the program, an ill-tempered truck driver from Klamath Falls, Oregon, told Mulkey, "I'm gonna whoop your friend after the show." He offered no reason other than that he wanted to brag to his friends back in Klamath Falls that he had "whooped a star."

Sure enough, after the gig the driver followed Lefty and Abe to their car. "Lefty, I'm gonna whoop your ass," he announced. Startled, Lefty asked why. The trucker said something about his friends back in Klamath Falls. Lefty took a closer look at the big guy's shoulders, and said, "Well, I don't believe you can do it. But let's have a drink first."

That sounded like a fair deal. They each took a shot of vodka, then Lefty said, "Well, I guess we're gonna do it." But the trucker had changed his mind. Disarmed by the drink and Lefty's fearless good humor in the face of an ass-whooping, he said, "Lefty, I was gonna whoop your ass, but you're a heckuva nice guy. I just wanna be your friend."

The truck driver followed the tour to Oklahoma City, where Lefty and Abe played the Trianon Ballroom the next night. It's a minor miracle he didn't follow them all the way back to Hendersonville. Lefty never did know such a thing as a stranger; waiting to see who he and Abe might bring home from the road was always high adventure for his family. Once it was a mangy dog that had jumped in the car when they stopped to pick up a hitchhiker. Another time, it was a mysterious one-armed man. Alice eventually had to throw him out of the house. Lefty sure wasn't going to. He had turned his den into a playpen for rowdy friends. A dart board went up, a pool table, too. Kilgore hung out. Mel Tillis hung out. Wayne Walker. Faron Young. George Jones. Faron, of course, was expected to watch his language if Alice was in the room. And George . . . well . . . in those days there was only so much you could do with George Jones.

The Frizzells found that out the first time Lefty brought Jones home. The two greatest country singers of their time stumbled in off the road after bingeing for no one knew how many days. Not missing a beat (though perhaps missing a step or two) they camped out in the downstairs den, each with a bottle, each refusing to pass out and leave the family in peace. They roared and laughed, argued and howled. From time to time, Alice would pound on the kitchen floor with a broom handle and yell: "Hold it down, Sonny!" Cringing, Lefty would put his fingers to his lips: "George! Shhh!" Then the two would step lightly around the room, whispering, a conspiratorial glint to their eyes. Day turned into night, night into a new day. Every time pretty redheaded Lois passed through the den, George would wonder who she was. Exasperated, slapping his fingers against the palm of his other hand, Lefty would say to his bleary-eyed friend, "I told you . . . and told you . . . and told you—this is my *daughter*. Don't be an *ass*."

As Lois recalls it, they ran out of booze on the second day. Hammered though they were, Lefty and George had sense enough to know they would never make it to the liquor store on their own. Still whispering, the two conspirators put their heads together and devised an ingenious plan. Lefty called a sympathetic liquor store, put in their order, and told the clerk he'd be sending his daughter to pick it up. Then he called Lois downstairs, and George handed her a nice crisp twenty-dollar bill to cover the cost of his bottle. Lefty threw in a few dollars for his own vodka. According to Lois, in order for her to slip past the Cerebus standing guard with a broom upstairs, Lefty then "made some story up, I don't know, about I was gonna go do something, and he was gonna loan me his car, 'cause I was his pretty little girl.

"So I got in that long blue Cadillac. You know, two blocks long? Drove up there, and you can barely see me over the steering wheel."

Back at the house, as Lefty later told her, George began to worry about that twenty-dollar bill he gave up. "Who the hell is that girl, anyway, that you sent with my twenty-dollar bill to a liquor store?" George demanded. "She ain't come back yet. She took my twenty and left town. I'll never see her again."

"George, by God," Lefty groaned, "I told you, and told you — it's my daughter! She's coming back with your whiskey!"

After a couple more days like that, Alice insisted that George had to go. That's all there was to it. Knowing he had overstepped the line this time — and not a little relieved himself — Lefty acquiesced. Again, he drafted Lois as their chauffeur. He and George poured themselves into the backseat of the Caddy and they all headed to Nashville. "Daddy had a bottle of vodka, and George had a bottle of vodka. And they were both sitting there, just drinking it from the bottle. They didn't need chasers or nothing. Nothing. You know they were embalmed."

Lefty and Lois dropped George off in front of Tootsie's. The minute they got back to Hendersonville, Alice marched Lefty off to Madison Hospital to dry out. They say no one saw George Jones for weeks.

For a while, Lefty's drinking got so bad Alice was checking him into Madison Hospital every few months. It didn't help much, for some of his friends didn't mind smuggling booze into his room. Moreover, Lefty's ulcers also flared up — eventually to the point of hospitalizing him. His general decline may have had to do with career idleness. Through the early months of 1963, he worked as he had the previous fall — enough to pay his bills and maintain a decent lifestyle, but no-where near as steadily as some of his friends. He played the Louisiana Hayride in March and guested a couple more times on the Opry, but in Lefty's case, Opry spots were usually no more than a sign he couldn't find a better gig on Saturday night. Most alarming of all was his record-ing silence. He had cut a mere four sessions in four years' time — none since moving to Nashville. In June, when he finally did return to the studio, the results were none too auspicious. The song chosen for single release was one of Lefty's own, "Don't Let Her See Me Cry." Newly written, it was not one of his more imaginative guilt-trip ballads. For the B-side, Lefty cut "James River," a Merle Kilgore–June Carter composition that, unfortunately, totally lacked the imagistic punch of another Kilgore-Carter composition ablaze all over American radio that very moment: Johnny Cash's "Ring of Fire."

As the summer progressed, Lefty's bookings picked up—at least in quantity, if not exactly quality. A typical date was his July 23 outing to Vernal, Utah, where he fronted "Wayne Hall and the Drifters" at the Vernal Rod and Gun Club Lounge. In August, Lefty worked five coast-to-coast dates in the span of nine days. After playing Denver on August 16, he was due in Portland, Oregon—a thousand miles across the Rockies—the next night. No one could have blamed him if he showed up late.

Trying to get in synch with the new Nashville, between tours Lefty roamed 16th Avenue in search of songs, and to check in with the Moellers at the Denny Bureau/Cedarwood complex. He even placed a few of his own songs with Cedarwood. As a Denny Bureau client, Lefty may have also been courted as a Cedarwood staff writer, though it's doubtful he ever signed. Lefty loved the creative vitality of Music Row, but loathed the song factory methods. He wanted no part of a 16th Avenue writer's cubicle with pressure to churn out songs on demand. Good songs, Lefty maintained, were written from the heart, not the head; and the heart knew no corporate timetable. Still, the frequent contact with other professionals inspired Lefty's muse. He wrote "Don't Let Her See Me Cry" shortly after moving to Hendersonville; and in February, on an airplane, he and country star Cowboy Copas co-wrote "Goodbye Kisses." A month later, Copas died in the same devastating plane crash that also killed Patsy Cline and Hawkshaw Hawkins. Released posthumously, "Goodbye Kisses," written with Lefty, gave Cowboy Copas one last goodbye hit.

At his next studio session, on October 1, Lefty supplied two new songs: "Lonely Heart," and "What Good Did You Get (Out of Breaking My Heart)." He lifted the latter title from a song he had written years before on stationery from the Hotel Marion in Little Rock. Yet despite Lefty's efforts, Don Law was not pleased with the results. He declined to release a single from any of the material Lefty cut that evening. Instead, three weeks later, he booked his former meal ticket back into Columbia's 16th Avenue studio for another try. Perhaps aware of the precariousness of his position—his recording contract had rolled over to a series of one-year options, allowing Columbia to pull the plug any time they felt his career was played out—Lefty entered the studio with much stronger ammunition. Early in the year, Merle Kilgore had recorded a Lefty original called "When It Rains the Blues." A relaxed little number more melodic than bluesy, Lefty wrote it while still living in California. He knew it was one of the most engaging songs he had authored in years; genuine hit material. Since Kilgore's version had run its course with surprisingly little impact, Lefty felt no qualms about cutting "When It Rains the Blues" himself at the second October date. With Grady Martin's acoustic lead setting the laid-back mood of the song, Lefty's slippery phrasing—and by now almost flawless timing—ensured that the mood held. There was still no question that the better the song, the better Lefty would sing it.

For a second number, Lefty picked up "I'm Not the Man I'm Supposed to Be" from his friend Wayne Walker. As the title suggests, if Walker didn't actually write it for Lefty, he may as well have. The session's third song was a pure novelty, the kind of peppy commercial fare Lefty rarely had much success with. Called "Saginaw, Michigan," it was a story-song written by Nashville tool and die maker Don Wayne (with a little help from Bill Anderson). Don Wayne knew nothing about the real life Saginaw, Michigan, except that Lufkin depth micrometers, important tools of his trade, were made there. Having read the words "Saginaw, Michigan" at his tool bench every day for eons, he thought they might make a great song title. So he crafted a harmless, lightweight tale typical of the era—poor boy loves girl; girl's rich father hates boy—and he structured the tale around the dactylic beauty of the city's name. Lefty found the song at Tree Publishing, one of Cedarwood's principal rivals, and thought it had hit potential.

If he could figure out how to sing it. Much wordier than Lefty was used to, "Saginaw, Michigan" cramped his style, forcing clearer articulation and disallowing him room to riff on the vowels. The session was already going badly when, to further distract Lefty, Merle Kilgore showed up with actor George Hamilton. Hamilton was in town filming *Your Cheatin' Heart,* the Hank Williams biopic so blithely unconcerned with Hank's reality that most Nashvillians viewed it as hillbilly science fiction. Nevertheless, though Kilgore and Hamilton took seats unobtrusively in the rear, Lefty could not concentrate on "Saginaw, Michigan" with the star of *Where the Boys Are* in the studio. Already frustrated, session leader Grady Martin finally told Kilgore, "Merle, you and your actor friend will have to leave." Kilgore said Lefty was crushed. Apologizing, he took Hamilton's hand in both of his and squeezed his eyes shut till they squirted tears. Hamilton told Lefty not to take it so hard, he understood. He swore if Lefty Frizzell walked on the set while he was shooting, the same thing would have happened to him.

On November 26, Columbia released the torturously recorded "Saginaw, Michigan" with "When It Rains the Blues" as the B-side. Within days, the record broke, naturally enough, in Saginaw. But soon enough Lefty's new single took off everywhere, and it was scaling the national charts by Christmas. In early January, Norfolk talent buyer Sheriff Tex Davis reported to *Billboard* that "Saginaw, Michigan" was "tearing 'em up in the Norfolk area at the moment." A navy man from Saginaw wrote in a letter to his hometown paper: " 'I just left Cuba and our ship put in at Mayport (Fla.), and in a few days we leave for Europe. Guess what song is played more than any other. . . . Saginaw, Michigan! In Cuba (Guantanamo Naval Base) they wear out a record every few days.' "

Lefty's novelty, the song he initially could barely sing, hit number one in early March and held that position for four weeks. It even cracked the pop chart — the first time that had happened for Lefty since "I Want to Be with You Always." The song received such saturation-level airplay that even the *Saginaw News* grew weary of it. "It may surprise the natives," wrote a staff reporter, "but 'Saginaw, Michigan,' sounded as a three-beat couplet, is considered beautiful euphony." The reporter further noted that hearing Lefty's hit was "no monumental musical experience. . . ."

For Lefty, though, the experience of "Saginaw, Michigan" was indeed monumental. Nearly five years had passed since "The Long Black Veil" last rated him a top-ten artist, and "Saginaw, Michigan" was ten times the hit "The Long Black Veil" had been. The latter had done little to change Lefty's affairs. "Saginaw, Michigan" changed everything. Lefty's stock skyrocketed at the Jim Denny Artists Bureau (which, with Denny's passing, had been renamed Denny-Moeller Talent) and with promoters nationwide. Lucky Moeller now added Lefty to his agency's top package tours, confident that his old friend's name would boost the prestige of a lineup that already included Webb Pierce, Faron Young, Bill Anderson, and Billy Walker. True enough, one of those tours grossed five-figure receipts at a series of February dates in Minneapolis, Des Moines, and at the Keil Auditorium in St. Louis. Lefty Frizzell was back in the big time.

In fact, Lefty's chart resurgence took him by total surprise. He nearly missed the comeback opportunity it afforded him. Whether because of his ulcers, or his other, more constant, ailment, he was out of commission in early December as "Saginaw, Michigan" started to break. On the fifteenth of the month, Alice scribbled a note to a "Mr. Thurston": "Sorry to be so late in sending enclosed check. Lefty has been in the hospital, and I'm just now getting caught up with my book keeping." Lefty's illness, whatever it was, may have cost him a few dates scheduled for early December in Chicago and Springfield, Illinois.

But a much more serious problem revealed itself when Lefty hooked up with the Denny-Moeller package tour. He still couldn't sing his hit. Bill Anderson told James Elliot what happened when the tour played St. Louis:

> Lefty was on the show and "Saginaw, Michigan" was number one in St. Louis and everywhere. And Lefty went out on the show that afternoon at the Keil Auditorium and did his great hits, "Always Late" and "I Love You a Thousand Ways" and "Mom and Dad's Waltz," all the great things from the fifties, and he left the stage. Then the people started hollering, " 'Saginaw, Michigan'! 'Saginaw, Michigan'!" and the emcee brought him back out. And the people are screaming, "Sing 'Saginaw, Michigan'!" and Lefty stood there in front of those people, number one record in the country, and said, "I don't know it."

After five full months on the charts, however, Lefty did, if nothing else, learn "Saginaw, Michigan" by heart. At least one mid-sixties film clip shows him rocking on his boot heels while gliding through the song. In early March, he broke away from the Denny-Moeller package tour to play a series of one- and two-nighters through Alabama and Mississippi. Then it was up the Atlantic Coast from Virginia to Worcester, Massachusetts, and west to Toronto. He covered Texas in early April and the Midwest later that month. On April 29, Lefty, Johnny Cash, and several other major stars played to 20,000 horse-racing fans during Derby Week in Louisville. Columbia Records flew in equipment to capture the Derby show live. Lefty was so hot again that when a reporter asked him how much road work he'd been doing, Lefty responded: "I have been on the road so much lately, that the other day, when I had a couple days off, I had just climbed in bed and fallen asleep when the wife walked in and turned on the light. I sat up in bed and was half way through my theme song before I realized where I was."

On May 23, he finally hit Saginaw, Michigan, itself. Along with Bobby Bare, Hank Snow, Billy Walker, and the Willis Brothers, Lefty played the downtown auditorium in the northern city the mere name of which hundreds of thousands of country fans considered beautiful euphony. Billy Walker rode to Saginaw with Lefty. He remembers the city so overrun with fans that the two of them couldn't find a vacant hotel room anywhere. Shut out of one too many Saginaw lodgings, Lefty told Walker he had an idea. At the next hotel, he told Billy to stay in the car while he disappeared inside. A few minutes later, Lefty reappeared and told Walker everything was fixed. "Just be sure to limp real bad when you walk through the lobby," he said. Lefty had scored them a room with a story about Walker being a wounded war veteran. Later that night, when the Nudie-suited pair left the hotel to head for the show, Walker forgot about his debilitating wound. He cruised on past the front desk in standup country style. Realizing the blunder, Lefty smiled at the desk clerk. "See what a little rest can do?" he drawled.

That night, during Lefty's turn on the bill, the grateful mayor of Saginaw surprised him with a commemorative trophy: a silver gavel-like hammer. Still singing, Lefty didn't understand what was happening. As the beaming politician approached, all Lefty could see from the corner of his eye was a stranger, possibly a heckler, coming at him with a hammer. When the mayor reached him, Lefty threw him into a left-handed headlock and wrestled him to the stage floor. The boys at the Dallas Sportatorium would have been proud. "I wouldn't have done it if it had been the key to the city," Lefty said. "But no, they gave me a damn hammer."

Chapter 26

YEARS HAD PASSED since Lefty received as much attention or made as much money as he did in the wake of "Saginaw, Michigan." Easily one of the year's top country hits, it earned Lefty his one and only Grammy nomination. (He lost to Bobby Bare and "Detroit City." All things considered, it was a good year for Michigan.) A Lefty album called *Saginaw, Michigan* was also a hit, reaching number two on the country LP list the same week Lefty bulldogged the mayor of Saginaw. Lefty's talent fee increased, record royalties poured in, and so did writer royalties from album cuts and the single's B-side, "When It Rains the Blues." Had deejay practices been as wide open as they were in 1951, had the jocks been willing to flip the record over just to see what would happen, the refined "When It Rains the Blues" might have given Lefty another double-sided hit.

The turnaround in his fortunes also provided Lefty with more video exposure. He started getting calls from syndicated programs like Porter Wagoner's, and he cameoed in a couple of country exploitation flicks, *Second Fiddle to an Old Guitar* and *The Road to Nashville*. Both were of the C-grade type that pickers referred to as "hay-balers."

But the major difference between 1951 and 1964 was that Lefty better appreciated the value of the money he was bringing home. He had already known the exhilaration of heedless spending, the instant gratification of owning a long black Cadillac within hours of seeing it. But he had also known what it was like to come down from that high to work Barstow boneyards for thirty-five dollars a night, to have to jump rent on a $125 suburban shack with a broken living room lamp. When the money poured in from "Saginaw, Michigan," Lefty invested in property. In November of '64, he bought a pair of verdant side-by-side lots at Station Camp on Old Hickory Lake. Two months later, he and Merle Kilgore went in on a couple of Victorian houses on 18th Avenue in Nashville, two blocks west of the very heart of Music Row. The purchase was a gamble. But Lefty and Kilgore had seen the kind of money hotshots like Owen Bradley and Chet Atkins made playing the Music Row real estate game.

Within a year of buying the two buildings, Lefty expanded his music industry dealings to include a publishing company. Started with Mulkey, and with Houston singer-songwriter Eddie Noack hired to run the office, it was every bit as sound a decision as buying up Music Row property. As 16th Avenue grew more economically sophisticated, many of the top songwriters developed sufficient business savvy to realize they'd be better off controlling their own copyrights. Not all agreed. Some figured the tradeoff in low administrative hassle was worth giving up their publishing rights, but others jumped headlong into the fray by starting their own small firms to compete with the Trees and Cedarwoods. Marijohn Wilkin, for instance, left Cedarwood and created Buckhorn Music with Bill Justis. Harlan Howard started Wilderness. Lefty called his company Golden Eye. Supposedly, he got the name from a one-eyed Music Row hanger-on who liked to pop his glass eye out and show it off to musician friends. "Here's the real golden eye," he'd say.

Ironically, the first Golden Eye song Lefty would record — "Writing on the Wall" — was not one he or Abe had written. It was by Bruce Delaney, "an old ranch kid from Montana" who David Frizzell had befriended while the two were both in the Air Force. David and Delaney had played in a country band together while stationed in Klamath, California, and would move to Nashville in the fall of 1965. After staying with Lefty for a time, Delaney and David went their separate ways. Delaney moved back to Montana, and was surprised when Lefty called him at Christmas that year and said he was going to cut "Writing on the Wall."

"That Christmas he called me up," Delaney recalls, "and said that he was gonna cut the song and asked me if I'd like to come back. He said he was starting Golden Eye, and would I like to come back and go to work for him."

In some respects it was an unlikely alliance. Ranch kid or not, Delaney had pronounced countercultural tendencies ("His hair was way longer than the Beatles'," says Marlon Frizzell) at a time when such fashion was not exactly the norm in Music City. Nevertheless, Lefty, who no one ever accused of being a conformist, hired Delaney to write for Golden Eye, and eventually to run the company and pitch songs after Noack (who was an excellent, well-liked writer but had a terrible drinking problem) proved ineffective. Thus, with his small support staff in place, Lefty rented a first-floor office on 16th Avenue and entered the publishing business.

Of course, Lefty Frizzell, music industry player, was still the same ol' Lefty. His twenty-mile business treks from Hendersonville to Nashville were often no more than a cover for his need to get out of the house. After an epic battle with Alice, he'd head to the Row and drop in on writers and song pluggers—ostensibly looking for material, but really just looking for company. Sometimes he'd check into a motel and stay in town overnight. Other times, he would crash at the East Nashville home of his old friend Judy Baker, who, with Hank Snow's help, had moved from Corpus Christi several years before Lefty arrived in town. Lefty doted on Judy's son, Rocky, teaching him string stricks and card tricks and—who but Lefty would try this on a kid?—how to emcee a show. Another of Lefty's favorite hideouts was Harlan Howard's 17th Avenue office. Lefty and Howard's manager, Don Davis, "cracked each other up," according to Howard, with combat stories of life on the road. But Lefty also enjoyed telling combat stories from life on Old Hickory Lake. "He'd come in with his bottle of vodka," said Howard, "griping about how Alice had been abusing him again just because he come home late at night drunk.

"He had a great sense of humor," Howard adds, "I mean aside from his singing, which I thought was some of the most original I've ever heard. I always thought he was strange and unique. He sang hard, he played hard. But to me, I just remember how much he made me laugh. He didn't tell jokes; his ad-libs, or even just talking about his domestic troubles was funny. You know, and I mean just his description of what Alice said to him, and what he said, and blah blah blah. Just his story-telling was great."

One of Lefty's favorite stories to tell was of a war he and Alice waged with a bamboo stick. It started after he and several of his cronies, out whooping it up one night, came back to Lefty's house to continue the party. Rickey Frizzell met his father at the door and told him to watch out for Alice. While he was out, she had opened some of his fan mail and found a few letters from women who were obviously more than fans. "I'm telling you," Rickey warned him, "don't go in there; she's mad." Lefty wasn't about to be scared away from his own house with his friends watching, so while they headed into the den, he went look-ing for Alice. As he entered their bedroom, the door closed behind him and something whizzed past his ear. He spun around and saw his wife coming at him with a thick bamboo stick. Lefty grabbed the stick, trying to fend her off, but Alice kept swinging. As he later told the story, he held on for dear life, his flailing legs waving behind him. Finally, Alice buckled and counter-thrust with the bamboo, catching her husband square in the nuts. Lefty hit the floor. Moaning in agony, his ear pressed to the carpet, all he could hear was one of his friends downstairs asking over and over again, in a mock—Peter Lorre accent, "Wheeerz Lef-tee? Wheeerz Lef-tee?"

While Lefty reveled in telling such tales, he did manage to work business into his cheery days on the Row. Howard, for one, was too smart to let Lefty's visits pass with no more than comedy routines. He'd pitch a song, and if Lefty liked it, he'd turn around and pitch it to Don Law for double impact. "When I had 'em both liking the song, chances are I was on the session," he says. And so it was that in February 1965, preparing for a two-day album session at the Columbia studio, Howard had Lefty and Law liking three of his songs. One would be Lefty's next hit; another would be as transcendent a non-hit as he ever recorded.

The hit-to-be was an uptempo, self-explanatory number called "She's Gone Gone Gone." Like so many of Lefty's mid-sixties productions, it kicked off with a clear-rung guitar intro melding into the opening line. But this time, what really lingered was the chorus—a powerful harmony duet that Lefty and Mulkey cut live in the studio. Lefty's style was so unique and specific, so easy to imitate in theory but impossible to duplicate in actuality, that he had rarely had much luck with harmony. But he and Mulkey now had spent over two years together to perfect a tandem sound. With Law's blessing, they eschewed the tired vocal chorus for most of the album and instead exploited their harmonic finesse. Howard was impressed by the partners' on-mike precision, and startled by how completely Mulkey had absorbed Lefty's sound. "God, he almost sang more like Lefty than Lefty did," Howard said.

Abe and Lefty were also well-represented as songwriters, as were Kilgore and Wayne Walker. The album (which would be released that summer as *The Sad Side of Love*) even included a remake of "Stranger" that was better than the original. But of all the songs included, the most staggering was "How Far Down Can I Go," a slow, honky-tonk drinker's confession that Howard provided. When he wrote it (with co-writer J. C. Barney), Howard was thinking of his father, a West Virginia native who moved to Detroit to take a job with General Motors. The city, says Howard, "kind of blew him away." A philanderer and heavy drinker, the old man came to a tragic end on Skid Row. "I mean, lost a beautiful woman and three good kids . . . and wound up drinking Thunderbird."

Though Lefty had reached a point where he no longer felt comfortable addressing his drinking in song, something about Howard's plainspoken hard country lyrics—something in the visceral honesty of the story of a man who knows his life is "out of control"—commanded his attention and inspired one of the most harrowing performances of his life. Part of the credit was due Don Law and his young partner, Frank Jones. They stripped the production of all showy gloss and extraneous sound, permitting Lefty's voice, buoyed by Pete Drake's mordant steel guitar, to utterly enfold the lyrics. When he sang, "my hands get to trem . . . bl . . . ing . . . so . . . ," it was as if he was staring straight into his shaky palms, trying to read some larger meaning in the betrayal their violent tremors revealed. Lefty could always laugh aside his most dangerous problems because part of him existed in a dream world of childlike whimsy. ("I'm a professional puker," he told his nephew Jimmy. "I can puke out one side of my mouth and tell a joke out the other.") If he didn't function in the real world, he didn't have to acknowledge when it was killing him. But singing was a different matter. Singing *was* his real world. All the suffering he denied on a day-to-day basis could be confronted with guitar in hand, which was why his most volcanic emotions were often spent in the play of his quietest numbers, and why on a song like "How Far Down Can I Go," Lefty Frizzell had no equal. None. In fifteen years on record to that point, his voice had stitched sincere emotion into the hearts of all who would hold their breath long enough truly to listen. But never had that voice sounded quite so scarily self-aware.

And yet, in a repeat of what was becoming a disturbingly frequent occurrence, Lefty's uncompromising work on "How Far Down Can I Go" went virtually unheard. "Stranger" had been met with radio silence in 1962. "When It Rains the Blues" had been ignored amid the commotion caused by the novelty "Saginaw, Michigan." Lefty's best work from the "Saginaw" follow-up session in January 1964, a tune he wrote with Mulkey called "Hello to Him (Goodbye to Me)" had been held back as an album cut while Don Wayne's unimpressive "The Nester" got the nod as a single. Likewise, "How Far Down Can I Go" was buried as an album track while the less intense, though by no means undeserving, "She's Gone Gone Gone" got the deejay push. Lefty probably didn't mind. Especially not as "She's Gone Gone Gone" cruised up the charts to a crest just shy of the top ten. But there was no denying that he had put his soul on the line with "How Far Down Can I Go," and no ignoring that someone—maybe Law, maybe his superiors—would not release it to radio.

Once "She's Gone Gone Gone" fell out of sight, after a solid three-month run, Lefty again lost his career momentum. His name, despite the continued high quality of his singles, sunk lower and lower on the charts. "A Little Unfair," "Writing on the Wall," "I Just Couldn't See the Forest (For the Trees)" and "You Gotta Be Puttin' Me On" were all recorded in 1965–66. All were worthy of Lefty's voice. None cracked the top forty. The disappointment struck at every financial level. The fine but weak-selling "Writing on the Wall," provided by Delaney, and "I Just Couldn't See the Forest (For the Trees)," co-written by Delaney and Lefty, were both Golden Eye songs. The tunes Delaney co-wrote with Lefty and/or Abe were among the strongest in Golden Eye's catalog, but without airplay or sales, they garnered little money for Lefty's publishing company. Neither did the songs that Lefty and Mulkey co-wrote, most of which were set aside as album cuts, B-sides, or unreleased takes. By 1967, it was clear that Golden Eye was about as functional as the glass eye for which it was named.

"It was really a shame," says Delaney, "because I was a long-haired old kid . . . and led kind of a guarded existence because it was during the war. You know, Lefty needed somebody in there that knew what they were doing, and also that was much more gregarious than I was. So I didn't do much good for him. I went down there and went in the office every day, and I took some songs around, but I didn't do him much good."

The failure of Golden Eye aside, Lefty's career took its deadliest shot in early 1967, when Don Law retired as head of Columbia's Nashville office. The good-humored Englishman had been an advocate for Lefty since the day they met in Dallas. He had heard the uniqueness in Lefty's style and signed him when others only wanted his songs. He had championed Lefty's career throughout, selflessly advising the confused young singer, and fighting for him when Columbia's front office lost faith. For many singers, not just Lefty, Law had been the consummate artist's producer, a man whose hit-making prowess had everything to do with respecting the musical integrity of the performers he signed. "That was the beauty of Don Law," Ray Price once said. "He let an artist be an artist, and not what he wanted them to be."

And yet it wasn't just a matter of professional relationships. The two of them, producer and artist, were above all else great friends. Lefty loved Don Law, and the feeling was mutual.

"Of all the artists I have worked with during my 40 years with Columbia Records," Law would one day write, "Lefty Frizzell was the most colorful and exhilarating. He was really a unique person; warm, lovable, generous, funny and extremely talented." Looking back on their early years together, Law said of Lefty, "He was never on time for a session and sometimes did not show up at all, having fallen by the wayside somewhere. However, once we got organized, the sessions were a riot. Thanks to Lefty's exuberance and keen sense of humor everyone had a ball, and we made some darned good records."

They would make them no more. Having reached compulsory retirement age, Law stepped aside for the modernist Bob Johnston, who produced Bob Dylan's Nashville records. Though a few of Columbia's better-selling acts were able to retain Law as an independent producer, Lefty was not among them. It would take a while for the new Columbia power relationships to shake down (ultimately resulting in the ascendency of the moody commercial wizard Billy Sherrill), but in March 1967, as Johnston took over as number one man, it was not he, or Sherrill, but Law's handpicked successor, Frank Jones, who produced Lefty's first session under the new regime.

Which made for an initially smooth transition. Triumphant, in fact. For the first song Lefty cut that evening was among his most emotionally charged recordings of the entire decade. Called "Get This Stranger Out of Me," the song is a plea for passion's renewal. It was written by A. L. "Doodle" Owens, a Waco, Texas, transplant just then starting to make his mark on Music Row. Known to hang around the Beck studio in the old days, he hadn't actually met Lefty till after a Waco concert in 1963, when he nervously introduced himself as a songwriter. At the time, Lefty cut right through Owens's shyness to befriend him. "I'm not like the rest of the singers," Lefty said. "I don't push songwriters away." About a year later, fed up with scraping by as a sign painter in Texas, Owens moved to Nashville to try to make it instead as a 16th Avenue tunesmith. "I waited till everybody in Waco said I'd never move," he recalls, "and I got a trailer one morning, about six o'clock in the morning, went up and got my wife, and said 'We're moving to Tennessee.' "

Signed to Forest Hills Music, Owens wrote "Get This Stranger Out of Me" for torrid-voiced Connie Smith, who turned it down. "She thought it was kind of dirty," he says. It wasn't till later, after Owens had moved to Hill & Range's Nashville office, that Lefty heard it. "I played that song for him," Owens says, "and he just bottomed out over it. And he played it for George Jones, and a couple other people. He loved the song."

What Lefty was thinking while singing "Get This Stranger Out of Me" is impossible to know. But he surely must have heard echoes of his own tormented life within Owens's simple lyrics and haunting melody. His delivery sounded like he meant the song as a naked plea to Alice to save his soul—and their marriage—not through holy spirit but through blessed earthly desire. The same lines Connie Smith heard as dirty, Lefty sang as supernal. "I never will forget that, when he did 'Get This Stranger Out of Me,' " Owens says. "I was getting chills."

Released during hippie America's so-called "Summer of Love," "Get This Stranger Out of Me" peaked at number sixty-three on the country charts and fell off after four weeks, the single most inexplicable commercial failure of Lefty's career. As for Alice, whether she considered his plea sincere or not didn't make much difference. For she was headed down a different path of righteousness, where Lefty could not follow.

Chapter 27

IN THE YEARS IMMEDIATELY after he received an original Jimmie Rodgers guitar at the first annual Rodgers Memorial Festival, Hank Snow's son, Jimmie Rodgers Snow, (or Jimmy, as he would later spell his name), grew to manhood in the spirit of rock-and-roll prodigality, indulging his habit of pills and booze while befriending the likes of Elvis Presley, Bill Haley, and Gene Vincent. After one especially soul-rending binge, he later wrote, he fell to his knees by his parents' mailbox and prayed to God to forgive him. God did more than that; He called Jimmy Snow to His divine service. From that day forward, the former Nashville gadabout walked a spiritual path, taking to evangelical ministry with the same resolve that had fired his father's rise to country stardom. In 1961, Brother Jimmy Snow made national headlines when one of his favorite sermons — a fire and brimstone blast against the demonic music called rock and roll — precipitated a bonfire of burning records in Plant City, Florida.

After four more years of Bible-thumping tent revivals, Jimmy Snow came home to Nashville to start Evangel Temple, an Assembly of God church located on Dickerson Road, not far from the Starday complex. Initial services were held in an office building while Brother Snow solicited bond money from his Opry acquaintances to pay for construction of a real church. He envisioned one with "good acoustics [and] with plenty of electrical outlets around the platform for a band." As soon as the foundation was laid, Jimmy Snow moved his congregation to the construction site and began holding services at what would, in short time, come to be nicknamed the "Church of the Stars." Billy Walker was the first of the stars to join Evangel Temple. Then, as

Brother Snow told it in his autobiography: "Lefty and Alice Frizzell came next. Alice was saved but Lefty never joined."

Actually, Lois Frizzell came next, not Alice—and definitely not Lefty. And before Lois came Barbara Miller, wife of soon-to-be-saved-himself Eddie Miller. As Lois recalls:

> Barbara Miller invited me to come to church. And I went. We'd always gone to Presbyterian churches. We never were into religion. I mean we were into God. We were taught to believe in God, because Mama and Daddy believed in God. And they were just normal, you know, they weren't extreme. We were taught to say our prayers at night, and we went to Presbyterian Bible—vacation Bible school—and stuff like that.
>
> But when Barbara invited me I went. And I got saved. It was powerful. I mean it was something I'd never experienced in my whole life. It filled such a void, it just . . . it was bigger than I was, and it was so magnificent to me that I had to go home and tell everybody, you know. It was like I wanted to tell the world what God really was.
>
> I'm gonna tell you, up to this day, it was real . . . he was incredible. Man, he was an awesome preacher when he was young, and vibrant, and full of fire.

Lois came back to the house that day and solemnly gathered her family around her in the living room. "My whole life is changed," she announced. Lefty, a bit exasperated by the big production, impatiently demanded, "What? What is it?"

"My whole life is changed," Lois repeated. "I've—I've got saved."

She then proceeded to proselytize on behalf of Evangel Temple and its pastor, Brother Jimmy Snow. "Of course Daddy immediately was critical," says Marlon Frizzell. " 'Cause he knew him, and said that the only reason Jimmy was a preacher was 'cause he couldn't make it in music." Alice, too, thought her daughter had fallen off her rocker. But Lois kept after her lost and forsaken family ("I hassled 'em, and hassled 'em, and hassled 'em") until Alice relented. Warily, she and the boys, but not Lefty, attended an evening service at Evangel Temple. There, with the Lord working through Jimmy Snow, the spirit hit them hard. When Brother Snow issued the altar call, the Frizzells didn't walk, they ran—with Alice out front—down the aisle to salvation. Life at Lefty's house would never be the same.

The initial impact was monetary. Despite his recent attempts to act businesslike, Lefty never knew how much money he had in his pocket, let alone in the bank. Alice handled their personal finances—which now included church offerings. Some say very *large* church offerings.

One of Lefty's friends estimated a total of approximately $30,000. Brother Snow, on the other hand, recalled that Alice may have bought $2,000 worth of construction bonds, but that otherwise she rarely had much money to give the church if, indeed, she had wanted to. "[Lefty] got upset about her coming to service, period," Snow said. "And if she gave five dollars, it would have been five million to him."

Lefty, of course, had a long history of merrily giving money away. But having earned it with his own sweat, he considered it his prerogative to waste it himself, as he saw fit. And tithing to a church, the minister of which was a man he did not respect, was not Lefty's idea of appropriate spending. But how could a sinner like him object? All he could do was grumble as the church rose on Dickerson Road, much as he grumbled every time he drove past the Starday building.

And money was only half the issue anyway. Dollars came and dollars went as they always had. Such was the life of a country singer born behind an oil well. Lefty had no real need of riches. As he approached his fortieth birthday, all he really wanted was to write, sing, and fish on the lake. ("Spit on the worm," he'd advise a novice, "it gets him used to the water.") Stationed with rod and reel behind the house, drinking beer instead of the straight vodka that meant trouble, Lefty could unwind and enjoy life. A barbecue in the park did him wonders, as did a ride on one of his boats, even the one he called "the submarine" in honor of its seaworthiness. Often he wanted less than that—just to sit with his arm around Alice, watching TV, or maybe to read one of the newspapers and history books with which he educated himself, or the *Fate* magazines on which he'd come to rely to ease the tedium of the road. He had changed since he lived in Northridge in the 1950s, when he wanted to stay at home but wanted his backyard blowouts too. He still loved to drink and shoot the bull with his buddies, but now part of him ached for an easy, peaceful life. After twenty years, for all the madness their love could resemble, he and Alice knew how to live with each other. They had their fights. But they loved each other, and understood each other, and nothing could ever really come between them.

Or so Lefty thought. But Evangel Temple upset their singular twenty-year balance. Alice's rebirth in Christ confronted Lefty with a spiritual rift that neither his drinking and infidelity, nor Alice's volatile temper, had ever produced. "They were great until I messed things up," Lois says with a sigh.

With his children saved, and growing older anyway, Lefty found himself totally isolated within his own family. At times he could barely recognize his wife and kids. For instance, one night Rickey came home all aglow from a Bible trip during which he'd been filled with the holy spirit to the point of speaking in tongues. When he told his family the wondrous good news, Lefty, disgusted, threw up his hands, and said, "They're brainwashed. Rickey could walk across the road and get hit by a car, 'cause he don't know what he's doing. He's out of his head."

Another time, it was Marlon who tormented him. Lefty's son came home from church and could tell his father had been drinking. "Daddy, man, you might go to hell or something," he said. Lefty spat, "Daddamn it!" and disappeared into the bedroom, slamming the door behind him. But Marlon would not be ignored so easily. He pounded on the door, and yelled, "You're demon possessed!"

The door flew open. Lefty, just as he had done with Lois many years before, grabbed Marlon by the throat and threw him to the floor. Marlon kept yelling, "You've a demon in you! Demon!" But this time Lefty didn't need anybody to pull him off his child. More disgruntled than angry, he let go of Marlon and stormed back into his room.

As for Alice, it was as if her twenty years of strained tolerance had finally given way. Throwing herself into church life with a late convert's fervor, she could no longer countenance Lefty's behavior at all. Drinking around her was now completely out of the question. "Mama used to drink beer and smoke cigarettes," says Marlon, ". . . but after that Mama got to where it was like, 'Lefty's going to hell.' And her whole life became consumed by that. Forever. To the very end."

To his credit, Lefty did make a few conciliatory gestures. He attended a few Evangel Temple services and even sang in the Opry-swelled choir. Once, at home, he fell to his knees in the kitchen and was saved right there among the pots and pans. He signed and dated a Bible that Alice kept, and noted: "I was saved this day."

"He meant it," Marlon says. "He meant it."

But by and large, Lefty responded to his family's newfound holiness with bitter resentment. With Alice intolerant of his vices, he sought more and more frequent refuge at friends' houses, or alone in the den with his bottle. While he drank no harder than he ever had, his isolation added a paranoid edge to his heaviest bouts. In 1967, after activist Stokely Carmichael spent two days making speeches in Nashville, riots broke out in one of the city's major black neighborhoods. The same happened, though on a lesser scale than in many cities, a year later when the Reverend Martin Luther King Jr. was assassinated. During that unrest, a curfew was declared and the Grand Ole Opry was canceled for the first time in its history. Twenty-five miles away in suburban Hendersonville, Lefty heard teenage laughter and voices drifting through his back window from Sanders Ferry Park, a popular hangout across the narrow cove from his house. In his disoriented state, Lefty thought the rioters would be swimming across the water any minute. Preparing for the worst, he strapped on a pistol, a blackjack, a .22 rifle, and a pair of handcrafted Mexican knives he had bought on one of his trips south of the border. When Alice and Marlon arrived home that night from an Evangel Temple prayer meeting, they wondered why all the lights were out in the house. They walked into the garage and turned one on. There was Lefty, decked out like a warrior. "Turn that light out!" he yelled, and warned them of the impending nautical attack. "That's ridiculous," Alice snorted. Lefty responded by throwing one of the mini-machetes past her into the wooden door. Alice marched him straight to the hospital.

Lefty knew it did him no good to drink alone. And he hated to be by himself anyway, so he would drop in on Judy Baker, sometimes staying for a week or two. Their relationship had, according to Judy, been platonic for many years. "There was lovemaking going on until I met my husband," she says, "then it was just a deep love, 'cause I realized then that Lefty was married. See, and I didn't want to break that up. No, I wouldn't have done that. No, the feeling was there, but it was such a deep feeling . . . but it was all sort of understood. Just bein' together. Whether we held hands, or just looked at each other, or sang. It was a deep, understanding love." Judy was grateful that Alice seemed to accept the friendship without much protest. Lefty was grateful, too, for Judy and Rocky provided him with a separate, more tolerant home environment where he could retreat from the world, have a drink, and speak his mind without fear of reprisal. For he, no less than Alice, had ideas about such high philosophical matters as faith, preachers, and evolution. (Lefty: "If we had developed from the apes, why do we still have the damn apes?")

One night at Judy's, he and a couple of buddies got together over homemade wine to debate precisely those issues — and others — down to such fine points as the meaning of birthmarks, and "where our people of different colors come from." While others proffered various bizarre anthropological theories, Lefty's basic position was scriptural non-argument. "We shouldn't be concerned with these things," he said, "since [the Bible] don't tell about it." (On the other hand, Lefty, married himself to a woman at least one quarter Cherokee, did wonder if this was the first time in history that there had been mixing of the races.)

Discussion then turned to other matters, such as whether Abraham

Lincoln had been assassinated because he freed the slaves. "No, no, no!" Lefty said. "He wasn't assassinated on account of he freed a few colored people. Oh no. That was politics of other things in the future. They killed him on account of bills to be passed. . . . He didn't even free the damn slaves, if you wanna know a fact. . . . He had nothin' to do with it actually. But he got credit for it. That's another fact. Abraham Lincoln never freed a damn slave in his life."

The talk of slavery opened a whole new topic. "Today it's no different," said one of Lefty's sparring partners. "Big corporations has got the working man under a thumb like that today; the people aren't even free. They're slaves. There's just as many white people enslaved today."

"Oh, hell—more!" interjected Lefty, the roughneck's son. "There's more white people, so there's more. No, no, we're not—no one's differin' with you there a-tall. We've known that since when I was a little bitty child; I knew that. See, you're bringin' up something here that we've all known, and we've lived with, but we don't talk about it no more. There ain't nothin' free. Nothin's free.

"Washington never did free the country," Lefty added. "They all fought for their ideals, but it's never happened and never will. They tried. So we keep strugglin' along, we talk about it, and it won't happen till the good Lord comes down, and the final battle."

Back home, some sort of battle was unavoidable. And sure enough, Lefty's resentment of Brother Snow's hold on his family turned to white-hot anger when Alice returned from church one day, walked through the door, and told her husband: "I want a divorce."

Certainly, marriage counseling is one of the valuable functions a good minister performs for his congregation. In Brother Snow's case, the counseling demands were compounded by the difficulties of administering to a star-studded flock. "Marriage trouble is a disease in this music community," he once told a fellow preacher. "I wish I had a dollar for every hour I've listened to marriage problems."

Over time, though, many in the Nashville music community started to note what they thought, rightly or wrongly, was a rather high incidence of divorce among the Evangel Temple worshipers. People started to wonder just what sort of advice Jimmy Snow was giving. Lefty had at least one close friend whose marriage had abruptly ended, allegedly thanks to the reverend's "counseling," so when his own wife walked in from church one day and demanded a divorce, Lefty felt pretty sure he knew who put the idea in her head. Sure enough, Alice freely acknowledged that Brother Snow had advised her.

It's impossible to pin down precisely what happened next, though a basic chain of events emerges from the variant versions of a story gleefully told and retold by nearly every last person who knew Lefty in the sixties and seventies. In his autobiography, Snow himself quoted a Nashville wag who said, "[Jimmy] Snow stories are almost as common as Polish jokes." The story involving Lefty is among many musicians' favorites. According to Marlon, who was at the house the day of the confrontation, Lefty sat and fumed in silence for a while, drinking alone while contemplating the reverend's gall. It was one thing to take his hard-earned money — but now to tell Alice to divorce him . . . After Lefty had sufficient time to think about that, he called the church. When Snow got on the line, Lefty said, "Jimmy, this is Lefty. Why did you tell my wife to get a divorce?"

"God told me to," Snow solemnly answered.

"Oh yeah?" Lefty said. "Well did God tell you I was gonna come kick your ass?"

Lefty hung up and headed for the front door. Alice tried to stop him, as did Marlon, who grabbed at his father and pleaded, "Please don't beat up Brother Snow, Daddy! Please don't beat up the minister!" Half an hour or so later, as certain versions of the story go, Lefty crashed a prayer meeting at Evangel Temple. Brother Snow saw him coming and acted quickly to defuse Lefty's rage. He suggested they step into his back office, where they could talk about the problem like adults. Whether because Lefty never really meant to kick the reverend's ass, or because, once there, he felt too keenly the sacrilege of pounding a preacher inside the House of God, Lefty apparently chewed out Brother Snow but didn't beat him up. Whether Jimmy Snow continued to counsel Alice about her marriage after that is unknown. He insists he never counseled her in the first place, and also says he has no recollection of the incident with Lefty. In his autobiography, though, he does offer that Lefty "was a real old-timer around Nashville and had a lot of big hits."

DISCOVERY II

Chapter 28

THE 1960S had but a few months left when one totally accidental smash hit record brought the decade's cultural fragmentation into clear, final, dispiriting focus in America. It wasn't by the Beatles and it wasn't by Jimi Hendrix and it wasn't by Bob Dylan either. The song was by Merle Haggard. It was called "Okie from Muskogee," and the blue-collar roadhouse din of it rose above the "smile on yer brother" and "give peace a chance"'s of the decade's close like notes bent and slung from an ugly American underground. People didn't request it, they reached out and yanked it from Haggard's throat. It terrified him. The first time he sang "Okie from Muskogee" live was to Green Berets at the Fort Bragg, North Carolina, NCO club. The brave men "who jump and die" jumped and stormed the stage.

Musically speaking, it was as if Haggard had enfranchised the guardians of an entire cultural underclass, the homesick boys with a war to fight and no one to sing them "Soldier's Last Letter." These were the men who cared less about Bob Hope or the Doors than they did about whatever ragtag cover band braved the jungle to sing them "Ode to Billie Joe." If humidity killed the amplifiers, so be it. The same men cheered for young Barbara Mandrell, known as the "Sweetheart of Steel," when she toured Vietnam. One of them—a black soldier—asked her to sing "Danny Boy" as he lay dying before her. They raised their bottles to Christine Kittrell, a Nashville R&B singer who nearly lost her leg when the makeshift club she was stomping the blues inside of was shelled. And the same men screamed and hollered when into their midst, momentarily deflecting their fear, came Lois Frizzell with her father, Lefty.

Lois talked Lefty into coming. She was already a seasoned veteran of the fire base entertainment circuit, having arrived in Vietnam during the bloody Tet Offensive of 1968, when fighting reached the American Embassy in Saigon and the marines were pinned down at Khe Sanh. Using her stage name, Leta Frizzell, and decked out in miniskirt and go-go boots, she fronted a Las Vegas outfit called the Donny James Band that specialized in covering the country hits of the day, just as Lefty had done back in Big Spring and Roswell. The band toured seven days a week, playing flatbed truck shows at bases where Hope's USO entourage dared not travel, jungle camps where the imperiled clubs took VC mortar like everything else during the Tet Offensive. Riding in their rickety VW bus, trying to reach their Saigon villa, Lois and the band would break through barricades, everybody except the hunched-over driver stretched across the floorboard while tracer bullets buzzed through the windows.

Lefty's daughter saw men she had partied with at night get blown from the sky come morning. She worked morale gigs at the medicine tents where "guys would come up in their wheelchairs, their pajamas, and half their intestines in plastic bags pinned to the pajamas." Her job was to cheer them up. One soldier Lois never forgot was a nineteen-year-old boy who'd lost half his face and body when he fell on a mine.

I could see him over there across the room, and he wouldn't look at me.

Because he was humiliated, because he was tore all to pieces. And I waltzed over there in my miniskirt, and boots-were-made-for-walking boots, and I jumped up on his lap, and put my arm around him, and I said, "Man, what's your favorite song, what do you wanna hear? Or do you just wanna sit and talk and hang out?" 'Cause I was the same age as these guys. So, he got to crying, and he just said, "I'm embarrassed, I didn't want you to see me." And I said, "Why?" He said, "Well look at me. Half of me's gone, and missing. I'm only nineteen years old. Have nothing to live for. Nothing to go home for." And I told him basically he was full of shit, you know. And I laughed, I said, "Ho! You've got to be kidding! You're only nineteen? Man, you can do a million, billion things with your life, you know?" And he was sittin' in that wheelchair, and by the time I left, and I had told him jokes, and messed with him for a long time. Singin' and carryin' on. And by the time I left he was laughin' and carryin' on, 'cause I told him dirty jokes, and all kinds of stuff. Told him he was full of shit, you know. . . . Then before I left, I went back over and hugged his neck, kissed him, and I said, "So how long you got before you go home?" And he said, "You know, I'm gonna go home now." I said, "Cool, man, that's great."

And now Lois was back with Lefty for more. When she suggested playing Vietnam, he didn't hesitate to accept. The in-country tours, deadly though they were, paid well. And Lefty was bored anyway. Not exactly bursting with swelled-chest patriotism (though not completely lacking it either), Lefty knew that Vietnam would be much more dramatic and interesting than the blue highway state fair circuit. And certainly more dramatic than the tour of Germany he had completed in 1968, when he and Frankfurt backup band Frank Yonco and the Texas Drifters barnstormed the American military bases. The German tour had torn him up. By the time he hit the NCO club in Nelligen, he had "a bad case of flu" and could hardly speak. "He really did a fine job in spite of his hoarseness," noted a local reporter. "This was possible because he selected his songs very carefully." (The song "requested constantly" by Lefty's overseas audience was "Cigarettes and Coffee Blues." He did not "select" it.)

Lois's Vietnam agent was Lee Maynard of VIP Shows, one of the largest outfits supplying talent to the military bases. He booked Lefty a room at the Embassy Hotel, a politicos' hangout next to the presidential palace in Saigon, and arranged his jungle gigs. Donny James, not Maynard, did the actual promoting. The billing read "Donny James Presents Lefty Frizzell." A sharp leader, James had worked with Buck Owens and Merle Haggard in Bakersfield. In Vietnam he organized a weekly AFRTS-TV show called "The Nashville Vietnam Show." The variety program aired all over South Vietnam on Saturday night from nine to ten. James, Lois, and the rest of the band were the mainstays; each week adding, as volunteer headliners, any big-time acts who were in Saigon. It didn't matter who they were, or what kind of entertainment they offered. "The Nashville Vietnam Show" hosted anyone from Russian choristers to Lefty Frizzell, to Mr. French himself, Sebastian Cabot.

Lefty was so bored at home he actually arrived in Vietnam *early*. His tour was booked for all of March 1969, but he and Lois flew in a month ahead, the two of them stopping in Alaska along the way. From Alaska to Saigon, they played cards. Lefty cheated. "Do you see me cheating?" he would say, ever so righteously indignant.

Lefty and Lee Maynard, like Lefty and most human beings he met, became instant friends, and spent the entire month of February carousing in Saigon. It wasn't, says Maynard, the same Vietnam that people saw in their stateside living rooms, at least not yet. "When they watch the Vietnam War on television . . . ," he said, "they can't picture a scenario like this: Lefty and I sitting with a couple of GI's in a gourmet French restaurant, in Saigon, with waiters with white jackets on." Lefty was drinking, of course, but left the women alone—even when sorely tempted to do otherwise. Basically, says Maynard, they were just having a monthlong carefree good time. "Just runnin' wild and loose." He and Lefty even fooled around with writing a song together. It was called "I'm Runnin', But I'm Goin' Nowhere." They wrote it on Embassy Hotel stationery. "We never got around to finishing the bridge," Maynard said.

Once the tour started, it was a different world altogether. Maynard and James had Lefty booked into officers' clubs all through the country, with a couple of shows back in Saigon. Maynard traveled with Lefty, acting as his de facto road manager. "I tried to stick to him," he says, " 'cause he was the only name act I had in-country at the time." The way the lineup was set, Donny James opened, with Lois taking the lead vocals on songs like Tammy Wynette's "D-I-V-O-R-C-E" and Jeannie C. Riley's "Harper Valley P.T.A." She sang the latter so many times she could see past the Widow Jones's window shades and smell Shirley Thompson's breath in her sleep. After Lois's segment was through, James would introduce Lefty, and he'd step out to sing his tried-and-true hits.

It took Lefty all of two shows to figure out that following his beautiful red-haired, miniskirted, go-go-booted daughter before a crowd of sex-starved GIs was the worst gig he'd taken since skating-rink days. Come time for the third date, Lois walked into the dressing room and found her daddy sulking over a drink. What's wrong, she asked him. "I don't want you going on before me ever again," he said. "I want you to go on and sing—I'll bring you on, you come on *after* I go on."

"But you're the star," Lois protested.

Lefty didn't care. "You wear those miniskirts, and those boys out there—they're *screaming*, and hollerin' for you. . . . I try to come on stage, and they're screaming for you back. Now, I want 'em to scream and be—and be wild about you, but not till I get on and get off. Because, you know, they don't wanna see an old hard-legged boy like me, after seeing you."

"No, Daddy, I'm not gonna do it," Lois insisted, "because you're the star. This is getting petty and ridiculous."

That got Lefty mad. In a rage, he ripped his pearl-buttoned western shirt open. "Buttons flew everywhere," Lois laughs, "and I had to duck 'em, like they were like bullets. 'Cause he was *mad*."

Lefty won the argument, though, and from then on he would sing first and introduce Lois with, she says, "a nice little spiel." The ego crisis put away, Lefty was able to immerse himself in the stark yet vivifying reality of his job. Says Lois:

> The shows were great. The guys were crazy about it. I mean, they went berserk. They were swinging from the rafters. They appreciated it so much. It was like—I can't explain, because there's no words for that kind of emotions. You know, 'cause they were dying every day, and I can't explain how incredible it was to be with 'em. You know I discovered one thing—that when people are so close to death, they feel the most alive. It was a twenty-four-hour-a-day deal over there, to feel so alive constantly, that you didn't care about rules. And that's why guys would let themselves go, and grow their hair long, and smoke pot. Because they were so alive, because they were so close to death . . . and so they were animated, and vivid, and real, and they didn't care. . . .
>
> And they all gave me their medals. I had purple hearts, I had every single medal you could find, and Daddy'd mention anything, and the next thirty minutes he'd have it. You know, if it was something to eat or drink, you know, they were so good to us. And we became—you become instant friends. Instantaneously. Because they were dying right and left.

The immediacy of the gigs, and the fervency of the GIs' appreciation in the face of death, completely overwhelmed Lefty. The soldiers idolized him. "They took him under wing," Lois says. "All the guys. Everywhere he went. And they'd just hang around him and stay with him. They treated him so good, and he was so appreciated. And the guys—it was like no other shows he'd done in the States, you know, because there was no war on. So, it was so intense when they applauded and screamed and hollered."

Maynard noticed the same thing. He was watching Lefty work at a GI club in Saigon when he overheard a soldier in the next booth exclaim to his companion: "Man, that guy is God!"

"This is what GIs thought of him," Maynard says. "Gave me goose bumps to hear somebody say that."

There was no way for Lefty to repay the soldiers but to give them his best work and to act himself around them. "Oh, man, yeah he partied with everybody . . . ," says Lois. "He dealt with them like he dealt with Marlon or me or anybody else. He was just—he was *real!* He was not much of a phony. I rarely in my whole life saw him ever do anything real phony."

They had their scares, of course. During a Vietcong attack on Danang, the Donny James crew was penned into a beach house there. For four or five days, they huddled inside—Lefty and Lois and the rest of the band—boards and furniture blocking the windows to catch stray bullets. They subsisted on C rations till a search of the house uncovered not food but cases and cases of stashed liquor. Lefty, jokes his daughter, "would have stayed there forever."

Another time, Lefty and Lois were on a military flight between gigs when they were both stricken with near-fatal cases of dysentery. Flown by chopper to a tent hospital, they were unloaded by stretcher and laid on cots, side by side. As Lois recalls:

> We almost died. They had to carry us each one at different times to the outhouse. They didn't have plumbing. Then we were looking at each other, and he reached over—we were in a cot next to each other—and he reached over and took my hand. And we thought we were dying because they said we were dehydrating so bad, and vomiting so much. Well they didn't think they were gonna be able to help us, you know. Daddy said, "We're not gonna make it." I said, "I know it, Daddy." He just shook his head, and he held my hand and squeezed it.

Later, they were falsely accused of canceling the next show because Lefty was drunk.

Lefty's Vietnam tour ended shortly thereafter. Lois stayed in Asia, though she was still so sick she had to check into a hotel in Hong Kong to recuperate before resuming her jungle gigs. Lefty was in little better shape. By the time he returned stateside, he had lost over thirty pounds. Says Marlon Frizzell, "When Daddy did get back from Nam, he was so damn sick that it scared everyone. We all thought he was gonna die, man, he looked so bad. He was so incredibly sick."

Six months after Lefty returned from Southeast Asia, the song about Muskogee, Oklahoma, USA, catapulted Merle Haggard from standard country music star to full-fledged media sensation. It raised his talent fee to nine thousand dollars a night, won him the admiration of Richard Nixon, and made him the object of the most intense political scrutiny any country singer has ever had to weather. Longhairs, rednecks, and journalists hung on Haggard's every word—the longhairs seeking justification for their middle-class condescension, the rednecks seeking affirmation of their working-class jingoism, and the writers seeking insight into a man many sensed might have more on his mind than kids' disrespect for the college dean.

No one seemed to notice that even before he released "Okie from Muskogee" Haggard had said that he didn't care how people dressed or wore their hair, as long as they were thankful they lived in a country that allowed them the choice. Lefty Frizzell felt much the same, as Porter Wagoner, who at the time didn't necessarily see things that way, had discovered when the two were booked together on a hillbilly package show a couple of years earlier. Lefty opened, followed by Porter. As usual, Lefty traveled light to the gig. It was just him, Mulkey, and Bruce Delaney, the Golden Eye songwriter who David Frizzell had brought from California, on bass. Several members of the Wagonmasters, Wagoner's well-creased backup band, were expected to sit in with Lefty, giving him a full lineup. Trouble was, the Wagonmasters refused to share the stage with longhaired Delaney.

"They wouldn't come on," Marlon says, "and Daddy found out why. He says, 'I don't give a damn what someone looks like, as long as he can play.' You know, that was Daddy's thing. As long as he's doing his job, what's the problem? And so he got out, and he stopped the show."

Irritated with Porter for not ordering his boys to cooperate, Lefty reached for the mike and gestured backstage. His voice twanging hard and sarcastic, Lefty said, "Porter Wagoner . . . and the Wagonmasters." Then he turned to the audience. "Just what," he asked, "is a wagonmaster?"

Lefty gave everybody a moment to ponder the question. Then he threw his arms open, indicating the majestic sweep of the elite designation "wagonmaster."

"Why," Lefty marveled, "he's master of the wagon!"

According to Delaney, Lefty "sung his ass off that night." Nevertheless, "they brought the curtain down on us right while we were playing. They weren't being polite about it; they were letting everybody know that 'we're running these motherfuckers off.'

"I had people come up to me and say, 'You know, I booed you, and the only reason I booed you is 'cause you got that goddamn long hair.' And I'd say, 'That's your right as an American.' But after that happened, it really kind of spooked and shook Lefty, and he went back to the motel without us, and Abe had to get his money."

In March 1970, the era's ugliness struck even closer to home when Lefty's son Rickey was savagely beaten by a carload of Hopkinsville, Kentucky, rednecks straight out of the movie *Easy Rider*. They dragged him through a field with a belt around his neck and left him for dead. Rickey (who, for a time, was married to Merle Kilgore's daughter) had moved from Jimmy Snow's church to the long hair, music, and leather-fringe outlook of the age. His best friend Danny Husky, country star Ferlin Husky's son, was with him in Hopkinsville the day he was beaten within an inch of his life. Danny Husky "was into Gothic poetry," says Marlon Frizzell. "He had a lot of poems he wrote about death and dying."

The poems were nightmarishly prophetic. On the way back from Hopkinsville, traveling without Rickey, whom Lois had already taken home, Danny Husky and two other teens were killed in a head-on collision on U.S. Highway 68. Both fathers, Lefty and Ferlin, went to pieces. "Daddy was tore up," Lois says. "He was completely devastated. To see Rickey nearly dead, plus Danny being dead, it just . . . reached him all the way to his soul."

As for Merle Haggard, he wanted no part of the hippie-bashing monster he inadvertently blessed with the gift of tongues. The more people tried to pin him down to a firmly articulated political stance (reporters *still* do that to him), the more they learned about his musical influences instead. He claimed Jimmie Rodgers and Bob Wills as heroes, and recorded tribute albums to both of them to prove it. But the man whom Haggard idolized the most — and he made no secret of his admiration — was Lefty Frizzell. It was to see Lefty perform that he had fought through an overflow crowd at the Rainbow Gardens in Bakersfield in 1951, and Lefty whose single "Always Late" he had worn clear through to "Mom and Dad's Waltz" on the other side. Indeed, Haggard covered "Mom and Dad's Waltz" for his *Sing Me Back Home* album of 1968, and years later he was "very honored" when Lefty brought Naamon and A.D. to his house for a visit. "Lefty liked me," Haggard said, "and he brought his mother and father there knowing that I wouldn't insult them, or talk down to them in any way. He put a lot of faith in me, I thought, by bringing his parents and his family there." By then, Lefty's mother had already become a Merle Haggard fan. "She said there was just two voices that the Lord made like that: her son's and mine."

But most important, it was Lefty who touched young Merle at the gut level at which lifelong allegiances are forged. Quite simply, the first time the peerless country artist Merle Haggard ever played to a real audience — at the Rainbow Gardens — it was thanks to Lefty Frizzell. As Haggard recalled:

It was 1953, and Lefty was on his second trip through Bakersfield. I was sixteen years old. It was the second time I'd seen him [at the Rainbow Gardens]. The first time was in 1951. But during those two years I'd learned how to play guitar and sing, and had been on — maybe a little

beer stage or two was all I'd ever been on—and was backstage at the
Rainbow Gardens. Lefty had already made one appearance, and he and
Wayne Raney, and Alice and Wayne's wife, were all back there. And me
and a friend of mine—the friend's name being Bob Teague—walked
back there.

Teague "was sort of a boisterous, brassy sort of guy." He went straight
up to Lefty and said, "This is a friend of mine here, see. Sings a lot like
you. You'd probably enjoy hearing him sing." Lefty politely answered,
"Well I sure would," and handed Merle his personalized Gibson.

I sang two or three songs, which I couldn't really tell you which ones
right now. I'm not sure. I think I just sang one or two verses of this and
that, hunkered down there on my knee. And a guy named Joe Snead,
who owned the Rainbow Gardens, came walking through. He's a big
cigar-smoking guy—you know, the big promoter/club-owner sort. Tom
Parker–type guy. And [Snead said], "Hey Lefty! Time for you to go back
on for your second show." And [Lefty] said, "Well I want to let this local
boy go on first before I go on." And [Snead] said, "No! People wouldn't
pay to hear no goddamn kid!" And Lefty said, "Well I'll put it to you this
way: I'm not going back on until this kid goes on." So the guy said, "Well
get out there then."

With Lefty's firm backing, sixteen-year-old Merle, playing Lefty's
Hall of Fame Gibson (the same guitar that Hank Williams had played
onstage two years earlier), stepped out in front of thousands of country
fans crammed into the Rainbow Gardens, none of them having a clue
as to the historic moment they were about to witness. "I sang two or
three songs," Haggard said. "And the audience response was more than
just nice. It was really, really nice. It was great. That was a real tight
spot, I'd say. That was the first time, and I was hooked."

Haggard's idolization of Lefty was so great that, according to Marlon
Frizzell, the first time he visited Lefty in Hendersonville, Merle was so
overwhelmed he could hardly speak. Once the two became good
friends, however, Haggard was forever seeking Lefty's approbation,
even as he selflessly deflected attention away from himself and toward
his hero in the press. For instance, after Merle finished his brilliant
Rodgers tribute album, he asked Lefty to come by his motel room just so
he could give him a copy of the record (Later, Lefty paid Haggard what
was, for him, a supreme compliment, affirming that Merle did "a marvelous job" on the Rodgers numbers.) Another time, after Lefty had just
completed a session produced by Harlan Howard's manager, Don Da-

vis, Lefty and Merle stopped off at Howard's Music Row office and started trading Rodgers tunes. Howard walked in and discovered the two of them, Lefty and Merle, wrestling over who would get to pick the guitar next. "It was better than that session I'd recorded earlier," Lefty said of their Rodgers contest.

Nevertheless, Lefty was every bit as disconcerted as he was flattered by such adulation. He had a great respect for Haggard, and couldn't help but be honored that the 1970 Country Music Association Entertainer of the Year considered him the number one influence on his music. But Haggard's success made Lefty ill at ease, and—if he was being honest with himself—slightly resentful. It was bad enough touring with Hank Williams Jr. (as Lefty had been doing a great deal), which couldn't help but make Lefty, who had shared a stage with Hank Sr., feel a bit like a hillbilly relic. Now, to hear Merle Haggard, only nine years his junior, slay the fans with vocal mannerisms some of which Lefty knew he had personally invented—and to hear Merle refer to him as a "living legend"—perturbed Lefty and reminded him of his own mortality, something he didn't particularly want to face. And Haggard was not alone. He just happened to be the most talented, visible, and articulate member of a growing generation of country singers who owed a stylistic debt to Lefty. As early as 1964 or '65, in a promotional interview, Columbia producer Frank Jones commented to Lefty that many of the green young singers auditioning for Columbia had "that Lefty Frizzell style."

Said Jones, "I think you would probably advise any aspiring vocalists—"

"I can advise them to—"

"—not to copy," Jones continued.

"—cut it out. To cut it out," Lefty drawled.

"To originate their own style."

"Absolutely."

"Because there's only one Lefty Frizzell, and—"

"I'm having trouble with him," Lefty said.

Chapter 29

As MUCH AS THE "living legend" designation bothered Lefty, the admiration of young comers was the least of the troubles he had with himself. As his singing career reached the quarter-century mark, his attitude toward that career turned ever more ambivalent. He was simply getting tired. The road no longer held any romance for Lefty. It was only another distance to travel, another motel night to kill, another old-timer's request for "Mom and Dad's Waltz," and another pickup band that didn't know the song. Sometimes respect itself was hard to come by. Merle Kilgore remembers a night that he, Lefty, and Abe Mulkey traveled to a show in Indianapolis, Lefty just coming down from a vodka high as the three of them hit the backstage door. As Kilgore walked in carrying Lefty's guitar, the door security man brightened. "Merle, I didn't know you were playing tonight," he said. But when Lefty, disheveled and grumpy, tried to follow, the guard put up his hand. Never one to lose his sense of humor, no matter how foul his mood, Lefty pointed ahead at Kilgore and said, "I am the starrah, and that's my guitarrah. If I don't go through that do', there ain't gonna be no show."

Layovers were the worst. Two nights in one town drove Lefty insane. So did the clubs themselves, the very sort of honky-tonks in which he had made his name. The smoke irritated his sensitive throat and sinuses, as did the post-concert table banter that country star manners required of him. He took self-administered allergy shots (at times letting the needle hang from his flesh in order to horrify friends and family), but still his laryngitis was forever flaring up, and his body wearing down. To deal with both—laryngitis and fatigue—he learned to rely on the pills that were the number one item in many musicians' survival kits. One of Music City's favorites was a wicked capsule nicknamed a "California Turnaround"—supposedly two would get you to the West Coast and back. More common were the no-nonsense "bennies," a handful of which a burned-out hillbilly would never hesitate to drop. For many in Nashville, the most popular picker's little helper was Didrex. As prescribed by the beloved Dr. Landon B. Snapp II, Didrex attacked the "depression" to which road musicians were susceptible. Lefty frequented Dr. Snapp's East Nashville office, sometimes sending one of his kids to pick up his prescription. His appointments with the good doctor (whose one-man assault on hillbilly gloom would eventually earn him three years in the pen) wreaked havoc with Lefty's chronic high blood pressure. For every brief lift, there was always the inevitable crash. One time in California, crashing with neither Didrex nor turnaround in sight, Lefty asked a friend to help him score some bennies. The friend made a quick phone call, and a while later his dealer showed up. Lefty and his friend squeezed into the front seat of the dealer's car. The curbside pharmacist extended his cigarette pack toward Lefty. "No thanks, I don't smoke," Lefty said. The dealer then shook the pack until Lefty realized there was something other than cigarettes inside. "But I'm starting now!" he said, and reached for the pack.

Wired or straight, drunk or sober, Lefty found it harder and harder to roust himself out of his den chair to make his weekend dates. His family dreaded his trips to the airport, which Lefty invariably delayed to the last minute. At that point, he would draft someone to drive him, always pressuring the unfortunate chauffeur to ignore such minor irritants as speed limits. Not that anyone wanted to see Lefty behind the wheel. It wasn't just his drinking, for even sober, he had an unnerving policy of straddling the yellow line as he drove. "That way," said Lefty, "if anything happens I can go either way."

Lefty's apathy toward his career had a predictable impact on his recorded work. From the end of his Vietnam tour in 1969 to June 1972, he went to the studio for only six sessions. All produced mediocre records, especially by Lefty's standards. There was no question he suffered the loss of Don Law. Changing times or no, rock and roll or no, Nashville Sound or no, Law had always, at some crisis point, recognized the need to return Lefty to his natural environment of spare ballads and steel guitars. But other than Frank Jones (whose efforts were hit-or-miss) the producers who followed Law seemed at a loss about what to do with Lefty. Try as they might, they couldn't seem to figure out how to match his earthy voice with the glossy sound taking over Nashville again.

But you couldn't blame only the producers. Lefty wasn't contributing his own material—he had, in fact, completely ceased writing songs—and he wasn't giving his best vocally. Nothing symbolized his artistic doldrums more than what happened at a 1970 session with Don Davis. With their history of war stories told in Harlan Howard's office to bind them, Lefty and Davis were old pals. There was no question Davis was a sympathetic producer. But Lefty, probably having throat trouble, couldn't carry the songs from start to finish. For one of the singles cut that day (possibly Howard's "Watermelon Time in Georgia") Davis had to resort to what had been unthinkable where Lefty Frizzell was concerned: spliced vocals. Unable to get one completely solid take out of Lefty, Davis had to mix and match excerpts from several takes to make for one seamless, though falsified, vocal track. In the digital 1990s, an electronic version of the technique is common. But in those days, especially for a man of Lefty's background, it had to be humiliating—like an aging Babe Ruth getting the sacrifice bunt sign.

Although for Lefty superlative work was no guarantee of commercial success, indifferent work guaranteed commercial defeat. His late-sixties and early-seventies singles rattled around the lower reaches of the *Billboard* charts, then disappeared before anyone had time to notice. Lasting ten weeks in the summer of 1970 and peaking at number forty-nine, "Watermelon Time in Georgia" was practically a hit. It would be two more years before Lefty saw *Billboard* action at all.

Disinterested in his music, and unnerved by the echoes of his own style creeping into country radio at every turn of the dial, Lefty reacted by withdrawing from Music Row. He had struck up a close friendship with Doodle Owens after cutting "Get This Stranger Out of Me," and he now took to killing time at Owens's house, which was only a few miles away from his own in Hendersonville. Their friendship brought Lefty into contact with Doodle's songwriting collaborators—notably Dallas Frazier, a former kiddie act on the West Coast country TV circuit who had grown to wider fame as one of Nashville's preeminent honky-tonk songwriters. Frazier, also one of George Jones's favorite writers, had a deep, mystical streak that Lefty respected. He was disinclined to play jokes on Frazier the way he did on other friends. The Hendersonville circle also included guitarist Shorty Hall, who had backed Lefty on many L.A. club dates in the California days, and Rusty Adams, an Opry act who in a former incarnation was known to children far and wide as Ko-Ko the Clown. Lefty's new friends were a bunch of roaring good old boys whose company insulated him from the mess his home life had become. With Doodle's house so close by (and with his den conveniently equipped with a beer tap), Lefty no longer needed to drive twenty-five miles to Music Row to tell his tales of life with Alice or to soak up the creative iconoclasm of gray-templed hillbilly song men. Without ever asking for the honor, Lefty became the spiritual center of their songwriters' world, the star among them, the one whose triumphs and tribulations most affected them all. As writers, Owens and Frazier were turning out more country hits than Lefty had seen in fifteen years, yet he remained the standard by which they measured not only success, but the rightness of all they did. They had codes to live by—songwriters' honor. They would not write a tune unless the idea was theirs, even if the idea was no more than a phrase forgotten the moment uttered. Or, if one of them did want to run with the phrase, he would first ask permission of the one who uttered it. While ducking the public praise of Haggard and others, Lefty could not escape the force of his own private example, the impact he had on whomever he reached. He could not help but remain the star wherever he walked. For all the boisterous beer-drinking fun Lefty had at Doodle Owens's house, every now and then, Owens says, "he'd pick up that guitar over there, and he'd start singin', and everybody'd just hush."

Lefty loved those sessions in Owens's den, as he did his refuge at Judy Baker's house. But neither provided him with a space all his own, a place where he could live as he wished, free of Alice's watchful, disapproving eye. Lefty solved that problem when he acquired what would go down in honky-tonk history as the legendary "little house." It all started in September 1968, when the real estate kingpins Lefty and Kilgore sold one of their 18th Avenue houses to Hill & Range for $33,000. The following June, not long after Lefty returned from Vietnam, they sold the other building, also to Hill & Range. Four years after speculating on Music Row, Lefty was out of the property business.

A month after Lefty and Kilgore sold the second house, Lois bought a tiny yellow brick bungalow on Cline Court in Hendersonville, just a few blocks from Owens's place, with money she made in Vietnam. She moved in but didn't stay long. When her own finances grew dangerously thin, she sold the Cline Court house to Lefty. With two houses on his hands, Lefty turned the smaller one over to his son Rickey's care. Rickey lived there while working for Dallas Frazier. That didn't last long either. When Rickey moved out, Lefty was stuck with an empty suburban bungalow at the crest of a quiet cul de sac—far, far from Music Row.

Which, he discovered, was exactly how he wanted it. The nondescript cottage became, quite literally, his home away from home. The family started calling it the "little house," which distinguished it from the "big house" on the lake. Lefty didn't stay there full-time, at least not at first. Once the shock and marital confusion wrought by Alice's rededication to Christ had worn off, she and Lefty found a newer, if less involved, equilibrium. Things were not the same between them, but they discovered they could still get along at some basic level; they could at least enjoy a quiet evening together watching *Columbo*, Lefty's favorite show. Yet such moments were peaceful but ephemeral, ever threatened by an underlying tension that drove Alice churchward and Lefty down to the little house.

Really, the Cline Court cottage was more like a clubhouse. Lefty went there to meet friends, drink, and generally not take care of himself. The little house soon replaced Doodle Owens's den as Hendersonville songwriters' central. Besides the core group of Lefty's close friends, there was always an extra warm body or two, a hanger-on eager to brag that he drank and threw knives at the wall with Lefty Frizzell. A Waco friend of Owens's, confident he could keep up, spent an entire day at the little house while traveling through Nashville, only to limp back to Texas with a new nickname — "Gimme Ten" — bestowed upon him by Lefty after the unfortunate ol' boy passed out in the bathtub. His last words, as day turned to night, had been: "Gimme ten minutes, I'll be out. Just gimme ten."

The company also sometimes included friends, like George Jones, whose promised visits, given past experience, would send a shudder through otherwise stout-hearted Lefty. Lit up and sequestered in Alabama, Jones would telephone ahead, only to suffer Lefty's mischievous taunting across the lines. "Who in the hell told you you could sing, you old Popeye?" Lefty would say. "I never have thought you could sing." After tormenting Jones long enough, Lefty would finally admit, "You know I love you, you sonofagun. Everything you do. I think you're one of the greatest singers that's ever been." (Lefty was sincere. Never free with his praise, he once scolded his teen nephew Jimmy for naively poking fun at Jones's style. Lefty firmly reminded him that George "may be the best country singer of all time.")

However content he felt with his friends, and apathetic toward his music, the other greatest singer that's ever been, Lefty, had to at least make a token effort to maintain his career. In early summer 1972, Columbia prepared another session for Lefty, this time with hotshot producer Billy Sherrill — who had just started working with George Jones — slated to man the boards. Sherrill met with Lefty and told him he thought Lefty should cover Mel Street's "Borrowed Angel," an independent release just starting to catch fire. But when Lefty declined,

Sherrill, probably annoyed, turned him over to staff producer Glenn Sutton.

A fan of Lefty's who, as a kid growing up in East Texas, had actually seen him perform on the Louisiana Hayride, Sutton was not about to dictate song choice to Lefty. "At this stage of the game," Sutton told him, "you know you oughta be able to do anything you wanna do." One of the songs Lefty wanted to do, and which he cut with Sutton at the session that June, was a piano-driven ditty called "You, Babe." Released as a single, it actually showed signs of radio life. Lefty lifted himself from his professional torpor and started to make the promotional rounds. He got out on the street a bit, toured, and made himself available for interviews. In September, deejay T. Tommy Cutrer aired a five-day segment of his hourlong "Music City USA" radio talk show with Lefty as cohost. Relaxed and enjoying himself, Lefty spent the five hours cracking jokes, roasting his friends, and telling stories nonstop. About Mel Tillis, known for his stuttering, he joked: "They charge him long distance to make a local call." Discussing "Always Late," T. Tommy mentioned that the song apparently only had eight lines. "Have you ever counted them?" he asked.

"No," Lefty mused, "but, um, first chance I get I ain't doin' nothin'. . . ."

Between spinning records and plugging sponsors, Cutrer pressed the right buttons to get Lefty talking at length about his career, both the good old days in Dallas and the recent hard times in Nashville. "It can be a problem sometimes, gettin' into Columbia studio, and you're a Columbia artist," Lefty said. "Sometimes it's not as easy as you think." He mentioned that his current producer was his friend Glenn Sutton, and that the two of them worked well together on "You, Babe."

"I think I can predict right now that there'll be many, many Lefty Frizzell hits coming out, with Glenn Sutton producing them," Cutrer intoned.

"I got a good feeling about it," Lefty agreed.

The five hours of programming ended on a strange, enigmatic note, however, when Lefty chose the depressing, seven-year-old-non-hit "How Far Down Can I Go" as his closing selection. After the intensely downbeat number played through, deejay Cutrer was clearly discomfited. "I just sort of felt like we ought've played 'Mom and Dad's Waltz,' or 'I Love You a Thousand Ways,' " he said.

And if Lefty really did wonder how far down he could go, he was about to find out. For when T. Tommy Cutrer predicted "many, many Lefty Frizzell hits coming out, with Glenn Sutton producing them," he

could not have shot wider of the mark. Columbia Records, for whom
Sutton worked, quietly dropped Lefty from the label roster. Twenty-two
years after shaking Don Law's hand in Dallas, Lefty's Columbia contract ran out for good in July. Considering that the radio interviews
were taped in September, Lefty probably already knew he'd been
dropped. If not, he certainly must have seen it coming. He had not
scored a top-forty hit in seven years or recorded anything that hit the
charts in two. The record industry, even the country record industry,
does not run on sentiment.

Chapter 30

THOUGH IT WAS small consolation, Lefty was in good company. In the 1970s, the Nashville labels purged many of their twenty-year stars. In 1972, the same year Lefty lost his Columbia deal, Webb Pierce and Kitty Wells both released their final sides for Decca. Carl Smith was through with Columbia by 1973, Ray Price a year after that. Some august members of the hillbilly old guard, RCA's Porter Wagoner and Columbia's Johnny Cash, for instance, hung tough into the 1980s before the axes fell. The most remarkable story was that of George Jones, whose 1970s label change led to his 1980 masterpiece "He Stopped Loving Her Today." But Cash and Wagoner and Jones were exceptions. By and large, the Watergate decade was ruled by Merle Haggard, Charley Pride, Tammy Wynette, Loretta Lynn and Conway Twitty, Waylon Jennings and Willie Nelson—artists who didn't hit their career strides until "Always Late" was distant memory.

Fortunately, the end of a long-term label affiliation rarely meant the end of a country singer's career. A rival company would usually sign the artist—if not another major label, then at least an overachieving independent of some kind. Lefty managed to combine the two. As soon as Columbia released him, Lefty, instead of closeting his boots and guitar, reentered the ranks of the industry entrepreneurs. He formed Frizzell-Spicer Enterprises with Ralph Spicer, a North Carolinian whom Lefty had befriended. A textile dealer by trade, Spicer knew how to move towels and underwear but had little, if any, music industry know-how. Just what the "enterprises" were to be remained a mystery to those close to Lefty. But Lefty liked Spicer, which in his book mattered more than expertise. So as a subsidiary of Spicer-Frizzell Enterprises, they started their own record label: Tellet Country. The name derived from Spicer's enthusiastic "Tell it! Tell it!," chanted one night when he and Lefty were outside staring at the stars, Lefty telling whatever came to mind. By the end of 1972, Tellet Country boasted a catalog of two 45s—one by Bobby Mackey, the other by staff producer Eddie Noack. In addition, Lefty cut song demos at Spicer's North Carolina recording studio. According to Marlon Frizzell, the studio was just "a big corrugated metal building, with a reel-to-reel tape recorder in there."

Of far more import to Lefty, if not to Ralph Spicer, was a new major label connection. Columbia had declined to pick up Lefty's option in July 1972. By November, he had signed with ABC Records, which had only recently opened a Nashville office. "The offer the company made, I couldn't refuse," Lefty told a Wichita reporter. "I'll make several LP albums and singles will be taken from them."

A part of Lefty may have wanted to refuse. Physically, he wasn't in very good shape. The Wichita writer, who miraculously caught up with Lefty to talk about an upcoming three-night stand at the town's Longbranch Club, noted it "was hot and raining in Nashville and Lefty Frizzell was so hoarse he could barely talk above a whisper." Lefty had just come in from a withering Texas rodeo tour, which in turn had followed a series of West Coast one-nighters. He confided that "after the first of the year I plan to do just about half as much club work as I have been doing."

Apparently, Lefty decided to cut back sooner than that. A pair of early December shows—one in Dayton, Ohio, the other in Flint, Michigan—were both canceled. Lefty may have been protecting his strained voice, for his first ABC album session was slated four days after the Dayton gig. But that couldn't have been the whole story. For in January, a month *after* the album sessions, Lefty dropped a pair of back-to-back dates at the Playboy Lounge in Amarillo. He was flat worn out and sick.

Alcoholism was no longer his only affliction. Rather it was the central malady around which other problems orbited. He put on excess weight, all of it from drinking, for he was notoriously unwilling to eat while hitting the bottle. His blood pressure soared. Alarmed by Lefty's hypertension, his doctor prescribed medicine that Lefty refused to take. He set the bottle on the highest shelf at the little house. Every now and then he'd glance up and say to his friends, "See those pills up there? One day I'm gonna take one of those pills." Later, when the same doctor saw how thoroughly Lefty had ignored his instructions, he nearly threw Lefty out of the office for wasting both their time, telling him he could have a stroke right there on the examining table. As a Band-Aid treatment, Lefty started patronizing a local spa. It didn't help much, for it was Lefty's way to put on a good buzz before hitting the steam and sauna. The main reason he liked the spa was that the Euca- lyptus room cleared his throat and sinuses.

With his body in such a sorry state, it was no wonder Lefty prioritized his sessions over roadwork. At the close of 1972, amid the canceled club dates, his ABC recording career commenced with three separate evening stints at Woodland Sound Studio in East Nashville. Don Gant, the head of ABC's Nashville office and the man who signed Lefty to the label, elected to produce. Dallas Frazier and Doodle Owens provided songs, as did a relatively unknown writer named Jimmy Buffett. Other material came from Whitey Shafer, a new friend of Lefty's who had also written "You, Babe." Recorded on the second of the three days, squeezed into the middle of the song lineup, was a pleasant upbeat number called "Lucky Arms." It, too, was a Whitey Shafer tune. Except it was co-written by Lefty Frizzell. Very quietly, very unceremoniously—and despite all the turmoil of his label change and worsening health—Lefty's bone-tired muse had awakened.

No one knows exactly when, or how, or why Lefty stopped writing songs in the first place. For him, the only thing worse would have been to disown Jimmie Rodgers. Perhaps Golden Eye's lack of success dis- heartened him, and no doubt his drinking had reached the point of subverting his artistic focus. Lefty blamed it on career distraction. "You start off with a beautiful idea, and you're pretty excited with it, and all of a sudden you have to catch a plane and head out for Canada, or somewhere for a job," he explained to Cutrer. "And sometime you just, you say I'll finish this later. And you never can. You never get back into the same mood or the same feeling that you have."

But Lefty had also lost his confidence. Country music was changing, modernizing both thematically and musically. The social turmoil of the 1960s had a profound effect on country music songwriting at almost every level. "Harper Valley P.T.A." (written by Tom T. Hall) and "Okie from Muskogee" were but two of the more glaring examples of an outward vision, of country writers' attempts to wed the simple verities of commercial country music to the complexities of Vietnam-era Amer- ica. As a writer, Mel Tillis evolved from the homesick country boy of "Detroit City" to the bitter, paralyzed veteran of "Ruby, Don't Take Your Love to Town." John D. Loudermilk moved from "Waterloo" to "Indian

Reservation." Even George Jones's best friend, songwriter Peanut Mont-gomery, got in the act by giving his pal a hair-raising Armageddon number called "Unwanted Babies." The song so spooked Pappy Daily that he made Jones release it under the name "Glen Patterson."

In other words, being always late with your kisses and wanting more, more, more of your kisses would no longer do. Lefty understood that and accepted it. As close as he was to hard country writers like Frazier and Owens, he also paid attention to singer-songwriters like Jackson Browne, whose "Ready or Not" would soon be a particular favorite of his. But it stifled his own output. In 1972, ironically the year he was elected to the Nashville Songwriters Hall of Fame and the year Columbia dropped him, he told journalist John Pugh that he considered all the changes in country music to be for the better. "There are so many more things to write and sing about," he said. "When I had my number one records, a lot of subjects were off-limits. So I just cut regular com-mercial songs; there was no real depth to them, such as you have in many of today's songs."

But Lefty was wrong if he thought a return to form would require of him a more topically sophisticated lyric range. The only thing called for was a lyric shift, a slight turn away from the love and infidelity themes that had dominated his life's work. Lefty's best songs had always been those written from closest to his country boy's heart. But his life, if not his unchanging heart, had long since ceased to be so simple. For him to write well again, he would have to quit thinking of what love had once meant, or of how it had been betrayed. Instead, he'd have to start facing the reality of where love, betrayed or not, had led him in desolation. It would not be an artistic move he could make on his own. He needed someone to help him along, someone whose collaboration and com-pany would cut against the despairing loneliness of such introspective material. Someone had to motivate Lefty to write again, and to write it like he felt it. Which is precisely where Whitey Shafer came in.

Raised in Whitney, Texas, about fifty miles east of Corsicana, Sanger D. "Whitey" Shafer had idolized Lefty since the first time he heard Lefty's debut record on a Whitney café jukebox. Shafer was in high school at the time. "I heard that 'If You Got the Money, I Got the Time,' I knew I'd found me a he-ro," he says. "I started keepin' up with him from then on after; every record he put out, I knew about it. I lived it."

Shafer's parents sang gospel in the Stamps Blue Jacket Quartet (a satellite of the famed Stamps Quartet). But they were not so musically strict as to tune out the sounds of the Texas dancehalls. Blessed with a fine, full voice of his own, Whitey grew up hearing Ernest Tubb and

Bob Wills on the radio, and after high school he started singing and playing piano in local honky-tonks. One particular favorite was the Night Owl, a county-line joint where his occasional bandstand partner was the teenaged Willie Nelson. Through the early 1960s, Shafer held a variety of jobs, among them raising turkeys and "busting rods" in the steel industry, while playing weekly gigs at the Circle R, the same Waco roadhouse Doodle Owens had haunted in younger days. Not long after Owens decided to go for broke and move to Nashville, thirty-three-year-old Shafer made the same decision. His friends pitched in to loan him $850 seed money. In Nashville, he hooked up with Owens and Dallas Frazier, had a couple songs cut by George Jones, including the B-side of "Unwanted Babies," and released a 45 or two under his own name. In 1969, his hero, Lefty Frizzell, recorded a song called "Honky Tonk Hill" that Shafer and Owens had co-written. It was released on one of the worst-selling records of Lefty's career.

Eventually, Shafer moved to the country star ghetto of Hendersonville. He didn't know that his idol lived only a block and a half away, until one day Owens drove him by Lefty's house. Not long afterward, Shafer took a songwriter's gamble that would, within a year's time, pay artistic dividends he would not have even dreamed about. One fateful summer day in 1972, having just completed a demo tape that included "You, Babe," and thinking that Lefty might like the song, Shafer said to himself, "Well, I think I'm just gonna go down there to his house, knock on his door, and see what happens." Resolved but scared, he did just that. Apparently he telephoned ahead, for Lefty later recalled waiting an hour while Shafer, who had lost his copy of the demo tape, raced to his publisher to get a new one. Either way, Lefty answered the door, beer in hand, and Shafer introduced himself. "I told him he was my hero, and all that stuff, you know, like people do. He said, 'Well come on in, knucklehead. Why don't you just play all four of 'em that you got on that tape.' "

He had caught his hero in "just exactly the right mood." Lefty listened to the tape, picked out "You, Babe" without Shafer's prompting, and to the songwriter's amazement (things aren't supposed to work this way in Music City) said, "I'll do that tomorrow." Shafer says he had no idea that Lefty had a Columbia session scheduled the following day. Lefty, on the other hand, had no idea that the upcoming session would be his last for Columbia.

A couple of days later, Shafer dropped by Lefty's house again, this time just to visit. They drank a few beers, joked around, and just like that, another of Lefty's easy friendships had been formed. He and

Whitey threw the usual "we oughtta get together and write sometime" line at each other (people in Nashville say "we'll write" the way others say "let's do lunch"), but the difference was Shafer meant it. He had already started "Lucky Arms," and the next time Lefty came by his house, Shafer said, "Why don't you help me finish this song." Lefty wrote the second verse, by himself, in fifteen minutes. "Second verse is kind of, I don't know, it's kind of romantic," Shafer says. "And the way he phrased things was, like, in a romantic style. He always wrote things from a woman's side of view, most of the time. He said, 'Always remember that.' "

Neither the best or worst song to which Lefty ever put his name, "Lucky Arms" served as a confidence builder, a reminder to Lefty that he still had music of his own left inside him. But it would take another half year of working with Whitey for that confidence, and his acute musical self-awareness, to return completely.

"I think it was Whitey's enthusiasm that helped Lefty wanna produce something again," says David Frizzell. "Whitey and Lefty just kinda hit it off, just the right personalities clickin' at the right time, and they were both incredibly creative people. Very, very witty. Both of them. Right on top of it, you know? And they were just an incredible songwriting team."

Already tight with Owens and Dallas Frazier, Shafer fit right in with all the beer-drinking mayhem at the little house. Peering through a living room window of the Cline Court bungalow, a stranger would never have guessed that the men inside, laughing and joking and ranting and raving, might have represented the highest concentration of hillbilly songwriting talent anywhere in the country at that moment. As for the writers themselves, through all the bottles and hijinks and childish antics at the little house, the one point they never overlooked was the seriousness of their lives' work. They all maintained a reverent belief in the righteousness of a good country song. Frazier and Owens and Shafer were masters of the honky-tonk heartache idiom, a juke-joint, roughhouse, spilt-tears style of writing to which they bravely adhered no matter what the Music Row trends. But to produce, they knew they had to get away from their homes. Frazier, who owned a farm outside Hendersonville, set up a furnished trailer on a hill over his land as a retreat for his closest songwriting friends. Out there in the peace of the countryside, he and Owens, or he and Shafer, or Shafer and Owens, would escape. "It was just a beautiful place for work," Owens says. "Piano, and guitars. Had us a gun up there. . . ."

One summer day in 1973, about a year after Lefty and Whitey first met, the two of them decided to try their luck writing at Frazier's retreat. It was the first time they had gotten together specifically to work, as opposed to letting a few beers naturally lead them into a few lines and licks. Owens, who had encouraged Lefty to write with Whitey, showed up while the pair were at the trailer. As Owens recalls:

> Lefty said, "Why don't you stay and write a song with us?" And I said, "Lefty . . . I've been up over two days and a night. I've been—I've really been drinkin', and I'm sobered up now, and my head's hurtin', and I don't feel good, and I just can't think. . . . That's the way life goes." Lefty said, "No, that's the way *love* goes." And he says, "Can I have that for an idea?" And I said, "You sure can." He said, "Well, why don't you stay and write it with us?" And I didn't do it.

As it just so happened Whitey was already fretting over a lovely three-line snippet of a verse he had written and liked, but didn't know what to do with. Sadly romantic, the verse was about the lifelong, wistful folly of good luck sought but never found. "I'd had it for months," Shafer says, "I didn't know where to go with it, or even what I was singin' about hardly. You know, and [Lefty] just spoke up and said, 'That's the way love goes.' We wrote the other four lines in about fifteen minutes. The song's only got eight lines in it."

On the surface, "That's the Way Love Goes" is so short, simple, and direct, it seems oddly naive, the kind of song Lefty might have written when he was eighteen years old and thumbing across West Texas. But the closer one pays attention, the more multilayered meaning the song delivers, and the more complex the emotions expressed reveal themselves to be. "That's the Way Love Goes" is equal parts hope and resignation, true love and lost love, a tight composite of opposite attitudes fused in a melody as soulful as Lefty's timeworn, forgiving voice.

And they still weren't done. Whitey had another long-incubated idea he wanted to fool around with that afternoon—something to do with mirrors and self-reflection. He and Lefty hammered the amorphous idea into final form as a near-dirge about the ravages of middle age and lovelorn dissipation. Initially called "I've Got a Heartache to Hide," it would go down in history under the title "I Never Go Around Mirrors." Written from a bleak spot in their souls the two men were in no hurry to confront, the song didn't come as easily as "That's the Way Love Goes" had.

"That took a little work," Shafer says, his voice suddenly quiet. "We had to go ahead and drink a few extra more beers 'fore we got into that one too deep."

On July 17, producer Don Gant booked Lefty into Woodland Sound Studio to record the two songs written on Dallas Frazier's farm, as well as a third astounding song from the Frizzell-Shafer team, "I Can't Get Over You to Save My Life," which Lefty readily acknowledged was written to Alice, and that featured him humming segments of the melody before croaking lines like "let me die." Juxtaposed against the harsh lyrics, the lament of a doomed man whose drinking buddies are his only salvation, the starkly beautiful, wordless hum served much the same balancing purpose the yodel had for Jimmie Rodgers. It was Lefty's way of keeping his head up. He cut "I Can't Get Over You to Save My Life" first, followed by "I Never Go Around Mirrors" and "That's the Way Love Goes." As a three-act cycle, it was damn near cinematic. Lefty set the stage with the two heart-wrenching numbers, only to show what the pain really meant through the kind, accepting tone of "That's the Way Love Goes." When Lefty sang "losing makes me sorry," and followed it with his laughing "say, 'Honey, now don't you worry,' " you could hear all the anger and guilt that poisoned his love for Alice — and hers for him — wash away in the grooves.

Chapter 31

BOLSTERED BY THE three new songs, Lefty's debut ABC album, *The Legendary Lefty Frizzell*, hit the record racks in August 1973. Lefty was so overwhelmed by how good it turned out, he reportedly cried the first time he heard it. In hindsight, critics have been quick to point to *The Legendary Lefty Frizzell* as an astounding return to form, a record on which Lefty, completely out of the blue, and against the industry's every expectation, delivered a late-career masterpiece. Of course, at the time there were no pundits around to sing the record's praises. The trade press totally ignored the album, and in a couple of instances opted to review a Columbia reissue of his Jimmie Rodgers tribute LP instead. The only significant mention his first ABC work received did not come till almost a year later, when a *Country Music* blurb listed *The Legendary Lefty Frizzell* as one of Merle Haggard's favorite new releases.

As little attention as the album as a whole received, by September the single "I Can't Get Over You to Save My Life" had snuck onto the charts. It was an apt release, for if ever Lefty had meant a song as much as "I Love You a Thousand Ways," it was "I Can't Get Over You to Save My Life." He and Alice could hardly live with each other; neither could they let each other go. Alice had left Evangel Temple, but her fundamentalist attitudes had not softened; nor had Lefty's drinking lessened. With the big house a site of constant confrontation, the little house, at first no more than a refuge and songwriters' club, was turning into Lefty's real home.

Physical separation didn't stop him and Alice from fighting. They were both too attached to their battles. Talking on the phone to each other was a petty game; they practically kept score of who could hang up on whom the most, or the quickest. The sound of the receiver slamming into its cradle was part of the daily soundtrack of life at Lefty's little house. "If that phone had been slammed down one time, it's been slammed down a thousand," says Shafer. Impish to the end, Lefty would involve his friends in the game against their will. Pretending to want reconciliation, he'd beg Owens or Shafer or Hall to call Alice for him, to talk her into listening to him. When one of them gave in and did his part, Lefty would say a word or two to his wife, then slam the receiver down, pleased to have won that round.

Surrounded by his friends like that, Lefty could usually maintain his sense of humor, devilish though it could be. "He was pretty dad-gum happy around me," Shafer says. "Most of the time." But not all the time. And never when he was alone. Lefty could not bear solitude. It wrecked him. His worst moments were those he spent completely by himself. One night, Lefty was drinking alone at the big house when he heard Marlon call out for Rickey across the water. The two brothers were simply hanging out in the park. But Lefty, drunk, paranoid, and perhaps tormented by the memory of Rickey's near-fatal beating, heard Marlon's voice as a cry of pain. He later told Marlon that in his mind he saw him tied to a tree and tortured. With that vision haunting him, Lefty picked up his rifle, drove around the lake to the park, and bore down on a small group of kids he found partying there. "I want my boys," he said. "Where's my boys?"

"Lefty, man, they're not here," said one, who knew Lefty and liked him. "They're all right, though. They're with friends."

But another kid, a local punk, picked up a rock and fired it at Lefty, hitting him square in the forehead and opening a huge gash over his eye. Staggering and bleeding, Lefty made it to Whitey's house for the night.

Loathing solitude, knowing what it did to him, Lefty hated to see his friends leave the little house to go home to their families at the end of the day. He loved his songwriter friends with a kind of love no one had ever written a song about, as Lefty himself once put it. Often as not, the last one to leave was Shorty Hall, the gentlest soul in Lefty's inner circle ("He laughed at bad news," says Owens) and the one to whom Lefty grew closest the last couple years of his life. Sitting at the kitchen table, Lefty would shyly ask if Hall thought his wife would mind if he spent the night at the little house.

"So I asked him one night," says Hall, "I said, 'How come you don't wanna stay by yourself?' He said, 'I don't wanna die by myself.' "

For all of Lefty's fraying nerves and fear of seclusion, the months following the release of *The Legendary Lefty Frizzell* were tumultuous careerwise. At almost the same time "I Can't Get Over You to Save My Life" cracked the low end of the charts, dropping off was a minor hit called "Hank and Lefty Raised My Country Soul." Written by Owens and Frazier, it was only the latest in the barrage of tributes to Lefty as living legend. But hearing someone sing *about* him was much more moving than hearing someone sing *like* him. And there was a further twist—the singer was Stoney Edwards, who is black. Edwards had, indeed, grown up listening to Hank and Lefty, and when his producer, Biff Collie, played him "Hank and Lefty Raised My Country Soul," Edwards flipped over it. "I felt like it was just words taken out of my mouth," he said.

Not long after the single broke, Edwards was given the opportunity to meet Lefty. One day, at a popular country hangout on West End Avenue in Nashville, Edwards was being interviewed for a live remote radio broadcast from the bar. After talking to Edwards, the deejay played his new record, "Hank and Lefty Raised My Country Soul." Biff Collie then asked him, "Stoney, you ever meet Lefty?" "No, man, but I'd sure love to meet him," he answered. "Well, he's right around the corner there, sitting in a booth," Collie said.

Lefty had a couple of friends with him, but he was drunk, weeping, listening to the song and mumbling about how it was a tribute to him, how he'd thought no one cared anymore, and how, Edwards recalls him saying, he'd heard it was a black man singing and that it had to be a black man to pay a tribute. In a previously published version of their encounter, Lefty says with apparent bitterness, "Wouldn't you know it? It had to be by a nigger." But Edwards insists that Lefty's tone and attitude weren't bitter or insulting at all. Quite the contrary. "He didn't insult me about the record, no," Edwards says. "He acted like he was glad that somebody would do a tribute to him. And he did say that it had to be a black man to do it. . . . He meant like it was an honor to him. . . . The way I got it is: 'More people cared than I thought. A black man made a tribute to me.' He felt like it was a great thing that some-body paid tribute to him."

In fact, Lefty was so drunkenly absorbed in the song that Collie couldn't manage to make the introduction. "Biff said, 'You like to meet the guy that sang the song?' And Lefty said, 'I sure would.' And he said, 'Well, this is him right here.' And Lefty said, 'Well I'd sure like to meet him.' " When it became obvious that Collie hadn't gotten through to Lefty, Edwards, not about to lose the thrill of meeting one of his idols, reached over and shook Lefty's hand. Lefty looked up, said hi, and went back to concentrating on the song.

Edwards's record had no concrete effect on Lefty's fortunes. Few fans bought the ABC album, and as a single—a too real for radio single—"I Can't Get Over You to Save My Life" topped out three places shy of the top forty. But during the winter of '73, red-hot Johnny Rodriguez, an upstart Texas singer whose style bore more than passing resemblance to Lefty's own, recorded "That's the Way Love Goes" for his second album, which arrived almost on top of Lefty's. Rodriguez had first heard the song when he, Lefty, Merle Haggard, and several other friends were hanging out at Nashville's Continental Inn, trading songs. After Lefty sang "That's the Way Love Goes," according to Rodriguez, "Merle wanted to cut it, but he'd just finished doing an album." In December, Mercury Records released Rodriguez's strong but less compelling version of Lefty's song as a single. By mid-February, the Frizzell-Shafer tune was the number one country song in America. The same week Rodriguez topped *Billboard*, Lefty popped in at number ninety with the other song he and Shafer wrote on Dallas Frazier's farm: "I Never Go Around Mirrors." Lefty's B-side was "That's the Way Love Goes."

As if that weren't enough, in March, Connie Smith released an LP for Columbia Records the *title cut* of which was "That's the Way Love Goes." Normally one would be ecstatic to have the feature song on a Connie Smith record. At her best, she's made other female country singers sound like Edith Bunker. But in the spring of '74, Smith was fresh off an Evangel Temple marriage (she and Alice were church lady friends), and her version of Lefty and Whitey's song was pure sap. The lyrics were rewritten, though not by her, to emphasize conjugal bliss as opposed to Lefty's bittersweet sense of loss.

Perhaps it was all for the best, however, for some of the action, distressing though it was, rubbed off on Lefty. At the end of April, when he returned to the studio for ABC, "I Never Go Around Mirrors" was still on the charts. It had, in fact, risen to number twenty-five—Lefty's first top forty appearance since 1965. Starting work on his second ABC album, Lefty cut three songs, including two more that he and Whitey co-wrote. Whitey had become such a fixture on Cline Court that Lefty took to teasing him about owing rent. When he'd finally heard enough, Whitey wrote a check for fifty-one dollars and noted in the memo corner: "place to cowrite with Lefty." Amused, Lefty never cashed it.

Whatever their arrangement, they continued to be a formidable songwriting duo. Drinking at the little house, they rarely had to wait long for inspiration. It tended to fall in their laps. When Lefty changed the lock on the little house door, he gave a copy of the key to Alice, who promptly threw it in the front yard and drove off. When Lefty entered the studio in April, one of the new Frizzell-Shafer songs he brought with him was "She Found the Key" (". . . that you threw away"). He recorded another of their songs that day, "My Wishing Room," the lyrics of which Lefty wrote on the back of a *TV Guide*. The thematic inverse of "She Found the Key," it was almost as gorgeous as "That's the Way Love Goes."

From the standpoint of creativity, Lefty was a new man. He had even made the bold move of switching roles in the studio, producing a pair of singles for Lois and Abe Mulkey, respectively, on the tenacious Tellet Country label. Recorded in December 1973, the Mulkey 45, especially, was a revelation. Not only did Abe's style sound completely his own, but the vigorous arrangements built around Lloyd Green's steel guitar and Bill Pursell's piano were pure 1950s honky-tonk. Given the chance to run the show, Lefty turned the clock back twenty years to Jim Beck's Dallas sound.

Lefty may have been a new man artistically, but he was not one physically. He could only handle so much work, of any quality, at one time. Begun in April, the vocal tracks for his second ABC album were not completed until October. Don Gant was a patient producer, and he allowed Lefty the time he felt he needed to rest his throat between sessions. Shorty Hall says Lefty had his own private voice test to tell him when he was ready for the studio. Every morning, says Hall, Lefty would get up and try out his Jimmie Rodgers yodel. "If he ever got his yodels right, that early in the morning, he'd call Don Gant and say, 'I'm ready.' So Don would set the session." Three or four songs would be cut, then a couple more months would pass before Lefty's liquid yodel told him he was ready again.

In the meantime, much as he wanted to cut back on touring, Lefty had to survive the road in order to make a living. His fee held steady in the six- to seven-hundred-dollar range, but his gigs were nothing but pain. He worked three days in Bermuda. He headlined the "Kiamichi Owa-Chito Festival of the Forest," in McCurtain County, Oklahoma. (As guest of honor, Lefty introduced the lovely "Miss Kiamichi Owa-Chito 1973.") He worked from one end of the country to the other, just like he always had, still enduring the indignities of poor promotion and intermittently disrespectful audiences. At one outdoor show, an ill-mannered biker kept interrupting Lefty's set by revving his Harley Hawg. Lefty finally called the uneasy rider to the stage, then brained him with his guitar. "Well. I guess I can sing now," Lefty said.

But it wasn't just the fatigue and physical waste that took their toll on Lefty. After so much time, he had come around to where every whistle-stop harbored ghosts—flashback memories of glory and friendship and fun, of wild nights spent knowing Alice would forgive him. The highway brought reunion but also sad reminiscence, shows where old pals were seen or missed for what Lefty might have guessed would be the last time. At a gig in Pennsylvania, Lefty and rocker Sleepy Labeef blew away the audience, then sat around trading honky-tonk horror stories about the old days in El Dorado. At the Longhorn Ballroom in Dallas, Lefty turned around in the middle of his set and noticed Clay Allen, who had played on the original Jim Beck demo, and who had worked the Pierce Brooks political tour with him, backing him up on guitar. "Well, well, Eddy Arnold, I'd know you anywhere," Lefty said, picking up an ancient joke between them as if decades passed meant nothing but a pause before the punch line. Out in West Texas, Lefty's Big Spring buddy Grady Kilgore, the erstwhile bartender at the Ace of Clubs, showed up for a gig with his wife and seven nurses accompanying him. And when Lefty and Kilgore's former Ace of Clubs boss Hugh Simpson died in Houston, Lefty flew in for the funeral wearing blue jeans and a work shirt, arriving just in time to help carry the salty ex-sailor's casket.

Some dates were harder on Lefty's friends than they were on him. When Lefty booked a two-night stay in Lafayette, Louisiana, he invited J. D. Miller to drive over from Crowley to see him. Miller couldn't make it the first night, but showed up the second, only to be informed that Lefty had taken ill and gone back to Nashville. Grievously disappointed, Miller ran into steel player Pee Wee Whitewing, who sat in with Lefty the night before. Whitewing shook his head and told Miller, "You oughta be glad you didn't see him." And out in California, when Junior Cox saw his cousin for the last time, Lefty, says Cox, was the "most saddest, loneliest, unhappiest man I ever met."

Every gig seemed a lesson in time. For one 1972 tour, Lefty hit the road again with his brother David. Except this time there was a third brother, Allen, who was five years younger than Lefty's daughter. David, no longer "Little David (Rock and Roll Sensation)," emceed the shows. He'd sing a few numbers, do impressions, introduce his brothers in turn, basically holding things together. "I'd have Allen come up, and he'd do one or two songs maybe," says David, "then I'd go up and help him do the last one, get him off, bring Lefty up, you know, and I played the harmonica with him, and sang a little harmony with him, and that sort of stuff." For the most part uninspired, Lefty stuck with "Always

Late" and "Mom and Dad's Waltz" and a few of his other twenty-year-old hits. "Let's face it . . . he'd been out there for many years," David says, "playing small little places, you know, and working with a different band every night. How much fun can that be? And most of the time these bands didn't take time enough to even learn one of the songs."

But once in a while, Lefty would pull out the stops, lean into his set, and completely dominate the room as he had in the 1950s. The last concert of the tour—the last time David shared a stage with his older brother—Lefty turned on the charisma and stopped all motion in the audience. The crowd squeezed in tight around the stage, every eye on Lefty, all riveted by a voice and star presence that never did learn how to quit. It was, says David, "unbelievable."

As the 1974 tour season wound down, Lefty's yodel cleared long enough for him to make two last stops at Woodland Sound Studio—one in August, the other in October. The sessions produced mixed results. The low point was Lefty's cover of Charlie Rich's "Sittin' and Thinkin'," an interesting song choice that Gant ruined by laying the backup vocals on far too thick. The high point was "Yesterday Just Passed My Way Again," a tender song about tenuous reunion that Whitey Shafer wrote with his wife, Darlene. Lefty loved the song and did it total justice. He followed with "Life's Like Poetry," a Merle Haggard tune that Hag had played for Lefty at one of his own recording sessions. It would be the last song Lefty Frizzell ever sang on record.

But of all the material cut those final two dates, the shocker was an astoundingly strong, poignant remake of "I Love You a Thousand Ways." A quarter century after scratching them out in pencil in the Chaves County Jail, lines like "please wait until I'm free" not only still resonated through Lefty's life; as sung to Alice, they had acquired all new meaning.

Merle Haggard arrived at the studio just as Lefty was finishing the vocal track for "I Love You a Thousand Ways" and was immediately struck by how great the remake turned out. "I was watching," Haggard said, "and he got through with it, and he played the whole album back for me, and we sit down, flat out on our butts right on the floor out there, and listened to his album. And I thought it was very good, you know, I thought there was very little sign of age. And we talked about that. We talked about people like Tommy Duncan we'd both listened to, and wondered at what age that would begin to take effect on us."

Stitched together from several sessions, over several years' time, Lefty's second ABC album, *The Classic Style of Lefty Frizzell*, turned out to be a slightly more uneven work than the first. Intent on giving Lefty an updated seventies sound, Gant, on a couple of songs, made the fatal error of drowning Lefty's voice in saccharine overdubbed strings. But where Lefty had room to breathe in the mix, he was, as always, incomparable. When he received his pre-final mix tape of the album, he and his pals held a listening party at Rusty Adams's house. Marlon was there and remembers watching his father's reaction as the tape rolled. Lefty was listening to every note through the din of the party. When "Yesterday Just Passed My Way Again" came over the speakers, the most sorrowful, unforgettable look Marlon had ever seen passed through Lefty's eyes. Stunned, Marlon crossed the room and said to his father, "That's the greatest stuff you've ever done."

With the tour season over and the new album in the can, Lefty had time on his hands for the holidays. That, for him, was always a mixed blessing. Not long before Christmas, he taped another weeklong radio series with T. Tommy Cutrer, who introduced Lefty as an artist "about as much imitated . . . by country music singers as anybody ever has or ever will be." That was in 1974; Cutrer didn't know how right he was. Rusty Adams accompanied Lefty to the studio and shared the interview load. Close listeners to Cutrer's show may have noticed more wear on Lefty's voice than was evident three years earlier, but he held up well, making wisecracks and telling entertaining stories. Lefty was also more reflective this time around, particularly when commenting on his new album, a preview copy of which he brought along for the program. He talked about how "I Never Go Around Mirrors" derived from years of partying on the road, of having to stay up all night with old friends, no matter the next day's schedule, lest they think he considered himself too good for them. "You get up after that," Lefty said, "and you walk to that mirror, and you look and say, 'No, that cain't — that cannot — that cannot be me." Lefty's running commentary had moments of considerable poignancy. He dedicated "Yesterday Just Passed My Way Again" to Darlene Shafer's mother, and confided to Cutrer, sincerely, that he considered his new version of "I Love You a Thousand Ways" better than the original. Without going into the circumstances of the song's genesis (Lefty had dodged that question for almost thirty years) he explained, "At the time, I didn't write it. It was the heart inside that did all the work."

Some time after the taping, Lefty's state of mind took a turn for the worse. On Christmas Eve, Whitey and Doodle were appearing on a different Nashville radio program when a call came through from Lefty. For reasons he never explained, he was staying at a motel near the radio station and invited his friends to come by when they were through. At the motel, Lefty surprised Owens by asking if he could borrow thirty or forty dollars. "Lefty never borrowed money off of nobody," Owens says. But Lefty, with no cash on his person, hadn't bought Alice a Christmas present yet. Doodle gladly loaned him the money, but felt uneasy when Lefty insisted they all drink a couple beers before heading back to Hendersonville. Sure enough, by the time they got to town, the store where Lefty intended to pick up a present for Alice was closed. "I felt sorry for him," Owens says. "He almost cried. He said, 'Man, I really wanted to get my wife something for Christmas.' "

The next day, Owens paid a holiday call to the big house. He found Lefty in a deeply sad mood. Lefty gave him back the money and the two friends drank a quiet holiday beer or two. Then Lefty said, "Doodle, I'm coming off the road. I can't stand it anymore. I wanna be home."

Chapter 32

LEFTY RANG IN the new year, 1975, with Judy Baker in Johnstown, Pennsylvania. He had called her a couple of days before at her mother's house there, and told her if she and Rocky would meet him at the airport, he would fly in to spend New Year's Eve with them. "He just come to relax with us, is what he wanted to do," Judy says. Warned by her not to risk the Johnstown airport in winter, Lefty landed in Pittsburgh, where Judy and Rocky drove to pick him up. Arriving late, they found him in the baggage area, sitting on his suitcase. He had left his guitar at home. "Isn't it wonderful where you can get on a plane, and not carry your guitar?" he said. The three of them made it back to Judy's brother's house in Johnstown in time for a snowy evening's merriment. The party started on New Year's Eve and never really quit for the next three weeks. They ate, drank, laughed, carried on, walked the mountain land, and hunted deer. One morning, about seven o'clock, Alice called Johnstown and spoke to Judy. "Is Lefty all right, Judy?" she asked. "Yeah, Alice, he's okay," she said. "You wanna talk to him? He's asleep. You want me to wake him up?" "Oh, no, no," Alice said. "I just wanna know that he's okay."

After three weeks, Lefty and the Bakers drove back to Nashville with trunk and trailer loaded down with deer meat. The one-day drive took three days. "We would go so far and just stop," Judy says. "We would go another hundred miles and just stop. We just never wanted it to end. We just never wanted to say goodbye."

Lefty intended the trip as a relaxing holiday getaway, but it took a lot out of him. He came back feeling sick and retreated once more to the little house to rest and to work on some new songs with Whitey and plan his next recording project. He already knew what it was to be: a gospel album, composed not of old standards, but of new songs he hoped to write with his Hendersonville friends. He talked about the idea constantly. It was no sudden conversion, for in his way, Lefty was every bit as sincerely religious as he was suspicious of old-fashioned Bible-thumping. "I'll tell you what," he once said to Shorty Hall, "I don't want 'em worrying about me, because me and The Man are right. They'd better be worried about theirselves."

Meanwhile, the first single pulled from Lefty's new secular album was the Haggard number, "Life's Like Poetry." It hit the charts in February but failed to ignite. Lefty probably didn't notice. He rarely played the radio anymore, and if someone else did, he was liable to reach over and turn it off. If they asked why he did it, he'd say, "I don't wanna hear myself repeated again." Nevertheless, with a new record to push, he had to muster enough strength to make the promo rounds. He stopped in Dallas in early April, where a well-meaning reporter made the mistake of calling him a living legend. "I always thought someone was supposed to be dead to be a legend," Lefty said. Still, much as he hated such interviews, Lefty was capable of candor and insight when speaking with someone he liked and trusted. One such writer was *Country Music* journalist Geoff Lane, who spent a couple of long evenings with Lefty at the little house, drinking Bloody Marys and interviewing him for what may have been the last time. Lane described Lefty as a man with "pain lines etched deep in his forehead, and around his eyes," but who also appeared to be a survivor with the worst behind him. Opening up to Lane, Lefty talked about the old days and the new, both in terms of his career and his personal life. "I was too young to be a husband or a father," Lefty said, looking back on his early years with Alice. "That was the hardest thing and I couldn't take care of it." He volunteered that "I Love You a Thousand Ways" had been written in the county jail, but when Lane asked if Lefty wanted to tell what he'd been in for, Lefty, exhibiting marvelous dissembling powers, responded, "Might as well be truthful, fightin' and carryin' on."

Throughout the interview sessions, Lefty made it clear that he and Alice were as good as completely separated. He went so far as to describe his singing style — his caressing, lingering way with a single note — as reflecting his having not wanted "to let go of the woman I loved." In fact, his and Alice's situation was worse than separation. On April 30, Alice, needing no nudge from a self-aggrandizing preacher, filed for divorce.

The petition was brief and relatively bloodless. Alice charged "cruel and inhuman treatment" as her grounds, but did not elaborate. She listed their date of separation as "January 1975." Besides alimony, she asked for their 1970 Oldsmobile station wagon, a vacant lot they owned in Winnsboro, Texas (her birthplace), a sixty-eight-acre tract of undeveloped land in Collinwood, Tennessee, that she and Lefty had recently purchased, and a trailer in which to live. She also requested that the big house be put on the market and the proceeds applied to the mortgage on the Collinwood land.

No one will ever know if Alice was serious. She had every reason to want to divorce Lefty. Then again, she had always had those reasons. It would not have been out of character for her to threaten divorce as heavy artillery in their thirty-year battle of wills. "I don't think she would have gone through with it," Lois says. "He was still hangin' out at the big house. They were still buds." If the petition was merely a bluff, a ploy to get Lefty to straighten up, it was effective. For the next couple of months, he often talked about a reconciliation, about retreating to Collinwood himself. He wanted to set up a trailer like Dallas Frazier's, not only for Alice but also so that he could have a quiet place to live and write his gospel album. For Lefty, reorganizing his life and working out his differences with Alice were all of a piece.

And yet, no matter how desperately he wanted to, he could not get off the road. At some point early that summer, Lefty, Shorty Hall, and singer Bill Phillips drove to Indianapolis for a package show at the city auditorium. Someone on the tour had canceled, so at the last minute the agent asked Lefty to fill in. Another summer season was about to begin. "Lefty laid in the backseat," says Hall, "and every thirty or forty minutes, would raise up and say, 'You think I can do it?' I said, 'How many millions of times have you done it? What are you worried about?' He was worried that he could not perform as good as some of the artists that was on there. I think he was already sick, you know."

Once they hit Indianapolis, Lefty's mini-entourage received the red carpet treatment. The local cops even met them at the city limits to escort them downtown. The concert—apparently the last of Lefty's life—proved to be a repeat of a scene played over and over since Lefty first broke out of Jim Beck's studio. Says Hall, "The crowd danced, and had a ball, you know, when the other people were performing. And come Lefty's time, he got out there, he hit that guitar one time . . . and them people stopped everything. Their dancin', the whole works. And he got standing ovations."

Lefty's next scheduled gig was for July 19 at the Delaware State Fair. A few days before that, he, Shorty, and Doodle Owens were all at a friend's house talking about the intended gospel album. "Lefty had a lot of good things to say about everybody that day," says Owens.

Hall remembers that the men were seated at a table, and in the middle of the conversation "Lefty reached up and grabbed his head right along . . . just above the eye. Felt a terrific pain." Adds Owens, "It was really strange. I had a strange feelin' that something was going on. He went in the bathroom . . . and didn't come out for about twenty, twenty-five minutes. I told Shorty, I said, 'Go check on Lefty, man, there's something wrong.' He went back there and Lefty was really having a bad time."

Hall took Lefty back to the little house that evening and saw to it that he ate a meal before going to bed. Later that week, on July 18, Lefty was preparing to leave for his Delaware gig when Alice and Lois came over to the little house to see him. They found him in a horribly distraught, depressed state, knowing that the road was about to swallow him again. Lois never forgot the conversation that ensued.

> Mama was sittin' on the couch, and he was sittin' on the couch facing her. And I was sittin' in the recliner chair that they had against the wall. Then he started telling about how he'd done everything, he'd been everywhere, he'd accomplished more than he ever set out to accomplish. That's what he said. He never dreamed — he never dreamed he'd get that far in life, and never dreamed he'd accomplish that much. And he'd seen everything there was to see. Been around the whole world and saw everything. He'd met kings, queens, and peasants. And hung out and drank with all of 'em. And he'd just done more than he ever wanted to do, actually. He said, "I've done more than I even wanted to do. And I'm so tired, I can't hardly stand it."

That evening, after Alice and Lois left, Shorty Hall came over. He didn't stay long, however, for he and Lefty had a redeye to Delaware booked for three o'clock in the morning. At about eight o'clock, Shorty went out and picked up an eight-pack of Miller ponies, Lefty's preferred beer, and brought it back to the little house. Then he went home to get ready for the flight.

Lefty was all alone.

Several hours later, at some point just after midnight, Lefty woke up on the floor next to his bed. He discovered he'd been sick to his stomach. He fumbled for a shirt and tried to put it on, but found he couldn't do it; he had no movement on his left side. Realizing what had happened, he managed to get to the phone. He called Alice and told her he thought he'd had a stroke. She called an ambulance and rushed over to

Cline Court. Once there, she could do little for Lefty. He asked her to help him up; he didn't want to be found on the floor. She told him to lie still. When the ambulance arrived, there wasn't much the crew could do for Lefty either. They were community volunteers, not trained paramedics, and had no way to stabilize his condition. They put him in the ambulance and took off for Music City. Alice followed in her own car.

Along the way, Lefty suffered a second stroke, a massive cerebral hemorrhage. By the time the ambulance reached Nashville's Memorial Hospital, Lefty was in a coma.

Around seven in the morning, Alice called Lois at Lois's mother-in-law's house. "She was crying, and I knew instantly something was wrong. Said, 'What's wrong, Mama, what's going on?' She said, 'Your daddy's real sick. He's gonna be okay, though. Come down here right now. Get here right now.' And I said, 'Well, I ain't even got dressed, Mama.' And she said, 'Throw something on and come now. Immediately.' And man, it freaked me out. And I thought, my God, some'n's real bad."

It took longer to notify Marlon and Rickey. They were camping out on their parents' Collinwood land, down by the Tennessee-Alabama border, with no phone nearby. "The sheriff's department came down there, told us that Daddy had had a heart attack," Marlon says. "I didn't even know if he was still alive." He and Rickey made it to Nashville by late afternoon. Lefty was still in a coma in intensive care. His eyes were open, though, and the nurse told Marlon to go ahead and talk to him, that somewhere back there Lefty could hear. Marlon held his father's hand, and said, "I love you. Please come out of it. Do. I understand if you don't want to, but I love you. I hope you will." Sitting by his father's side, Marlon told him if he was so tired, and ready to go on, to go ahead and do it. "Go on," he said, "but if not, we want you to stay with us."

All through the day and into the night, the family sat, waiting. "Most of the time I spent on my knees, bargaining with God," Lois says. At one point, a doctor came out and talked to them all. When he told Lois that her father wasn't going to make it, she threw a fit. "I practically cussed the poor man out. I told him he didn't know how strong my daddy was. I actually called him a liar." A few hours later, at 11:20, Lefty's family was jolted from their prayers by the electronic code signaling cardiac arrest. They watched from the frozen distance of stop-time shock as the nurses and doctors ran to Lefty's room. "It was too late," Lois says. "He had decided he'd go on down the road."

Lefty's sudden passing—so unexpected, but in hindsight so pre-dictable—nearly destroyed everyone around him. It was so much more than the death of a loved one; it was the death of a leader. He was only forty-seven years old. Among family and friends, singers, and fans, Lefty was the star, the dominant personality, the center of every universe he inhabited. When he died, it was like a black hole opened and sucked the light out of everyone's lives. Outside his imme-diate family, it seemed like practically everyone he had known found out while onstage. Whitey Shafer was working in Waco when the call came through; people waited till he finished his show to tell him. Lefty's brother Allen and nephew Jimmy, gigging in Yuma, Arizona, heard the news between sets. Merle Haggard learned Lefty had died five minutes before he was due onstage. The despair of the "show must go on" hypocrisy he endured that night stayed with him for years, finally surfacing in a song he wrote called "Footlights" that may be the most honest, bitter comment on the plight of a midlife country entertainer anyone has ever sung.

Immediately after Lefty died, Alice became physically sick and was bedridden. "There wasn't a cell in her body that didn't feel the pain," her daughter says. Shorty Hall went over to the little house the next day. He looked at the lone Miller pony sitting on the mantel in the living room and experienced a grieving epiphany that he never could put into words. Lefty was placed in his casket—Lois nearly fainted when they had to pick one out—and taken to the Cole and Garrett funeral home for public visitation. The children were given a half hour alone with Lefty before the doors were opened to the fans. The three of them, crying, put a gold charm shaped like a guitar in Lefty's hand. Then they thought of something funny he might have said, had he been able, and started to laugh. By the time the public was allowed inside, the laughter had turned to suffocating sobs. People say Lois, out of her mind with grief, kept repeating, "Where's my daddy? Where's my daddy?" while her nine-year-old son, Christopher, echoed at her side, "Poppa, Poppa!"

Strong woman that she was, Alice recovered from her collapse and maintained her quiet composure as she greeted the musicians, fans, and relatives—Frizzells, Coxes, Harpers, and strangers—who soon arrived from all across the country. Many showed up to weep at Lefty's side, others for the spectacle only. One family actually posed by the open casket, cameras clicking. Rickey Frizzell, the most mild-mannered of Lefty's children, threw them out of the parlor.

Held in stifling heat at antiseptic Forest Lawn Cemetery in Good-lettsville, Tennessee, the funeral turned into a mad circus. Lefty was to be buried near country stars Hawkshaw Hawkins, who died in the same plane crash that killed Patsy Cline, and Stringbean, who was murdered, in a dismal section of the cemetery known, perversely, as "Music Row." Chosen as active pallbearers were Rusty Adams, Dallas Frazier, Abe Mulkey, Doodle Owens, Whitey Shafer, and Lois's husband, Tommy Smith. The honorary pallbearers included virtually every middle-aged man who ever sang on the hillbilly music circuit and survived. The procession was so long the city had to block off Dickerson Pike, a major suburban artery. As the hearse passed through town, Lefty's family looked out the window and saw tears streaming down the face of the motorcycle cop directing traffic. The number of lives that Lefty had touched seemed limitless.

At graveside, Lefty's family sat at the front, surrounded by a silent sea of friends and fans pouring across the grass. His parents, Naamon and A.D., held to their chairs in blinking stoicism while someone played "Mom and Dad's Waltz." They barely moved a muscle as Lefty's coffin was lowered into the ground. The dirt was shoveled in before anyone left. Riveted in horror, no one could believe what was happening as the first clods hit the casket, sounding to the singers' and songwriters' ears like cymbals rung into emptiness.

ENERGY DEPENDENCE

March 31, 1992. Jester Park. Corsicana, Texas.

Highway 167 runs a claustrophobic timber gauntlet south from Little Rock to El Dorado, Arkansas. The trees close in and night falls fast. About twenty miles north of El Dorado, the air thickens and gives off a swampy, industrial odor that stays with you into town. Heat lightning—at least you hope it's heat lightning—arcs on the horizon, the soundless explosions flashing gold above the Ouachita River.

Around El Dorado's town square, yellow pennants hang from the streetlights, each printed with the silhouette of an oil derrick. A little ways on, a pair of two-lane highways crisscross before one dead-ends at the railroad tracks. A baby Doberman guards a lumberyard there. Motels at the crossroads. A pair of police cruisers idle side-by-side in a gas station parking lot.

At the Days Inn bottle club, the barmaid wonders if I'm with one of the construction crews in town since the tornado hit last week. The twister cut a swath through the outskirts of El Dorado, just a few feet off the path of another that hit the year before. At that time, the barmaid was running a "redneck beer bar" out where the funnel touched down. She and her customers were trapped between the highway and the tornado, waiting for the roof to fly off over their heads. It wasn't much of a bar, anyway, she says, just a place to serve beer in cans. "Don't want to give those people bottles," she says. "Learned my lesson the hard way."

It's several more hours to Corsicana, where U.S. 287 skirts the factory side of town past Nutrena Feeds, the Anchor Glass Container Factory,

National Incinerator, and "Joy's Place," a "Game Room with Jukebox." On the door to Joy's juke joint (which is part of a converted roundhouse) a handwritten sign reads: "Friday   Country & Rap $2.00."

Downtown, Corsicana lacks El Dorado's air of menace, but makes up for it in dusty stillness. Country craft boutiques and children's clothing stores appear to be struggling against a leaden local economy reflected in the inordinate number of pawnshops. I don't think Corsicana has seen much oil lately. The two or three people I ask have never heard of Tuckertown. Nor do they seem to have heard of Lefty Frizzell, though at that very moment, a few thousand fans are gathering in Jester Park for the unveiling of the Lefty Frizzell Memorial on what would have been his sixty-fourth birthday, the day proclaimed by the mayor himself as "Lefty Frizzell Day."

One man I overhear at the public library knows there's a hubbub at Jester Park, he just doesn't know what it's all about. "I guess I just didn't pay attention, follow up on it," he says, to a gray-haired woman sitting near him.

The woman tells him they're holding a tribute to Lefty Frizzell, the country singer. Lefty was born in Corsicana, you know.

Oh yeah, Lefty Frizzell—now the man gets it. "I see him every now and then on TV, at those Nashville functions," he says.

Lefty has been dead for over sixteen years.

The mood at the park is of a Pierce Brooks county fair campaign stop. The pickups parked in a line on the grass all have stickers in their windows for one of the three people running for Navarro County sheriff. Judging by the distribution of slogans, it looks like a close race. A bored flatfoot whistles cars this way and that. Local pickers parade on and off a bandstand lined with stars-and-stripes bunting. Families spread picnic blankets in the sun. The elderly wear visors. Their grandchildren sport T-shirts that say things like: "I've Fallen and I Can't Reach My Beer" and "Guns N' Roses Was Here."

A tour bus belonging to Shelly West, former duet partner of David Frizzell, is parked in the center of the action. In fact, her bus *is* the center of the action. Camera hounds wait by the door for a Frizzell, any Frizzell, to emerge. The star this lazy day is eighty-three-year-old Naamon, Lefty's father, in poor health, yet showing no sign of wear as he stands by the bus for hours on end, dressed in solid black, signing every piece of paper in sight. He has outlived his oldest son by almost seventeen years, his daughter-in-law by eight. Alice passed on in 1984. She died of cancer. Some say it is the disease of great sorrow. "She was the saddest person I ever saw," says Lois. "You can't even describe that kind of sadness. It was so deep, it went through her physically."

Mingling near the bus are pockets of middle-aged former deejays, managers, and producers, men who once ran the country music business, but for whom the business now has no use. They are here from Dallas or Tyler, Shreveport or Monroe, all shaking hands and telling Lefty stories, mostly there just because it's so rare to see one of their own get his day. A few of the boys from Bob Wills's band are drifting about. Abe Mulkey is here. A ten-year-old Dodge station wagon pulls to a stop, and out steps Floyd Tillman. He takes a look around, then reaches into the trunk and hauls out his guitar case. Inside is a black and tan 1957 Gibson arch-top—the most beautiful guitar I have ever seen in my life.

At three o'clock, the crowd closes in around the memorial itself, a life-size statue of Lefty with a mural behind depicting the red-letter days of his life and career. The statue is draped in blue cloth and strapped tight with a yellow cord. A number of Corsicana citizens—people who have worked incredibly hard for four years to bring this day about—have things to say, and there are long lists of people deserving thanks. An assortment of guests are brought to the microphone: Madge Suttee, the Beck studio piano player; Irene Smith, Hank Williams's sister. A middle-aged woman, a doctor, tells of meeting Lefty when she was working on Music Row in the old days. Her father died while she was in Nashville and she had no way to get home. Lefty, whom she hardly knew at the time, showed up at her office with a plane ticket and fifty dollars. He told her to get out of the music business, that it would only cause her grief. Choked with emotion, she says Lefty Frizzell is part of the reason she's a doctor today.

A heretofore unheard Lefty demo from the Beck studio is played for the crowd, the sound system so weak it remains largely unheard. A local radio reporter talks into his live remote, trying gamely, as the speeches drag on, to keep up interest, to explain to the folks back home that even if they don't recognize Lefty's name, they know his influence. What he means is that in 1984, two years after Lefty was voted into the Country Music Hall of Fame, Merle Haggard took yet another version of "That's the Way Love Goes" to number one, and that same year, Whitey and Darlene Shafer gave young comer George Strait a number one hit called "Does Fort Worth Ever Cross Your Mind." Lefty's style slid wholesale from car speakers across America as Strait sang, "I wonder now if it may-aykes a difference. . . ." By the mid-1980s, if it hadn't been already, Lefty's sound was the dominant force in commercial country music. With Strait, Randy Travis, and Keith Whitley at the forefront, an army of young hillbilly singers descended on 16th Avenue, all breaking up syllables, all rolling their vowels in the gravelly low end of their vocal registers to prove they had country soul. Travis and Strait meant it. Whitley *really* meant it. Prior to recording a contemporary version of "I Never Go Around Mirrors," lengthened by new lines from Shafer, Whitley sang it over Lefty's grave. But he and Travis were exceptions. Most who have swallowed Lefty's style, and there are more of them every day, appear to have no idea where they got it. Some have said Haggard, others Whitley. But what the reporter at Lefty Frizzell Day in Corsicana should emphasize is that you cannot listen to a 1990s country music station for fifteen minutes without hearing echoes of Lefty Frizzell.

The statue stays covered. The stories are moving, the tribute sweet. But half the crowd, mostly standing, can't hear it. As speaker after speaker steps to the mike, the people in back start to grumble. They look at their watches, then at the veiled statue, then back at their watches. They shift on their feet, which are starting to ache. Some head back to the stage. Others drift off into the side streets of Corsicana. Most, though, are happy to stick it out to see Lefty's face. They've been through this kind of gig before. Seems like they're never on time.

Sources

THE DOCUMENT CITED as "Frizzell, Lefty. Deposition for: 'Jack Starnes, Jr. vs. Wm. Orville Frizzell, known as Lefty Frizzell,' # 6550[3], District Court, Jefferson County, Texas, October 10, 1952," is the defendant's personal copy of the deposition, given to Lefty at the time and preserved by his family since his death. No copy of the document exists in the Jefferson County Court records. Through an apparent clerical error, Lefty's copy is numbered 65501, instead of 65503, which was the actual Starnes/Frizzell case number. Also, throughout the document, Art Satherley's last name is consistently misspelled "Satterlee." The correct spelling has been used in the text.

"Frizzell, Lefty. MSS and papers," is a catchall citation that refers to the bewildering hodgepodge of preserved private letters, unpublished song lyrics, doodlings, tour itineraries, telegrams, ad clippings, receipts (a vacuum cleaner purchase, for instance), telephone bills, and other items, both dated and undated, in custody of the Frizzell heirs and of such varied nature as to constitute their own bibliographic nightmare. Some I have separated out to cite individually. Most, however, I have happily lumped together under "MSS and papers."

The letter quoted in its entirety on page 62 is as read aloud by Alice Frizell during an interview taped in 1984. The letter has since been lost, which is unfortunate as it would almost certainly have dated Lefty's Louisiana Hayride audition.

GENERAL SOURCES

Billboard, 1948–1975. Particularly helpful was the weekly "Folk Talent and Tunes" column written by, in succession, Johnny Sippel, Joel Friedman, and Bill Sachs. Select individual articles cited below.

Country Music Reporter/Music Reporter, September 22, 1956–March 14, 1964.

Gentry, Linnell. *A History and Encyclopedia of Country, Western, and Gospel Music.* Nashville: McQuiddy Press, 1961.

Kingsbury, Paul, and Alan Axelrod, eds. *Country: The Music and the Musicians.* New York: The Country Music Foundation/Abbeville Press, 1988.

Malone, Bill C. *Country Music U.S.A.* 1968. Rev. ed. Austin: University of Texas Press, 1985.

Music City News, July 1963–July 1975. Select individual articles cited below.

Except where otherwise noted, discographical and sessional information is from:

Weize, Richard. Discography in *Lefty Frizzell: Life's Like Poetry.* Vollersode, West Germany: Bear Family Records, 1992.

Chart information not drawn from original Billboard *sources is taken from:*

Whitburn, Joel. *Top Country Singles 1944–1988.* Menomonee Falls, Wis.: Record Research, Inc., 1989.

———. *The Billboard Book of Top 40 Hits.* New York: Billboard Publications, 1987.

PROLOGUE

Amburn, Ellis, *Dark Star: The Roy Orbison Story,* New York: Lyle Stuart, 1990.

Frizzell, Alice. Interviewed by Lois and Marlon Frizzell, 1984.

Frizzell, Lefty. MSS and papers.

Haggard, Merle. From radio specials produced by Larry Daniels and Bill Mack. Quoted in notes to *The Lefty Frizzell Story: His Life, As Told by Mom and Dad Frizzell.* Visalia, Calif.: 2×4 Record Corp., 1980.

Miller, Joseph, ed. *New Mexico: A Guide to the Colorful State.* Compiled by Workers of the Writers' Program of the Work Projects Administration in the State of New Mexico. 1940. Rev. ed. New York: Hastings House, 1962.

Utley, Robert M. *Billy the Kid: A Short and Violent Life.* Lincoln and London: University of Nebraska Press, 1989.

Author interviews
Lucky Cook

CHAPTER 1

Batton, Billy, and Wyvonne Putman. "Tuckertown." Unpublished manuscript. Navarro County Historical Society, Corsicana, Texas.

Fielder, Donna. "Honky-tonk Melody Brought Dexter Fame," *Denton (Tex.) Record-Chronicle,* June 27, 1980.

Fluker, Bobby. "Lefty Frizzell: A Story of Rags to Riches." Special to the *Corsicana (Tex.) Daily Sun,* March 31, 1992.

Franks, Kenny A., and Paul F. Lambert. *Early Louisiana and Arkansas Oil: A Photographic History 1901–1946.* College Station, Tex.: Texas A&M University Press, 1982.

Frizzell, Lefty. Deposition for: "Jack Starnes, Jr. vs. Wm. Orville Frizzell, known as

Lefty Frizzell," # 6550[3], District Court, Jefferson County, Tex., October 10, 1952.

Murchison, William, Jr. "Oil—Navarro County." In *Navarro County History*, Vol. 2. Corsicana, Tex.: Navarro County Historical Society, Pioneer Village, 1978.

Rister, Carl Coke. *Oil! Titan of the Southwest*. Norman: University of Oklahoma Press, 1949.

Stinger, Tommy. "The American Well and Prospecting Company." In *Navarro County History*, Vol. 5. Corsicana, Tex.: Navarro County Historical Society, Pioneer Village, 1985.

Tosches, Nick. "Al Dexter." *Old Time Music* 22 (Autumn 1976).

———. *Country: The Biggest Music in America*. New York: Stein and Day, 1977.

"Wine, Women, Song." *Denton (Tex.) Record-Chronicle*, February 11, 1973.

Yergin, Daniel. *The Prize: The Epic Quest for Oil, Money and Power*. New York: Simon & Schuster/Touchstone, 1991, 1992.

Author interviews

Junior Cox, Betty Frizzell, Marlon Frizzell, Naamon Frizzell, Blanche Whaley (for Frizzell geneology)

CHAPTER 2

Dixon, Robert M. W., and John Godrich. *Recording the Blues*. New York: Stein and Day, 1970.

Doty, Carl. "Tune Wranglers of Texas." *Rural Radio*, May 1938.

Everson, William K. *The Hollywood Western: 90 Years of Cowboys and Indians, Train Robbers, Sheriffs and Gunslingers, and Assorted Heroes and Desperados*. New York: Citadel Press, 1969, 1992.

Fowler, Gene, and Bill Crawford. *Border Radio*. New York: Limelight Editions, 1990.

Frizzell, Alice. Interviewed by Lois and Marlon Frizzell, 1984.

Green, Douglas B. "The Singing Cowboy: An American Dream." *Journal of Country Music*, 7, no. 2, May 1978.

Lane, Geoff, "The Last of Lefty Frizzell," *Country Music* 4, no. 2, November 1975.

The Lefty Frizzell Story: His Life: As Told by Mom and Dad Frizzell. Visalia, Calif.: 2 X 4 Record Corp., 1980.

Lynch, Vincent, and Bill Henkin. Photographs by Kazuhiro Tsuruta. *Jukebox: The Golden Age*. Berkeley, Calif.: Lancaster-Miller, 1981.

Pahls, Marty, and Smiley Jaxon. Liner notes to *Devil with the Devil: Hot Western Swing from the 1930s*. San Francisco: Rambler Records, n.d.

Porterfield, Nolan. *Jimmie Rodgers: The Life and Times of America's Blue Yodeler*. Urbana: University of Illinois Press, 1979.

Porterfield, Nolan. Liner notes to *Jimmie Rodgers: The Singing Brakeman*. Vollersode, Germany: Bear Family Records, 1992.

Pugh, Ronnie. Liner notes to *Jimmie Davis: Country Music Hall of Fame Series*. University City, Calif.: MCA Records, 1991.

Tosches, Nick. "Honky-Tonkin': Ernest Tubb, Hank Williams, and the Bartender's

Muse." In *Country: The Music and the Musicians*, edited by Paul Kingsbury and Alan Axelrod. New York: The Country Music Foundation/Abbeville Press, 1988.

Townsend, Charles R. *San Antonio Rose: The Life and Music of Bob Wills*. Urbana: University of Illinois Press, 1976.

Author interviews

Marlon Frizzell, Naamon Frizzell, Bob Pinson

CHAPTER 3

Adams, Susan. "Meet Lefty Frizzell." *The Official Lefty Frizzell Fan Club Journal* 1, no. 1, July 1956.

Coffey, Kevin Reed. "Indelible Ink: The Life and Times of Songwriter Ted Daffan," *Journal of Country Music*, 16, no. 2, 1994.

Fehrenbach, T. R. *Lone Star: A History of Texas and the Texans*. New York: American Legacy Press, 1968.

Frizzell, Alice. Interviewed by Lois and Marlon Frizzell, 1984.

Frizzell, Lefty. Deposition for: "Jack Starnes, Jr. vs. Wm. Orville Frizzell, known as Lefty Frizzell," # 6550[3], District Court, Jefferson County, Texas, October 10, 1952.

———. MSS and papers.

Guralnick, Peter. "Ernest Tubb: The Texas Troubadour." In *Lost Highway*. New York: Harper & Row/Perennial, 1979, 1989.

Harrison, W. Walworth. *History of Greenville and Hunt County Texas*, Waco, Tex.: Texian Press, 1976.

Larsen, Lawrence H. *The Urban South: A History*. Lexington: University Press of Kentucky, 1990.

The Lefty Frizzell Story: His Life: As Told by Mom and Dad Frizzell. Visalia, Calif.: 2 X 4 Record Corp., 1980.

Kingston, Mike, ed. *1992–93 Texas Almanac*. Dallas: *Dallas Morning News*, 1991.

Patoski, Joe Nick, and Bill Crawford; *Stevie Ray Vaughan: Caught in the Crossfire*. Boston: Little, Brown and Company, 1993.

Roden, Jim. "Lefty Frizzell—A Living Legend." *Dallas Times Herald*, April 3, 1975.

Tosches, Nick. "Honky-Tonkin': Ernest Tubb, Hank Williams, and the Bartender's Muse." In *Country: The Music and the Musicians*, edited by Paul Kingsbury and Alan Axelrod. New York: The Country Music Foundation/Abbeville Press, 1988.

Author interviews

Betty Frizzell, Marlon Frizzell, Naamon Frizzell, Dorothy Locke

CHAPTER 4

Frizzell, Alice. Interviewed by Lois and Marlon Frizzell, 1984.

Frizzell, Lefty. Deposition for: "Jack Starnes, Jr. vs. Wm. Orville Frizzell, known as

Lefty Frizzell," # 6550[3], District Court, Jefferson County, Texas, October 10, 1952.

————. MSS and papers.

Ginell, Cary. Liner notes to *Bill Boyd and His Cowboy Ramblers 1934–47*. Sugarland, Tex.: Texas Rose Records, 1982.

————. Liner notes to *Milton Brown & his Musical Brownies 1934*. Sugarland, Tex.: Texas Rose Records, 1982.

————. Liner notes to *Roy Newman & His Boys Vol. 1: 1934–8*. Santa Monica, Calif.: Origin Jazz Library Records, 1981.

————. Liner notes to *W. Lee O'Daniel and His Hillbilly Boys 1935–38*. Sugarland, Tex.: Texas Rose Records, 1982.

Govenar, Alan. *Living Texas Blues*. Dallas: Dallas Museum of Art, 1985.

————. *Meeting the Blues*. Dallas: Taylor Publishing Company, 1988.

Hansen, Harry, ed. *Texas: A Guide to the Lone Star State*. Originally Compiled by the Federal Writers' Program of the Work Projects Administration in the State of Texas. 1940. Rev. ed. New York: Hastings House, 1969.

Kingston, Mike, ed. *1992–93 Texas Almanac*. Dallas: Dallas Morning News, 1991.

The Lefty Frizzell Story: His Life: As Told by Mom and Dad Frizzell. Visalia, Calif.: 2 X 4 Record Corp., 1980.

Pahls, Marty, and Smiley Jaxon. Liner notes to *Devil with the Devil: Hot Western Swing from the 1930s*. San Francisco: Rambler Records, n.d.

Rogers, John William. *The Lusty Texans of Dallas*. New York: E. P. Dutton and Company, Inc., 1951, 1960.

Russell, Tony. Liner notes to *Milton Brown & His Musical Brownies: Taking Off!* London: Topic Records, 1977.

Strickland, Ron. *Texans: Oral Histories from the Lone Star State*. New York: Paragon House, 1991.

Townsend, Charles R. *San Antonio Rose: The Life and Music of Bob Wills*. Urbana: University of Illinois Press, 1976.

Author interviews

Junior Cox, Betty Frizzell, Naamon Frizzell, Leon Rhodes

CHAPTER 5

Fleming, Elvis E. "Lefty Earned 'Paid Dues' Here." *Roswell (N.M.) Daily Record*, August 10, 1992.

————. "The Maturing Period: 1903–1940." In *Roundup on the Pecos*, edited by Elvis E. Fleming and Minor S. Huffman. Roswell, N.M.: Chaves County Historical Society, 1978.

Frizzell, Alice. Interviewed by Lois and Marlon Frizzell, 1984.

Frizzell, Lefty. Interviewed by T. Tommy Cutrer. "Music City USA" radio program, #624, September 14, 1972.

Miller, Joseph, ed. *New Mexico: A Guide to the Colorful State*. Compiled by Workers of the Writers' Program of the Work Projects Administration in the State of New Mexico. 1940. Rev. ed. New York: Hastings House, 1962.

Wolfe, Charles. Liner notes to *Lefty Frizzell: Life's Like Poetry*. Vollersode, Germany: Bear Family Records, 1992.

Author interviews

Lucky Cook, Junior Cox, Betty Frizzell, Smiley Mauldin, Ray and Ina Patterson

CHAPTER 6

Adams, Susan. "Meet Lefty Frizzell." *The Official Lefty Frizzell Fan Club Journal* 1, no. 1, July 1956.

"Charge Four with Rape." *Roswell (N.M.) Daily Record*, July 13, 1947.

Fleming, Elvis E. "Lefty Earned 'Paid Dues' Here." *Roswell (N.M.) Daily Record*, August 10, 1992.

Frizzell, Alice. Interviewed by Lois and Marlon Frizzell, 1984.

Frizzell, Lefty. MSS and papers.

"Plead Guilty to Rape Charge." *Roswell (N.M.) Daily Record*, August 8, 1947.

"RAAF Captures Flying Saucer on Ranch in Roswell Region." *Roswell (N.M.) Daily Record*, July 8, 1947.

"Six Are Given Terms in Prison on Two Charges." *Roswell (N.M.) Daily Record*, August 22, 1947.

Wolfe, Charles. "Lefty Frizzell." *The Journal of the American Academy for the Preservation of Old-Time Country Music* 1, no. 4, August 1991.

Author interviews

Lucky Cook, Junior Cox, Betty Frizzell, Lois Frizzell, Marlon Frizzell, Smiley Mauldin

CHAPTER 7

Bartlett, Kim. *Gulf Star 45*. New York: Norton, 1979.

Frizzell, Alice. Interviewed by Lois and Marlon Frizzell, 1984.

Frizzell, Lefty. Deposition for: "Jack Starnes, Jr. vs. Wm. Orville Frizzell, known as Lefty Frizzell," # 6550[3], District Court, Jefferson County, Texas, October 10, 1952.

————. MSS and papers.

Hansen, Harry, ed. *Texas: A Guide to the Lone Star State*. Originally Compiled by the Federal Writers' Program of the Work Projects Administration in the State of Texas. 1940. Rev. ed. New York: Hastings House, 1969.

The Lefty Frizzell Story: His Life: As Told by Mom and Dad Frizzell. Visalia, Calif.: 2 X 4 Record Corp., 1980.

Rister, Carl Coke. *Oil! Titan of the Southwest*. Norman: University of Oklahoma Press, 1949.

Strickland, Ron. *Texans: Oral Histories from the Lone Star State*. New York: Paragon House, 1991.

Tucker, Steve. "The Louisiana Hayride, 1948–1954." *North Louisiana Historical Association Journal* 8, no. 5 (Fall 1977).

Waltrip, Rufus, and Lela Waltrip. "Loco Hills." In *Artesia: Heart of the Pecos*, Canyon, Tex.: Staked Plains Press, 1979.

Author interviews

Junior Cox, Tillman Franks, Betty Frizzell, Marlon Frizzell, Naamon Frizzell, Horace Logan, Olen Thurman

CHAPTER 8

Frizzell, Alice. Interviewed by Lois and Marlon Frizzell, 1984.

Frizzell, Lefty, deposition for: "Jack Starnes, Jr. vs. Wm. Orville Frizzell, known as Lefty Frizzell," # 6550[3], District Court, Jefferson County, Texas, October 10, 1952.

———. Interviewed by T. Tommy Cutrer. "Music City USA" radio program, #621, September 11, 1972.

———. MSS and papers.

The Lefty Frizzell Story: His Life: As Told by Mom and Dad Frizzell. Visalia, Calif.: 2 X 4 Record Corp., 1980.

Martin, Robert L. *The City Moves West: Economic and Industrial Growth in Central West Texas.* Austin: University of Texas Press, 1969.

Myres, Samuel D. *The Permian Basin: Petroleum Empire of the Southwest.* El Paso, Tex.: Permian Press, 1973.

Pickle, Joe. *Gettin' Started: Howard County's First Twenty-five Years.* Big Spring, Tex.: Heritage Museum, 1980.

Author interviews

Clay Allen, Naamon Frizzell, Grady Kilgore, Sleepy Labeef, Don Lambert, Ben Nix, Olen Thurman

CHAPTER 9

"Amusements." *Dallas Daily Times Herald*, April–August 1950.

Catalog of Copyright Entries: Third Series: Volume 4, Part 5b, Number 2: Unpublished Music: July–December 1950. Copyright Office, the Library of Congress, Washington, D.C.

Coffey, Kevin Reed. "Indelible Ink: The Life and Times of Songwriter Ted Daffan." *Journal of Country Music* 16, no. 2, 1994.

"Dallas Hopefuls for Lt. Governor Stumping Texas." *Dallas Daily Times Herald*, July 9, 1950. Also, related articles July 20–22, August 26, 1950.

Frizzell, Alice. Interviewed by Lois and Marlon Frizzell, 1984.

Frizzell, Lefty. Columbia contract records. From Don Law logs. Files of the Country Music Foundation Library and Media Center, Nashville, Tennessee.

———. Deposition for: "Jack Starnes, Jr. vs. Wm. Orville Frizzell, known as Lefty

Frizzell," # 6550[3], District Court, Jefferson County, Texas, October 10, 1952.

———. Interviewed by T. Tommy Cutrer. "Music City USA" radio program, #621, September 11, 1972.

———. MSS and papers.

Hawkins, Martin. "Bullet Records: A Shot in the Dark." *Journal of Country Music* 8, no. 3.

Hawkins, Martin, and Colin Escott. "Bullet Records: A Shot in the Dark," *Country Sounds*, October 1986.

Hurst, Jack. "Music City Pioneer Toasted, Roasted." *The Nashville Tennessean*, January 27, 1971.

Law, Don. Interviewed by Douglas Green. Country Music Foundation Oral History Project, May 14, 1975.

Roden, Jim. "Lefty Frizzell—A Living Legend." *Dallas Times Herald*, April 3, 1975.

Wilonsky, Robert. "Big D Jamboree." *Dallas Observer*, May 20–26, 1993.

Wolfe, Charles. "Honky-tonk Starts Here: The Jim Beck Dallas Studio." *Journal of Country Music* 11, no. 1, 1986.

———. Liner notes to *Lefty Frizzell: Life's Like Poetry*. Vollersode, Germany: Bear Family Records, 1992.

Author interviews

Clay Allen, Mary E. Beck, Boots Bourquin, Ted Daffan, Jimmy Fields, Buddy Griffin, Jimmy Kelly, Grady Kilgore, J. D. Miller, Ben Nix, Ray Price, Leon Rhodes, Billy Walker, Chuck Wiginton

CHAPTER 10

Catalog of Copyright Entries: Third Series: Volume 4, Part 5b, Number 2: Unpublished Music: July–December 1950. Copyright Office, the Library of Congress, Washington, D.C.

Churchill, Allen. "Tin Pan Alley's Git-Tar Blues." *New York Times Magazine*, July 15, 1951.

"Dallas 'Hillbilly' Singer Going Good." *Dallas Daily Times Herald*, September 21, 1950.

Frizzell, Alice. Interviewed by Lois and Marlon Frizzell, 1984.

Frizzell, Lefty, deposition for: "Jack Starnes, Jr. vs. Wm. Orville Frizzell, known as Lefty Frizzell," # 6550[3], District Court, Jefferson County, Texas, October 10, 1952.

———. Interviewed by T. Tommy Cutrer. "Music City USA" radio program, #621, September 11, 1972.

———. MSS and papers.

The Lefty Frizzell Story: His Life: As Told by Mom and Dad Frizzell. Visalia, Calif.: 2 X 4 Record Corp., 1980.

Wolfe, Charles. Liner notes to *Lefty Frizzell: Life's Like Poetry*. Vollersode, Germany: Bear Family Records, 1992.

Author interviews

Clay Allen, Marlon Frizzell, Naamon Frizzell, Grady Kilgore, Abe Mulkey, Ben Nix, Doodle Owens, Billy Walker

CHAPTER 11

Catalog of Copyright Entries: Third Series: Volume 4, Part 5b, Number 2: Unpublished Music: July–December 1950. Copyright Office, the Library of Congress, Washington, D.C.

Cherry, Hugh. Letter to the editor. *Los Angeles Times*, May 31, 1993.

Fleming, Elvis E. "Lefty Earned 'Paid Dues' Here." *Roswell (N.M.) Daily Record*, August 10, 1992.

Frizzell, Alice. Interviewed by Lois and Marlon Frizzell, 1984.

Frizzell, Lefty. Columbia contract, November 8, 1950.

———. Columbia contract records. From Art Satherley logs. Files of the Country Music Foundation Library and Media Center, Nashville, Tennessee.

———. Columbia contract records. From Don Law logs. Files of the Country Music Foundation Library and Media Center, Nashville, Tennessee.

———. Deposition for: "Jack Starnes, Jr. vs. Wm. Orville Frizzell, known as Lefty Frizzell," # 6550[3], District Court, Jefferson County, Texas, October 10, 1952.

———. Interviewed by T. Tommy Cutrer. "Music City USA" radio program, #623, September 13, 1972.

———. MSS and papers.

Henderson, Frame. "Art Satherly [sic], Talent Scout." *The Mountain Broadcast and Prairie Recorder*, new series, 5, September 1945.

Hurst, Jack. "Music City Pioneer Toasted, Roasted." *The Nashville Tennessean*, January 27, 1971.

Kahn, Ed. "Pioneer Recording Man: 'Uncle' Art Satherley," n.d. Files of the Country Music Foundation Library and Media Center, Nashville, Tennessee.

Law, Don. Interviewed by Douglas Green. Country Music Foundation Oral History Project, May 14, 1975.

Starnes, Jack, Jr. *Souvenir Album: Lefty Frizzell and the Tune Toppers.* Beaumont, Tex., circa 1951.

Wolfe, Charles. Liner notes to *Lefty Frizzell: Life's Like Poetry.* Vollersode, Germany: Bear Family Records, 1992.

"WSM's Grand Ole Opry: Prince Albert Show." Radio script, December 30, 1950. Files of the Country Music Foundation Library and Media Center, Nashville, Tennessee.

Zolotow, Maurice. "Hillbilly Boom." *Saturday Evening Post* 216, no. 33, February 12, 1944.

Author interviews

Clay Allen, Bill Callahan, Jesse Ezell, Naamon Frizzell, Buddy Griffin, Jimmy Kelly, Ray Price, Ken Ritter, Olen Thurman

CHAPTER 12

Case records: "Jack Starnes, Jr. vs. Wm. Orville Frizzell, known as Lefty Frizzell," # 65503, District Court, Jefferson County, Texas, June 11, 1952.

Case records: "Neva Starns [sic] v. Jack Starns [sic]," #3322-C, Criminal District Court of Jefferson County, Texas, March 20, 1941.

Clark, James A., and Michel T. Halbouty. *Spindletop*. New York: Random House, 1952.

Daily, H. W. (Pappy). "Pappy Daily Speaks His mind." *Billboard*, November 14, 1964.

Frizzell, Lefty. Deposition for: "Jack Starnes, Jr. vs. Wm. Orville Frizzell, known as Lefty Frizzell," # 6550[3], District Court, Jefferson County, Texas, October 10, 1952.

————. MSS and papers.

Ginell, Cary. Liner notes to *Cliff Bruner's Texas Wanderers*. Van Nuys, Calif.: Texas Rose Records, 1983.

Hansen, Harry, ed. *Texas: A Guide to the Lone Star State*. Originally Compiled by the Federal Writers' Program of the Work Projects Administration in the State of Texas. 1940. Rev. ed. New York: Hastings House, 1969.

Hawkins, Martin. "Martin Hawkins on the Starday Label, and 'Pappy' Daily, Its Founder." *Country Music Review*, December 1976.

Property records, Jefferson County Courthouse, Beaumont, Texas.

Seay, Gina. "H. W. 'Pappy' Daily Winds Up Fifty Years as a Country Music Legend." *The Houston Leader* 28, no. 25, May 20, 1982.

Silverman, Dwight. "Profiles 1980: Bill Starnes." *Beaumont (Tex.) Enterprise-Journal*, March 9, 1980.

Yergin, Daniel. *The Prize: The Epic Quest for Oil, Money, and Power*. New York: Simon & Schuster/Touchstone, 1991, 1992.

Author interviews

J. D. Miller, Ken Ritter

CHAPTER 13

Baker, Judy. Letter to author. June 1993.

Frizzell, Lefty. Deposition for: "Jack Starnes, Jr. vs. Wm. Orville Frizzell, known as Lefty Frizzell," # 6550[3], District Court, Jefferson County, Texas, October 10, 1952.

————. Hill and Range contract. In case records: "Jack Starnes, Jr. vs. Wm. Orville Frizzell, known as Lefty Frizzell," # 65503, District Court, Jefferson County, Texas, June 11, 1952.

————. MSS and papers.

Lane, Geoff. "The Last of Lefty Frizzell." *Country Music* 4, no. 2, November 1975.

Law, Don. Liner notes to *Remembering . . . The Greatest Hits of Lefty Frizzell*. New York: Columbia Records, 1975.

Sievert, Jon. "Country Classics: Legendary Guitars from the Country Music Hall of Fame." *Guitar Player* 20, no. 10, October 1986.

Starnes, Jack, Jr. *Souvenir Album: Lefty Frizzell and the Tune Toppers*. Beaumont, Tex., circa 1951.

Wilonsky, Robert. "Big D Jamboree." *Dallas Observer*, May 20–26, 1993.

Wolfe, Charles. Liner notes to *Lefty Frizzell: Life's Like Poetry*. Vollersode, Germany: Bear Family Records, 1992.

Author interviews

Judy Baker, Mary E. Beck, Bill Callahan, David Frizzell, Freddie Hart, Horace Logan, Abe Manuel, J. D. Miller

CHAPTER 14

Escott, Colin, with George Merritt and William MacEwen. *Hank Williams: The Biography*. Boston: Little, Brown and Company, 1994.

Frizzell, Lefty. Deposition for: "Jack Starnes, Jr. vs. Wm. Orville Frizzell, known as Lefty Frizzell," # 6550[3], District Court, Jefferson County, Texas, October 10, 1952.

———. Hill and Range contract. In case records: "Jack Starnes, Jr. vs. Wm. Orville Frizzell, known as Lefty Frizzell," # 65503, District Court, Jefferson County, Texas, June 11, 1952.

———. Interview on *Hank Williams: Reflections by Those Who Loved Him*. MGM PRO 912, 1975.

———. Interviewed by T. Tommy Cutrer. "Music City USA" radio program, #621, September 11, 1972.

"Fugitive Charge Faces Opry Star." *The Nashville Tennessean*, August 12, 1951.

Haggard, Merle, with Peggy Russell. *Sing Me Back Home: My Story*. New York: Simon & Schuster/Pocket, 1981.

Hopson, Don. Lefty Frizzell discography, 1979. Files of the Country Music Foundation Library and Media Center, Nashville, Tennessee.

Lane, Geoff. "The Last of Lefty Frizzell." *Country Music* 4, no. 2, November 1975.

Larson, Salle. "Reo Palm Isle Celebrates Fifty-five Years of Fame." *Longview (Tex.) News-Journal*, February 9, 1990.

Pinson, Bob. Hank Williams itinerary, April 2–5, 1951. The Country Music Foundation, Nashville, Tennessee.

Property records, Gregg County Courthouse, Longview, Texas.

Silverman, Dwight. "Profiles 1980: Bill Starnes." *Beaumont (Tex.) Enterprise-Journal*, March 9, 1980.

Wolfe, Charles. Liner notes to *Lefty Frizzell: Life's Like Poetry*. Vollersode, Germany: Bear Family Records, 1992.

"WSM's Grand Ole Opry: Prince Albert Show." Radio script, June 16, 1951. Files of the Country Music Foundation Library and Media Center, Nashville, Tennessee.

Author interviews

Judy Baker, Bill Callahan, Curley Chalker, Dr. Joe Dickerson, Tillman Franks, Betty Frizzell, Marlon Frizzell, Naamon Frizzell, Buddy Griffin, Don Helms, Horace

Logan, Merle Kilgore, Abe Manuel, Ray Price, Pee Wee Reid, Ken Ritter, Joe Tonahill, John G. Tucker, Billy Walker

CHAPTER 15

Case records: "Jack Starnes, Jr. vs. Wm. Orville Frizzell, known as Lefty Frizzell," # 65503, District Court, Jefferson County, Texas, June 11, 1952.

Case records: # 49987, Pulaski Circuit Court, Pulaski County, Little Rock, Arkansas.

Frizzell, Lefty. Deposition for: "Jack Starnes, Jr. vs. Wm. Orville Frizzell, known as Lefty Frizzell," # 6550[3], District Court, Jefferson County, Texas, October 10, 1952.

————. MSS and papers.

"Fugitive Charge Faces Opry Star." *The Nashville Tennessean*, August 12, 1951.

Lane, Geoff. "The Last of Lefty Frizzell." *Country Music* 4, no. 2, November 1975.

"Lefty Frizzell." Partial manuscript circa September 1951. Author and date unknown. Files of the Country Music Foundation Library and Media Center, Nashville, Tennessee.

Pinson, Bob. Hank Williams discography. In Roger M. Williams, *Sing a Sad Song: The Life of Hank Williams*. 2d Edition. Urbana and Chicago: University of Illinois Press, 1981.

Property records, Jefferson County Courthouse, Beaumont, Texas.

"Texans Hang Ten-Gallon Hats Here for Night." *The Nashville Tennessean*; August 12, 1951.

Author interviews

Bobbie Cohn, Junior Cox, Lois Frizzell, Marlon Frizzell, Abe Manuel, Pee Wee Whitewing

CHAPTER 16

Bastin, Bruce. Liner notes to *Honky Tonkin' with Lefty Frizzell*. West Sussex, England: Flyright Records, 1983.

Bleeden, Joe. "Hollywood Now Hillbilly H.Q." *Billboard* 63, no. 47, November 24, 1951.

Broven, John. *South to Lousisana: The Music of the Cajun Bayous*. Gretna, La.: Pelican Publishing, 1983.

Case records: "Jack Starnes, Jr. vs. Wm. Orville Frizzell, known as Lefty Frizzell," # 65503, District Court, Jefferson County, Texas, June 11, 1952.

"Court Puts Off Frizzell Case." *Billboard*, July 19, 1952.

Frizzell, Lefty. Deposition for: "Jack Starnes, Jr. vs. Wm. Orville Frizzell, known as Lefty Frizzell," # 6550[3], District Court, Jefferson County, Texas, October 10, 1952.

————. MSS and papers.

"Jack Starnes Files 25G Frizzell Suit." *Billboard*, July 5, 1952.

Sippel, Johnny. "Country & Western." In "The Billboard 1952 Juke Box Special." *Billboard*, March 15, 1952.

Wolfe, Charles. Liner notes to *Lefty Frizzell: Life's Like Poetry*. Vollersode, Germany: Bear Family Records, 1992.

Author interviews

Abe Manuel, Rose Lee Maphis, J. D. Miller, Ray Price, Pee Wee Whitewing

CHAPTER 17

Allen, Bob. *George Jones: The Saga of an American Singer*. Garden City, N.Y.: Doubleday & Company/Dolphin, 1984.

Braun, Bert. "Jimmy [sic] Rodgers' Day: Folk Artists and Execs Stage Great Tribute." *Billboard*, June 6, 1953.

Case records: "Jack Starnes, Jr. vs. Wm. Orville Frizzell, known as Lefty Frizzell," # 65503, District Court, Jefferson County, Texas, June 11, 1952.

Fowler, Gene, and Bill Crawford. *Border Radio*. New York: Limelight Editions, 1990.

Frizzell, Alice. Interviewed by Lois and Marlon Frizzell, 1984.

Frizzell, Lefty. Deposition for: "Jack Starnes, Jr. vs. Wm. Orville Frizzell, known as Lefty Frizzell," # 6550[3], District Court, Jefferson County, Texas, October 10, 1952.

————. MSS and papers.

"Juno, Starday Disk Labels Make Bow." *Billboard*, June 27, 1953.

Raney-Sutherland, Wanda. "Saying Goodbye to a Country Music Legend: Wayne Raney: 1921–1993." Private publication, 1993.

Snow, Hank, the Singing Ranger, with Jack Ownbey and Bob Burris. *The Hank Snow Story*. Urbana and Chicago: University of Illinois Press, 1994.

Thileen, Vincent. "Grand Ole Opry Singer Appeals to Bobby-Soxer." *Memphis Commercial-Appeal*, November 14, 1949.

Author interviews

Junior Cox, Betty Frizzell, Lois Frizzell, Freddie Hart, Abe Manuel, J. D. Miller, Abe Mulkey, Ken Ritter, John G. Tucker

CHAPTER 18

Autry, Gene, with Mickey Herskowitz. *Back in the Saddle Again*. Garden City, N. Y.: Doubleday & Company, 1978.

Bleeden, Joe. "Hollywood Now Hillbilly H.Q." *Billboard* 63, no. 47, November 24, 1951.

Everson, William K. *The Hollywood Western: 90 Years of Cowboys and Indians, Train Robbers, Sheriffs and Gunslingers, and Assorted Heroes and Desperados*. 1969. Rev. ed. New York: Citadel Press, 1992.

Frizzell, Alice. Interviewed by Lois and Marlon Frizzell, 1984.

Frizzell, Lefty. Deposition for: "Jack Starnes, Jr. vs. Wm. Orville Frizzell, known as

Lefty Frizzell," # 6550[3], District Court, Jefferson County, Texas, October 10, 1952.

Fulford, D. G. "Hometown Jamboree." *Pasadena (Calif.) Weekly*, April 2, 1987.

Green, Douglas B. "The Singing Cowboy: An American Dream." *Journal of Country Music* 7, no. 2, May 1978.

Haggard, Merle, with Peggy Russell. *Sing Me Back Home: My Story*. New York: Simon & Schuster/Pocket, 1981.

Nelson, Norman. "Spotlight on Southern California: The Hard to Believe Market." *Billboard*, April 25, 1953.

"Personal Appearances Boom Along the Suburban Trails: Rural Stars Thrive As City Acts Strive." *Billboard*, September 19, 1953.

Property records, Jefferson County Courthouse, Beaumont, Texas.

"72G Guarantee for Frizzell." *Billboard*, March 20, 1954.

Sippel, Johnny. "Country & Western." In "The Billboard 1952 Juke Box Special." *Billboard*, March 15, 1952.

Stogner, Dave, with Judy Pybrum Malmin. "It Wasn't Easy, Was It!: A Chronicle of Western Swing Music." Unpublished ms.

"Tops in Radio and T.V.: Cliffie Stone." *Country Song Roundup*, October 1950.

Tosches, Nick. *Country: The Biggest Music in America*. New York: Stein and Day, 1977.

Author interviews

Junior Cox, Shorty Hall, Freddie Hart, Cliffie Stone, Chuck Wiginton

CHAPTER 19

Adams, Susan. "Meet Lefty Frizzell." *The Official Lefty Frizzell Fan Club Journal* 1, no. 1, July 1956.

Baker, Judy. Letter to author, June 1993.

Bowman, Lynn. *Los Angeles: Epic of a City*. Berkeley, Calif.: Howell-North Books, 1974.

Frizzell, Alice. Interviewed by Lois and Marlon Frizzell, 1984.

Frizzell, Lefty, MSS and papers.

Los Angeles: A Guide to the City and Its Environs. Compiled by Workers of the Writers' Program of the Works Project Administration in Southern California. New York: Hastings House, 1941.

Shaffer, Gina. "Northridge: Early Day Oasis." *Northridge (Calif.) Daily News*, n.d.

Author interviews

Judy Baker, Junior Cox, Floyd Cramer, Betty Frizzell, Lois Frizzell, Marlon Frizzell, Horace Logan, Rose Lee Maphis, Howard Vandevender (Van Howard), Chuck Wiginton

CHAPTER 20

"Alan Freed Attracts Mob in Newark." *Billboard*, May 15, 1954.

Allen, Bill "Hoss." Interviewed by John Landes, 1985. Files of the Country Music Foundation Library and Media Center, Nashville, Tennessee.

Amburn, Ellis. *Dark Star: The Roy Orbison Story*. New York: Lyle Stuart/Carol Publishing, 1990.

Baxter, Gordon. *Village Creek: The First and Only Eyewitness Account of the Second Life of Gordon Baxter by Himself*. New York: Summit Books, 1979.

Escott, Colin, with Martin Hawkins. *Good Rockin' Tonight: Sun Records and the Birth of Rock 'n' Roll*. New York: St. Martin's, 1991.

Fielder, Donna. "Honky-tonk Melody Brought Dexter Fame." *Denton (Tex.) Record-Chronicle*, June 27, 1980.

Hemphill, Paul. *The Nashville Sound: Bright Lights and Country Music*. New York: Simon and Schuster, 1970.

Martin, Joe. "Country Music Field Full of Green Stuff—Folding Kind, That Is." *Billboard*, May 22, 1954.

Nashville Tennessean, September 11–18, 1955.

"Ohio Deejay Skeds Ball in Newark." *Billboard*, April 17, 1954.

Schickel, Steve. "R&B Music Invades Pop Market: Jukes, Disk Stores Feeling Trend." *Billboard*, August 14, 1954.

"Teenagers Demand Music with a Beat, Spur Rhythm-Blues." *Billboard*, April 24, 1954.

Tosches, Nick. "Al Dexter." *Old Time Music* 22, (Autumn 1976).

———. *Country: The Biggest Music in America*. New York: Stein and Day, 1977.

Turner, Robert. "Concert Comments." *Hollywood Bowl Magazine*, August 2, 4, 6, 1955.

"Western Night" schedule. *Hollywood Bowl Magazine*, August 2, 4, 6, 1955.

White, Glenn P. Letter to Bob Pinson, November 17, 1993.

"Wine, Women, Song." *Denton (Tex.) Record-Chronicle*, February 11, 1973.

Wolfe, Charles. "Honky-tonk Starts Here: The Jim Beck Dallas Studio." *Journal of Country Music* 11, no. 1, 1986.

Author interviews

Hoss Allen, Mary E. Beck, David Frizzell, Marlon Frizzell, Earl Gaines, Freddie Hart, Jolly Joe Nixon, Pop Staples, Billy Walker

CHAPTER 21

Adams, Susan. "Meet Lefty Frizzell." *The Official Lefty Frizzell Fan Club Journal* 1, no. 1, July 1956.

Frizzell, David. "Lefty Frizzell: A Powerful Man." *Country Music*, January/February, 1984.

Frizzell, Lefty, MSS and papers.

O'Donnell, Red. "Eddie Miller." *BMI: The Many Worlds of Music*, October 1969.

Pugh, John. "Lefty and the Fabulous Fifties." *Music City News*, March 1972.

Selvin, Joel. *Ricky Nelson: Idol for a Generation*. Chicago: Contemporary Books, 1990.

Author interviews

Hillous Butrum, Betty Frizzell, David Frizzell, Lois Frizzell, Marlon Frizzell, Freddie Hart, Don Law Jr., Rose Lee Maphis

CHAPTER 22

Elliott, James Isaac. "The Life and Legacy of Lefty Frizzell: Music, Media and Modern Country Singing." Master's thesis, Austin Peay State University, 1990.

Frizzell, Alice. Interviewed by Lois and Marlon Frizzell, 1984.

Frizzell, David. Columbia contract. Don Law logs. Files of the Country Music Foundation Library and Media Center, Nashville, Tennessee.

————. "Lefty Frizzell: A Powerful Man." *Country Music*, January/February, 1984.

Hicks, Darryl E. *Marijohn: Lord, Let Me Leave a Song*. Nashville: Message Press, 1978.

Horstman, Dorothy. *Sing Your Heart Out, Country Boy*. 1975. Rev. ed. Nashville: The Country Music Foundation, 1986.

Jim Denny Artist Bureau records. Files of the Country Music Foundation Library and Media Center, Nashville, Tennessee.

Probate records, Sumner County, Gallatin, Tennessee.

Author interviews

Lucky Cook, Junior Cox, David Frizzell, Lois Frizzell, Marlon Frizzell, Harlan Howard, Marijohn Wilkin

CHAPTER 23

Cooper, Daniel. "Boogie-Woogie White Boy: The Redemption of 'Hossman' Allen." *Nashville Scene* 11, no. 5, March 4, 1993.

Cunniff, Albert. "Muscle Behind the Music: The Life and Times of Jim Denny." *Journal of Country Music* 11, nos. 1–3, 1986–7.

Doyle, Don H. *Nashville in the New South 1880–1930*. Knoxville: University of Tennessee Press, 1985.

————. *Nashville Since the 1920s*. Knoxville: University of Tennessee Press, 1985.

Greene, Lee S. *Lead Me On: Frank Goad Clement and Tennessee Politics*. Knoxville: University of Tennessee Press, 1982.

Hemphill, Paul. *The Nashville Sound: Bright Lights and Country Music*. New York: Simon and Schuster, 1970.

Henderson, Jerry. "Nashville's Ryman Auditorium." *Tennessee Historical Quarterly* 27, no. 4 (Winter 1968).

Ivey, Bill. "The Bottom Line: Business Practices That Shaped Country Music." In *Country: The Music and the Musicians*, edited by Paul Kingsbury and Alan Axelrod. New York: The Country Music Foundation/Abbeville Press, 1988.

Kienzle, Rich. "Grady Martin: Unsung and Unforgettable." *Journal of Country Music* 10, no. 2, 1985.

Minnix, Kathleen. " 'That Memorable Meeting': Sam Jones and the Nashville Revival of 1885." *Tennessee Historical Quarterly* 47, no. 3 (Fall 1989).

Oermann, Robert K. "Nashville's golden soul era." *The Nashville Tennessean*, February 18, 1988.

———. "Roy [Acuff] on Roy." *The Nashville Tennessean*, November 24, 1992.

Rumble, John Woodruff. "Fred Rose and the Development of the Nashville Music Industry,1942–1954." Ph.D. diss., Vanderbilt University, 1980.

Smith, W. O. *Sideman: The Long Gig of W. O. Smith*. Nashville: Rutledge Hill Press, 1991.

Thomason, Philip. "The Men's Quarter of Downtown Nashville." *Tennessee Historical Quarterly* 41, no. 1 (Spring 1982).

Warden, Margaret Lindsley. "The Southern Turf." *The Nashville Tennessean*, May 25, 1952.

White, Howard, with Ruth White. *Every Highway Out of Nashville*. Nashville: JMP Productions, 1990.

Wolfe, Charles. Liner notes to *Lefty Frizzell: Life's Like Poetry*. Vollersode, Germany: Bear Family Records, 1992.

———. *Tennessee Strings: The Story of Country Music in Tennessee*. Knoxville: University of Tennessee Press, 1977.

Author interviews

Arthur Alexander, Hoss Allen, Harlan Howard, Jolly Joe Nixon, Marijohn Wilkin

CHAPTER 24

Frizzell, Alice. Interviewed by Lois and Marlon Frizzell, 1984.

Frizzell, Lefty. Interviewed by T. Tommy Cutrer. "Music City USA" radio program, #625, September 15, 1972.

———. Letter to Merle Kilgore. March 25, 1963.

Grand Ole Opry programs, September 1, 1962; September 8, 1962. Files of the Country Music Foundation Library and Media Center, Nashville, Tennessee.

Hatch Show print records. Files of the Country Music Foundation Library and Media Center, Nashville, Tennessee.

Jim Denny Artist Bureau records. Files of the Country Music Foundation Library and Media Center, Nashville, Tennessee.

Property records, Sumner County, Gallatin, Tennessee.

Author interviews

Lois Frizzell, Merle Kilgore, Abe Mulkey

CHAPTER 25

Elliott, James Isaac. "The Life and Legacy of Lefty Frizzell: Music, Media and Modern Country Singing." Master's thesis, Austin Peay State University, 1990.

Frizzell, Alice. Letter to "Mr. Thurston." December 15, 1963. Files of the Country Music Foundation Library and Media Center, Nashville, Tennessee.

Grand Ole Opry programs, February 16, 1963; February 23, 1963; April 20, 1963. Files of the Country Music Foundation Library and Media Center, Nashville, Tennessee.

Hatch Show print records. Files of the Country Music Foundation Library and Media Center, Nashville, Tennessee.

Henderson, James W. " 'Saginaw, Michigan,' Hits Top." *The Saginaw News*, March 15, 1964.

Horstman, Dorothy. *Sing Your Heart Out, Country Boy*. 1975. Rev. ed. Nashville: The Country Music Foundation, 1986.

Jim Denny Artist Bureau records. Files of the Country Music Foundation Library and Media Center, Nashville, Tennessee.

Smith, Jonathan Guyot. "Cowboy Copas: One of Country Music's Finest." *Discoveries* 66, November 1993.

Wolfe, Charles. Liner notes to *Lefty Frizzell: Life's Like Poetry*. Vollersode, Germany: Bear Family Records, 1992.

Author interviews

Lois Frizzell, Marlon Frizzell, Merle Kilgore, Abe Mulkey, Billy Walker

CHAPTER 26

Cooper, Daniel. "Being Ray Price Means Never Having to Say You're Sorry." *Journal of Country Music* 14, no. 3, 1992.

Elliott, James Isaac. "The Life and Legacy of Lefty Frizzell: Music, Media and Modern Country Singing." Master's thesis, Austin Peay State University, 1990.

Hicks, Darryl E. *Marijohn: Lord, Let Me Leave a Song*. Nashville: Message Press, 1978.

Law, Don. Interviewed by Douglas Green. Country Music Foundation Oral History Project, May 14, 1975.

Law, Don. Liner notes to *Remembering . . . The Greatest Hits of Lefty Frizzell*. New York: Columbia Records, 1975.

Millar, Bill. Liner notes to *Eddie Noack*. London: Ace Records, n.d.

Property records, Davidson County, Nashville, Tennessee.

Property records, Sumner County, Gallatin, Tennessee.

White, Howard, with Ruth White. *Every Highway Out of Nashville*. Nashville: JMP Productions, 1990.

Author interviews

Judy Baker, Bruce Delaney, Jimmy Frizzell, Lois Frizzell, Marlon Frizzell, Harlan Howard, Don Law Jr., Abe Mulkey, Doodle Owens, Marijohn Wilkin

CHAPTER 27

"Nashville Racial Tensions Cancel 'Grand Ole Opry.' " *Billboard*, April 20, 1968.

Nashville Tennessean, April 5–8, 1968.

Snow, Jimmy, with Jim and Marti Hefley. *I Cannot Go Back*. Plainfield, N.J.: Logos International, 1977.

Author interviews
Judy Baker, Jimmy Frizzell, Lois Frizzell, Marlon Frizzell, Rev. Jimmy Snow

CHAPTER 28

Allen, Bob. "Looking Forward into the Past." *Country Song Roundup*, December 1981.

Cooper, Daniel. "Sittin' Here Bleedin' [Christine Kittrell]." *Riff*, April 1993.

Deen, Dixie. "Merle Haggard: 'Someone Told My Story in a Song.' " *Music City News* 4, no. 11, May 1967.

Eng, Steve. *A Satisfied Mind: The Country Music Life of Porter Wagoner*. Nashville: Rutledge Hill Press, 1992.

Foster, Alice. "Merle Haggard: 'I Take a Lot of Pride in What I Am,' " *Sing Out!*, March/April 1970.

Frizzell, Lefty. Interviewed by T. Tommy Cutrer. "Music City USA" radio program, #625, September 15, 1972, and #1231, January 13, 1975.

———. Interviewed on *Columbia Artists' Interviews with Frank Jones*. New York: Columbia Records, circa 1964–5.

Hemphill, Paul. *The Good Old Boys*. New York: Simon and Schuster, 1974.

Lane, Geoff. "The Last of Lefty Frizzell." *Country Music* 4, no. 2, November 1975.

Litchfield, Ken. "Wreck Kills Husky's Son, Two Others." *The Nashville Tennessean*, March 4, 1970.

Mandrell, Barbara, with George Vecsey. *Get to the Heart: My Story*. New York: Bantam, 1990.

Pugh, John. "Lefty and the Fabulous Fifties." *Music City News*, March 1972.

Shuman, E. Reinald. "Frizzell's Flu Fails to Dampen Crowds." *Music City News*, March 1968.

Author interviews
Bruce Delaney, Lois Frizzell, Marlon Frizzell, Merle Haggard, Lee Maynard

CHAPTER 29

Eng, Steve. *A Satisfied Mind: The Country Music Life of Porter Wagoner*. Nashville: Rutledge Hill Press, 1992.

"Frizzell Decides to Slow His Pace." *Wichita (Kans.) Beacon*, November 3, 1972.

Frizzell, Lefty. Interviewed by T. Tommy Cutrer. "Music City USA" radio program, #s 621–625, September 11–15, 1972.

Property records, Davidson County, Nashville, Tennessee.

Property records, Sumner County, Gallatin, Tennessee.

White, Howard, with Ruth White. *Every Highway Out of Nashville*. Nashville: JMP Productions, 1990.

Wolfe, Charles. Liner notes to *Lefty Frizzell: Life's Like Poetry*. Vollersode, Germany: Bear Family Records, 1992.

Author interviews

Jimmy Frizzell, Lois Frizzell, Marlon Frizzell, Shorty Hall, Harlan Howard, Merle Kilgore, Abe Mulkey, Doodle Owens, Glenn Sutton

CHAPTER 30

"Frizzell Decides to Slow His Pace." *Wichita (Kans.) Beacon*, November 3, 1972.

Frizzell, Lefty. Interviewed by T. Tommy Cutrer. "Music City USA" radio program, #s 621–625, September 11–15, 1972, and #s 1231–1235, January 13–17, 1975.

———. MSS and papers.

Hurst, Jack. "Fame Is Elusive for an Original Country Giant." *Chicago Tribune*, August 15, 1982.

Law, Don. Interviewed by Douglas Green. Country Music Foundation Oral History Project, May 14, 1975.

Pugh, John. "Lefty and the Fabulous Fifties." *Music City News*, March 1972.

Wolfe, Charles. Liner notes to *Lefty Frizzell: Life's Like Poetry*. Vollersode, Germany: Bear Family Records, 1992.

Author interviews

David Frizzell, Lois Frizzell, Marlon Frizzell, Doodle Owens, Whitey Shafer, Ralph Spicer

CHAPTER 31

American Federation of Musicians, Local #257, contract records. Files of the Country Music Foundation Library and Media Center, Nashville, Tennessee.

Frizzell, Lefty. Interviewed by T. Tommy Cutrer. "Music City USA" radio program, #s 1231–1235, January 13–17, 1975.

———. MSS and papers.

"Hag's Favorites." *Country Music* 2, no. 10, June 1974.

Lane, Geoff. "The Last of Lefty Frizzell." *Country Music* 4, no. 2, November 1975.

Roland, Tom. *The Billboard Book of Number One Country Hits*. New York: Billboard Books, 1991.

Snow, Jimmy, with Jim and Marti Hefley. *I Cannot Go Back*. Plainfield, N.J.: Logos International, 1977.

Wolfe, Charles. Liner notes to *Lefty Frizzell: Life's Like Poetry*. Vollersode, Germany: Bear Family Records, 1992.

Woods, Jeff. "Color Me Country: Tales from the Frontlines." *Journal of Country Music* 14, no. 2, 1992.

Author interviews

Clay Allen, Junior Cox, Stoney Edwards, David Frizzell, Jimmy Frizzell, Lois Frizzell, Marlon Frizzell, Merle Haggard, Shorty Hall, Grady Kilgore, Sleepy Labeef, J. D. Miller, Whitey Shafer, Connie Smith

CHAPTER 32

Chancery Court records, Sumner County, Gallatin, Tennessee.

Frizzell, Lefty. Obituary. *The Nashville Tennessean*, July 21, 1975.

Guralnick, Peter. "Haggard at the Crossroads: A Portrait of the Artist in Mid-life." *Country Music* 9, no. 5, January/February 1981.

Lane, Geoff. "The Last of Lefty Frizzell." *Country Music* 4, no. 2, November 1975.

"Lefty Frizzell Dies Before Date at Fair." *Delaware State News*, July 21, 1975.

Roden, Jim. "Lefty Frizzell — A Living Legend." *Dallas Times-Herald*, April 3, 1975.

Author interviews

Judy Baker, Jimmy Frizzell, Lois Frizzell, Marlon Frizzell, Shorty Hall, Abe Mulkey, Doodle Owens, Whitey Shafer

Epilogue

Author interview

Lois Frizzell

Discography

The following is an abridged, and slightly amended, version of Richard Weize's Frizzell discography, which appears in *Lefty Frizzell: Life's Like Poetry* (Vollersode, Germany: Bear Family Records, 1992; BCD 15550). Unlike Weize's complete discography, which includes EP, reissue, and various artist entries, the present version, due to space limitations, lists only the original 45 and/or LP release number. Thus readers should be aware that many of the songs that appear here as unreleased did, in fact, surface in various reissue formats over the years. Indeed, every last one of these recordings is included in the Bear Family boxed set. (As of this writing, the best available single-disc compilation of Lefty's music is *The Best of Lefty Frizzell* [Santa Monica, Calif.: Rhino Records, 1991; RZ 71005].)

Regarding session personnel, occasional changes have been made, mostly to accommodate information gathered by the author and by independent researchers Don Hopson and Clay Allen. All subsequent author notes are per the original discography.

This discography is a chronological listing of Lefty's Columbia & ABC recordings by master number. The exact format of the chronological discography is as follows:

1. date; 2. location; 3. producer; 4. personnel; 5. discography opus number; 6. original master number; 7. title; 8. 45/78RPM releases; 9. LP release; 10. New York master number; 11. composer/writer

JULY 25, 1950; Jim Beck Studio, Dallas, Texas; Producer: Art Satherley & Don Law
LEFTY FRIZZELL: vocal/guitar; NORMAN STEVENS: lead guitar; possibly JIMMIE CURTIS: steel guitar; BOBBY WILLIAMSON: bass; PEE WEE STEWART: fiddle; MADGE SUTTEE: piano

001.	RHCO 4188-1	I LOVE YOU A THOUSAND WAYS (Lefty Frizzell)	Co 20739-4	HL 9021
002.	RHCO 4189-1	IF YOU'VE GOT THE MONEY, I'VE GOT THE TIME (Lefty Frizzell–Jim Beck)	Co 20739-4	HL 9021
003.	RHCO 4190-1	SHINE, SHAVE, SHOWER (IT'S SATURDAY) (Lefty Frizzell–Jim Beck)	Co 20772-4	

004.   RHCO 4191-1   COLD FEET
                     (Lefty Frizzell–Aubrey Freeman–Jim Beck)

       NOTE: According to Joe Knight, the above songs were recorded in two sessions, and both Jimmy Rollins (lead
       guitar) and Buddy Griffin (rhythm guitar) played on RHCO 4190 and RHCO 4191.

SEPTEMBER 21, 1950; Jim Beck Studio, Dallas, Texas; Producer: Don Law
       LEFTY FRIZZELL: vocal/guitar; probably LEON RHODES: lead guitar; BUDDY GRIFFIN: rhythm
       guitar; JIMMY KELLY: steel guitar; EDDIE DUNCAN: bass; EDDIE CALDWELL: fiddle; MADGE
       SUTTEE: piano

005.   RHCO 4280   DON'T THINK IT AIN'T BEEN FUN DEAR
                   (Lefty Frizzell–Elizabeth Jane Cozza–Jim Beck)
006.   RHCO 4281   WHEN PAYDAY COMES AROUND
                   (Lefty Frizzell–Aubrey Freeman–Jim Beck)
007.   RHCO 4282   MY BABY'S JUST LIKE MONEY
                   (Lefty Frizzell–Jim Beck)
008.   RHCO 4283-1 LOOK WHAT THOUGHTS WILL DO   Co 20772-4   HL 9021
                   (Lefty Frizzell–Jim Beck–Dub Dickenson)

JANUARY 11, 1951; Jim Beck Studio, Dallas, Texas; Producer: Don Law
       LEFTY FRIZZELL: vocal/guitar; NORMAN STEVENS: lead guitar; BUDDY GRIFFIN: rhythm
       guitar; C. B. WHITE: steel guitar; BILL CALLAHAN: bass; EDDIE CALDWELL: fiddle; VERNON
       "Chubby" CRANK: drums; MADGE SUTTEE: piano

009.   CO 45062   MY BABY'S JUST LIKE MONEY   Co 20799-4
                  (Lefty Frizzell–Jim Beck)
010.   CO 45063   YOU WANT EVERYTHING BUT ME
                  (Aubrey Freeman)
011.   CO 45064   WANT TO BE WITH YOU ALWAYS   Co 20799-4   HL 9021
                  (Lefty Frizzell–Jim Beck)
012.   CO 45065   GIVE ME MORE, MORE, MORE (OF YOUR KISSES)   Co 20885-4
                  (Ray Price–Lefty Frizzell–Jim Beck)

Personnel information on sessions from July 25, 1950, until December 7, 1955, derives principally from
Joe Knight's recollections, augmented by interviews with musicians and a little guesswork. The studio
location for the October 19, 1951, session was provided by Ray Topping from the Gold Star session logs.
We were unable to locate an AFM contract for the second session on February 24, 1958, but the personnel
was probably identical or similar to the first session.
     Personnel information for 1965–69 derives from Grady Martin's diaries. The "Agnes and Orville" session
details were confirmed from an AFM contract.
     This discography is based on information originally published with "Lefty Frizzell—His Life, His Music"
(BFX 15100). We haven't updated it to the point of including all releases since 1984 that have contained
Lefty's repertoire. We have, however, included two CDs: "American Originals" (Columbia CK 45067) and
"The Best of Lefty Frizzell" (Rhino R271005).

MAY 24, 1951; Jim Beck Studio, Dallas, Texas; Producer: Don Law
       LEFTY FRIZZELL: vocal/guitar; probably TAWNEE HALL: lead guitar; probably BLACKIE
       CRAWFORD: rhythm guitar; HAROLD L. "Curly" CHALKER: steel guitar; PEE WEE REID: bass;
       JIMMY DENNIS: drums; JERRY ROWLEY: fiddle; EVELYN ROWLEY: piano

013.   JB 37   HOW LONG WILL IT TAKE (TO STOP LOVING YOU)   Co 20885-4
       CO 46263   (Lefty Frizzell)
014.   JB 38   ALWAYS LATE (WITH YOUR KISSES)   Co 20837-4   HL 9021
       CO 46264   (Lefty Frizzell–Blackie Crawford)
015.   JB 39   MOM AND DAD'S WALTZ   Co 20837-4   HL 9021
       CO 46265   (Lefty Frizzell)
016.   JB 40   YOU CAN GO ON YOUR WAY NOW
       CO 46266   (Lefty Frizzell)

JUNE 1, 1951; Jim Beck Studio, Dallas, Texas; Producer: Don Law
       LEFTY FRIZZELL: vocal/guitar/prob. harmonica; probably TAWNEE HALL: lead guitar; proba-
       bly BLACKIE CRAWFORD: rhythm guitar; possibly HAROLD L. "Curly" CHALKER: dobro; PEE
       WEE REID: bass; JERRY ROWLEY: fiddle; EVELYN ROWLEY: piano

017.   JB 45   TREASURE UNTOLD   Co 20840-4   HL 9019
       CO 46353   (Cozzens–Rodgers)
018.   JB 46   BLUE YODEL #6   Co 20842-4   HL 9019
       CO 46354   (Rodgers)
019.   JB 47   TRAVELLIN' BLUES   Co 20842-4   HL 9019
       CO 46355   (Jimmie Rodgers–Shelly Lee Alley)
020.   JB 48   MY OLD PAL   Co 20841-4   HL 9019
       CO 46356   (Jimmie Rodgers–Elsie McWilliams)

JUNE 1, 1951; Jim Beck Studio, Dallas, Texas; Producer: Don Law
LEFTY FRIZZELL: vocal/guitar/prob. harmonica; probably TAWNEE HALL: lead guitar; probably BLACKIE CRAWFORD: rhythm guitar; HAROLD L. "Curly" CHALKER: dobro; PEE WEE REID: bass; JERRY ROWLEY: fiddle; EVELYN ROWLEY: piano

021.	JB 49 CO 46357	BLUE YODEL #2 (Jimmie Rodgers)	Co 20840-4	HL 9019
022.	JB 50 CO 46358	LULLABY YODEL (Jimmie Rodgers–Elsie McWilliams)	Co 20843-4	HL 9019
023.	JB 51 CO 46359	BRAKEMAN'S BLUES (Jimmie Rodgers)	Co 20841-4	HL 9019
024.	JB 52 CO 46360	MY ROUGH AND ROWDY WAYS (Jimmie Rodgers–Elsie McWilliams)	Co 20843-4	HL 9019

OCTOBER 19, 1951; ACA Studio, Houston, Texas; Producer: Don Law
LEFTY FRIZZELL: vocal/guitar; R. L. "Blackie" CRAWFORD: guitar; JOE CALLAHAN: guitar; HAROLD L. "Curly" CHALKER: steel guitar; PEE WEE STEWART: bass; UNKNOWN: fiddle; JIMMY DENNIS: drums; MADGE SUTTEE: piano

025.	ACA 2054 CO 46994	I LOVE YOU (THOUGH YOU'RE NO GOOD) (Lefty Frizzell)
026.	ACA 2055 CO 46995	IT'S JUST YOU (I COULD LOVE ALWAYS) (Lefty Frizzell)
027.	ACA 2056 CO 46996	(DARLING NOW) YOU'RE HERE SO EVERYTHING'S ALRIGHT (Lefty Frizzell)
028.	ACA 2057 CO 46997	I'VE GOT REASONS TO HATE YOU (Lefty Frizzell–Boots Bryan–Jack Starnes Jr.)

JANUARY 8, 1952; Jim Beck Studio, Dallas, Texas; Producer: Don Law
LEFTY FRIZZELL: vocal/guitar; probably TAWNEE HALL: lead guitar; probably BLACKIE CRAWFORD: rhythm guitar; PEE WEE WHITEWING: steel guitar; ARTIE GLENN: bass; JOHNNY GIMBLE: fiddle; HAROLD CARMACK: piano

029.	JB 69 CO 47607	I LOVE YOU (THOUGH YOU'RE NO GOOD) (Lefty Frizzell)	
030.	JB 70 CO 47608	DON'T STAY AWAY (TILL LOVE GROWS COLD) (Lefty Frizzell–Sutherland)	Co 20911-4
031.	JB 71 CO 47609	IT'S JUST YOU (I COULD LOVE ALWAYS) (Lefty Frizzell)	Co 20950-4
032.	JB 72 CO 47610	(DARLING NOW) YOU'RE HERE SO EVERYTHING'S ALRIGHT (Lefty Frizzell)	Co 20911-4

APRIL 4, 1952; Jim Beck Studio, Dallas, Texas; Producer: Don Law
LEFTY FRIZZELL: vocal/guitar; AS ABOVE: lead guitar; AS ABOVE: rhythm guitar; PEE WEE WHITEWING: steel guitar; ARTIE GLENN: bass; JOHNNY GIMBLE: fiddle; HAROLD CARMACK: piano

033.	JB 94 CO 47788	IF YOU CAN SPARE THE TIME (I WON'T MISS THE MONEY) (Lefty Frizzell–Guidry Tassin)	Co 20950-4
034.	JB 95 CO 47789	A KING WITHOUT A QUEEN (Bob Wills–D. Moore–B. J. Wills)	Co 21241-4
035.	JB 96 CO 47790	FOREVER (AND ALWAYS) (Lefty Frizzell–Lessie Lyle)	Co 20997-4
036.	JB 97 CO 47791	I KNOW YOU'RE LONESOME (WHILE WAITING FOR ME) (Lefty Frizzell)	Co 20997-4

c. JULY 10, 1952; (REHEARSAL SESSION) Miller's Shop, 218 North Parkerson, Crowley, Louisiana
LEFTY FRIZZELL: vocal/guitar; WOODY GUIDRY: guitar; HERBY HALL: steel guitar; BOB HENDERSON: fiddle; BENNY FRUGE: piano

000.	none	LOST LOVE BLUES (Lefty Frizzell)
000.	none	THAT'S ME WITHOUT YOU (J. D. Miller–Bennett Wyatt)
000.	none	SEND HER HERE TO BE MINE (Lefty Frizzell)

JULY 14, 1952; Fort Worth, Texas; Producer: Don Law
LEFTY FRIZZELL: vocal/guitar; WOODY GUIDRY: guitar; J. D. MILLER: rhythm guitar; HERBY HALL: steel guitar; BOB HENDERSON: fiddle

| 037. | FW 10 CO 48232 | LOST LOVE BLUES (Lefty Frizzell) | |
| 038. | FW 11 CO 48233 | THAT'S ME WITHOUT YOU (J. D. Miller–Bennett Wyatt) | |

OCTOBER 7, 1952; Jim Beck Studio, Dallas, Texas; Producer: Don Law
LEFTY FRIZZELL: vocal/guitar; JIMMY ROLLINS: lead guitar; JOE KNIGHT: rhythm guitar; EDDIE DUNCAN: bass; JACK YOUNGBLOOD: fiddle; HAROLD CARMACK: piano

039.	JB 110 CO 48461	I WON'T BE GOOD FOR NOTHIN' (Lefty Frizzell)	
040.	JB 111 CO 48462	IF I LOSE YOU (I'LL LOSE MY WORLD) (Lefty Frizzell)	
041.	JB 112 CO 48463	I'M AN OLD OLD MAN (TRYIN' TO LOVE WHILE I CAN) (Lefty Frizzell)	Co 21034-4
042.	JB 113 CO 48464	YOU'RE JUST MINE (ONLY IN MY DREAMS) (Lefty Frizzell)	Co 21034-4

FEBRUARY 6, 1953 (18:30–21:30); Jim Beck Studio, Dallas, Texas; Producer: Don Law
LEFTY FRIZZELL: vocal/guitar; JIMMY ROLLINS: lead guitar; JOE KNIGHT: guitar; PAUL BLUNT: steel guitar; EDDIE DUNCAN: bass; JACK YOUNGBLOOD: fiddle; FRED CANTU: drums; HAROLD CARMACK: piano

043.	JB 1 CO 48962	I'LL TRY (Lefty Frizzell)	
044.	JB 2 CO 48963	(HONEY, BABY, HURRY) BRING YOUR SWEET SELF BACK TO ME (Lefty Frizzell)	Co 21084-4
045.	JB 3 CO 48964	TIME CHANGES THINGS (Lessie Lyles–Lefty Frizzell)	Co 21084-4
046.	JB 4 CO 48965	ALL OF ME LOVES ALL OF YOU (Lefty Frizzell)	

FEBRUARY 7, 1953 (20:30–23:30); Jim Beck Studio, Dallas, Texas; Producer: Don Law
LEFTY FRIZZELL: vocal/guitar; ROY NICHOLS: lead guitar; LOU MILLET: guitar; ERNIE HARVEY: steel guitar; LUM YORK: bass; JACK YOUNGBLOOD: fiddle; WAYNE RANEY: harmonica; TOMMY PERKINS: drums

047.	JB 13 CO 48974	CALIFORNIA BLUES (BLUE YODEL, #4) (Jimmie Rodgers)	Co 21102-4
048.	JB 14 CO 48975	NEVER NO' MO' BLUES (Jimmie Rodgers–Elsie McWilliams)	Co 21101-4
049.	JB 15 CO 48976	WE CRUCIFIED OUR JESUS (Lefty Frizzell)	Co 21118-4
050.	JB 16 CO 48977	WHEN IT COMES TO MEASURING LOVE (Lefty Frizzell)	Co 21118-4

MARCH 9, 1953; poss. Jim Beck Studio, Dallas, Texas; Producer: Don Law
LEFTY FRIZZELL: vocal/guitar; ROY NICHOLS: lead guitar; LOU MILLET: guitar; ERNIE HARVEY: steel guitar; LUM YORK: bass; JACK YOUNGBLOOD: fiddle; WAYNE RANEY: harmonica; TOMMY PERKINS: drums

| 051. | CO 49087 | SLEEP BABY SLEEP (Jimmie Rodgers) | Co 21101-4 |
| 052. | CO 49088 | (I'M) LONELY AND BLUE (Elsie McWilliams–Jimmie Rodgers) | Co 21102-4 |

JUNE 4, 1953 (15:00–18:00); Jim Beck Studio, Dallas, Texas; Producer: Don Law
LEFTY FRIZZELL: vocal/guitar; JIMMY ROLLINS: lead guitar; JOE KNIGHT: guitar; PAUL BLUNT: steel guitar; ARTIE GLENN: bass; JACK YOUNGBLOOD: fiddle; FRED CANTU: drums; HAROLD CARMACK: piano

053.	JB 47 CO 49503	BEFORE YOU GO, MAKE SURE YOU KNOW (Lefty Frizzell)	Co 21142-4
054.	JB 48 CO 49504	TWO FRIENDS OF MINE IN LOVE (Lefty Frizzell)	Co 21142-4
055.	JB 49 CO 49505	HOPELESS LOVE (Lessie Lyle–Frizzell)	Co 21169-4

056.   JB 50   THEN I'LL COME BACK TO YOU   Co 21169-4
        CO 49506   (Lefty Frizzell–Tassin S. Burton)

NOVEMBER 14, 1953 (21:00–24:00); Jim Beck Studio, Dallas, Texas; Producer: Don Law
    LEFTY FRIZZELL: vocal/guitar; WAYNE RANEY: duet vocal; JIMMY ROLLINS: lead guitar; JOE
    KNIGHT: rhythm guitar; PAUL BLUNT: steel guitar; ARTIE GLENN: bass; JACK YOUNGBLOOD:
    fiddle; FRED CANTU: drums; HAROLD CARMACK: piano

057.   JB 104   THE TRAGIC LETTER (THE LETTER THAT YOU LEFT)
        CO 50463   (Lefty Frizzell–H. P. Willis)

NOVEMBER 15, 1953 (01:00–04:00); Jim Beck Studio, Dallas, Texas; Producer: Don Law
    LEFTY FRIZZELL: vocal/guitar; WAYNE RANEY: duet vocal; JIMMY ROLLINS: lead guitar; JOE
    KNIGHT: rhythm guitar; PAUL BLUNT: steel guitar; ARTIE GLENN: bass; JACK YOUNGBLOOD:
    fiddle; FRED CANTU: drums; HAROLD CARMACK: piano

058.   JB 105   TWO HEARTS BROKEN NOW   Co 21284-4
        CO 50464   (Lefty Frizzell–H. P. Willis)
059.   JB 106   YOU CAN ALWAYS COUNT ON ME   Co 21241-4
        CO 50465   (Lefty Frizzell–H. P. Willis)
060.   JB 107   I'VE BEEN AWAY WAY TOO LONG   Co 21208-4
        CO 50466   (Lefty Frizzell–H. P. Willis)

NOVEMBER 17, 1953; Jim Beck Studio, Dallas, Texas; Producer: Don Law
    LEFTY FRIZZELL: vocal/guitar; JIMMY ROLLINS: lead guitar; JOE KNIGHT: rhythm guitar;
    PAUL BLUNT: steel guitar; ARTIE GLENN: bass; WAYNE RANEY: harmonica; JACK
    YOUNGBLOOD: fiddle; FRED CANTU: drums; HAROLD CARMACK: piano

061.   JB 120   RUN 'EM OFF   Co 21194-4
        CO 50382   (Onie Wheeler–Tony Lee)
062.   JB 121   THE DARKEST MOMENT (IS JUST BEFORE THE Co 21194-4
        CO 50383   LIGHT OF DAY)
                           (Lefty Frizzell)
063.   JB 122   YOU'RE TOO LATE   Co 21284-4
        CO 50453   (Lefty Frizzell–H. P. Willis)
064.   JB 123   MY LITTLE HER AND HIM   Co 21208-4
        CO 50454   (Lefty Frizzell)

        NOTE: Break in New York Master numbers.

OCTOBER 5, 1954; possibly Jim Beck Studio, Dallas, Texas; Producer: Don Law
    LEFTY FRIZZELL: vocal/guitar; JIMMY ROLLINS: lead guitar; JOE KNIGHT: rhythm guitar;
    PAUL BLUNT: steel guitar; GRUNDY "Slim" HARBERT: bass; JOHNNY GIMBLE: fiddle; FRED
    CANTU: drums; WILLIAM "Bill" SIMMONS: piano

065.   CO 52607   I LOVE YOU MOSTLY   Co 21328-4
                           (Lefty Frizzell–B. Adams)
066.   CO 52608   YOU'RE THERE, I'M HERE
                           (Lefty Frizzell)
067.   CO 52609   LET IT BE SO
                           (Lefty Frizzell)
068.   CO 52610   MAMA!   CO 21328-4
                           (Jesse Ashlock)

JANUARY 19, 1955 (13:30–16:30 & 17:00–20:00); Jim Beck Studio, Dallas, Texas; Producer: Don Law
    LEFTY FRIZZELL: vocal/guitar/leader; JIMMY ROLLINS: lead guitar; JOE KNIGHT: rhythm
    guitar; PAUL BUSKIRK: mandolin; DALE GILLEY: steel guitar; GRUNDY "Slim" HARBERT:
    bass; EUGENE "Buddy" BRADY: fiddle; FREDDIE CANTU: drums; WILLIAM "Bill" SIMMONS:
    piano

069.   JB 259   MAKING BELIEVE   Co 21366-4
        CO 52987   (Jimmie Work)
070.   JB 260   MOONLIGHT, DARLING AND YOU   Co 21393-4
        CO 52988   (Lefty Frizzell–Adams)
071.   JB 261   I'LL SIT ALONE AND CRY   Co 21393-4
        CO 52989   (Wooten–Potter–Sharp)
072.   JB 262   A FOREST FIRE (IS IN YOUR HEART)   Co 21366-4
        CO 52990   (Lefty Frizzell–Adams)

        NOTE: Joe Knight is not listed on the AFM contract, but remembers that he played on the session.

JUNE 18, 1955 (13:00–17:00); Jim Beck Studio, Dallas, Texas; Producer: Don Law
    LEFTY FRIZZELL: vocal/guitar/leader; JIMMY ROLLINS; lead guitar; JOE KNIGHT: rhythm guitar; PAUL BUSKIRK: mandolin; HARLAND POWELL: steel guitar; PAUL BRAWLEY: bass; EUGENE "Buddy" BRADY: fiddle; WILLIAM PECCHI: drums; WILLIAM "Bill" SIMMONS: piano

073.	JB 309 CO 53573	SWEET LIES (J. Ross–J. Organ)	Co 21433-4
074.	JB 310 CO 53574	YOUR TOMORROWS WILL NEVER COME (Harper–L. Hayes)	Co 21458-4
075.	JB 311 CO 53575	IT GETS LATE SO EARLY (Lefty Frizzell–L. Hayes)	Co 21458-4
076.	JB 312 CO 53576	I'M LOST BETWEEN RIGHT AND WRONG (Lefty Frizzell–L. Hayes)	Co 21433-4

    NOTE: Joe Knight is not listed on the AFM contract, but remembers that he played on the session.

DECEMBER 6, 1955 (15:00–18:00); Jim Beck Studio, Dallas, Texas; Producer: Don Law
    LEFTY FRIZZELL: vocal/guitar/leader; JIMMY ROLLINS: lead guitar; PAUL BUSKIRK: mandolin-guitar; BOB MEADOWS: steel guitar; PAUL BRAWLEY: bass; EUGENE "Buddy" BRADY: fiddle; WILLIAM PECCHI: drums; WILLIAM "Bill" SIMMONS: piano

077.	JB 335 CO 54332	PROMISES (PROMISES, PROMISES) (J. Tucker)	Co 21506-4
078.	JB 336 CO 54333	MY LOVE AND BABY'S GONE	
079.	JB 337 CO 54334	TODAY IS THAT TOMORROW (I DREAMED OF YESTERDAY) (J. Johnson)	Co 21506-4
080.	JB 338 CO 54335	FIRST TO HAVE A SECOND CHANCE (Teddy Wilburn–Webb Pierce)	Co 21488-4

DECEMBER 7, 1955; Jim Beck Studio, Dallas, Texas; Producer: Don Law
    LEFTY FRIZZELL: vocal/guitar/leader; JIMMY ROLLINS: lead guitar; JOE KNIGHT: rhythm guitar; poss. PAUL BUSKIRK: mandolin; poss. BOB MEADOWS: steel guitar; poss. PAUL BRAWLEY: bass; EUGENE "Buddy" BRADY: fiddle; poss. WILLIAM PECCHI: drums; poss. WILLIAM "Bill" SIMMONS: piano

081.	JB 339 CO 54336	THESE HANDS (Eddie Noack)	Co 21488-4
082.	JB 340 CO 54337	YOU CAN'T DIVORCE MY HEART (Chuck Rogers)	
083.	JB 341 CO 54338	TREAT HER RIGHT (Buck Bryant)	

MAY 22, 1956 (19:30–22:30); Music City Recording, 804 16th Avenue South, Nashville, Tennessee; Producer: Don Law
    LEFTY FRIZZELL: vocal/guitar/leader; LOREN OTIS "Jack" SHOOK: guitar; SAMUEL PRUETT: guitar; DONALD HELMS: steel guitar; RAY EDENTON: bass; JERRY RIVERS: fiddle; FARRIS COURSEY: drums

084.	OB 1133 CO 56199	HEART'S HIGHWAY (E. Miller–A. Harper)	Co 21554-4
085.	OB 1134 CO 56200	I'M A BOY LEFT ALONE (Peshoff–G. Miller)	Co 21554-4
086.	OB 1135 CO 56201	JUST CAN'T LIVE THAT FAST (ANYMORE) (Lefty Frizzell–J. Johnson)	Co 21530-4
087.	OB 1136 CO 56202	THE WALTZ OF THE ANGELS (D. Reynolds–J. Rhodes)	Co 21530-4

NOVEMBER 7/8, 1956 (22:45–02:15); Music City Recording, 804 16th Avenue South, Nashville, Tennessee; Producer: Don Law
    LEFTY FRIZZELL: vocal/guitar/leader; THOMAS GRADY MARTIN: guitar; JOHNNY SIBERT: steel guitar; BOB L. MOORE: bass; WALTER LENK: drums; MARVIN H. HUGHES: piano

088.	OB 1218 CO 56978	LULLABY WALTZ (J. D. Miller)	Co 40818-4
089.	OB 1219 CO 56979	GLAD I FOUND YOU (Joe E. Johnson–Lefty Frizzell)	Co 40818-4
090.	OB 1220 CO 56980	NOW THAT YOU ARE GONE (W. Walker)	Co 40867-4
091.	OB 1221 CO 56981	FROM AN ANGEL TO A DEVIL (R. Nail)	Co 40867-4

MARCH 13, 1957 (10:00–13:00) Radio Recorders, 7000 Santa Monica Boulevard; Hollywood, California; Producer: Don Law
LEFTY FRIZZELL: duet vocal; JOHNNY BOND: duet vocal/leader; JOSEPH "Joe" MAPHIS: guitar; MARIAN HALL: steel guitar; ENOS "Skeets" MCDONALD: bass; MARIAN ADAMS: drums; WILLIAM A. WARDLE: piano

092.	RHCO 40152	LOVER BY APPOINTMENT (Lefty Frizzell)	Co 4-40934	
		BREAK IN MASTER NUMBERS		
093.	RHCO 40154	SICK, SOBER AND SORRY (Tex Atchison–Eddie Hazelwood)	Co 4-40934	

NOTE: This is a split-session with FREDDIE HART, who recorded masters RHCO 40151 & RHCO 40153.

MAY 10, 1957 (18:00–21:00); Bradley Film & Recording Studios, 804 16th Avenue South, Nashville, Tennessee; Producer: Don Law
LEFTY FRIZZELL: vocal/guitar; SHIRLEY CADDELL: duet vocal; THOMAS GRADY MARTIN: guitar/leader; WALTER "Hank" "Sugarfoot" GARLAND: guitar; RAY EDENTON: guitar; ROY M. "Junior" HUSKEY JR.: bass; MURRAY M. "Buddy" HARMAN JR.: drums; MARVIN H. HUGHES: piano; UNKNOWN: vocal chorus

094.	OB 1348 CO 58007	NO ONE TO TALK TO (BUT THE BLUES) (W. Walker–Cherry)	Co 40938-4	
095.	OB 1349 CO 58008	IS IT ONLY THAT YOU'RE LONELY (Schroeder–Weissman)	Co 40938-4	CL 1342
096.	OB 1350 CO 58009	MAILMAN BRING ME NO MORE BLUES (Clayton–Roberts–Katz)		

OCTOBER 25, 1957 (12:30–15:30); Bradley Film & Recording Studios, 804 16th Avenue South, Nashville, Tennessee; Producer: Don Law
LEFTY FRIZZELL: vocal/guitar; THOMAS GRADY MARTIN: guitar/leader; WALTER "Hank" "Sugarfoot" GARLAND: guitar; EDDIE HILL: guitar; FLOYD T. "Lightnin'" CHANCE: bass; MURRAY M. "Buddy" HARMAN JR.: drums; MARVIN H. HUGHES: piano; UNKNOWN: vocal chorus

097.	OB 1438 CO 59154	YOU'VE STILL GOT IT (Loy Clingman)	
098.	OB 1439 CO 59155	TELL ME DEAR (F. Hart)	Co 4-41080
099.	OB 1440 CO 59156	TO STOP LOVING YOU (MEANS CRY) (Lefty Frizzell)	

OCTOBER 25, 1957 (21:30–00:30); Bradley Film & Recording Studios, 804 16th Avenue South, Nashville, Tennessee; Producer: Don Law
LEFTY FRIZZELL: vocal/guitar; THOMAS GRADY MARTIN: guitar/leader; WALTER "Hank" "Sugarfoot" GARLAND: guitar; HAROLD RAY BRADLEY: guitar; FLOYD T. "Lightnin'" CHANCE: bass; MURRAY M. "Buddy" HARMAN JR.: drums; MARVIN H. HUGHES: piano; UNKNOWN: vocal chorus

100.	OB 1441 CO 59157	THE TORCH WITHIN MY HEART (F. Hart)	Co 4-41161
101.	OB 1442 CO 59158	TIME OUT FOR THE BLUES (D. Hart–B. Starcher)	Co 4-41080

FEBRUARY 19, 1958 (20:00–23:30); Radio Recorders, 7000 Santa Monica Boulevard; Hollywood, California; Producer: Don Law
LEFTY FRIZZELL: vocal/guitar; BOBBY BRUCE: leader; KENNETH R. BAKER: guitar; NEIL K. LEVANG: guitar; WAYNE L. BURDICK: steel guitar; JOHN M. KELLEHER: bass; M. C. "Muddy" BERRY: drums; EDWIN R. CARVER: piano; UNKNOWN: vocal chorus

102.	RHCO 40672-5	I LOVE YOU A THOUSAND WAYS (Lefty Frizzell)
103.	RHCO 40673-13	IF YOU'VE GOT THE MONEY, I'VE GOT THE TIME (Lefty Frizzell–Jim Beck)
104.	RHCO 40674-5	I WANT TO BE WITH YOU ALWAYS (Lefty Frizzell)
105.	RHCO 40675-7	MOM AND DAD'S WALTZ (Lefty Frizzell)

FEBRUARY 24, 1958; Radio Recorders, 7000 Santa Monica Boulevard; Hollywood, California; Producer: Don Law
  LEFTY FRIZZELL: vocal/guitar; with poss. BOBBY BRUCE: leader; KENNETH R. BAKER: guitar; NEIL K. LEVANG: guitar; WAYNE BURDICK: steel guitar; DONALD PAUL DUFFY: bass; M. C. "Muddy" BERRY: drums; EDWIN R. CARVER: piano; UNKNOWN: vocal chorus

106.	RHCO 40662-9	(DARLING) LET'S TURN BACK THE YEARS (Williams)	
107.	RHCO 40663-5	YOU WIN AGAIN (H. Williams)	
108.	RHCO 40664-1	WHY SHOULD I BE LONELY (Lovell–Rodgers)	CL 1342
109.	RHCO 40665-1	SIGNED, SEALED AND DELIVERED (Cowboy Copas–Lois Mann)	CL 1342
		BREAK IN MASTER NUMBERS	
110.	RHCO 40688-3	NOBODY KNOWS BUT ME (Jimmie Rodgers–Elsie McWilliams)	CL 1342

FEBRUARY 24, 1958 (20:00–23:00) Radio Recorders, 7000 Santa Monica Boulevard; Hollywood, California; Producer: Don Law
  LEFTY FRIZZELL: vocal/guitar; BOBBY BRUCE: Leader; KENNETH R. BAKER: guitar; NEIL K. LEVANG: guitar; WAYNE L. BURDICK: steel guitar; DONALD PAUL DUFFY: bass; M. C. "Muddy" BERRY: drums; EDWIN R. CARVER: piano; UNKNOWN: vocal chorus

111.	RHCO 40691-3	IF YOU'RE EVER LONELY DARLING (Lefty Frizzell)	
112.	RHCO 40692-11	SILENCE (B. Barton–Wranack)	Co 4-41161
113.	RHCO 40693-4	RELEASE ME (Miller–Williams–Yount)	CL 1342
114.	RHCO 40694-14	OUR LOVE'S NO BLUFF	

SEPTEMBER 12, 1958 (14:00–18:00); Bradley Film & Recording Studios, 804 16th Avenue South, Nashville, Tennessee; Producer: Don Law
  LEFTY FRIZZELL: vocal/guitar; THOMAS GRADY MARTIN: guitar/leader; WALTER "Hank" "Sugarfoot" GARLAND: guitar; HAROLD RAY BRADLEY: guitar; CHARLES EUGENE O'NEAL: steel guitar; BOB L. MOORE: bass; MURRAY M. "Buddy" HARMAN JR.: drums; FLOYD CRAMER: piano; UNKNOWN: vocal chorus; JACK GREGORY: saxophone (14:00–17:00)

115.	OB 1674-6 CO 61588	YOU'RE HUMBUGGIN' ME (J. Miller–R. Morgan)	Co 4-41268
116.	OB 1675-5 CO 61589	SHE'S GONE (Wayne Walker)	Co 4-41635
117.	OB 1676-8 CO 61590	CIGARETTES AND COFFEE BLUES (Marty Robbins)	Co 4-41268
118.	OB 1677-5 CO 61591	I NEED YOUR LOVE (Sonny Woods–Willie Jennings)	

DECEMBER 2/3, 1958 (19:30–01:30); Bradley Film & Recording Studios, 804 16th Avenue South, Nashville, Tennessee; Producer: Don Law
  LEFTY FRIZZELL: vocal/guitar; THOMAS GRADY MARTIN: guitar/leader; HAROLD RAY BRADLEY: guitar; DONALD HELMS: steel guitar; BOB L. MOORE: bass; THOMAS LEE "Tommy" JACKSON JR.: fiddle; MURRAY M. "Buddy" HARMAN JR.: drums; FLOYD CRAMER: piano; UNKNOWN: vocal chorus

119.	OB 1713-3 CO 61861	MY BUCKET'S GOT A HOLE IN IT (Williams)	CL 1342
120.	OB 1714-8 CO 61862	I LOVE YOU A THOUSAND WAYS (Lefty Frizzell)	CL 1342
121.	OB 1715-2 CO 61863	IF YOU'VE GOT THE MONEY, I'VE GOT THE TIME (Lefty Frizzell–Jim Beck)	CL 1342
122.	OB 1716-5 CO 61864	MOM AND DAD'S WALTZ (Lefty Frizzell)	CL 1342
123.	OB 1717-6 CO 61865	I WANT TO BE WITH YOU ALWAYS (Lefty Frizzell)	CL 1342
124.	OB 1718-3 CO 61866	ALWAYS LATE (WITH YOUR KISSES) (Lefty Frizzell)	CL 1342
125.	OB 1719-5 CO 61867	IF YOU'RE EVER LONELY DARLING (Lefty Frizzell)	CL 1342

MARCH 3, 1959 (19:00–23:00); Bradley Film & Recording Studios, 804 16th Avenue South, Nashville, Tennessee; Producer: Don Law
    LEFTY FRIZZELL: vocal/guitar; THOMAS GRADY MARTIN: guitar/leader; HAROLD RAY BRADLEY: guitar; DONALD HELMS: steel guitar; JOSEPH S. ZINKAN: bass; MURRAY M. "Buddy" HARMAN JR.: drums; MARIJOHN WILKIN: piano; UNKNOWN: vocal chorus

126.	OB 1765-6 CO 62449	SIN WILL BE THE CHASER FOR THE WINE (Lefty Frizzell–Eddie Miller)	
127.	OB 1766-16 CO 62450	KNOCK AGAIN, TRUE LOVE (Walker)	Co 4-41384
128.	OB 1767-9 CO 62451	THE LONG BLACK VEIL (Marijohn Wilkin–Danny Dill)	Co 4-41384
129.	OB 1768-4 CO 62452	ONE HAS-BEEN TO ANOTHER (Harlan Howard)	

JULY 22, 1959 (14:30–18:00); Bradley Film & Recording Studios, 804 16th Avenue South, Nashville, Tennessee; Producer: Don Law
    LEFTY FRIZZELL: vocal/guitar; THOMAS GRADY MARTIN: guitar/leader; HAROLD RAY BRADLEY: guitar; JOSEPH S. ZINKAN: bass; MURRAY M. "Buddy" HARMAN JR: drums; FLOYD CRAMER: piano; UNKNOWN: vocal chorus

130.	OB 1888-7 CO 62828	FARTHER THAN MY EYES CAN SEE (Freddie Hart)	Co 4-41455
131.	OB 1889-9 CO 62829	MY BLUES WILL PASS (Lefty Frizzell)	Co 4-41635
132.	OB 1890-6 CO 62830	BALLAD OF THE BLUE AND GREY (Harlan Howard)	Co 4-41455

MAY 26, 1960 (19:30–23:00); Bradley Film & Recording Studios, 804 16th Avenue South, Nashville, Tennessee; Producer: Don Law
    LEFTY FRIZZELL: vocal; THOMAS GRADY MARTIN: guitar/leader; HAROLD RAY BRADLEY: guitar; DONALD HELMS: steel guitar; JOSEPH S. ZINKAN: bass; MURRAY M. "Buddy" HARMAN JR.: drums; FLOYD CRAMER: piano; UNKNOWN: vocal chorus

133.	OB 2221-9 CO 64931	THAT'S ALL I CAN REMEMBER (Marijohn Wilkin–Mel Tillis)	Co 4-41751
134.	OB 2222-9 CO 64932	SO WHAT! LET IT RAIN (Lefty Frizzell)	Co 4-42253
135.	OB 2223-6 CO 64933	WHAT YOU GONNA DO, LEROY? (Mel Tillis)	Co 4-41751

FEBRUARY 7, 1961 (19:30–23:30); Bradley Film & Recording Studios, 804 16th Avenue South, Nashville, Tennessee; Producer: Don Law
    LEFTY FRIZZELL: vocal; THOMAS GRADY MARTIN: guitar/leader; WALTER "Hank" "Sugarfoot" GARLAND: guitar; HAROLD RAY BRADLEY: guitar; JOSEPH S. ZINKAN: bass; DALE POTTER: fiddle; MURRAY M. "Buddy" HARMAN JR.: drums; FLOYD CRAMER: piano; UNKNOWN: vocal chorus

136.	OB 2437-12 CO 66320	I FEEL SORRY FOR ME (Lefty Frizzell)	Co 4-42253
137.	OB 2438-8 CO 66321	HEAVEN'S PLAN (Wayne Walker)	Co 4-41984
138.	OB 2439-5 CO 66322	LOOKING FOR YOU (Lefty Frizzell)	Co 4-41984

MAY 9, 1962 (14:00–17:30); Columbia Studios, 804 16th Avenue South, Nashville, Tennessee; Producer: Don Law
    LEFTY FRIZZELL: vocal; THOMAS GRADY MARTIN: guitar/leader; HAROLD RAY BRADLEY: guitar; RAY EDENTON: guitar; JOSEPH S. ZINKAN: bass; MURRAY M. "Buddy" HARMAN JR.: drums; FLOYD CRAMER: piano; UNKNOWN: vocal chorus

139.	CB 164-7 CO 75325	STRANGER (I. Stanton–W. Walker)	Co 4-42521	CL 2169/CS 8969
140.	CB 165-2 CO 75326	A FEW STEPS AWAY (Eddie Miller)	Co 4-42676	
141.	CB 166-5 CO 75327	FORBIDDEN LOVERS (I. Stanton–W. Walker)	Co 4-42676	
142.	CB 167-5 CO 75328	JUST PASSING THROUGH (Dan Wolf)	Co 4-42521	

JUNE 26, 1963 (14:00–18:00); Columbia Studios, 804 16th Avenue South, Nashville, Tennessee; Producer: Don Law
    LEFTY FRIZZELL: vocal; THOMAS GRADY MARTIN: guitar/leader; WAYNE MOSS: guitar; RAY EDENTON: guitar; JOSEPH S. ZINKAN: bass; WILLIAM PAUL ACKERMAN: drums; WILLIAM WHITNEY PURSELL: piano; UNKNOWN: vocal chorus

143.	CB 737-6 CO 79057	THAT REMINDS ME OF ME (Mel Tillis)		
144.	CB 738-3 CO 79058	DON'T LET HER SEE ME CRY (Lefty Frizzell)	Co 4-42839	CL 2169/CS 8969
145.	CB 739-5 CO 79059	THROUGH THE EYES OF A FOOL (Williams–Bare)		CL 2169/CS 8969
146.	CB 740-2 CO 79060	JAMES RIVER (Merle Kilgore–June Carter)	Co 4-42839	CL 2169/CS 8969

OCTOBER 1, 1963 (19:00–22:00); Columbia Studios, 804 16th Avenue South, Nashville, Tennessee; Producer: Don Law & Frank Jones
    LEFTY FRIZZELL: vocal; THOMAS GRADY MARTIN: guitar/leader; HAROLD RAY BRADLEY: guitar; RAY EDENTON: guitar; JOSEPH S. ZINKAN: bass; MURRAY M. "Buddy" HARMAN JR.: drums; FLOYD CRAMER: piano; UNKNOWN: vocal chorus

147.	NCO 80058-5	PREVIEW OF COMING ATTRACTIONS (Harlan Howard)	
148.	NCO 80059-4	LONELY HEART (Lefty Frizzell)	CL 2169/CS 8969
149.	NCO 80060-1	WHAT GOOD DID YOU GET (OUT OF BREAKING MY HEART) (Lefty Frizzell)	CL 2169/CS 8969

OCTOBER 21, 1963 (19:00–23:00); Columbia Studios, 804 16th Avenue South, Nashville, Tennessee; Producer: Don Law & Frank Jones
    LEFTY FRIZZELL: vocal; THOMAS GRADY MARTIN: guitar/leader; HAROLD RAY BRADLEY: guitar; RAY EDENTON: guitar; JOSEPH S. ZINKAN: bass; MURRAY M. "Buddy" HARMAN JR.: drums; FLOYD CRAMER: piano; UNKNOWN: vocal chorus

150.	NCO 80061-5	WHEN IT RAINS THE BLUES (Lefty Frizzell)	Co 4-42924	CL 2169/CS 8969
151.	NCO 80062-4	I'M NOT THE MAN I'M SUPPOSED TO BE (Wayne Walker)		CL 2169/CS 8969
152.	NCO 80063-13	SAGINAW, MICHIGAN (Don Wayne–Bill Anderson)	Co 4-42924	CL 2169/CS 8969

JANUARY 22, 1964 (18:00–21:00 & 21:30–00:30); Columbia Studios, 804 16th Avenue South, Nashville, Tennessee; Producer: Don Law & Frank Jones
    LEFTY FRIZZELL: vocal; THOMAS GRADY MARTIN: guitar/leader; HAROLD RAY BRADLEY: guitar; RAY EDENTON: guitar; JOSEPH S. ZINKAN: bass; MURRAY M. "Buddy" HARMAN JR.: drums; FLOYD CRAMER: piano (18:00–21:00); UNKNOWN: vocal chorus

153.	NCO 80131-5	THERE'S NO FOOD IN THIS HOUSE (Merle Kilgore)		CL 2169/CS 8969
154.	NCO 80132-4	THE RIDER (W. Tubb)	Co 4-43051	
155.	NCO 80133-6	THE NESTER (D. Wayne)	Co 4-43051	
156.	NCO 80134-7	I WAS COMING HOME TO YOU (Hayes–Rule)		CL 2169/CS 8969
157.	NCO 80135-4	HELLO TO HIM (GOODBYE TO ME) (Lefty Frizzell–Abe Mulkey)		CL 2169/CS 8969

OCTOBER 16, 1964 (18:30–22:30); Columbia Studios, 804 16th Avenue South, Nashville, Tennessee; Producer: Don Law & Frank Jones
    LEFTY FRIZZELL: vocal; THOMAS GRADY MARTIN: guitar/leader; HAROLD RAY BRADLEY: guitar; RAY EDENTON: guitar; JOSEPH S. ZINKAN: bass; MURRAY M. "Buddy" HARMAN JR.: drums; FLOYD CRAMER: piano; ABE MULKEY: harmony vocal

158.	NCO 80792-4	I CAN TELL (Lefty Frizzell–Abe Mulkey)		CL 2386/CS 9186
159.	NCO 80793-3	MAKE THAT ONE FOR THE ROAD A CUP OF COFFEE (F. Hart)	Co 4-43169	
160.	NCO 80794-9	'GATOR HOLLOW (Mel Tillis)	Co 4-43169	
161.	NCO 80795-3	IT COSTS TOO MUCH TO DIE (J. A. Balthrop)		

FEBRUARY 10, 1954 (14:00–17:00); Columbia Studios, 804 16th Avenue South, Nashville, Tennessee; Producer: Don Law & Frank Jones

LEFTY FRIZZELL: vocal; THOMAS GRADY MARTIN: lead guitar/leader; RAY EDENTON: rhythm guitar; HAROLD RAY BRADLEY: guitar; PETE DRAKE: steel guitar; JOSEPH S. ZINKAN: bass; MURRAY M. "Buddy" HARMAN JR.: drums; WILLIAM WHITNEY PURSELL: piano; ABE MULKEY: harmony vocal

162.	NCO 82530-3	SHE'S GONE GONE GONE (Harlan Howard)	Co 4-43256	CL 2386/CS 9186
163.	NCO 82531-2	RUNNING INTO MEMORIES OF YOU (Mel Tillis–Wayne Walker–B. Joy)		CL 2386/CS 9186
164.	NCO 82532-3	CONFUSED (Abe Mulkey–Lefty Frizzell–Merle Kilgore)	Co 4-43256	CL 2386/CS 9186
165.	NCO 82533-4	HOW FAR DOWN CAN I GO (Harlan Howard–J. C. Barney)		CL 2386/CS 9186

FEBRUARY 11, 1965 (14:00–17:00); Columbia Studios, 804 16th Avenue South, Nashville, Tennessee; Producer: Don Law & Frank Jones

LEFTY FRIZZELL: vocal; THOMAS GRADY MARTIN: lead guitar/leader; RAY EDENTON: rhythm guitar; HAROLD RAY BRADLEY: guitar; PETE DRAKE: steel guitar; JOSEPH S. ZINKAN: bass; MURRAY M. "Buddy" HARMAN JR.: drums; WILLIAM WHITNEY PURSELL: piano; ABE MULKEY: harmony vocal

166.	NCO 82534-1	IT'S BAD (WHEN IT'S THATAWAY) (Lefty Frizzell–Abe Mulkey)		CL 2386/CS 9186
167.	NCO 82535-3	I DON'T TRUST YOU ANYMORE (Lefty Frizzell–Abe Mulkey)		CL 2386/CS 9186
168.	NCO 82536-2	A LITTLE UNFAIR (Hank Cochran–C. Howard)	Co 4-43364	CL 2386/CS 9186
169.	NCO 82537-1	WOMAN LET ME SING YOU A SONG (Harlan Howard)		CL 2386/CS 9186

MARCH 1, 1965 (14:00–17:00); Columbia Studios, 804 16th Avenue South, Nashville, Tennessee; Producer: Don Law & Frank Jones

LEFTY FRIZZELL: vocal; THOMAS GRADY MARTIN: lead guitar/leader; RAY EDENTON: rhythm guitar; WAYNE MOSS: electric guitar; PETE DRAKE: steel guitar; JOSEPH S. ZINKAN: bass; MURRAY M. "Buddy" HARMAN JR.: drums; WILLIAM WHITNEY PURSELL: piano; ABE MULKEY: harmony vocal

170.	NCO 82595-9	PREPARATIONS TO BE BLUE (D. Reeves–E. Reeves)		CL 2386/CS 9186
171.	NCO 82596-3	STRANGER (I. Stanton–W. Walker)		CL 2386/CS 9186
172.	NCO 82597-3	LOVE LOOKS GOOD ON YOU (J. Shook)	Co 4-43364	CL 2386/CS 9186

JANUARY 17, 1966 (14:00–17:00); Columbia Studios, 804 16th Avenue South, Nashville, Tennessee; Producer: Don Law & Frank Jones

LEFTY FRIZZELL: vocal; THOMAS GRADY MARTIN: lead guitar/leader; ABE MULKEY: harmony vocal; possibly BEN KEITH: steel guitar; other details unknown

173.	NCO 83088-4	MAMA (Jesse Ashlock)	Co 4-43590
174.	NCO 83089-5	IT'S HARD TO PLEASE YOU (Lefty Frizzell–Abe Mulkey)	
175.	NCO 83090-3	YOU DON'T WANT ME TO GET WELL (Lefty Frizzell–Abe Mulkey–Jack Kirch)	

		BREAK IN MASTER NUMBERS	
176.	NCO 83229	WRITING ON THE WALL (B. Delaney)	Co 4-43590

MARCH 31, 1966 (18:00–21:00); Columbia Studios, 804 16th Avenue South, Nashville, Tennessee; Producer: Don Law & Frank Jones

LEFTY FRIZZELL: vocal; THOMAS GRADY MARTIN: lead guitar/leader; RAY EDENTON: rhythm guitar; HAROLD RAY BRADLEY: guitar; PETE DRAKE or BEN KEITH: steel guitar; JOSEPH S. ZINKAN: bass; MURRAY M. "Buddy" HARMAN JR.: drums; WILLIAM WHITNEY PURSELL: piano; ABE MULKEY: harmony vocal

177.	NCO 83384-3	I JUST COULDN'T SEE THE FOREST (FOR THE TREES) (Lefty Frizzell–B. Delaney)	Co 4-43747	CL 2772/CS 9572

178.	NCO 83385-4	I'M NOT GUILTY (Lefty Frizzell–Abe Mulkey)	
179.	NCO 83386-2	IT COULDN'T HAPPEN TO A NICER GUY (Hank Cochran)	
180.	NCO 83387-2	EVERYTHING KEEPS COMING BACK (BUT YOU) (Lefty Frizzell–Abe Mulkey)	Co 4-43747

NOVEMBER 11, 1966 (14:00–17:00); Columbia Studios, 804 16th Avenue South, Nashville, Tennessee; Producer: Don Law & Frank Jones
    LEFTY FRIZZELL: vocal; THOMAS GRADY MARTIN: lead guitar/leader; RAY EDENTON: rhythm guitar; HAROLD RAY BRADLEY: guitar; "Buddy" EMMONS: steel guitar; UNKNOWN: bass; UNKNOWN: drums; HARGUS "Pig" ROBBINS: piano; ABE MULKEY: harmony vocal

181.	NCO 80474-4	HEART (DON'T LOVE HER ANYMORE) (A. C. Solberg–B. Delaney–Abe Mulkey)	CL 2772/CS 9572
182.	NCO 80475-2	YOU DON'T HAVE TO BE PRESENT TO WIN (J. Alsup)	CL 2772/CS 9572
183.	NCO 80476-2	MY FEET ARE GETTING COLD (Barbara Cummings–Bob Cummings)	
184.	NCO 80477-3	IS THERE ANYTHING I CAN DO (Abe Mulkey–Bruce Delaney)	

SEPTEMBER 15, 1966 (18:00–21:00); Bradley's Barn, Mount Juliet, Nashville, Tennessee; Producer: Don Law & Frank Jones
    LEFTY FRIZZELL: vocal; THOMAS GRADY MARTIN: lead guitar/leader; BOBBY CISCO: unknown; BILL EDWARDS: unknown; ABE MULKEY: harmony vocal; other details unknown

185.	NCO 80478-4	THE OLD GANG'S GONE (Bobby Cisco–Bill Guess)		
186.	NCO 80479-3	A SONG FROM A LONELY HEART (E. Noack)	Co 4-44023	
187.	NCO 80480-4	YOU GOTTA BE PUTTIN' ME ON (M. Vickery)	Co 4-44023	CL 2772/CS 9572
188.	NCO 80481-3	THERE IN THE MIRROR (Abe Mulkey–Bruce Delaney)		

MARCH 8, 1967 (18:00–21:00); Columbia Studios, 804 16th Avenue South, Nashville, Tennessee; Producer: Frank Jones
    LEFTY FRIZZELL: vocal; THOMAS GRADY MARTIN: lead guitar/leader; RAY EDENTON: rhythm guitar; JAMES L. WILKERSON: guitar; LLOYD GREEN: steel guitar; WALTER HAYNES: guitar/fiddle; JOSEPH S. ZINKAN: bass; LEONARD B. MILLER: drums; WILLIAM W. PURSELL: piano; ABE MULKEY: harmony vocal

189.	NCO 120448-3	GET THIS STRANGER OUT OF ME (A. L. Owens)	Co 4-44205	CL 2772/CS 9572
190.	NCO 120449-4	MONEY TREE (Wayne P. Walker)		CL 2772/CS 9572
191.	NCO 120450-3	HOBO'S PRIDE (Lefty Frizzell–Abe Mulkey)	Co 4-44205	

AUGUST 15, 1967 (14:00–17:00); Columbia Studios, 804 16th Avenue South, Nashville, Tennessee; Producer: Frank Jones
    LEFTY FRIZZELL: vocal; THOMAS GRADY MARTIN: lead guitar/leader; RAY EDENTON: rhythm guitar; HAROLD RAY BRADLEY: guitar; LLOYD GREEN: steel guitar; JOSEPH S. ZINKAN: bass; CHARLES R. "Charlie" MCCOY: harmonica; MURRAY M. "Buddy" HARMAN JR.: drums; HARGUS "Pig" ROBBINS: piano; ABE MULKEY: harmony vocal
*OVERDUB: OCTOBER 17, 1967; Columbia Studios, 804 16th Avenue South, Nashville, Tennessee;
    Producer: Frank Jones
    LEFTY FRIZZELL: vocal

192.	NCO 120258-4	WHEN THE ROOSTER LEAVES THE YARD (E. Pleasant–A. Solberg)		CL 2772/CS 9572
193.	NCO 120259-4	ANYTHING YOU CAN SPARE (Harlan Howard)	Co 4-44390	CL 2772/CS 9572
194.	NCO 120260-3	ONLY WAY TO FLY (without overdub) (E. Miller)		
194A.	NCO 120260-3	ONLY WAY TO FLY* (E. Miller)	Co 4-44738	

NOVEMBER 3, 1967 (14:00–17:00); Columbia Studios, 804 16th Avenue South, Nashville, Tennessee; Producer: Frank Jones
LEFTY FRIZZELL: vocal; other details unknown

195.	NCO 120871	A PRAYER ON YOUR LIPS IS LIKE FREEDOM IN YOUR HANDS (A. L. Owens)	Co 4-44390	CL 2772/CS 9572
196.	NCO 120872	LITTLE OLD WINEDRINKER ME (H. Mills–D. Jennings)		Cl 2772/CS 9572
197.	NCO 120873	A WORD OR TWO TO MARY (Vance Bulla–Peter Cotton)		
198.	NCO 120874	ALMOST PERSUADED (Billy Sherrill–Glenn Sutton)		CL 2772/CS 9572

DECEMBER 5, 1967; Columbia Studios, 804 16th Avenue South, Nashville, Tennessee; Producer: Frank Jones
LEFTY FRIZZELL: duet vocal; JUNE STEARNS: duet vocal; THOMAS GRADY MARTIN: electric guitar/leader; HAROLD RAY BRADLEY: guitar; RAY EDENTON: guitar; JOSEPH S. ZINKAN: bass; MURRAY M. "Buddy" HARMAN JR.: drums; FLOYD CRAMER: piano

| 199. | NCO 120911 | HAVE YOU EVER BEEN UNTRUE (V. McAlpin–R. Drusky) | Co 4-44449 |
| 200. | NCO 120912 | IF YOU'VE GOT THE MONEY, I'VE GOT THE TIME (Lefty Frizzell–Jim Beck) | Co 4-44449 |

NOTE: The above two recordings were issued as AGNES & ORVILLE

APRIL 29, 1968 (14:00–17:00); Columbia Studios, 804 16th Avenue South, Nashville, Tennessee; Producer: Frank Jones
LEFTY FRIZZELL: vocal; other details unknown

201.	NCO 98532	WHEN THE GRASS GROWS GREEN AGAIN (C. Putman–J. Hartman–J. Barlow)	Co 4-44563
202.	NCO 98533	THE MARRIAGE BIT (Don Wayne)	Co 4-44563
203.	NCO 98534	I'LL REMEMBER YOU (A. L. Owens)	

SEPTEMBER 18, 1968 (18:00–21:30); Columbia Studios, 804 16th Avenue South, Nashville, Tennessee; Producer: Frank Jones
LEFTY FRIZZELL: vocal; other details unknown

204.	NCO 98623	WASTED WAY OF LIFE (Vic McAlpin)	Co 4-44692; 4-44984
205.	NCO 98624	KEEP THEM FLOWERS WATERED WHILE I'M GONE (Don Wayne)	Co 4-44692
206.	NCO 98625	AN ARTICLE FROM LIFE (without overdub) (J. Wilson)	
206A.	NCO 98625	AN ARTICLE FROM LIFE (J. Wilson)	Co 4-44738

MAY 15, 1969 (14:00–17:00); Columbia Studios, 804 16th Avenue South, Nashville, Tennessee; Producer: Frank Jones
LEFTY FRIZZELL: vocal; other details unknown

207.	NCO 100826	BLIND STREET SINGER (D. DeChillis)	
208.	NCO 100827	HONKY TONK HILL (without overdub) (A. L. Owens–Sanger D. Shafer)	
208A.	NCO 100827	HONKY TONK HILL (A. L. Owens–Sanger D. Shafer)	Co 4-44984

FEBRUARY 19, 1970 (18:00–21:30); Columbia Studios, 804 16th Avenue South, Nashville, Tennessee; Producer: Don Davis
LEFTY FRIZZELL: vocal; FRED F. CARTER JR.: electric guitar/leader; WALTER HAYNES: guitar/fiddle; WELDON M. MYRICK: rhythm guitar/dobro; BILLY LINNEMAN: bass; KARL T. HIMMEL: drums; JOHNNY GIMBLE: fiddle; JERRY D. SMITH: piano
*OVERDUB: MARCH 11, 1970; Columbia Studios, 804 16th Avenue South, Nashville, Tennessee; Producer: Frank Jones
DOLORES D. EDGIN, ROBBIE HARDIN, HURSHEL WAYNE WIGINTON: vocal chorus

| 209. | NCO 101337 | MY BABY IS A TRAMP (Harlan Howard) | Co 4-45145 |
| 210. | NCO 101338 | SHE BROUGHT LOVE SWEET LOVE* (J. Crutchfield) | Co 4-45145 |

MAY 26, 1970 (18:00–21:00); Columbia Studios, 804 16th Avenue South, Nashville, Tennessee; Producer: Don Davis
    LEFTY FRIZZELL: vocal; FRED F. CARTER, JR.: electric guitar/leader; WALTER HAYNES: guitar/fiddle; WELDON M. MYRICK: rhythm guitar/dobro; BILLY LINNEMAN: bass; JERRY K. CARRIGAN: drums; JOHNNY GIMBLE: fiddle/guitar; JERRY D. SMITH: piano; JIM GLASER, ROBBIE H. BOWEN, ANITA CARTER: vocal chorus

211.	NCO 104539	WATERMELON TIME IN GEORGIA (Harlan Howard)	Co 4-45197
212.	NCO 104540	I MUST BE GETTING OVER YOU (L. Reynolds)	Co 4-45310
213.	NCO 104541	OUT OF YOU (Dallas Frazier)	Co 4-45197

OCTOBER 19, 1970 (18:00–21:00); Columbia Studios, 804 16th Avenue South, Nashville, Tennessee; Producer: Don Davis
    LEFTY FRIZZELL: vocal; FRED F. CARTER JR.: electric guitar/leader; WALTER HAYNES: guitar/fiddle; WELDON M. MYRICK: rhythm guitar/dobro; BILLY LINNEMAN: bass; JERRY K. CARRIGAN: drums; JOHNNY GIMBLE: fiddle/guitar; JERRY D. SMITH: piano; ABE MULKEY: harmony vocal

214.	NCO 108693	IT'S RAINING ALL OVER THE WORLD (Harlan Howard)	
215.	NCO 108694	THERE'S SOMETHING LONELY IN THIS HOUSE (L. J. Dillon)	
216.	NCO 108695	THREE CHEERS FOR THE GOOD GUYS (Harlan Howard)	Co 4-45310

JULY 19, 1971 (18:00–21:00); Columbia Studio, 804 16th Avenue South, Nashville, Tennessee; Producer: Larry Butler
    LEFTY FRIZZELL: vocal; THOMAS D. "Tommy" ALSUP: guitar/leader; JERRY W. SHOOK: guitar; BILLY R. SANFORD: guitar; JERRY "Chip Young" STEMBRIDGE: guitar; STUART H. BASORE: steel guitar; ROY M. "Junior" HUSKEY JR.: bass; JOHNNY GIMBLE: fiddle; JAMES C. ISBELL: drums; LARRY BUTLER: piano; GEORGE RICHEY: piano; SONJA MONTGOMERY, HOYT H. HAWKINS, NEAL MATTHEWS JR., RAYMOND C. WALKER, DUANE WEST: vocal chorus

| 217. | NCO 108204 | HONKY TONK STARDUST COWBOY
(D. Statler) | Co 4-45347 |
| 218. | NCO 108205 | WHAT AM I GONNA DO
(Lefty Frizzell) | Co 4-45347 |

JUNE 14, 1972; Columbia Studios, 804 16th Avenue South, Nashville, Tennessee; Producer: Glenn Sutton
    LEFTY FRIZZELL: vocal; JAMES "Jimmy" CAPPS: guitar; RAY EDENTON: guitar; GLENN SUTTON: guitar; ROBERT THOMPSON: banjo/bass; PETE DRAKE: steel guitar/leader; BOB L. MOORE: bass; MURRAY M. "Buddy" HARMAN JR.: drums; HARGUS "Pig" ROBBINS: piano; ALBERT BRUNEAU: unknown; HOYT H. HAWKINS, NEAL MATTHEWS JR., RAYMOND C. WALKER, HUGH GORDON STOKER: vocal chorus

219.	NCO 114371	GIVE ME MORE, MORE, MORE (OF YOUR KISSES) (Lefty Frizzell–Ray Price–Jim Beck)	
220.	NCO 114372	YOU BABE (Sanger D. Shafer)	Co 4-45652
221.	NCO 114373	THIS JUST AIN'T A GOOD DAY FOR LEAVIN' (Dallas Frazier–Sanger D. Shafer)	

DECEMBER 14, 1972 (18:00–21:30); Woodland Sound Studio, 1011 Woodland Street, Nashville, Tennessee; Producer: Don Gant
    LEFTY FRIZZELL: vocal; HERMANN B. "Pete" WADE: guitar; JAMES D. "Jimmy" CAPPS: guitar; ROBERT C. "Bobby" THOMPSON: guitar; HARALD "Hal" RUGG: steel guitar; BOBBY DYSON: bass; JAMES C. ISBELL: drums/leader; GORDON TERRY: fiddle; RON OATES: piano; HURSHEL WAYNE WIGINTON, JUNE EVELYN PAGE, DOLORES D. EDGIN, JOSEPH T. BABCOCK, RICKY PAGE or HOYT H. HAWKINS, NEAL MATTHEWS JR., HUGH GORDON STOKER, RAYMOND C. WALKER: vocal chorus

222.	none	DOWN BY THE RAILROAD TRACK (Dallas Frazier)		ABCD 861
223.	none	LET ME GIVE HER THE FLOWERS (G. Terry)	ABC 11350	ABCX 799
224.	none	IF I HAD HALF THE SENSE (A FOOL WAS BORN WITH)	ABC 11442	ABCX 799
		(D. Pearce)		

DECEMBER 15, 1972, (18:00–21:30); Woodland Sound Studio, 1011 Woodland Street, Nashville, Tennessee; Producer: Don Gant

LEFTY FRIZZELL: vocal; JERRY "Chip Young" STEMBRIDGE: guitar; JAMES D. "Jimmy" CAPPS: guitar; ROBERT C. "Bobby" THOMPSON: guitar; HARALD "Hal" RUGG: steel guitar; BOBBY DYSON: bass; JAMES C. ISBELL: drums/leader; NORMAN KEITH "Buddy" SPICHER: fiddle; GORDON TERRY: fiddle; RON OATES: piano; HURSHEL WAYNE WIGINTON, JUNE EVELYN PAGE, DOLORES D. EDGIN, JOSEPH T. BABCOCK, RICKY PAGE or HOYT H. HAWKINS, NEAL MATTHEWS JR., HUGH GORDON STOKER, RAYMOND C. WALKER: vocal chorus

225.	none	SOMEBODY'S WORDS (Eddy Raven)	ABC 11387	ABCX 799
226.	none	LUCKY ARMS (Sanger D. Shafer–Lefty Frizzell)	ABC 12023	ABCX 799
227.	none	TRUE LOVE NEEDS TO BE IN TOUCH (Dallas Frazier–Sanger D. Shafer)		
228.	none	MY HOUSE IS YOUR HONKY TONK (Sanger D. Shafer)		ABCD 861

DECEMBER 19, 1972 (18:00–21:30); Woodland Sound Studio, 1011 Woodland Street, Nashville, Tennessee; Producer: Don Gant

LEFTY FRIZZELL: vocal; JERRY "Chip Young" STEMBRIDGE: guitar; JAMES D. "Jimmy" CAPPS: guitar; JOHN LEE CHRISTOPHER: guitar; HARALD "Hal" RUGG: steel guitar; BOBBY DYSON: bass; JAMES C. ISBELL: drums/leader; NORMAN KEITH "Buddy" SPICHER: fiddle; GORDON TERRY: fiddle; RON OATES: piano; HOYT H. HAWKINS, NEAL MATTHEWS JR., HUGH GORDON STOKER, RAYMOND C. WALKER: vocal chorus

*OVERDUB SESSION: NOVEMBER 26, 1974 (18:00–21:00); Woodland Sound Studio, 1011 Woodland Street, Nashville, Tennessee; Producer: Don Gant

STRINGS: BERGEN D. WHITE (leader); SHELDON KURLAND, BRENTON BOLDEN BANKS, LENNIE HAIGHT, GEORGE BINKLEY III, MARTHA MCCRORY, GARY VANOSDALE, MARVIN D. CHANTRY, CHRISTIAN TEAL, STEVEN M. SMITH, MARTIN KATHAN, ROY CHRISTENSEN

229.	none	I BUY THE WINE (R. Burke–G. Barnhill)	ABC 11350	ABCX 799
230.	none	IF SHE JUST HELPS ME TO GET OVER YOU (A. Reynolds–D. Williams)	ABC 12023	ABCX 799
231.	none	FALLING* (Sanger D. Shafer–A. L. Owens)	ABC 12103	ABCD 861
232.	none	RAILROAD LADY (J. Buffett–J. Walker)	ABC 11442	ABCX 799

JULY 17, 1973 (18:00–21:00); Woodland Sound Studio, 1011 Woodland Street, Nashville, Tennessee; Producer: Don Gant

LEFTY FRIZZELL: vocal; THOMAS GRADY MARTIN: guitar/leader; JERRY "Chip Young" STEMBRIDGE: guitar; HAROLD RAY BRADLEY: guitar; PETE DRAKE: steel guitar; BOB L. MOORE: bass; MURRAY M. "Buddy" HARMAN JR.: drums; NORMAN KEITH "Buddy" SPICHER: fiddle; JOHNNY GIMBLE: fiddle; HARGUS "Pig" ROBBINS: piano; ABE MULKEY: harmony vocal; HOYT H. HAWKINS, NEAL MATTHEWS JR., HUGH GORDON STOKER, RAYMOND C. WALKER: vocal chorus

233.	none	I CAN'T GET OVER YOU TO SAVE MY LIFE (Sanger D. Shafer–(Lefty Frizzell)	ABC 11387	ABCX 799
234.	none	I NEVER GO AROUND MIRRORS (I'VE GOT A HEART- ACHE TO HIDE) (Sanger D. Shafer–Lefty Frizzell)	ABC 11416	ABCX 799
235.	none	THAT'S THE WAY LOVE GOES (Sanger D. Shafer–Lefty Frizzell)	ABC 11416	ABCX 799

APRIL 30, 1974 (14:00–17:00); Woodland Sound Studio, 1011 Woodland Street, Nashville, Tennessee; Producer: Don Gant

LEFTY FRIZZELL: vocal; JERRY W. SHOOK: guitar; JAMES D. "Jimmy" CAPPS: guitar; HAROLD RAY BRADLEY: guitar; JEFFREY P. NEWMAN: guitar; WELDON M. MYRICK: steel guitar: BILLY LINNEMAN: bass; JAMES C. ISBELL: drums/leader; NORMAN KEITH "Buddy" SPICHER: fiddle; HARGUS "Pig" ROBBINS: piano; ABE MULKEY: harmony vocal; HOYT H. HAWKINS, NEAL MATTHEWS JR., HUGH GORDON STOKER, RAYMOND C. WALKER: vocal chorus

236.	none	SHE FOUND THE KEY (Sanger D. Shafer–Lefty Frizzell)		ABCD 861
237.	none	I WONDER WHO'S BUILDING THE BRIDGE (A. L. Owens–Roger Burch)		
238.	none	MY WISHING ROOM (Sanger D. Shafer–Lefty Frizzell)		ABCD 861

AUGUST 14, 1974 (18:00–21:00); Woodland Sound Studio, 1011 Woodland Street, Nashville, Tennessee; Producer: Don Gant
    LEFTY FRIZZELL: vocal; KELTON "Kelso" HERSTON: guitar; JERRY "Chip Young" STEMBRIDGE: guitar; REGGIE YOUNG: guitar; JEFFREY P. NEWMAN: guitar; WELDON M. MYRICK: steel guitar; HENRY P. STRZELECKI: bass; JAMES C. ISBELL: drums/leader; NORMAN KEITH "Buddy" SPICHER: fiddle; BOBBY R. WOOD: piano; HOYT H. HAWKINS, NEAL MATTHEWS JR., HUGH GORDON STOKER, RAYMOND C. WALKER: vocal chorus
*OVERDUB SESSION: NOVEMBER 26, 1974 (18:00–21:00); Woodland Sound Studio, 1011 Woodland Street, Nashville, Tennessee; Producer: Don Gant
    STRINGS: BERGEN D. WHITE (leader); SHELDON KURLAND, BRENTON BOLDEN BANKS, LENNIE HAIGHT, GEORGE BINKLEY III, MARTHA MCCRORY, GARY VANOSDALE, MARVIN D. CHANTRY, CHRISTIAN TEAL, STEVEN M. SMITH, MARTIN KATHAN, ROY CHRISTENSEN

239.	none	I'M GONNA HANG OUT MY MIND TODAY (Sanger D. Shafer–Dallas Frazier)		ABCD 861
240.	none	SITTIN' AND THINKIN' (Charlie Rich)	ABC 12061	ABCD 861
241.	none	I LOVE YOU A THOUSAND WAYS (Lefty Frizzell–Jim Beck)	ABC 12103	ABCD 861
242.	none	I'M NOT THAT GOOD AT GOODBYE (Bob McDill–Don Williams)		ABCD 861

OCTOBER 22, 1974 (18:00–21:30); Woodland Sound Studio, 1011 Woodland Street, Nashville, Tennessee; Producer: Don Gant
    LEFTY FRIZZELL: vocal; KELTON "Kelso" HERSTON: guitar; DAVID C. KIRBY: guitar; JERRY W. SHOOK: guitar; JOHN LEE CHRISTOPHER JR.: guitar; JEFFREY P. NEWMAN: steel guitar; BILLY LINNEMAN: bass; JERRY K. CARRIGAN: drums; JOHNNY GIMBLE: fiddle; RON OATES: piano/leader; LOUIS D. NUNLEY, DOROTHY ANN DILLARD, WILLIAM GUILFORD WRIGHT, D. BERGEN WHITE: vocal chorus
*OVERDUB SESSION: NOVEMBER 26, 1974 (18:00–21:00); Woodland Sound Studio, 1011 Woodland Street, Nashville, Tennessee; Producer: Don Gant
    STRINGS: BERGEN D. WHITE (leader); SHELDON KURLAND, BRENTON BOLDEN BANKS, LENNIE HAIGHT, GEORGE BINKLEY III, MARTHA MCCRORY, GARY VANOSDALE, MARVIN D. CHANTRY, CHRISTIAN TEAL, STEVEN M. SMITH, MARTIN KATHAN, ROY CHRISTENSEN

| 243. | none | YESTERDAY JUST PASSED MY WAY AGAIN* (Sanger D. Shafer–Darlene Shafer) | | ABCD 861 |
| 244. | none | LIFE'S LIKE POETRY (Merle Haggard) | ABC 12061 | ABCD 861 |

THE 1983 DAVID FRIZZELL OVERDUB PRODUCTIONS

OVERDUB SESSION: JUNE 8, 1983 (14:00–17:00 & 18:00–21:00); Young'un Sound Studio, Nashville, Tennessee; Producer: David Frizzell
    LEFTY FRIZZELL: vocal; MICHAEL BLASUCCI: guitar/leader; BILLY J. WALKER JR.: guitar; TOM BRUMLEY: steel guitar; EMORY L. GORDY: bass; RALPH GALLANT: drums; CHARLES R. MCCOY: harmonica; HARGUS "Pig" ROBBINS: piano

165A.	NCO 82533	HOW FAR DOWN CAN I GO (Harlan Howard–J. C. Barney)	FC 38938
166A.	NCO 82534	IT'S BAD (WHEN IT'S THATAWAY) (Lefty Frizzell–Abe Mulkey)	FC 38938
187A.	NCO 80480	YOU GOTTA BE PUTTIN' ME ON (M. Vickery)	FC 38938
189A.	NCO 120448	GET THIS STRANGER OUT OF ME (A. L. Owens)	FC 38938
202A.	NCO 98533	THE MARRIAGE BIT (Don Wayne)	FC 38938

OVERDUB SESSION: JUNE 9, 1983 (14:00–17:00 & 18:00–21:00); Young'un Sound Studio, Nashville, Tennessee; Producer: David Frizzell
    LEFTY FRIZZELL: vocal; MICHAEL BLASUCCI: guitar/leader; BILLY J. WALKER JR.: guitar; TOM BRUMLEY: steel guitar; EMORY L. GORDY: bass; RALPH GALLANT: drums; HARGUS "Pig" ROBBINS: piano

| 180A. | NCO 83387 | EVERYTHING KEEPS COMING BACK (BUT YOU) (Lefty Frizzell–Abe Mulkey) | FC 38938 |

193A.	NCO 120259	ANYTHING YOU CAN SPARE (Harlan Howard)	FC 38938
211A.	NCO 104539	WATERMELON TIME IN GEORGIA (Harlan Howard)	FC 38938
212A.	NCO 104540	I MUST BE GETTING OVER YOU (L. Reynolds)	FC 38938
221A.	NCO 114373	THIS JUST AIN'T A GOOD DAY FOR LEAVIN' (Dallas Frazier–Sanger D. Shafer)	FC 38938

Index